T0294195

The Many Lives

of

MANGALAMPALLI BALAMURALIKRISHNA

The Many Lives

of

Mangalampalli Balamuralikrishna

AN AUTHORIZED
BIOGRAPHY

VEEJAY SAI

VINTAGE
An imprint of Penguin Random House

VINTAGE

USA | Canada | UK | Ireland | Australia
New Zealand | India | South Africa | China

Vintage is part of the Penguin Random House group of companies
whose addresses can be found at global.penguinrandomhouse.com

Published by Penguin Random House India Pvt. Ltd
4th Floor, Capital Tower 1, MG Road,
Gurugram 122 002, Haryana, India

First published in Vintage by Penguin Random House India 2022

Copyright © Veejay Sai 2022

All rights reserved

10 9 8 7 6 5 4 3 2 1

ISBN 9780670090426

Typeset in Adobe Caslon Pro by Manipal Digital Systems, Manipal
Printed at Thomson Press India Ltd, New Delhi

www.penguin.co.in

Dedicated to:

The great saint–composers, the generous royal patrons of arts, the unparalleled scholars and poets who enriched the language and countless musicians of the Telugu lands who kept the lamp of Shastreeya Sangeetam burning bright with their Vidwat, down the centuries . . .

In the words of Saint Tyagaraja:

ఎందరో మహానుభావులు అందరికీ వందనములు

(There are countless great people. I offer my salutations to them all.)

Contents

Preface

It was the start of summer in 2010. Precisely, 30 April. Bengaluru is usually cool at this time of the year. A short bout of spring gives way to the summer. The interim period is when Bengaluru's old trees pop up in thousands of sequential blooms. That particular evening, a concert of Dr Mangalampalli Balamuralikrishna (Dr MBK) was organized in a makeshift stage under a shamiana in the open lawns of Bangalore Club. The scenic colonial hub in the heart of the city was packed with club members and his fans. Jayaraj, a connoisseur of classical music who had served as the commissioner of Bruhat Bangalore Mahanagara Palike, was one of the organizers of the event. Dr MBK was accompanied that evening by Mysore Manjunath on the violin, Jayachander Rao on the mridangam and Giridhar Udupa on the ghatam. A couple of songs into the concert, he began a long Aalapana in Ragam Amritavarshini. Halfway through the Aalapana, the fragrance of petrichor enveloped the space. Clouds gathered in the sky showered down unexpectedly. 'Santatam Chintaye Amriteshwari, Salilam Varshaya Varshaya,' Dr MBK continued to sing with a wide grin on his face as the rain lashed outside the tent.

A few murmured that it was Bengaluru's first summer shower. Others were stunned. Could this have been the power of his music? One will never know. We live in times when sentiments like devotion are easily rationalized and open to countless arguments. But for a true devotee of music, nothing can be more powerful than its effect. For a society obsessed with consumerism and hungry for quick, visible results, the subtlety of what a form like Carnatic can offer is often lost.

The concert ended and everyone was returning home. The maestro and his manager were both being hosted at the club. They had retired into their rooms, and I went to bid them goodbye. The manager asked me to meet them the next morning instead as their flight out of the city was only at noon. The next morning, we chatted over breakfast. I asked the maestro if he felt his music had brought in the rain the previous evening. He smiled widely and shrugged. 'Whatever you believed happened, happened!' he said nonchalantly.

On an earlier occasion I had suggested making a full-length documentary on him, his music and his life. There were several but none of them were detailed. However, that didn't take off. His manager then asked me if I would write a special souvenir. It had to be kept a secret as it was supposed to be a surprise gift for the maestro's eighty-fifth birthday. I was more than excited to take this on. Over the next couple of years I interviewed him and got a good deal of information about his early life. The project was not meant to be done in a rush, so all of us kept at it whenever time permitted. In the midst of it, his manager suddenly died, and the project came to a halt. What made it worse was the maestro had completely withdrawn into himself. No amount of coaxing would help. 'What is there to say? You know everything. You can write whatever you want to!' he said on one occasion. Since it did not seem to be going anywhere, I paused the project.

It was not as if I was a huge fan of his music. In fact, at my home, where Carnatic music constantly blared from the radio or from cassettes, we rarely heard his music. My grandfather, a staunch conservative who kept up a colourful commentary about many musicians, would praise his voice but stay reserved about the music. Years later, when I spent time with the notorious critic 'Subbudu', he raved about his voice. My own meetings with Balamuralikrishna during the late 1990s began with formal interactions until we reached a point where he would nonchalantly crack raunchy jokes. Once he asked me what my birth star was and, on finding out, said, 'We are of the same star!'

I didn't know what that meant, but our interactions afterwards were absolutely delightful. Be it in Delhi, Mumbai, Hyderabad, Bengaluru or at his house in Chennai, one never tired of his company. Looking back now, I realize he had no reason to entertain a junior, up-and-coming journalist like me. But he did! That made a lot of difference. 'Meet Veejay. He is a Sanskrit scholar. You know, we both are of Visaka Nakshatram!' he would say and introduce me to anyone around him. It was embarrassing, to say the least. I was no scholar. I was just another student and fan(atic) of the language. It fascinated me no end. But his exaggerations in private gatherings felt unwarranted. Sometimes I felt he was pulling my leg. Those around him told me that he was always encouraging of youngsters. It could be both, in this case! But his fatherly concern, his penchant for wordplay and his patience while answering all kinds of questions gave him an unusual charm that one would rarely find in classical music maestros of his stature and calling.

His eighty-fifth birthday, on 6 July 2015, came and went, without that planned special souvenir. I went to Bengaluru and met him when he was honoured with a lifetime award by his spiritual guru, His Holiness the Jagadguru Shankaracharya of the Sringeri Sharada Peetham. This time he seemed more receptive to talking. He laughed and joked like his usual old self. And was he a master of wordplay! 'Padalaalityam' was child's play for him at any point of time.

In November 2016, he passed away. I decided to abandon the project, thinking it was a sign that I wasn't meant to do it. At the end of May the next year, I went to the Kamani Auditorium to attend a concert by Vidushi Kishori Amonkar, a great friend of his. 'When is the book coming out? You must write it! His story must be told. It is very important. Whenever you write it, send me a copy!' she ordered. Little did I know that that was going to be my last meeting with her. A week later, she made her final exit from this world, just like her friend Balamuralikrishna had, peacefully in her sleep.

Her words kept ringing in my ears. His story needed to be told. When literary agent Kanishka Gupta approached me, asking if I had any ideas, I suggested this biography. In a matter of days he found a publisher. While researching, I unearthed a mountain of information about Dr

MBK. His life has been public since his first concert, when he was barely seven! Countless press clippings, photographs, reviews, brickbats and more. Abundance of information is more dangerous than the lack of it. How does one decide what is important and what is not? How does one go beyond boring hagiographies? How does one encompass into words the work someone has done? I met so many of his fellow musicians, contemporaries, juniors whom he had encouraged, several others critical of his music, and the mountain in front of me only kept growing. It was going to be a humungous task to cherry-pick content. Meeting his warm and welcoming family gave me a different perspective, of the person he was at home. His sons and daughters, and grandchildren, Vibhu and Mahima, generously shared information and helped me navigate through the content.

We decided this biography would be a good tribute for his ninetieth birth anniversary that would fall in July 2020. By March, the dreaded pandemic stuck, and everything came to a grinding halt. Picking up strings and storylines from where I had left them, I somehow managed to complete this task.

So here is a story of this musical genius. I say 'a' story and not 'the' story because lives like his can never be covered in one book. There is so much more to the man, his genius and his life. A man who could connect with anyone with a song. A man who could make you feel the highly complicated genre of music he was singing was easy. Whoever encountered him had a memorable story to share. That was the effect he left on them. If it wasn't a personal meeting, it was his music that lingered on like an aftertaste.

He loved collecting and driving around in the latest cars and was too radical for a classical musician. He was never known to practise music, either at home or outside. To add to that, he loved ice creams and fried foods, two things many singers run away from. He never had a fever or a headache all his life. He loved watching cricket and stunt movies. He was unbelievably generous with his money and never knew how he was being used. He helped countless people get jobs. He was a man who was hated for his intellectual audacity as much as he was adored for his music. A complicated genius of a musical mind and an equally misunderstood person. His innocence was taken for granted, and his silence was assumed to be arrogance. A phenomenal virtuoso who hid behind his childlike smile. Someone who would easily fit into what the eighth-century Sanskrit dramatist Bhavabhuti wrote, probably about himself, in his play *Maalatimadhavam*:

ये नाम केचिदिह नः प्रथयन्त्यवज्ञां
जानन्ति ते किमपि तान्प्रति नैष यत्नः ।
उत्पत्स्यते तु मम कोऽपि समानधर्मा
कालो ह्ययं निरवधिर्विपुला च पृथ्वी ॥

(Those who deride or ignore my work—
let them know: my efforts are not for them.
There will come along someone who shares my spirit:
the world is vast, and time endless.)

This could be said of Balamuralikrishna too. It will take another era to understand his unfathomable musical imagination and how effortlessly he handled it. This is a story of Mangalampalli Balamuralikrishna.

1

The Music of the Telugus

What are today the states of Andhra Pradesh and Telangana were in the colonial era an extension of the larger Madras Presidency. Prior to that, there were numerous princely kingdoms in the Telugu-speaking regions. After the fall of the Vijayanagara Empire, there are theories of large groups of artistes migrating and scattering across far-flung areas in the south.

The region that is now Telangana was once home to some of the greatest scholars of Sanskrit language and literature. In his seminal work *Contribution of Andhra to Sanskrit Literature*, the great academician, scholar, translator and biographer Acharya Biruduraju Rama Raju (1925–2010) writes:

> A quick look at the works of famous poets who emerged from the Telugu-speaking regions will give yet another reason to understand the development of literary Telugu through Sanskrit. First the famous trio of poets—Nannayya Bhatta (1022–56), who took up the rendering of Vyasa Mahabharata into Telugu; Tikkanna, who continued the work up to leaving the Aranyaparva (thirteenth century); and Chadlavaada Errana (thirteenth century), who completed the work. Srinatha (1380–1445), the first poet duo Nandi Mallayya and his uncle Ghanta Singayya; Alasani Peddanna (1509–30), who was the first of the Ashta Diggajas of Krishnadevaraya's court . . .

1

When it came to the literature of music and dance, there were a number of works that were popular in the artiste communities. Listing out all might not be possible but at least the most popular ones that many veteran artistes continue to recollect make for an important part of performance history and oral traditions. *Manasollasa* of the Chalukya king Somesvara (1127–38) was hugely popular among the Telugu people. In the fourth chapter titled 'Vinoda Vimsati', Somesvara highlights various forms of entertainment, such as *Gita* (song), *Vaadya* (instrumental), *Nritya* (dance), *Katha* (storytelling) and *Chamatkara* (magic). It is no surprise that this text was quoted by various scholars in the Telugu-speaking region in the centuries that followed. *Manasollasa* was one of the earliest encyclopaedic works dealing with day-to-day life, including food and lifestyle, arts and culture, warfare and administration and more. The Gita Govinda of Jayadeva (twelfth century) was already famous in temple and court performances. The entire text, divided into cantos and songs called Ashtapadis, gained a new life in the oral tradition of songs. The dance communities of coastal Andhra have a long history of performing these Ashtapadis set to a number of ragas other than those mentioned by Jayadeva in his treatise. Does this mean there was already a different culture and maybe a different system of raga music prevalent in those regions?

There was also the *Nritta Ratnavali*, a treatise on dance written by Jayappa Senapati, an army chief in the Kakatiya kingdom in 1253. The Kakatiyas were the second major dynasty that ruled the Telugu countryside after the Satavahanas. Under the Kakatiya reign, art, culture and literature blossomed in new ways. Many great scholars of Sanskrit and Telugu have reflected on the glory of that era in their works. *Nritta Ratnavali* is one of the earliest works that deals with music and dance in the Telugu-speaking regions. The 1000-pillared temple in Warangal, the Ramappa temple, built by Racherla Rudradeva, a chief in the Kakatiya army in 1213, seems to have been the main inspiration behind *Nritta Ratnavali*. There were also other poets and writers like Paalakuriki Somanatha (1160–1240) who wrote *Basava Puranam* and *Panditaaraadhya Charitra* that give an extensive list of musical forms prevalent in that era.

The great philosopher and saint Sri Vidyaranya (1296–1386) one of the founders of the Vijayanagara Empire who later became the twelfth Jagadguru of the Sringeri Sharada Peetham, was a Telugu from Ekasila Nagaram (present-day Warangal) in the Trilinga Desam. In addition to authoring numerous philosophical works like *Sarvadarsanasangraha* and *Panchadasi*, he also authored *Sangita Sara*. This treatise is the first to mention the Melakartha system in Carnatic music. To quote senior musicologist Dr S. Ramanathan, 'The *Sangita Sara* has a very important place in the history of Indian music especially of the South. It serves as the link between *Sangita Ratnakara* (thirteenth century) on one hand and *Svaramelakaalanidhi* (sixteenth century) on the other. The Sangita Sara is really the first work on South Indian music or Carnatic music as it is called now.' The manuscripts of *Sangita Sara* are not available today. But we have enough information about its contents in the *Lakshana Granthas* or musical treatises like Sangita Sudhanidhi, written by Sri Govinda Dikshita in the early seventeenth century.

In the Vijayanagara Empire ruled by Sri Krishnadevaraya (1509–29) and earlier kings, art and music found great patronage. Great musicians like Purandaradasa and Kanakadasa emerged, spreading the concept of Bhakti through music. Purandaradasa (1484–1564), a disciple of the Dvaita philosopher Saint Vyasa Tirtha, was a prolific composer and is referred to as the Sangeeta Pitamaha. Around the same time, Atukuri Molla (1440–1530), who authored her interpretation of the Ramayana, became popular in performance traditions.

The rule of Krishnadevaraya saw an unprecedented blossoming of literature and culture. The Ashta Diggajas—Allasani Peddanna, Nandi Thimmana, Dhurjati Kavi, Madayyagari Mallana, Ayyalaraju Ramabhadrudu, Tenali Ramakrishna, Pingali Surana and Ramaraja Bhushanudu—whose works are categorized as the 'Prabandha Age' of Telugu literature, was one of the highlights of the literary history of the Telugus. Allasani Peddanna, whose magnum opus was *Manu Charitra*, was honoured with the title 'Andhra Kavita Pitamaha'. Then came the Tallapaka poets, out of whom Annamacharya (1408–1503) was one of the most prolific composers. His compositions, called Sankeertanas, numbering as many as 32,000 dedicated to Lord Venkateswara of Tirupati, deal with a number of musical and poetic sub-genres. Today only about 12,000 of them are available. He was given the honorary title of 'Pada Kavita Pitamaha'.

Then there were the songs of Bhadrachala Ramadasu. Born as Kancharla Gopanna (1620–80), he was yet another prolific composer who wrote a number of poems and songs in praise of Lord Rama enshrined at Bhadrachalam. His compositions, popular as Ramadasu Keertanalu, spread across the region very soon. Composer and poet Kshetrayya or Varadayya (1600–80) was born in Muvva in the Krishna district of Andhra Pradesh. He perfected the musical and poetic form called Padam, mostly songs of love and longing in praise of Lord Krishna of Muvva. These compositions highlighted the sentiment of *Shringara* or amorous delight. Following in his footsteps was Sarangapani in the seventeenth century. A minister in the court of the Karvetinagaram kings, Sarangapani composed over 200 Padams in praise of Lord Venugopalaswamy enshrined in the temple of Karvetinagaram. The dance community of Kalavantulu, which later came to be called Devadasis, perfected these Kshetrayya and Sarangapani Padams, popularizing them across the region. This genre became extremely popular within the modern Bharatanatyam repertoire even in the Tamil-speaking regions. One of the most popular families of Devadasis to which Veena Dhanammal (1867–1938) belonged further popularized these Padams both in Bharatanatyam and modern Carnatic music.

Shivanarayana Tirtha (1650–1745) authored the *Yakshaganam Sri Krishna Leela Tarangini*, the longest opera in the Sanskrit language. Born as Tallavajula Govinda Sastrulu in Andhra Pradesh, he lived in the village of Kaza in Guntur district. He migrated to Thanjavur in Tamil Nadu. A master of Sanskrit, music, dance and poetry, he wrote over fifteen books, the most popular of them being the *Sri Krishna Leela Tarangini*. Musicologists in later years have analysed this work as having been inspired by Jayadeva's *Gita Govindam*. The text as such utilizes a number of poetic meters and musical forms. The Tarangini is equally popular in both music and dance traditions as the content is flexible to song and dance. With twelve Tarangams that have 153 songs, 302 Shlokams and thirty-one Choornikas, Narayana Theertha summarized in song and poetry the tenth chapter of Shrimad Bhagavatam.

Then came the famous poet, saint composer and Advaita philosopher Sadasiva Brahmendra. Born into a Telugu Velanadu Brahmin family, he mostly wrote in Sanskrit. All his compositions have a strong subtext of the Advaita philosophy that he advocated. There were also composers like Tirupati Narayanaswamy Naidu (1873–1912), Cheyyur Chengalvaraya Sastri (1810–1900), the Singaracharyulu brothers, Toomu Narasimhadasa (1807–77), Munipalle Subramanya Kavi (1730–80), Narumanchi Janakiramaiah (1823–90), whose writings were extremely popular, both in concerts and in the *Bhajana Sampradayam*.

The glorious era of Carnatic music was ushered in with the trinity of Shyama Shastri (1762–1827), Tyagaraja (1767–1847) and Muthuswamy Dikshithar (1775–1835). Out of this trinity, Shastri and Tyagaraja belonged to families of Telugu origin. All three of them were born in the temple town of Thiruvarur, and lived and worked around the Thanjavur region, which was the cultural heartland of Tamil Nadu. They, in a sense, codified what reached us as *Karnataka Sangita* in the modern era. All of Carnatic music can be divided into two eras, pre-trinity and post-trinity. Enough has been written by great musicologists on this aspect. Post-trinity saw a large number of composers or *Vaggeyakaras*—Mahakavi Dasu Sriramulu (1846–1908), Tumarada Sangameshwara Sastry (1874–1931), Hari Nagabhushanam (1884–1959), Ogirala Veeraraghava Sarma (1908–89), Kocharlakota Ramaraju (1878–1950), Munuganti Venkata Rao Pantulu (1902–64), Mahendravada Bapanna Sastri (1904–79), Achyutanna Gopala Sarma (1908–68), and many more. The writings of these composers seemed to be inevitably influenced by the works of the trinity. However, they did not acquire the cult status enjoyed by the compositions of the trinity in the twentieth and twenty-first centuries.

In addition to all these was the rich folklore music tradition of the Telugu-speaking regions. While there might not be a visibly direct link with raga music, one cannot deny the influence of a large number of sub-genres from the folk tradition that made their way under the umbrella of modern classical music. The compositions of Annamacharya have clearly borrowed much from the existing folk traditions. Forms like Jajara, Suvvi, Lalipatalu, Elapatalu and so on existed in their folk variants. The godfather of Telugu folklore studies, Acharya Biruduraju Rama Raju, writes about a large number of poetic meters from Telugu that made their way into Carnatic music: 'Meters like "Madhuragati Ragoda", "Chathushpada", "Shatpada", "Dviradagati Ragada", "Hayaparachara

Ragada", "Vrushabagati Ragada", and others are Desi meters which are prevalent in a number of folk songs and can be seen in the compositions of many Vaggeyakaras.' In addition to these forms of folk music is the music for folk dance forms in Telugu-speaking regions. The Gusadi dance of the Gonds, mango dance of the Kondareddis, the peacock dance of Konds, the Dimsa dance of the Arakku valley, the Siddhi dance, the Lambani dance, the Tappeta Gundlu of the coastal districts, the Urumulu dance of Rayalaseema, the Goravayyalu dance of Karimnagar and other such forms have distinctly different music, the tunes of which migrated into the classical genre over centuries. A lot of music also travelled through oral traditions via wandering minstrels and balladeers.

I asked senior musician and musicologist Malladi Suribabu what music may have been like prior to the popularity of the Carnatic trinity of composers. He promptly rolled out the names of Annamacharya, Ramadasu, Sadasiva Brahmendra and a few others. The Telugu-speaking regions had a highly aware audience for music and literature accustomed to high standards of music and the traditional storytelling form of Harikatha.

The Thriving Harikatha Tradition

The earliest literary references to the art of storytelling can be found in the Upanishads and Puranas. Outside of that, the twelfth-century treatise *Manasollasa* of King Somesvara devotes a whole chapter to the art of storytelling. Post the decline and fall of the Vijayanagara Empire, we have several Telugu scholars who have mentioned numerous Harikathas in their works. The famous literary commentator and writer Kolachalam Mallinatha Suri mentions numerous Harikathas in both Sanskrit and Telugu. However, that tradition was very different from what emerged in the nineteenth and twentieth centuries. Like the performances of ancient 'Prabandha', it is a lost art form.

The modern form of public devotional oratory and singing emerged in the region of Thanjavur, the cultural heartland of modern-day Tamil Nadu. Under the Maratha rulers who were great patrons of the arts and culture, several *Keertankaars* visited and performed in and around the Thanjavur region. Many of these artistes came from Maharashtra, or northern cities like Gwalior. However, there are differences of opinion on this matter. According to Prof. T. Donappa, who authored *Telugu Harikatha Sarvaswamu*, the modern Telugu Harikatha was a clever formulation of Srimad Ajjada Adibhatla Narayana Dasu (1864–1945). It would be interesting to briefly run through the life and art of Dasu and see why he was acknowledged as the unparalleled genius of this art form.

Born in the village of Ajjada in the Vizianagaram district of Andhra Pradesh, Dasu was hailed as a child prodigy when he began reciting the Pothana Bhagavatamu at the age of seven or eight. A polyglot who was proficient in a dozen languages, including Arabic and Persian, Dasu was a poet, composer, dancer, instrumentalist, percussionist, playwright, and, last but not least, the grand old man of Harikatha. He was also proficient in the complicated art form of Avadhanam that played with rhythm, poetry, prosody and more. He authored numerous Kavyas, Prabandhas and translated a number of works. He was the first to translate the Rubaiyat of Omar Khayyam into Telugu and Sanskrit. His work *Navarasa Tarangini* is a comparative analysis of the scholarship of Kalidasa and William Shakespeare. His proficiency in Sanskrit saw him setting to music over 300 selected stanzas of the Rig Veda. Among his musical accomplishments was his expertise in the complicated Panchamukhi Taalam. Here the performer has to put five different Taalams to a song: two with his arms, two with his feet and one with his head. A panel of five other musicians sits as observers, keeping track of one Taalam each. Dasu gave innumerable Panchamukhi performances and earned the titles of 'Layabrahma' and 'Panchamukhi Parameshwara'. Putting together his vast knowledge of music, dance, rhythm, poetry and languages, he designed his own style of Harikatha. He authored over twenty original Harikatha performances. He was also the first principal of the Maharaja's Government College of Music and Dance, established by Pusapati Vijayarama Gajapathi Raju, the Maharaja of Vizianagaram, in 1919. It was Dasu who inspired Rabindranath Tagore to introduce music as a subject for students at Santiniketan.

Dasu visited Madras in 1894 and gave a number of Harikatha performances, winning the appreciation of everyone. A performance review in *The Hindu* dated 30 June 1894 states:

This pride of Vizianagaram was unfolding the story in his characteristic impassioned language with his inimitable skill. Not only was he applauded time after time but at the close there was a spontaneous and irresistible outburst of admiration from everyone present exclaiming that it was a rare and excellent treat. Of the gifted expounder, it may be well and truly said that he is entitled to be spoken of in glowing terms by best of Pandits, by the most ardent lovers of music and by the most reputed of elocutionists. The rhythmic cadences of his harmonious verse, the melodious intonations of his musical flight and snatches of vivid and pictorious representations of nature conjured up by his lively and constructive faculty of imagination and his powerful command of the language appealed to the listeners' spiritual sensibilities.

The fame of Dasu was to stay for long in the memories of the music lovers of Madras. In 1927, he was invited to perform at the first All India Music Conference, which later led to the creation of The Music Academy of Madras. In 1936, after seventeen years of great service, he retired as the principal of the Music College at Vizianagaram. In 1938, he was once again felicitated by the Chennapuri Andhra Mahasabha in Madras. Dasu passed away in 1945. By the time of his demise, he had managed to inspire over 100 Harikatha exponents in Andhra. Till today, the moment you mention Harikatha, Dasu's name is inevitably suffixed with it.

Dasu's era led to the art form of Harikatha spreading like wildfire across the Telugu-speaking regions. Several noteworthy names like Kaaruru Krishnadasu, Vajapeyajula Subbaiah, Vadalamani Narasimhadasu, Neti Lakshminarayan Sastry, Bankumalli Simhachaladasu, Hemani Varahalladasu, Ammula Vishvanatha, Peddenti Suryanarayanadasu, Banka Balakrishnana and others spread this art form in every nook and corner. One of the famous names that emerged was Musunuri Suryanarayana Bhagavathar.

Born on 9 September 1909 in a village called Dula near Kadiam to Ratnamma and Venkataramana Murthy, Bhagavathar belonged to the Kaundinyasa Gotra and Apastambha Sutra. His guru was Chellapilla Venkata Sastry, one of the famed poets of 'Tirupati Venkata Kavallu'. He trained in Harikatha Kalakshepam with Sriamana Peddinti Suryanarayana

Dikshita Dasu. He was honoured with the title of 'Gayaka Ratna'. His cousin was the famous stage actor Addanki Sriramumurthy, who learnt the art of Padyamu and Gadyamu from him. Suryanarayana Bhagavata passed away at the very young age of forty-one on 8 April 1949. Ammula Vishvanatha Bhagavathar, born in Rakamakrishnapuram, on the outskirts of Vijayawada in the Krishna district of Andhra Pradesh, on 23 January 1916 to the couple Narahar Amma and Gopala Rao, went to a regular school till Grade 10. He began training in music under Krova Satyanarayana and in Harikatha under Adibhattala Narayanadasu, Dikshitadasu and Musunuri Suryanarayana. He became a popular Harikatha performer during festivals and special occasions connected to temples. Panditaradhyula Sambamoorthy Bhagavathar was born in Rachawaram in Nellore district. He was an expert of the Pancha Maha Kavyas, the complete works of Kalidasa, and a singer and composer. His son was the famous playback singer S.P. Balasubramaniam (1946–2020).

This glorious art of Harikatha spread far and wide for a century and eventually began fading. One would have thought that with so many exponents this art form would have thrived for longer. However, this was not to be. With the advent of silent cinema and later the talkies, the audience found other forms of entertainment. The shift in focus also led to the gradual decline of serious practitioners. By the beginning of the twenty-first century, far and few authentic Harikatha exponents remained in the Telugu-speaking regions. Their counterparts in Tamil Nadu still continued to pursue this art form, even if there were only a handful.

The Modern Sabha Culture in Andhra

With so many musicians and Harikatha exponents around, it was obvious that a new crop of organizers too began business. One must remember that at this point, between 1850 till about 1950, the Telugu drama scene was thriving, with ticketed shows across the land. In his seminal work *Andhra Nataka Ranga Charitra*, the actor-turned-writer Mikkilineni Radhakrishna Murthy (1914–2011) lists hundreds of drama companies, district by district. In addition to those well-established in several villages and towns, there were large travelling drama companies that camped for months conducting performances. The success of the theatre economy might have inspired several organizers to look at classical music too. Until then, classical music was mostly limited to temples, temple festival performances and royal courts of smaller princely kingdoms. Several princely kingdoms patronized music and musicians. Vizianagaram, Bobbili, Karveti Nagaram, Venkatagiri, Pithapuram, Gadwal, Nuziveedu Samsthanam, Polavaram Samsthanam, Palluru Samsthanam, Challapalli Samsthanam, Srikalahasthi Samsthanam and smaller princely states all had great rulers with a fine taste for the arts like music, dance and drama. In addition to these were large temple organizations like the Tirumala Tirupati Devasthanam, Simhachalam, Annavaram, Bhadrachalam and Vemulawada which patronized music and artistes.

Several artistes in later years like Rallapalli Ananthakrishna Sarma and Srirangam Gopalaratnam were empanelled as Asthana Vidwans. A quick survey of all the various drama companies, organizations, the number of ticketed performances and the long list of artistes would give you an idea of the love for the arts that the Telugus once had. Inspired by the travelling Parsi drama companies, a large number of regional Telugu drama companies mushroomed across the region giving employment to hundreds of artistes. That was an era when a drama actor had to be well qualified in allied fields like classical music, percussion, *abhinayam* and so on to be able to have a successful career. These drama companies also sourced great musicians to give music for large productions. The theatre economy was largely sustained by mythological and historical dramas. Some of the greatest stars of the Telugu stage, like Vemuri Gaggaiah, Addanki Sriramamurthy, Yadavalli Suryanarayana, Bellamkonda Subbarao, Mangalagiri (Senior) Sriranjani, Dasari Kotiratnam, Parupalli Subbarao, Bezawada Rajaratnam and many others, were hailed as superstars on stage for acting as well as singing. Almost all the drama music was based on classical ragas. This saw a proliferation of a large number of teachers training students in these art forms.

Many organizations that were started to propagate music and dance became popular venues for staging dramas. At other times, they were popular for their music festivals. Tyagaraja Bhakta Sabha in Bheemavaram was started in 1919 by Sarvadharmayya Pantulu. Initially, it ran a three-day festival. In the first few years, among the celebrated participants of the first festival were violinist Bhamidipati Narasimha Shastry, vocalist Cherukumalli Lachiraju and flautist Mangalampalli Pattabhiramayya. By 1921, the Sabha became popular for conducting major festivals in the Someshvara temple and the premises of the Panchayat board. For the silver jubilee celebrations, several scholars, musicologists and musicians were invited from Tamil Nadu and Karnataka, with the celebrations being presided over by the famous vocalist Parupalli Ramakrishnaiyya Panthulu. Famous poet Sripada Krishnamurthy Shastry, and famous music *vidwan* Harinagabhooshanam were specially invited to participate in the festivities. The Sabha is the only one in all of Andhra Pradesh that has sustained itself for fifty years and successfully had a golden jubilee without any help from the Central Sangeet Natak Akademi or any government bodies. During the golden jubilee celebrations, several famous musicians participated. Among them were D.K. Pattammal, M.S. Subbulakshmi, Radha–Jayalakshmi, Maharajapuram Santhanam, Madurai Somasundaram, Sheikh Chinna Maulana and Andhra's own musical stars Dr M. Balamuralikrishna, Tirupati Ponnarao and Dandamuni Ramamohan Rao. In 1953, a statue of Saint Tyagaraja was unveiled in the Sabha.

Ramavilas Sabha in Chittoor began in August 1924 and was founded by Chittoor V. Nagaiah along with Madabhooshi Anantashayanam Iyengar. Subbarao Mudaliar of Arcot financed the Sabha. The main aim of this Sabha was to promote classical music concerts, musical dramas and Harikathas. Several prominent artists like Chittoor Subramania Pillai, Mahalingam Bhagavathar—the adopted son of Harikesanallur Muthaiah Bhagavathar—and Subbaraman were regular participants in the Sabha. The Vijaya Tyagaraja Sabha in Vishakapatnam was founded by Dr Sripada Pinakapani and Dr Brahmaiah Shastry in 1945. The Sabha would conduct competitions where students of music had to sing ten Tyagaraja Kritis, five Shyama Sastry Kritis, five Dikshitar Kritis and three Varnams. This list of items had to be given one day before the competition and the judge could change it overnight. The winners were given a gold medal and a cash prize. The first three winners in the years after the competition started were Nedunoori Krishnamurthy, Nukala Chinna Satyanarayana and Voleti Venkateshwarulu. All three grew to be great professional musicians in their respective careers in later decades.

There were several other Sabhas like Sangeeta Vidwat Sabha in Kakinada, which was started in 1946 by Manuganti Sriramamurthy, Kilambi Tatacharyulu, Peri Subbarao and others; Sri Sitarama Gana Sabha in Tenali that was established in 1947 by Narumanchi Subbarao; and Sri Tyagaraja Gana Sabha in Elluru that was established in 1947 by Kambammettu Venkatasubbarao who was a mridangam artiste himself. The Akashavani Office of All India Radio in Vijayawada began on 1 December 1948, with some of the most famous musicians of Andhra Pradesh participating from the very beginning. One of the first concerts played was by Parupalli Ramakrishnaiyya Panthulu. Following that, musicians and musicologists like Banda Kanakalingeshwara Rao, Balantrapu Rajanikantha Rao, Kandukuri Ramabhadra Rao, G.V. Krishna Rao, Pingali Lakshmi Kantam and Prayaga Narasimha Shastry associated themselves with regular programming in music, becoming extremely popular across the Andhra region. The evolution of Sabha culture in the Telugu-speaking regions further enhanced the awareness of Carnatic music in the region.

The gramophone era played a big role in the spread of music. Several stalwarts of that era saw their music being recorded by popular companies. Almost all the famous stage actors/singers were recorded and their discs released to huge commercial success. Theatre critic Modali Nagabhushana Sarma (1936–2019) edited a two-volume book titled Tolinaati Gramophone Gaayakulu where he listed over fifty famous drama artistes whose recordings were popular. Among the popular classical musicians of that era from Andhra were Cocanada Satyavathi Bai, violinist Dwaram Venkataswamy Naidu and vocalist Parupalli Ramakrishnayya Panthulu, who shared their names with their musical counterparts from Thanjavur, Salem, Coimbatore and Madras.

'Sundara Telugu'

It would be of great interest to study the unprecedented growth and popularity of the Telugu language, especially in connection with music and dance. Outside of the Telugu-speaking regions, the post-trinity era saw a large number of musicians and composers writing in Telugu. Many from the Tamil-speaking regions like Veena Kuppayyar (1798–1860), Patnam Subrahmanya Ayyar (1845–1902), Harikesanallur Muthaiah Bhagavatar (1877–1945), Ramanathapuram 'Poochi' Srinivasa Iyengar (1860–1919), Maha Vaidyanatha Aiyar (1844–93), Tiger Varadachariar (1876–1950), Dharmapuri Subbarayar (nineteenth century) and many others wrote and composed a number of songs in Telugu. Even traditional Harikatha scholars in Tamil Nadu like Thanjavur Krishna Bhagavatar (1841–1903), Thirupazhanam Panchapakesa Sastri (1868–1924), Mangudi Chidambara Bhagavatar (1880–1938) and others were experts in the Telugu language.

Until the Tamil Isai Movement began, a large part of what comprised Carnatic music Kacheri was in Telugu. The Tamil Isai Movement helped highlight the rich ancient music and dance history of Tamil Nadu before the arrival of Telugu. However, till the nineteenth century, a large part of the earliest published material, like books on Carnatic music, were in Telugu. One of the earliest publishing houses from this region was the Saraswati Mudraalayumu founded in 1854 by Telugu Pandit Vavilla Ramaswamy Sastrulu, who hailed from the Nellore district in Andhra. He started the Hindu Bhasha Sanjeevini in Chennai and published over fifty important books, both in Telugu and Sanskrit. After his demise, his son renamed the publishing house Vavilla Press and continued publishing hundreds of books in Telugu, Sanskrit, Tamil and English. As the national freedom struggle was gaining momentum, several books by noted Bengali writers, like *Anandamatha* by Bankim Chandra Chatterji (1907) were published by Vavilla Press. Hundreds of Telugu literary works came to light. The famous courtesan-singer Bangalore Nagaratnamma published Muddu Palani's *Radhika Santwanamu*, originally banned for obscenity, through Vavilla Press in 1910 amidst much controversy. In 1909, the nationalist Kasi Nathuni Nageshwara Rao founded the weekly Telugu language journal *Andhra Patrika*. In 1914, he moved his headquarters to Madras, as he found a larger readership in those regions. *Andhra Patrika* also gave significant coverage to the arts, particularly classical music, dance and drama.

The Thanjavur region, which also saw the revival and codification of the dance form that came to be known as Bharatanatyam, is another area where the influence of Telugu is visible. Codified by four brothers popularly known as the Thanjavur Quartet—Chinayya (1802–56), Ponnayya (1804–64), Sivanandam (1808–63) and Vadivelu (1810–47)— the modern repertoire of Bharatanatyam is largely influenced by their writings. A large part of their compositions are in Telugu. Whatever survived of the Quartet was from the private notebooks of Nellaiyappa Nattuvanar (1859–1905), the grandson of Ponnayya, which were Telugu compositions written in the Grantha script. Several other works from the nineteenth century, like *Chennapuri Vilasamu* by Narasimha Sastri, first published in 1863, gave details of cultural performances in the private gatherings of the elite. In 1904, Pandanallur Arunachala Pillai (1873– 1939), another descendant of the Quartet, published a Telugu work *Abhinayaabjodaya Sulochani* that detailed abhinyam in dance. In 1896, an anthology of Telugu Javalis by Dharmapuri Subbaraya Ayyar was published in the Tamil script in his own lifetime.

In 1915, the scholarly writer Devulapalli Veeraraghavamurti Sastri published the *Abhinaya Svyambodhini* that had a number of songs connected to the dance repertoire. The scholar P.S.R. Apparao writes: 'Dr Manomohan Ghosh studied six manuscripts of "Abhinaya Darpanam", collected from different places to decide his translation of the text that contains 328 verses. It is significant to note that all these manuscripts are in Telugu script only.' This is yet another testimony to the popularity of the Telugu language. In an older interview to the All India Radio, one of the greatest exponents of Bharatanatyam, Thanjavur Balasaraswati (1918–1984) mentions that all through her growing years, the only manuscript of dance her illustrious family and contemporaries adhered to was the Telugu manuscript of *Abhinaya Darpanam*.

The Yakshagana traditions of dance and drama that travelled from the regions of Andhra and settled down in the Thanjavur region was yet another art form that saw the spread of Telugu. The Bhagavata Mela Natakam was a Telugu language theatre performed mostly by Smartha Brahmin men. Having settled down in Melattur near Thanjavur, the art form survives till today, with generation after generation of practitioners. The famous Saraswati Mahal Library in the palace of Thanjavur published a number of literary works like the *Raghunathanayakaabhyudayamu* by Raghunatha Nayaka and *Rajagopala Vilasamu* by Chengalva Kalakavi.

They also published a lot of other works. Several other books like *Telugu Shringara Javali* were published using the Tamil script in 1924.

The *Sangita Sampradhaya Pradarsini*, an encyclopaedic work on music by Subbarama Dikshithar, was first published in Telugu in 1904 at the *Ettayapuram Samsthanam* in Tamil Nadu. In the section titled 'Vaggeyakara Charitam', Dikshithar lists a number of Vaggeyakaras who were of Telugu origin. Several later books—like *Gandharva Kalpavalli*, a self-instructor in music by one P.S. Ramulu Chetti, a harmonist, printed and published from Madras in 1911—were in Telugu. Many composers chose Telugu as the main language for composing music and music for dance. The linguistic technicalities of the language, suited to composition for Carnatic music, aided the unprecedented popularity that Telugu enjoyed within the classical performing traditions. Several other Telugu books were published using the Grantha script. One of the reasons for this unprecedented popularity of Telugu language in modern Tamil Nadu might be the settlement of various business communities like the Chettys and Naidus, whose mother tongue was Telugu. They were also big patrons of the arts and literature, and often funded the publication of works. Tamil songs, especially on the concert stage, became popular only by the early 1940s, when the Tamil Isai Sangam began its December music conference.

While speaking with the eminent art critic, author, translator and scholar Dr Prema Nandakumar, she quotes the great revolutionary Tamil poet Subramanya Bharati (1882–1921) who wrote:

"சுந்தரத் தெலுங்கில் பாட்டிசைத்து தோணிகளோட்டி விளையாடி வருவோம்"

(Sundara telunginil paatisaithu thonigalotti vilaiyadi varuvom)
(Let us sing songs in beautiful Telugu and play ferrying these oars . . .)

She mentioned the numerous kingdoms like the Vijayanagara Empire, the Nayak rulers of Madurai and Thanjavur, and the Rajas of Rajapalayam who patronized Telugu. Several Telugu compositions of the Nayak kings continue to be sung in rituals and festivals across ancient temples like Srirangam and Tirunelveli, till date.

In addition to that was the technicality of the language itself. Musicologist N. Balasubramanian enumerated these details further:

> The Telugu language has a natural flow of vowel endings that keeps within the poetic conventions unlike no other South Indian languages. In Tamil we have two variants, 'மெய் எழுத்து' (Mei ezhuthu) which are basically words that end in consonants and 'உயிர் மெய் எழுத்து' (Uyir mei ezhuthu) or words that break at odd syllables. While Tamil is an ancient language capable of great poetry, somehow it lacks the natural flow that Telugu has, when it comes to songs. Especially looking at compositions in classical music you will find all the songs end with elongated vowel sounds. This makes it easier for poetry to be translated into song within rhythmic cycles. A lot of the Telugu compositions also borrow from Sanskrit prosody.

Balasubramanian's two daughters Ranjani and Gayatri are popular Carnatic vocalists. Studying the important point that both Nandakumar and Balasubramanian made, if you look at the Tamil poetry of the likes of Saint Arunagirinathar (fifteenth century) or later composers like Gopalakrishna Bharati (1811–96), you find great poetry but a challenge for any composer to set those lines to tune. It is only in recent times that several ancient works in Tamil, like the poetry of the Vaishnava Azhwar saints and the Shaiva Nayanmar saints, has been set to music.

In the twentieth century, Carnatic music in its modern avatar was largely spread with the help of traditional Shishya Paramparas. Students belonging to numerous musical lineages carried forward the legacies of their teachers, orally or through the written medium. By the twentieth century, Andhra saw a proliferation of great musicians. If the first generation saw the likes of Naidu and Pantulu, they were followed by many more stalwarts like Rallapalli Ananthakrishna Sarma (1893–1979), Sripada Pinakapani (1913–2013), Voleti Venkateshwarlu (1928–89), Srirangam Gopalarathnam (1939–93), Nedunuri Krishnamurthy (1927–2014), Dr Mangalampalli Balamuralikrishna (1930–2016), and many others who spread the fragrance of classical music across the world.

Understanding the cultural milieu of the region would help in reading the various subtexts in the life stories of musicians of that era. They were products of their times and inherited the art from their predecessors. One can easily say that in all of South India, the Telugu-speaking regions had the widest variety of music available at any point of time.

However, this great glory did not seem to last for too long. A large number of factors, a few political and others socio-cultural, were responsible for the gradual decline of the classical music culture in Andhra. Many great artistes turned towards Tamil Nadu that continued to support and nourish the classical arts. In one of his older speeches, the famous Carnatic vocalist Dr Mangalampalli Balamuralikrishna said, 'Today Tyagaraja is alive because of the Tamils. They sing his songs regularly and keep him alive. The Telugus seem to have forgotten their own heritage.' This was furthered by Dr Nedunuri Krishnamurthy, who once said, 'I learn my music from the audiences of Madras and Tamil Nadu. They have safeguarded and kept a culture of music that we (Telugus) seem to have taken for granted.' The sentiment expressed by both these stalwarts is a grim reflection of the decline of classical culture in the Telugu-speaking regions.

In the last nine decades, The Music Academy, Madras, which grew to become a premier organization patronizing Carnatic classical music, has honoured many renowned artistes from the Telugu lands and from Telugu family backgrounds. The Academy's prestigious title of 'Sangita Kalanidhi' was bestowed upon several stalwarts with Telugu ancestry like Dwaram Venkataswamy Naidu (1941), Karur Chinnaswamiah (1950), Chittoor Subramania Pillai (1954), 'Papa' K.S. Venkataramiah (1962), Alathur Sivasubramania Iyer (1964), Rallapalli Ananthakrishna Sarma (1974), Mangalampalli Balamuralikrishna (1978), Sripada Pinakapani (1983), Nedunuri Krishnamurthy (1991), Sheikh Chinna Moulana (1998) and A. Kanyakumari (2016). Many others like Emani Sankara Sastry, Chitti Babu and Dandamudi Rammohan Rao, to name a few, were regular performers in all the Sabhas in Chennai in the famous December music season. The Telugus might swallow their pride but the fact is Chennai remains the Carnatic capital of India.

The once glorious chapter of Telugu drama, too, came to an end with the gradual decline of the theatre culture. Telugus eventually took to the more popular mediums of television and cinema for entertainment. The once thriving dance tradition also began its descent after the demise of a whole generation of traditional gurus like Nataraja Ramakrishna (1923–2011), Vempati Chinna Satyam (1929–2012) and Vedantam Satyanarayana Sarma (1935–2012). The artistes trained by these gurus might be the last of the generation that still pursues classical dance. The partition of the state into Andhra Pradesh and Telangana seems to have done less to enhance the classical arts. It would take a major renaissance before Telugus can get back the lost glory of their performance practices.

2

God in the Form of a Guru

*'A Guru alone will be able to protect one by administering, with love,
the medicine of spiritual initiation and enlightenment to keep the mind
free from attachment.'*

—Guru Leka Etuvanti

The status of a Guru is considered the highest in all the traditional systems
of knowledge in India. The Guru is someone who is closer to a student
than his own parents, who is responsible for the overall growth of the
student. He is a strict disciplinarian where it is needed and yet is loving,
accessible and caring at all times. The Guru's role is crucial to the growth
of a music or dance student. As young Murali started showing promise as
a musician, his father Pattabhiramayya set out to find an able Guru for
him. Being a musician himself, it wasn't difficult for Pattabhiramayya to
teach his son. For that matter, without much effort, Murali learnt to play
the flute, which his father played. But Pattabhiramayya felt the need for an
outside, more vigilant eye that could look beyond compassion. But in the
region around Srikakulam and the surrounding districts of coastal Andhra
where they lived, there were few teachers of classical music.

At the crack of dawn on 5 December 1883, as the Arudra star
ascended the skies, a second son was born here to a devout couple,

Brahmasri Sheshachala Amatya and Mangamamba. It was the holy month of Margaseersha in the traditional Vaishnava calendar when special prayers are offered to Lord Vishnu. Till date, thousands of devotees observe this month with much reverence and adoration.

Lord Krishna in the Bhagavad Gita, chapter 10, says:

बृहत्साम तथा साम्नां गायत्री छन्दसामहम्।
मासानां मार्गशीर्षोऽहमृतूनां कुसुमाकरः।।10.35।।

(Among the Vedic hymns, I am the Brihat Saama, among the Mantras, I am the Gayathri Mantra.
Of the twelve months, I am Margaseersha, of the seasons, I am the spring season.)

In other years, the couple would religiously make a pilgrimage to the temple of 'Andhra Maha Vishnu'. It was on the premises of this temple that the great king Sri Krishnadevaraya of the Vijayanagara Empire penned his epic poem 'Aamuktamalyada', a Telugu literary adaptation of the story of Saint Andal, the only female among the ancient Vaishanava Azhwars. In the auspicious month of Margaseersha, every morning, poems from Andal's magnum opus 'Thiruppavai' and 'Nachiyar Thirumozhi' are sung to the lord.

The couple had had a son earlier whom they named Hanumanta Rao. Their second son was named Ramakrishnayya. Mangamamba gave birth to a total of eight children—four sons and four daughters. After Ramakrishnayya, the other two sons were Subba Rao and Tirumala Rao. The four daughters were Rajyalakshmamma, Sowbhagyamma, Satyavatamma and Mahalakshmamma. In those days, having a large family was a sign of prosperity. Having lived the full life of a Grihasta, Sheshachala Amatya decided to head out for his spiritual journey. He took Sanyasa Ashrama and was rechristened Sri Sri Pradyumnananda Saraswati. He didn't live long enough to see the success of his son. After his demise, Mangamamba was left with the responsibility of taking care of the family. The eldest son, Hanumanta Rao, became a father figure for everyone at home.

Pantulu Garu, as Ramakrishnayya fondly came to be addressed very early in his life, grew up in this large joint family. There was a constant reminder of their great ancestors and his Srivatsa Gotram. One name that came up was Brahmasri Pundarikakshayya, who was a famed scholar of Sanskrit. In addition to having conducted numerous Yagnas and Yagas, he was known to be a great philanthropist who generously helped everyone who sought his solace and advice. He wrote a book titled Advaita Sudha Nidhi, which made him popular among the philosophers and intellectuals of his era.

Even as a child of five, Pantulu had already learned the Vedic mantras at home and could chant them effortlessly. As per the Telugu Vaidiki Brahmin tradition, most boys are initiated into the sacred thread ceremony or Upanayana Samskaram at the age of seven. However, for Pantulu, this was delayed until he turned thirteen, in 1896. All expenses in this large household were being borne by Hanumanta Rao, and they had to save to conduct the extravagant ceremony. Once this was successfully concluded, the teenager Pantulu was qualified to work and add to the household income.

One of the family members, a paternal aunt's son, Brahmasri Adivi Chinna Venkata Pattabhiramayya Pantulu, was working as the *thanedaar* in the Challapalli Samsthanam, a minor Zamindari settlement. Pantulu was sent to work here as a *musaddi* or a clerk. That year, Pantulu's boss took him to their native village of Peddakallepalli in Krishna district. The village was already famous as 'Kadalee Puram' and 'Dakshina Kashi'. The designation of a thanedaar was a respected one. All local issues were solved by him. Hence the villagers often feared and honoured anyone who sat in that position. Though Pantulu was only fourteen years old, his professionalism gave him the aura of a senior and experienced person. While living in the village, Pantulu's interest in culture grew, particularly so in music after watching various travelling drama companies.

His family boasted of great Sanskrit scholars, legal experts and even employees of royal kingdoms. But in his conservative Brahmin community, music was looked down upon as an art form meant for cheap entertainment. Still, Pantulu couldn't contain his curiosity and the search for a teacher began. In that remote village in Andhra Pradesh, there was only one person who was acknowledged as a teacher of 'Shastreeya Sangeetam'. Pantulu was drawn to him. In the summer of 1898, at the

Agraharam in Peddakallepalli, Pantulu sought him out. On reaching his home and presenting himself before the master, Pantulu bowed down in reverence and began chanting his Pravaram, the traditional way of introducing oneself to elders and seeking blessings. '*Abhivaadaye Chatussagara Paryantam Gobrahmanebhya Shubham Bhavatu. Srivatsa Gotrodbhavaha, Seshachalarya Putrah, Srikaakula Gramavaasi, Parupalli Ramakrishna Sharma Naamah, Aham Asmibhoh*,' he chanted, as both his palms touched his ears before he brought them down, crossed them on the floor and touched the feet of someone he had already considered as a Guru. The Guru was mighty pleased with his student already!

Susarla Dakshinamurthy Sastry: The Man Who Returned Tyagaraja to the Telugus

There is little biographical detail about Susarla Dakshinamurthy Sastry. When I interviewed violinist Annavarapu Ramaswamy in Vijayawada, he only had one thing to say. With great reverence he folded his hands and said, 'Aayina Oka Agrahaareekudu! (He belonged to an Agraharam!)' What seems to be a pretty innocuous statement was actually loaded with subtext. The ancient Agraharams, especially around the Andhra region, were notorious for their strictly disciplined lifestyle. Ramaswamy understood the life of a resident of an Agraharam in the nineteenth century, and the passion required for artistes to emerge out of that uncompromisingly orthodox lifestyle and follow their love for something like music, which was looked down upon. That was the reason Ramaswamy's eyes brimmed with tears even as he made that statement about his Guru's Guru.

Whatever we know about him is of an anecdotal nature. For the bi-centennial celebration of Saint Tyagaraja's birth, a commemorative souvenir was brought out. It contained articles by various musicians of that era. Among these is an essay by Pantulu Garu about his guru.

Dakshinamurthy Sastry was born on Ashada Shukla Trayodashi in the Roudri year of the traditional Telugu calendar. That correlates to 1 July 1860. His parents, Susarla Gangadhara Sastry and Lakshmamma, were residents of an Agraharam. Their oldest son, Krishnabrahma Sastry, had passed away at a young age. After him, a second son, Lakshminarasimha

Sastry, became a great scholar of the Telugu and Sanskrit languages. Dakshinamurthy was the third child. Having studied Sanskrit, Tarka, Nyaya and other traditional branches of education, Dakshinamurthy Sastry got interested in music. Those days, those who wanted to learn music had to travel to Thanjavur, the cultural heartland of Tamil Nadu. Legend goes that the determined seventeen-year-old Sastry walked from his village over several weeks to reach Thanjavur.

In Thanjavur, he sought out Venkatasubbayya, the first disciple and a relative of Saint Tyagaraja. Venkatasubbayya hailed from the village of Aakumalla in Andhra. Since he was staying in the Manambuchhavadi area in Thanjavur, over a period of time he came to be called 'Manambuchhavadi Venkatasubbayya'. Living in Thiruvaiyaru then, he was already teaching music to several students there. Noteworthy among them were 'Maha' Vaidyanatha Sivan, 'Patnam' Subrahmanya Ayyar, 'Lavani' Venkata Rao, Sharabha Shastry and Panchapakesha Iyer, the grandson of Saint Tyagaraja. Venkatasubbayya was also a composer in his own right. Some of his famous compositions like 'Mariyaada Kaadu' in Ragam Saraswati and several other Ragamalikas were popular in the concert circuit among the earlier generation of musicians.

Sastry went to him and sought his mentorship. In the tradition of the ancient system of Gurukula Vaasam, where the students live with their guru, Sastry stayed with Venkatasubbayya. In addition, he also trained under Tiruvottriyur Tyagayyar. After half a dozen years of intense training with his gurus, it was time for him to return to Peddakallepalli. But this time, his mission was different. Inspired by his guru, he wanted to set up a Gurukulam in Peddakallepalli. This was also the first time songs of Saint Tyagaraja were going to such remote places in Andhra. Sastry turned his own house into a Gurukulam. He not only began teaching for free, but also fed his students every day. Sastry had a large family of three sons and three daughters. In addition to his sons Krishna Brahmam, Nageshwara Sastry and Vishwapathy Sastry, he also took care of his brother Lakshminarasimha's son Susarla Gangadharam Sastry. He trained all of them to be musicians. In between, for a few years, the family migrated to Machilipatnam, so that his children could continue their higher studies. Once that finished, they returned to Peddakallepalli.

Sastry's only aim was to spread the music of Saint Tyagaraja. For that, he was ready to overcome any obstacles. He was a rebel of his time. Breaking the protocol of a rigid Agraharam, Sastry's was an open house. His students came from every caste and community, and he welcomed them with an openness that many of his time would have found difficult to digest. Anyone was welcome so long as they were interested in learning music. In addition to vocal music, Sastry also taught the veena, violin, and flute. Over a period of time, several illustrious students were trained in his Gurukulam. They included Challapalli Seetaramayya, Challapalli Subbayya, Chitta Purushottama Sastry, Rajanala Venkatappayya, Dvivedula Lakshmana Sastry, Duddu Seetaramayya, Prabhala Anjaneyulu, Tripuraneni Venkatadri Chowdhary, Dalipathri Ramaswamy and Nanduri Simhadri Appalacharyulu. The brightest star among all his students, though, was Ramakrishnayya Pantulu. While many students came and went, Pantulu, being the pet of his guru, trained under Sastry for a total of twelve years.

With such a large brigade of students, Sastry began organizing the Tyagaraja Aradhana Festival every year. A rare group image from the early 1900s shows Guru Susarla at the annual festival surrounded by his students. Pantulu can be seen holding his violin. This is probably the only surviving image of Sastry from when he was active as a festival organizer. Sastry had sown the seeds of Guru Bhakti in each of his students. One of his major contributions was to completely change the musical landscape of the Telugu-speaking regions. One can ascribe the unprecedented popularity of Saint Tyagaraja in remote corners of Andhra to the efforts of Sastry and his large contingent of disciples. After having trained many disciples and spread the music of Saint Tyagaraja in every corner of Andhra Pradesh, Sastry finally breathed his last on 30 July 1917 in the month of Bhadrapada.

Along with his music, Pantulu's job as thanedaar continued. He was now an eligible bachelor. Brahmasri Keshiraju Poornayya Pantulu of Repalle village offered his daughter Venkataramanamma in marriage to Pantulu. They lived happily but for a short while, as Venkataramanamma developed some health complications and passed away soon. Pantulu had only been married for a year, and this was a big shock for him. To keep his mind away from the depression enveloping him, in 1902, Pantulu took up the post of a *karanam* or accountant for the village of Telugurayunipalem. But belonging to a conservative family, he could not live as a young widower owing to the traditional *dosham* of *Anashramam*. According to the Shastras, for a young Brahmin to be able to participate in many important traditional rituals, he would have to strictly fit into one of the Ashramas: either be a Brahmachari or a bachelor, or a Grihasta or a householder. The role of his wife was of great importance for his home to function. Pantulu being a young widower was stuck in an odd position that would imply a dosham. To get out of this and fulfil his duties as a householder, he had to be married.

In 1906, Pantulu decided to give up his job and completely dedicate himself to music. Taking the permission of his guru, he travelled to Thanjavur. Renting a small house on the West Main Street in Thanjavur, Pantulu stayed there for a year. Those were the days when stalwarts of music performed regularly across villages nearby. Pantulu got the chance to attend numerous concerts by musicians like Ramanadapuram 'Poochi' Srinivasa Iyengar, Madurai Pushpavanam and Konerirajapuram Vaidyanatha Iyer. That was also the era of great Harikatha Vidwans. Pantulu regularly heard Harikatha concerts by stalwarts like Palakkad Anantarama Bhagavatar, Thirupazhanam Panchapakesha Sastrigal, Mangudi Chidambara Bhagavatar, Thirukodikaval Krishna Iyer and Tiruchi Govindaswami Pillai. In addition to attending their concerts, he sought out all these musicians and acquired a large number of Kritis or compositions from them. He also learnt to play the violin and flute.

The year he lived in Thanjavur transformed his mind and he became more determined to be a musician. Like his guru Susarla, he too decided to return to Andhra and recreate the culture of Thanjavur in his native place.

Meanwhile the family decided that Pantulu couldn't carry on as a widower and began looking for another alliance. This time, Kumari Venkataramanamma, the daughter of Brahmasri Maddali Seetaramayya Pantulu of Kaptaanpalem near Challapalli, married him. Re-entering Grihastashramam in 1908, Pantulu continued his music training and teaching on the side. Additional responsibility fell on his shoulders when the karanam or village head of Machilipatnam, Parupalli Venkatakrishnayya

Pantulu, decided to leave his job. This new responsibility was handed over to Pantulu. The Tahsildar of Telugurayunipalem, Bhaktavatsalam Naidu, had a keen interest in music. Breaking protocol, he became a student of his subordinate Pantulu. This news created a sensation across the region, making Pantulu famous as a musician for the first time.

In 1915, John Sinclair, first Baron Pentland, Governor of Madras Presidency, visited Tenali. A special program of music was organized in his honour. Pantulu gave a concert. The Governor was so pleased that he took the gold medallion he was wearing and gifted it to Pantulu. This news too spread across the region. In 1916, Pantulu became a father for the first time, to a beautiful girl child. At around the same time, Pantulu's Vedanta teacher, Kanukollu Trivikrama Rao, had decided to renounce the world and become a monk. He was rechristened Sri Vimalananda Bharati and appointed the pontiff of the Sri Siddheshwari Peetham at Courtallam. In addition to being a scholar of Sanskrit and Vedanta, he was a prolific writer. He was an authority on the works of Adi Shankaracharya. His speeches have been compiled into a seven-volume set titled *Sri Vimalananda Vignana Vilasanubandham*. The Pantulu couple found spiritual solace in Sri Vimalananda Bharati Swami (1878–1950). He was a great devotee of Sri Chandrashekhara Bharati Mahaswamiji III (1892–1954), the 34th Jagadguru of the Sringeri Sharada Peetham in Karnataka. Pantulu and his wife took the newborn to the Guru for blessings. Being a devotee of the Dakshinamnaya Sharada Peetham in Sringeri, he decided to name his daughter Sharada, after the goddess of learning. Though enjoying his family life, Pantulu continued with his musical journey.

The same year, the first All India Music Conference (AIMC) was held in Baroda. Under the able patronage of Maharaja Sayajirao Gaekwad III, Baroda had grown to be a centre for culture, especially classical music. Having heard of the fame of Pantulu, Diwan Thanjavur Madhava Rao brought it to the notice of Hindustani musician and scholar Pandit Vishnu Narayan Bhatkhande. He in turn wrote a letter to the Raja of Vizianagaram to send his most famous musicians to the conference. The Raja chose the great Veena Dhanammal, who was on his payrolls in the royal court as an Asthana Vidushi, and Pantulu. Author Janaki Bakhle writes in her book, 'In keeping with the format of the Indian National

Congress sessions, participants at the first AIMC delivered their speeches in English and the conference's standing committee was created to include a representative each from Southern Maratha country, Baroda, Tanjore, Gujerat, Mauslipatan, Mysore, Madras, Madura, Bengal, Lucknow, Nagpore and Karwar.' A total of nineteen performing musicians were invited, fourteen of them being Hindustani artistes and four Carnatic artistes. Out of the four, along with Abraham Pandithar and his daughter Maragathavalliammal, the iconic Veena Dhanammal and author M.S. Ramaswamy Iyer, was Pantulu. At the conference, they became great friends. In addition, Pandit Vishnu Digambar Paluskar, who founded the Gandharva Mahavidyalaya, and the great Abdul Karim Khan of the Kairana Gharana befriended Pantulu. Atiya Begum Fyzee Rahamin, one of the only women musicians invited to the first AIMC, spent a substantial time with him learning about Saint Tyagaraja. She was to write about this 'friendly acquaintance' later in one of her essays on music.

Pantulu was totally devoted to his Guru Susarla. He emulated him in every way possible. From the very year after his guru's demise, Pantulu began organizing a small music festival in his Guru's memory. This was to grow into a major event over the years.

It was around this time that Pantulu was invited to perform at the Saraswati Gana Sabha in Kakinada. Established in 1904 by Komireddy Suryanarayanamurthy Naidu during the festival of Dasara, the Sabha became a nerve centre for Carnatic music culture over a decade. What began as a three-day festival gradually grew into a festival of eleven days and nights. The zamindar of Polavaram was its president in the first decade. Being a man of refined tastes, he often travelled to the Thanjavur region and heard concerts. He invited the stalwarts of the era to perform in his Sabha. Musicians like Konerirajapuram Vaidyanatha Iyer, Kanchipuram Naina Pillai, Ramanadapuram 'Poochi' Srinivasa Iyengar, Thirukodikaval Krishna Iyer, Govindaswamy Pillai and Harikatha scholars like Mangudi Chidambara Bhagavatar performed there. From the kingdom of Mysore, musicians like Mysore Vasudevacharya, Bidaram Rachappa, Bidaram Krishnappa, Veena Seshanna and Subbanna were invited to perform regularly. In addition to these visiting musicians, there were several leading local musicians like Veena Venkataramana

Dass, Sangameshwara Shastry, Piratla Shankara Shastry, Mridangam *vidwans* like Ashwadhati Ramamurthy and many others who performed at the festival. Mangudi Chidambara Bhagavatar's Harikatha concerts that went on for several nights were highly appreciated. He was the first Harikatha exponent to compose an entire Katha Prasangam on the life of Saint Tyagaraja, using over seventy Kritis. The Rasikas and Telugu audiences were more than happy to welcome him. In addition to that, he was a great food lover. So the Sabha made elaborate food preparations for him and his entourage of musicians.

Around that time, the greatest Harikatha exponent in the Telugu region was Srimad Ajjada Adibhatla Narayana Dasu—a polymath, polyglot and versatile genius. It was Pantulu who arranged a meeting between Narayana Dasu and Chidambara Bhagavatar with the aim to bring together two different streams of musical scholarship. The Telugu press of the day reported this grand meeting as a 'Krishna–Kaveri Sangamam'. The eleven-day-long festival and the Sabha became a great centre for artistes to meet and interact with each other. Among all the artistes of Andhra, the one who got the highest praise for his vocal concerts was Pantulu. He also got invited to Madras, where a new music culture was brewing.

On 21 November 1921, Pantulu performed at the Gokhale Hall in Madras. Accompanying him was Mysore T. Chowdiah on the violin, Kumbakonam Azhaganambi Pillai on the mridangam and Kanchipuram Velayudha Mudaliar on the khanjira. All the musical stalwarts of Madras attended the concert. Towards the end, Gana Vidya Sundari Bangalore Nagarathnamma (1878–1952) went onto the stage and felicitated Pantulu. In the speech she made, she regretted not having heard him earlier and not being able to travel too much to remote Andhra to perform in the festivals he was organizing, owing to her health. In addition to honouring him with a silk *angavastram*, she took out an emerald necklace that she was wearing and presented it to him. This was to be the beginning of a friendship between Pantulu and Nagarathnamma, which would last till her demise. She invited him to Thiruvaiyaru where the annual Tyagaraja Aradhana was being conducted. Later, Pantulu was also made a board member of the Tyagabrahma Aradhana Mahotsava Sabha in Thiruvaiyaru. Mangudi Chidambara Bhagavatar (1880–1938) who already had a vast repository of Tyagaraja Kritis, announced to the august gathering that he would like to learn more Kritis from Pantulu. With such grand endorsements and praise, Pantulu's fame spread in Madras too.

Back home in Andhra, Pantulu travelled and performed extensively across the region. There was no village or temple he didn't sing in. There was no festival without his music. Several honours and recognitions came his way. The Saraswati Gana Sabha in Kakinada, which would honour stalwarts of music with a gold medal, a silver *kalasham* or ritualistic pot and a citation, decided to bestow the same on Pantulu in 1929. The same year in May, the Andhra Research University honoured him with the title of 'Bharathi Theerthopadhyaya'. He was made the President of the fourth Andhra Gayaka Mahasabha Festival that was conducted in Vijayawada in 1930.

In 1931, the Andhra Saraswata Parishad, under the leadership of veteran musician Piratla Shankara Shastry in Narsaraopeta, honoured him with the title of 'Gayaka Sarvabhowma'. This grand ceremony was right in the middle of their third music festival that ran for three days from 7–9 March. Several great stalwarts of music were invited to perform here. On the second evening, a grand function was organized and this honour was bestowed upon Pantulu. This was the title he was to be known by for the rest of his life.

Invitations poured in from Madras. C.R. Srinivasa Iyengar began the Tyagaraja Music Festival at the Gokhale Hall with Pantulu's inaugural concert. It was during that time that the Columbia Recording Company heard him and brought out gramophone records of his songs. Old posters of Columbia Records billed him alongside other musical stalwarts like K.B. Sundarambal, Chembai Vaidyanatha Bhagavatar, Palghat Rama Bhagavatar, Doraiappa Bhagavatar, violinist T. Chowdiah of Mysore, Nagaswaram and Thavil Vidwans Thiruveezhimalai Brothers and Needamangalam Meenakshisundaram Pillai and Pantulu's friend, the great Veena Dhanam. The only other artiste from Andhra on the same poster is Cocanada Satyavathi Bai, who was famous for her Harikathas. In this record, Pantulu sang two compositions of Saint Tyagaraja: 'Karuna Samudra' in Ragam Devagandhari and 'Paraloka Bhayamu' in Ragam Mandari.

As Pantulu's fame spread, he was also offered a home to stay in Madras. His musician friends would already address him as 'Ramakrishnayyar' as though he were a local Tamilian. While he was very tempted to shift, he remembered his responsibility to spread the music of his guru in Andhra. After all, he had promised Guru Susarla that he would continue the work of propagating the music of Tyagaraja. He returned and settled down in Vijayawada. He sold whatever he had inherited from his father and built a house. He got his daughter Sharada married to Purnachandra Rao, the son of Keshiraju Ramakrishnayya Pantulu. As he continued his services to music, he kept in touch with the music fraternity in Madras too.

The Music Academy of Madras was established in 1928. Pantulu was one of the few artistes from Andhra invited to perform regularly. On the invitation of his old friends Harikesanallur Muthaiah Bhagavatar and Mysore Vasudevacharya, Pantulu was made a member of the experts committee. Bhagavatar, who was fond of Pantulu, also introduced him to several big patrons of music in Madras. Old images of the Music Academy show him alongside the stalwarts of his era. The same year, the mid-year concert series was held in April. The venue was Gana Mandir, an extension of Dr U. Rama Rau's clinic on Thambu Chetty Street in George Town. On 13 April, Pantulu gave a vocal concert accompanied by Thriuparkadal Srinivasa Iyengar on the violin and Venu Naicker on the mridangam. Several well-known musicians of the city, including Pantulu's old friends, the ageing Veena Dhanammal and her family who were also residents of George Town, attended. Dhanammal, who rarely gave a nod of approval for anyone's music in public, is supposed to have showered great affection and praise on Pantulu's rendering of Tyagaraja Kritis. Recollecting her words, her grandson and writer T. Sankaran writes in an essay: 'For Dhanammal to praise anyone, they had to have the highest standards of music. Pantulu's rendering of Tyagaraja's "Vedalenu Kodandapani" in Ragam Thodi, was a topic of discussion for several days in Dhanammal's house. She only had high praise for him!'

Pantulu was invited to be on the advisory expert committee of the Music Academy in 1933. The conference of the Academy was inaugurated by Nobel Laureate C.V. Raman and was presided over by K. Ponniah Pillai. That same year, Pillai was honoured with the title of 'Sangita Kalanidhi'. Pantulu's name was featured with several great stalwarts of that era in the Academy's journal. From the entries in the journal we know that he lamented the deterioration of the quality of music due to neglectful teaching practices. On 24 December 1933, with the Kalanidhi 'designate' Ponniah Pillai in the chair, Pantulu read out a paper in Telugu titled 'Karnatic music and its Present Situation'. The Academy's journal quotes an excerpt:

> The ancients conceived music as an Upasana. Later on the art developed greatly in the hands of poets and master musicians. If one examines old treatises on music, he would find that at the times of the Ratnakara, Indian music had not divided itself into Hindustani and Karnatic styles. The theoretical basis of the present day Karnatic music might be said to be Venkatamakhin's 'Chaturdandi Prakasika' formulating the 72 Melakartas. But it would be found from the actual practice of the musicians that the guide for the musicians either in the singing of the Raga or of the Kriti, is the compositions of the musical trinity of South India, Thyagayya, Dikshitar and Syama Sastri. At the present, music has no doubt deteriorated, mostly because of the fastly dying Gurukula system of old. To prevent further deterioration and preserve the peculiar glory and grace of Karnatic music, an authoritative body like Music Academy should collect and publish an authorized version of Lakshana Gitas and recognized Kritis.

On the fourth day of proceedings, Ragalakshanas were taken up for discussion. Hindustani musician S.N. Ratanjankar, who was then serving as the principal of Morris College in Lahore, was also present. Twenty ragas were taken up for discussion. In his presentation, Pantulu said:

'Even individual Svaras have their particular Svabhavas or characteristics. For instance, it was laid down in the Sastra that the svabhava for Sadarana Gandhara was gamaka, whereas that of Antara Gandhara was fixed. If the latter was to be used with gamaka in any particular Raga, it was specially mentioned as an exception as in the case of Sahana.'

When the discussion led by Lakshmana Pillai of Travancore turned to Ragam Ghanta, Pantulu stated that Ghanta was different from Ghantaravam. He pointed out a mistake in the Sangita Sampradaya Pradarsini that morphed both the names. 'In the ancient treatise, as also in the Sangita Parijata, this Ghanta was classed under Hanumaththodi,' he added.

On the sixth day, the Lakshanas of Purnachandrika were taken up. The Academy journal mentions that Pantulu sang a Ragamalika of Manambuchhavadi Venkatasubbayya, which had the Prayoga *Dha-ni-sa-ri*. Another day on the Ragam Hindustani Kapi, Pantulu doubted the usage of Antara Gandhara or Kakali Nishada in the Ragam.

These detailed observations and arguments that brought out the finer nuances of music showed the musicians of Madras the in-depth study Pantulu had done on music and the immense knowledge he possessed. Being a master of Sanskrit, Pantulu would often quote Ragalakshana Slokas from various treatises, impressing everyone at the Academy. Over the period of this conference, a close friendship developed between Ratanjankar and Pantulu. In a letter written to him later, Ratanjankar invited Pantulu to Lahore to visit the college and requested him to deliver a few lectures on music and music theory.

In 1934, the Sangita Kalanidhi was given to T.S. Sabesha Iyer. Once again, Pantulu, being on the expert committee, actively participated in the day-to-day debates and discussions held at the Academy. A group photo of the members of the Academy shows Pantulu sitting in the front row beside his friend Harikesanallur Muthaiah Bhagavatar, Tiger Varadachariar, Saraswati Bai, Madurai Shanmugavadivu and her young daughter M.S. Subbulakshmi. In 1935, Pantulu was once again invited to be on the experts committee. That year, the Sangita Kalanidhi was given to Mysore Vasudevacharya, yet another old friend of Pantulu. That year in the December music festival, more recording companies approached Pantulu to bring out LPs and gramophone records.

In 1943, the large group of disciples decided to celebrate the Sashtiabdhipoorthi or the sixtieth birthday celebrations of Pantulu in a grand way. The town of Bezawada (modern-day Vijayawada) was all decked up for this event. The function on 26 October was inaugurated by Rajah Saheb Venkatadri Appa Rao Bahadur, a great patron of the arts and a literary figure who was already popular for his Telugu translation of the twelfth-century Sanskrit poetic work *Gita Govindam* authored by poet Jayadeva. As per the ancient Telugu tradition of honouring artistes, a large

Gajaarohanam ceremony was conducted where Pantulu was taken on an elephant in a procession. A grand function was organized at the Lakshmi Talkies theatre in Vijayawada. It was the talk of the town for months on end, as it saw the participation of all the famous cultural personalities of that era. Legend goes that the great guru of Saint Tyagaraja, Sonti Venkataramanayya, also had a Gajaarohanam in Thiruvotriyur.

A special souvenir with letters and messages from Pantulu's friends and admirers was published. Several notable writers, poets, Sanskrit scholars, dramatists and Rajas, zamindars, lawyers sent in special messages praising Pantulu and his dedication to spreading music in the Telugu countryside. Among those testimonials, there is a noteworthy poem written by the poet laureate Vishwanatha Satyanarayana who dedicated a poem in praise of Pantulu. He wrote:

చదువునకు నాల్గు దశలవి
యధీతి బోధాచరణములచట ప్రచారం
బెది నాళీట గొఱవడు న
య్యది సంపూర్ణంబు గాద యనవచ్చు గదా !

ఒకటి మూడును నొకరాశి ప్రకటమునకు
రెండు నాల్గును నొకరాశి రెండవాదియ
యుత్తమము, పదిమందికి నుపకరింప
నట్టి కళ యుండెనేమి లేదాయె నేమి?
ఈః నాల్గు దశలయందున
గానంబున చరమ దశయుగా మనె స్తుతికిన్
దానెంతో తగును దిక్కుల
నేనుగు పారుపలి రామకృష్ణ సుధి, ధరన్

Writing about his music, the famous musicologist Prof. P. Sambamurthi (1901–73) who was the head of the department of Indian music at the Madras University wrote:

Pantulu is a brilliant singer, a creative artiste of high degree and a person with extensive and varied repertoire. Every concert he gives some fresh food for thought. If there is the element of accuracy in his Raga expositions, and if there is the touch of classicism in his musical renderings, it is not in a small measure due to his detailed knowledge of the Sangita Sastra and the correct Sampradaya. Some professional musicians think that knowledge of musicology is not quite an indispensable thing. It is an erroneous notion. A musician who has studied musicology stands on a firmer ground and is able to sing or perform with greater confidence. He is able to tackle the most difficult Ragas and abstruse rhythms. Our Pantulu Garu deservedly attained eminence in the professional world and he can look back with legitimate pride and gratification at his long record of professional career. In the discussions in the Madras Music Academy Conferences, he has shown his grasp of the many subtle problems relating to music. He is a Lakshana–Lakshaya Vidwan in the truest sense of the term. One cannot hope to form a correct estimate of his genius by listening to a single concert of him. One should listen to a series of his concerts. The Gayaka Sarvabhauma is by nature, an unassuming, unostentatious gentleman. It is somewhat difficult to draw him out. He is a kind and good-natured friend. He has an open heart and never fails to recognize greatness from whichever source it comes. He has to his credit some brilliant disciples. Sri Ramakrishnayya Pantulu has maintained the standard of the ideal Gayaka, envisaged in the classical works on music. He has set a noble example for all future musicians to follow. He is a musician of sterling worth. He is a sincere performer. No accompanist can overpower him. He has always upheld the traditions of Kacheri Dharma. His concerts are not only pleasing but are also educative. May god vouchsafe to him a long, happy and prosperous life and help him serve the great heritage of ours for many more years to come.

Several musician contemporaries of Pantulu like Bangalore Nagarathnamma and Ariyakudi Ramanuja Iyengar sent long letters filled with lavish praise. Telugu literary giants like the Venkata–Parvatheesha poet duo, Shatavadhani Challa Pichayya Shastry, Avadhaana Bhooshana Potharaju

Lakshminarasimha Kavi, Shatavadhani Bhamidipati Appayya Shastry, Pouranika Shiromani Peeshupati Subrahmanya Shastry, Gaanakala Prapoorna Srimad Ajjada Adibhatla Narayana Dasu, Avadhaana Shiromani / Mahamahopadhyaya Kashi Krishnacharyulu, Chellapilla Venkata Sastry, and many more musician contemporaries showered their love and praise on Pantulu. No other musician in the modern history of Andhra Pradesh managed to gather the amount of goodwill from all sections of the society like Pantulu did.

The same year in December, the Music Academy bestowed the Sangita Kalanidhi award on the veteran flute Vidwan Palladam Sanjeeva Rao. That year's conference was inaugurated by Dr Sarvepalli Radhakrishnan, who was then the vice-chancellor of the Banaras Hindu University. The conference was held at the Sundareswarar Hall at the RR Sabha. A group photo from that year shows Pantulu sitting in the first row alongside his old friends Muthaiah Bhagavatar, K.V. Krishnaswamy Iyer, the president of the Music Academy and several other eminent musicians of that era.

At the silver jubilee celebrations of Sri Tyagaraja Bhakta Sabha in Bheemavaram, a grand function was organized to honour Pantulu on 20 January 1944. The same evening Pantulu gave a concert that went on from 6 p.m. up to midnight. The music loving audiences of Bheemavaram kept requesting for more. This concert made the news once again. In 1945, the Music Academy celebrated the Swati Tirunal day, presided over by Sir C.P. Ramaswami Iyer. In a group photo taken on the occasion, one can see Pantulu seated in the first row beside Violin Chowdiah, U. Rama Rau, Maharajapuram Vishwanatha Iyer, Sir C.P., Palghat Mani Iyer, G.N. Balasubramaniam, D.K. Pattammal and others.

In 1947, the Carnatic music world was celebrating the birth centenary of Saint Tyagaraja. The Andhra Ganakala Parishat in Rajamundry brought out a special souvenir edited by the scholar Vissa Appa Rao on 11 January. The souvenir carried articles by many noted musicians of the day—Kalluri Veerabhadra Sastry, Bangalore Nagarathnamma, Gayaka Ratna Piratla Sankara Sastry, Tiger Varadachariar, Prof. Dwaram Venkataswamy Naidu and others. In this, Pantulu also published an essay on the life of his Guru, Susarla. In addition to this, he was also a regular writer and contributor on music to numerous Telugu magazines and newspapers.

Until 1948, all the artistes who were performing in radio had only two choices—the All India Radio station in Madras and the Deccan Radio of the erstwhile Nizam's dominion. Artistes from coastal regions of Andhra would travel to Madras and give concerts. By then Pantulu was a regular at the Madras radio station. However, over a period of time it became tedious for artistes to keep travelling all the time. It was Pantulu who conducted a signature campaign bringing in all the artistes and organizations of the Andhra region and appealed for a station to be set up in Vijayawada. After endless letters, his efforts bore fruit. The Vijayawada station of the All India Radio was inaugurated on 1 December 1948 with a concert by Pantulu. At the inauguration, all the famous cultural personalities were present. Musicians, scholars, writers and poets like Vishwanatha Satyanarayana, Devulapalli Krishnasastri and others marked their presence at this historic event.

In 1951, as he did each year, Pantulu was conducting the music festival in memory of his Guru Susarla. All his students and many musicians had gathered for it. The huge event was more than just a series of concerts. It was a celebration on the scale of any wedding. Everyone who came was fed and taken care of. Pantulu took a personal interest in making sure all the arrangements were in place. It was hectic, but one would assume he was used to it. The day would begin in the morning with prayers. He would be in *madi*. On the third day of the festivities, in the morning, he woke up as usual and after going through daily ablutions, in madi, he came and prostrated in front of his Guru's photo placed on a little table. Spreading his arms folded in front, facing the earth below, he stretched his body out in *Saashtanga Namaskaram* and never got up. He had suffered a stroke. The news of his demise soon spread across the world of music. One of his senior-most students N.C.H. Krishnamacharyulu wrote: 'There couldn't have been a better way to make his final exit from this world. At the feet of his guru, doing a Saashtanga Namaskaram in madi. This was the sign from gods and a blessing from his Guru.' And thus the Atma of Pantulu merged at the feet of his beloved Guru Susarla.

Though Pantulu departed physically, his name was to stay on forever in the world of music. It is not possible to list out all his students here. The list is long and illustrious. But the most noteworthy students included Dalipathri Pichchari Brothers who played the Nagaswaram, Saride Subba Rao who played the violin, Rajanala Venkata Ramayya, the great Sanskrit poet and scholar, Sistla Rajashekharam, his cousin and the celebrated stage actor Addanki Srirama Murthy, Paturi Seetaramayya Chowdhary, Maddulapalli Lakshmi Narasimha Shastry, Singaraju Suryanarayana Raju, T.K. Yashoda Devi, M.V. Ramana Murthy, Tirupati Ponna Rao, violinist Chadalavada Satyanarayana, violinist and composer Nallan Chakravarthula Krishnamacharyulu, Annavarapu Ramaswamy, Juluri Arundhati Sarcar, and last but not the least, Mangalampalli Pattabhiramayya.

The Pantulu story doesn't end here. He will return later in the book. The stature of a 'Guru', in a sense, grants itself an afterlife. The very position of that elevated status gains a shade of immortality.

3

A Star is Born

The villages in the coastal districts of Andhra Pradesh are rather special and unique for their phenomenal cultural contribution. While you had the ancient temple towns, you also had several new urban settlements that got integrated into these towns over a period of time. Rajamahendrapuram, Antarvedi, Bheemavaram, Annavaram and so on were ancient settlements which gradually got extended into bigger cities over time. There were many more places that were already famous for their cultural output. The ancient town of Kuchelapuram which later became Kuchipudi, was famous for the community of Brahmin boys whose profession was to pursue classical dance. Tenali was famous for its most eminent citizen Tenali Ramakrishnayya, who adorned the court of Krishnadeva Raya, the emperor of Vijayanagar Empire. Further in, there was a long list of Agraharams or settlements of Brahmin communities. In places like Iragavaram, great scholars of various branches of Sanskrit like Vedam, Tarka, Vyakarana, Nyaya and Shastra emerged. There was a time, maybe half a century ago, when you just had to mention the village your family hailed from and your profession and scholarship would be assessed with much accuracy and reverence. Over time, the cultural heritage of a place became evident by its very name. The author and translator Prof. Ramaswamy of Bangalore, in one of his seminal essays on the greatness of Telugu language, wrote:

If one puts on a weighing scale all the Sanskrit manuscripts of rest of India on one side, just the amount of Sanskrit manuscripts produced between East and West Godavari regions in Andhra will weigh more.

This is a comment on the rich cultural life that the coastal regions once enjoyed. The village of Kuchipudi housed several Brahmin families dedicated to the art form of dance-dramas like Bhagavatam and Yakshagaanam. In the nearby smaller princely states of Pithapuram, Karvetinagaram and Bobbili, a separate culture of dance thrived in the Kalavantulu communities, much like the Devadasi tradition of the Thanjavur region of Tamil Nadu. Women from traditional Kalavantulu families would be dedicated to temples. A completely different repertoire of song and dance evolved from this community, adding to the existing corpus of literary texts and scholarship. However, for a large section of men, especially from the Brahmin communities, music and dance in public, remained a social taboo. Except for the traditional Brahmin families of Kuchipudi, no other Brahmin men took to performing in public. Even if they did, like in the Bhajana Sampradayam genre of music, it was often limited to temple festivals and special occasions.

Prayaga Ranga Sarma (1859–1927)

Ranga Sarma hailed from Rajole in the East Godavari district. His father Lakshmana Shastry was a renowned expert of *jyotishya* or astrology. Having trained in Sanskrit and other Shastras, Ranga Sarma took a keen interest in the Bhajana Sampradayam, or congregational singing of Bhajans, from an early age. He would sing songs of the Adhyatma Ramayanamu, Gita Govindamu, and Krishna Leela Tarangini with great passion. He also began writing poems and composing songs which became very popular with the local audience. He used the mudra or pen name Rangadasu in his songs.

At a very young age, Sarma went on a pilgrimage by foot to Kashi, Prayaga and other holy places, camping for a while at Prayaga before making a return. In those days Kashi Yatra was considered the final journey in one's life. If a person returned from the journey successfully, it was celebrated. On completion of his pilgrimage, Sarma earned the title

'Prayaga Ranga Sarma'. For the rest of his life, the holy city of Prayaga was prefixed to his name, giving him a unique identity.

As a composer, he travelled to several temples in remote villages and sang songs in praise of the local gods. However, from the existing corpus of works, it seems that Rangadasu composed his most memorable songs in a beautiful ancient temple of Lord Krishna in Gudimellanka. It's a remote village even today.

In 2017, I visited the temple, driving two hours into the rural landscape from the main city of Rajamundry in East Godavari district. Lord Krishna is worshipped as Venugopala here. The large temple pond and lush green surroundings would have surely inspired any musician. The composer's 'Ramaududbhavinchinaadu Ravikulambuna', 'Rama Rama Enaraada' and the folk songs 'Eme o chitti' and 'Krishnamma Gopalabala Krishnamma' became extremely famous. The first song is about Lord Rama, except for one line. He writes, '*Asudanu Gudimellankanu Velasina Vara Gopaludu Kaada*,' dedicating his song to Venugopala of Gudimellanka. In the folk song Krishnamma, he writes, '*Pudamilo Gudimellanka Puravasudaina Vara Rangadasuniki Ippudu Varamulichchina Tandri Krishnamma*,' mentioning that he was a resident of Gudimellanka. Over the decades, like many other folk songs, the song morphed, different lyrics were added to the tune, and these made their way into early Telugu cinema. Similar to these songs dedicated to the Gudimellanka temple, his song 'Bala Tripura Sundari' is dedicated to the goddess enshrined in a temple in the nearby village of Kadali.

Ranga Sarma's only daughter Sooryakantamma grew up in the shadow of her father. It wasn't a surprise to see her blossom into a musician of great merit in a short time. In addition to singing, she mastered the veena. As per the customs of the community, as she was turning eight, they began looking for a groom for her. That was an era when girls were married off early.

Today, child marriage is illegal. But a hundred years ago, it was common practice across the Andhra region. It was only much later that writers like Gurzada Appa Rao wrote 'Kanyasulkamu' and raised awareness against the practice. Even so, in remote villages, the practice continued to be followed.

Mangalampalli Pattabhiramayya (1892–1984)

Pattabhiramayya was a rebel of sorts for his time. Being the first in his huge family to take to music was in itself a great feat. It was unthinkable for conservative and traditional Brahmin boys to do so. That was meant for 'others'. Pattabhiramayya was born on 17 October 1892, as the sixth child and fourth son of his parents Venkataramayya and Seethamma. The couple had ten boys and three girls. Venkataramayya was a fifteenth generation migrant to Antarvedipalem, a hamlet in the Rajole Taluk of West Godavari district. They were Telaganya Brahmins, or the sect of Vaidiki Brahmins that hailed from the Telangana region. There is a village called Mangalampalli even in present-day Telangana. After the fall of the Kakatiya Empire, various communities migrated to coastal Andhra and settled there. Theirs was one such. However, they continued to maintain their old village name Mangalampalli. Going by the older interviews given by one of his most famous students, the musician and musicologist Nookala Chinna Satyanarayana (1923–2013) and the veteran violinist Annavarapu Ramaswamy (b. 1926), one knows that Pattabhiramayya's life was as dramatic as a movie script.

Pattabhiramayya was an oddball from his childhood. At the age of five, he was put in a *pathshala* where traditional subjects of the Shad Darshanas would be taught alongside modern-day subjects like maths, science and geography. At the age of eight, his sacred thread ceremony was performed. As per tradition, the father would not teach his son but get a professional teacher from outside. A teacher from a nearby village was invited to stay at their home for Pattabhiramayya to study the sacred texts. After a few months, the teacher decided to give up material life and become a Sanyasi. Venkataramayya's friend Krishnamacharyulu took pity on the little boy and began teaching him Sanskrit. He was also sent to learn Jyotishyam or Hindu astro-science from his older brother Somanna who was staying in Sakhinetipalli. It was while he was studying here that Pattabhiramayya observed the temple rituals and got attracted to music. A local teacher Pichchi Anantacharyulu was a regular performer at the temple festivals. Pattabhiramayya decided to risk approaching him for music lessons. But why was music considered a taboo then?

More than a taboo, conservative Brahmin families looked down upon it. In an era when there were very few performances and concerts outside of the usual temple rituals, most musicians had to accompany dancers. And since dancers came from the Kalavantula community, the profession came to be looked down upon. The common refrain in local Telugu is more colourful than what the English language can accurately translate: '*Mundalu Saanula Venta Dolu Dappu Kottukuntu Thirigevaadu*', meaning, 'One who keeps beating the drum behind whores and prostitutes'. In retrospect, one can only say such statements were the result of the prejudices about various communities. Pattabhiramayya decided his love for music was so great that he had to overcome the stifling orthodoxy around him. He began taking lessons from Anantacharyulu in secret.

Meanwhile, in 1903, Venkataramayya passed away, leaving the burden of the large family to Seethamma and his older son Seetharamayya. The family's finances were not in great shape either. Taking stock of everything at home, on the thirteenth day after the funeral, Seetharamayya realized his younger brother Pattabhiramayya was turning out to be a 'good for nothing'. Little fights among the siblings took a big turn when once Pattabhiramayya got late for a meal. In anger, Seetharamayya hurled a little brass tumbler at him, bursting out that he was an unlucky fellow feeding off the little remaining family wealth. In front of everyone, he asked him to leave the house, saying he was now on his own. Venkataramayya's younger brother Venkataratnayya was present at the time too. He worked as an Asthana Vidwan in the zamin of Alluri Pedda Suryanarayana Rao in nearby Chintalapalli. It was common among Princely kingdoms and feudal lords to appoint their popular artistes, poets and writers as 'Asthana Vidwans'. A decorative honour that would sometimes mean getting grants of land or grains from their patrons, and being felicitated at public events, temple festivals and other such traditional ceremonies. Taking pity on his nephew Pattabhiramayya, he decided to take the boy along with him.

Pattabhiramayya was entrusted with work in the zamin. Alongside, he was also learning Sanskrit and participating in the local Bhajana Mandali. Over time, he picked up songs from the Adhyatma Ramayana and other texts.

In the nearby village of Taatipaka lived a famous singer and violinist, Kocharlakota Rama Raju (1876–1946). Born in Upada village in 1876 to Venkatanarayana and Janakamma, he trained in music from Chebrolu Venkataratnam of Machilipatnam and later from C.S. Krishna Iyer, an early student of Patnam Subrahmanya Ayyar. He composed numerous Varnams, Kritis and Swarajatis and authored several books like *Gayaka Manoranjani* and *Sreerama Keerthana Karnamrutam*. Having heard about the greatness of Rama Raju, Pattabhiramayya left his uncle's house without informing anyone and sought his mentorship. This caused great trauma to Venkataratnayya, who had taken the responsibility of his nephew. They searched for the boy for a week and then gave up. A week later, though, Pattabhiramayya returned home, causing both joy and anger at the same time. He explained that he had sought Rama Raju out as a music teacher, but his style of teaching didn't suit him. The truth came out later, when a letter from Rama Raju seeking pardon for Pattabhiramayya's behaviour reached the house. Realizing that Pattabhiramayya was Venkataratnayya's nephew and had run away from home, Rama Raju reprimanded him and sent him back. Back in the zamin, Pattabhiramayya continued to work, promising his aunt and uncle that he would never vanish again. One day, the zamindar caught Pattabhiramayya off-guard and scolded him for running away when he could learn Sanskrit from his uncle.

In 1903, Venkataratnayya fell ill with the dreaded cholera and passed away. Pattabhiramayya was sent back to Antarvedipalem to his mother and brothers. Back home, and more or less back to square one, Pattabhiramayya was once again the point of worry for his mother. The oldest son-in-law of the house Bhagavatula Papayya Sastri was also a cousin by relation. He convinced Seethamma that music was not so bad after all. If the boy was really interested in it, he should be allowed to pursue it. Pattabhiramayya's mother sent him with Sastri to his home in Elamanchilli. In the same village, Seethamma's brother Bhagavatula Venappa was housing one Subramanyam Iyer, who hailed from Pakshitheertham in Chengalput district of Tamil Nadu. Other than the fact that he was a travelling musician who would live on his meagre earnings as a teacher, nothing else was known of him. He had arrived in the coastal Andhra region and kept moving from one village to another. He depended largely on the kindness and hospitality of the local Brahmins. He somehow found his way into Venappa's house and was given a room to stay. Around the same time, Pattabhiramayya was entrusted to his custody as a student. Now serious music lessons began. Though the family, especially the mother and older brother, were unsure about him taking up music, they were also at peace thinking the boy had finally settled on one thing. Little did they realize that this wouldn't last too long.

Iyer was good at teaching and the young boy really took a great liking to his new Guru. The music lessons kept going for days, and the Venappa family was getting used to this routine at home. One morning, both the Guru and the student went missing. Frantic searches began. Numerous letters were sent to different villages in search of these two. Seethamma had barely made peace with his love for music when this news came to cause her further anxiety. For weeks on end, nobody knew where they had gone. One day a letter arrived from Pakshitheertham. Iyer had written to the Venappa family saying the young boy was safe and with him. He had some urgent work and had to leave immediately, and the young student insisted on accompanying him since he didn't want the music lessons to end. So both of them set out urgently, thinking that they would return soon. Though the family heaved a sigh of relief, they were not totally convinced that everything was fine.

In Pakshitheertham, Iyer had incurred a huge debt. He had to pay off several people and his meagre earnings weren't enough. On top of this was a young stomach to feed. Iyer had a friend known as Tawker, a Gujarati Brahmin who worked as a cook in Kanchipuram. He invited Iyer to come there and seek opportunities for a new livelihood. Iyer and his student arrived at Kanchipuram. While Tawker expected his friend, he didn't know this little kid would tag along. He found him an unnecessary burden on them and threw him out. In an alien land where he knew neither the language nor the people, little Pattabhiramayya was left to the mercy of nature. Sleeping in temple choultries and eating free prasadams offered by kind priests, how long could he carry on? He was angry that the Guru he had trusted completely had let him down. He was also frustrated at the way things were unfolding in his life. He went from temple to temple in Kanchipuram, crying his heart out to the gods. He starved for days and turned weak till he fainted. When he woke up, he found himself surrounded by priests of the Varadaraja Perumal temple. He was murmuring something in Telugu, so they took him to the house of a Telugu Vaishnava scholar who lived nearby. After feeding him and taking care of him, the host heard his long story. He also helped him write a letter to Antarvedipalem.

There was a big sigh of relief on receiving a letter from Pattabhiramayya with a temporary address in Kanchipuram. Everyone at home had given up any hope of his return. Neighbours kept taunting them that he might not even be alive. They had managed to find Iyer's address and sent several letters to Pakshitheertham, but there was no response. This only made things worse. Seethamma began to curse herself for her carelessness and began ignoring her health. Once the letter arrived, they were finally at peace. It stated everything that had happened and requested money to go onwards to Thanjavur, the heartland of Carnatic music, so he could find a better teacher. Seetharamayya replied asking him to return home since their mother's health was not too good. He also said he could pursue music later. The kind scholar who had taken care of Pattabhiramayya put him on a train back home, packing him some food for his journey. The train went via Madras and left for Andhra only the next morning. Pattabhiramayya decided to sleep on the platform in Madras Central. He kept his only possessions under his head like a pillow. The next morning he was in for a rude surprise. The pillow had vanished and in its place was a brick! Whatever little money his brother had sent and his possessions had been stolen. On hearing his story, a kind stationmaster gave him some money and put him on the next train out.

He finally got home. While everyone was glad they had him back, they were equally worried about his future. It was around that time that someone who had heard the name of Susarla Dakshinamurthy Sastry mentioned it to them. He belonged to the Sishya Parampara of Saint Tyagaraja and was a resident of Bandar, or Machilipatnam, as it was called then. Pattabhiramayya, who had now lost trust in Gurus, was hesitant to take up yet another, but decided to give it a chance.

Once he reached Machilipatnam, at the house of Susarla, he was asked to prove himself. Pattabhiramayya, by then, had already reached a certain level of training in Geetams under Pakshitheertham Iyer. Susarla was impressed. The next question was his stay. Susarla was teaching students at his home. It was a traditional Gurukula Vasam. He already had ten disciples living with him and one more would be difficult to accommodate. Through an older connection, he found a friend who was a revenue inspector. They made an arrangement that Pattabhiramayya would teach his two daughters in return for accommodation. Thus, more serious music lessons began under the mentorship of the new Guru Susarla. The Guru's nephew Gangadhara Sastri was a co-student and a good flautist. So while Pattabhiramayya learnt vocals from the Guru, he also found himself drawn to the flute and very soon mastered that instrument too.

Guru Susarla would frequent Thanjavur, and on each of those trips he would take a few disciples along with him. This time he took Pattabhiramayya. In Thanjavur, they met the stalwart flautist Sarabha Sastry. Both Susarla and Sastry had trained under the same Guru. Pattabhiramayya was asked to perform in Sastry's presence. On hearing the young boy, Sastry blessed him. Pattabhiramayya met many more great musicians in the company of his Guru. He also began giving small concerts. The first half of his concert would be vocal and the rest would be on the flute. The audience connected well with this. However, in the summer of 1917, Guru Susarla passed away.

In the meantime, his flute Guru Gangadhara Sastri migrated to settle down in Vijayawada. Pattabhiramayya followed, since living in Machilipatnam after the demise of his Guru only enhanced his sense of loss. This opened a new door of opportunities. Since Gangadhara Sastri could not possibly teach all the students who approached him, he would send many to Pattabhiramayya. Soon Pattabhiramayya was also making some money from local concerts, and was able to send it home to his mother and older brother. They were finally happy that the boy had settled down, and started thinking of his marriage.

As was the custom, Pattabhiramayya's Jaatakam or horoscope was passed around to be matched with that of the probable bride and several alliances came forward. Finally, the family settled for Sooryakantamma, the daughter of Prayaga Ranga Sarma. That his bride was also interested in music was enough to convince Pattabhiramayya.

Pattabhiramayya and Sooryakantamma got married in 1918. She was only nine years old, and he was already in his mid-twenties! While such marriages were common, it was also normal for the girl to return to stay at her parents' home after the marriage. So Sooryakantamma returned to live with her husband in Vijayawada only eight years later, in 1926. By then, she was also a veena artiste giving concerts. His mother Seethamma visited the couple at Antarvedipalem and stayed with them for a while. She returned feeling satisfied that her son had settled well after all the troubles he had gone through. She was ageing and not very healthy. She breathed her last at the age of sixty-one at her native place.

The couple settled down in Vijayawada. While Pattabhiramayya had his performances and was also teaching students, Sooryakantamma got more active with her music practice. She would give veena recitals at local festivals and temples. Every Tuesday and Friday, she would walk up the steps with her veena to the top of the Indrakiladri Hill and perform inside the ancient temple of goddess Kanakadurga, the presiding deity of the city. Having a good knowledge of Sanskrit and Telugu, she would also sing various songs for the goddess. Over a period of time, this became a regular practice. Four years flew by, and then Sooryakantamma became pregnant. While women traditionally went to their parents' home for the course of the pregnancy, Sooryakantamma chose to stay on. Even into her sixth month of pregnancy she continued to climb the hill with her veena and offer her prayers to the goddess. This was getting to be a risky affair. Her parents, who were then living in the village of Shankaraguptam, decided to bring her home for the last trimester. Her only condition was that she would take her veena along with her. Pattabhiramayya tried to dissuade her saying it wouldn't be possible to sit down on the floor and perform in such an advanced stage of pregnancy. But Sooryakantamma was not one to be easily convinced. Back in her parents' home, Sooryakantamma was taken care of by her older sister Subbamma. Widowed at a young age, Subbamma decided to live a saintly life, immersed in prayers, and help about her parents' home. The two sisters would bond and Sooryakantamma would tell her if a boy was born, she would name him Krishna. She would laugh about leaving Krishna in Subbamma's custody if he troubled her when she got busy with her music. Subbamma would take care of her younger sister and when Sooryakantamma would lie down with the veena by her bedside, Subbamma would sit in the afternoons and read slokas or prayers by her side. The local doctors had given clear instructions to her parents that she must not sit on the floor. However, she would keep strumming the strings of the Veena while lying down in the afternoons and late into the night.

On 5 July, Sooryakantamma began having labour pains. The doctor and midwife were called in. During the auspicious twilight hours of the evening of 6 July 1930, a Sunday in the Gregorian calendar, Sooryakantamma gave birth to a boy. On the traditional Telugu Panchangam that the family followed, it was the month of Ashada and the auspicious day of Ekadasi, the last few days of the holy Uttarayana period, as the Vishaka Nakshatra ascended the skies. The delivery was a normal one. Subbamma sat by the bed chanting mantras even as the baby was washed and placed near Sooryakantamma. She held her son close to her and would often be seen whispering into his ears. The ladies of the house would laugh and tease her, asking if she was already planning to teach him the veena. The first ten days passed by quickly. Pattabhiramayya was sent a letter and he finished some of his pending music commitments and started for Shankaraguptam. On the tenth day, Sooryakantamma suddenly developed a fever. Being on a liquid diet, her body was still weak from the delivery. The fever worsened over the next couple of days. The local doctor was rushed in to see her. The body temperature didn't come down. On the third day, as though she had a premonition, she signalled to her sister Subbamma. It was 10 p.m. Subbamma brought some water and poured a few drops in Sooryakantamma's mouth. She gently held the baby by her side and the next moment she was gone.

Pattabhiramayya was barely able to get over the happiness of seeing his son when this unexpected catastrophe struck. What would happen now? Who would take care of the infant? What did the future hold? He had faced many troubles in his life as a budding musician but a personal trauma was difficult to get over.

A fortnight passed, the family was still dealing with the loss. But there was work and prior commitments; Pattabhiramayya couldn't wish them

away. He began packing his bags and some of the jewellery of his late
wife. A bunch of talkative relatives who saw him packing his bags began
gossiping loudly. Was he going to sever all connections with the family
now? If so, why did he want only his wife's jewellery? He should also
take his son. Yet another cursed the little boy for being an unlucky one,
causing the death of his mother. All this was intolerable. Pattabhiramayya
began crying. Subbamma, who overheard the conversation, threw a
huge fit of rage and reprimanded the relatives for their loose talk. She
consoled Pattabhiramayya and told him to leave the child in her care. She
remembered her late sister's words. She swore to take care of the child and
make him her priority as long as she lived. Leaving his son in Subbamma's
care, the heartbroken Pattabhiramayya returned to Vijayawada.

Though back in his routine of teaching, Pattabhiramayya's mind was in
disarray. It was around this time that Nookala Chinna Satyanarayana joined
him as a student. He had come to Vijayawada to learn violin from Akkaji
Rao. Alongside, he began taking vocal lessons from Pattabhiramayya. He
was one of the few students who had the habit of noting down everything
he considered important. Years later, his notes were a significant resource
of the musical culture of Andhra then.

However, everything about the place was alive with memories of his
wife. A few of his relatives suggested a second marriage. But he ruled that
out immediately. Nobody could replace Sooryakantamma. One day, he
walked up to the top of the Indrakiladri Hill to the temple of goddess
Kanakadurga. It was the same flight of steps Sooryakantamma had walked
up and down countless times to pray to the goddess. Hundreds of thoughts
flashed in his mind. By the time he reached the temple and faced the idol
of the goddess in the sanctum, he broke down completely. He prayed for
strength to carry on with his life and took a resolution not to remarry.
From now on, his sole aim in life would be to bring up his son as a good
musician. In the meantime, as per Sooryakantamma's wishes, the little boy
was being called Krishna at home.

On a trip to Eluru, a friend mentioned to him that Subbamma was
there with the child at her relative's place. Even as Pattabhiramayya was
entering the gate, the child began screaming as if he was familiar with
who was coming in. This surprised everyone. Pattabhiramayya held his

son in his arms and made a request. He turned to the elders at home and requested Subbamma to accompany him back with the child to Vijayawada. If Subbamma could continue to be a mother to his child, she was free to do whatever else she wanted, he said. Subbamma decided in the interest of the child that she would move to Vijayawada. Every day she would hold him in her lap and chant to put him to sleep. Pattabhiramayya made sure he provided his sister-in-law everything she required to take care of little Krishna.

As the boy began to walk, Pattabhiramayya would take him to the music classes he taught. On other days, Subbamma would take care of him at home. One day Pattabhiramayya returned home to find Subbamma upset. She had several grievances against the little boy. While Subbamma was busy with household chores, little Krishna had found his way to the room where Pattabhiramayya kept his tamburas. There he began playing with the strings. The next complaint was that he was a fussy eater. For Krishna to eat, someone had to sing or play music. Only then would he respond to food. Otherwise, he would go hungry and fall asleep from the fatigue of playing around the house. Pattabhiramayya began shedding tears of happiness knowing his little son was already showing an aptitude for music. In addition to that, little Krishna became the favourite of everyone in Pattabhiramayya's music classes. To keep him entertained, one only had to sing songs. He would watch them and smile without batting an eyelid.

It was around the same time that Parupalli Ramakrishnayya Pantulu migrated to Vijayawada and settled there, having purchased a house in the area that is now Satyanarayanapuram. There were many empty plots available around. Another musician Lanka Venkateshwarlu too had moved there. On the suggestion of a few friends, Pattabhiramayya managed to raise Rs 800, a princely amount for that time, and buy 400 square yards there. Having erected a small thatched roof hut on his plot, Pattabhiramayya invited his new neighbours to bless his house. His senior Guru-Bandhu Pantulu was also a neighbour now. Pattabhiramayya decided to continue his music training under Pantulu's mentoring. After his Guru Susarla's demise, he had always felt the need for another equally erudite and knowledgeable Guru. And Pantulu fit into that bracket well. Pantulu would organize the annual festival in memory of his Guru Susarla.

Mangalampalli Pattabhiramayya and Sooryakantamma, the parents of Balamuralikrishna.

Gayaka Sarvabhowma Parupalli Ramakrishnayya Pantulu, the guru from whom Balamuralikrishna learnt music.

Sri Vimalananda Bharati, the spiritual mentor to Guru Pantulu and Balamuralikrishna.

The revered polymath Vidwan Kashi Krishnacharyulu, whose guidance nurtured the child prodigy.

The only surviving image of Susarla Dakshinamurthy Sastry (*top row, fifth from left*) with his large batch of disciples, circa 1900. Parupalli Ramakrishnayya Pantulu can be seen to his right, playing the violin (*top row, second from left*).

Balamuralikrishna after his debut at the Susarla Aradhana Festival accompanied by Akkaji Rao on the veena and Radhakrishna Raju on the mridangam.

Ananda Vikatan, dated 18 January 1942, published a photo feature about Balamuralikrishna's debut at Thiruvaiyaru Tyagaraja Aradhana.

மாஸ்டர் பால முரளி கிருஷ்ண
பத்தே வயதான இந்தப் டை
பிரமாதமாகப் பாடி, பெரிய
வான் கஷ்டெயல்லாம் மூக்கின்(
விரல் வைக்கச் செய்து விட்ட

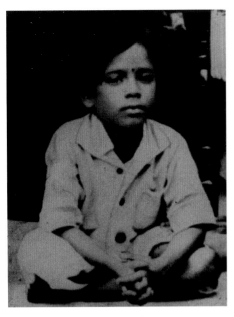

The child prodigy.

A studio portrait.

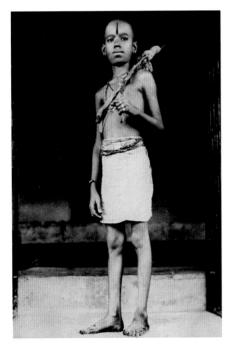

After his sacred thread ceremony.

On the lap of his father, Pattabhiramayya.

A young star with his jacket loaded with medals.

The little Balamuralikrishna (*centre*) with his Guru Pantulu at
the Susarla Aradhana Festival, where they take out a procession
of the portraits of Susarla and Saint Tyagaraja.

A concert announcement of Pantulu accompanied by Balamuralikrishna on the violin, 1945.

The famous Harikatha exponent Musunuri Suryanarayanamurthy Bhagavatulu (1909–1949), who rechristened him by adding the 'Bala' to 'Muralikrishna'.

A ticketed concert notice of Balamuralikrishna, accompanied by Saride Subbarao on the violin and Kovvidi Hanumantarao on the mirdangam, in a local newspaper, April 1945.

Little Balamuralikrishna, 'the senior-most disciple' of Guru Pantulu, along with other students.

Parupalli Ramakrishnayya Pantulu (*seated, fourth from right*) as an experts committee member of the Music Academy Madras, along with his contemporaries, including Tiger Varadachariar, Muthaiah Bhagavatar and Saraswati Bai.

Parupalli Ramakrishayya Pantulu (*seated, second from left*) along with Srimad Ajjada Adibhatla Narayanadasu, Kanchipuram Naina Pillai, Dwaram Venkataswamy Naidu and other stalwarts at a gathering in Kakinada in the 1920s.

Foster mother Subbamma, under whose love and care Balamuralikrishna spent his childhood years.

Sooryakanta Bhavanamu, the house in Vijayawada where Balamuralikrishna grew up.

Balamuralikrishna makes it to the cover of All India Radio's *Vaanoli* magazine in its August 1942 issue, the year he debuted at Thiruvaiyaru.

All his students would participate. A 1932 group image from this festival shows a young Pattabhiramayya standing right behind his Guru Pantulu along with other students, Vankadari Venkatasubbayya and Chilakalapudi Venkateshwara Sastry.

Over time, Pattabhiramayya managed to raise a three-storey bungalow with financial help from his friends and relatives. He named it 'Sooryakanta Bhavanamu' in fond memory of his late wife. The house-warming ceremony or Gruha Pravesham was done on the 22 August 1937. Several friends and students of Pattabhiramayya sang at the house on the occasion. Pattabhiramayya himself played the flute with his little son on his lap, and the gathering of elders, seeing the awestruck child, began calling him 'Muralikrishna'.

It was confirmed from the beginning that Muralikrishna would be a musician. However, nobody expected that he had a natural inclination to it. Pattabhiramayya himself was in for a surprise when Muralikrishna began to easily reproduce anything he heard, almost identically.

In Sanskrit there is a word for this: 'Eka Santaagraahi', or someone who can grasp anything in a single go. This is one of those rare unsolved mysteries of human nature where a child can grasp anything he/she hears or sees just once. Whatever they choose to grasp gets impressed on their memory forever. It was this nature of 'Eka Santaagraaham' that Muralikrishna displayed right from his fifth year.

He would repeat fairly difficult phrases in music on hearing them just once. This soon made news in the music circles in Vijayawada. Several of Pattabhiramayya's friends like Khambampati Akkaji Rao, a senior veena vidwan, would spend time with the little boy testing his memory. Now everyone around was convinced of the little boy's capabilities. Next came the question of formally teaching him music. While Pattabhiramayya was already giving lessons, it was advised that a more methodological training was needed. The only name that came up during these discussions was that of Pantulu.

Pantulu was not only the brightest student Susarla had, he was also an ace teacher. By then, he had trained a number of senior students. Pattabhiramayya sought him out as a teacher for his son. Initially, Pantulu refused to teach the little boy saying it was too young an age to trouble a child. If the boy had an aptitude for music, he should be brought to him after a few more years. In the meantime, Pattabhiramayya could continue teaching him at home. The other reason was that the boy was way too thin, weak and puny to have any stamina to put in the hours of practice required for the art. Pantulu tried to dissuade Pattabhiramayya. While this disheartened Pattabhiramayya, he insisted that Pantulu listen to the boy once before making a decision. Muralikrishna was brought in the presence of Pantulu and asked to sing. He sang a Geetam. On hearing him, Pantulu had a change of heart. He was not only impressed with his singing but also the way he presented that song. This was not a normal child, he realized. It was decided that on an auspicious day, he could formally join him as a student. However, Pantulu said he would have to learn Geetams all over again and began teaching him another Geetam. And thus Muralikrishna found the Guru who was to change his life forever.

An Impressive Debut

In 1938, like every year, Pantulu was busy organizing a music festival in memory of his Guru Susarla. The arrangements were elaborate, almost like a grand wedding. In addition to disciples of Susarla and Pantulu, several musicians from outside were invited to perform. Everyone was housed and fed for all the days of the festival. This was the one big event Pantulu personally monitored year after year. There was nothing more important to him than keeping alive the memory of his beloved Guru, year after year. This time around, Pantulu had an assignment to attend to and travelled out of town. The responsibility for making arrangements fell on his student Neti Lakshminarayana. He normally helped around the festival but this was the first time such a huge responsibility had fallen on his shoulders. He decided to include a few others of his Guru-Bandhus. Senior Mridangam artiste Radhakrishna Raju and Lanka Venkateshwarlu suggested he also include the name of little Muralikrishna in the festival. Pattabhiramayya was strictly against this. Moreover, Guru Pantulu was away. Without his permission, how could he possibly sing?! They kept playing around with the idea for many days. Other arrangements had to be made and invitations had to go to print. Without the knowledge of

Pattabhiramayya, Muralikrishna's name was printed for a performance scheduled on the 18 July 1938. Coincidentally it was Ashada Shuddha Ekadasi, the exact day on the traditional Telugu calendar that he was born on, eight years ago!

When Pantulu returned and saw the invitation, he was furious. He reprimanded Lakshminarayana saying this was no time to fool around. The child had barely joined as a student. Moreover, a Harikatha being performed by the great Musanuri Suryanarayana Bhagavatulu was to follow this performance. If the boy made any mistake, the Guru would be blamed. And Pantulu would have to hang his head in shame. Lakshminarayana sought pardon saying that it was too late and invitations had already been sent out. It was only a half-hour slot for Muralikrishna and if the boy's singing was really bad, they could cut it and request Bhagavatulu and his troupe to begin their concert right away.

On the morning of 18 July, senior artistes Akkaji Rao with his veena and Radhakrishna Raju with his mridangam got on to the stage. It was an Ekadasi and Pantulu was observing his ritual fast. Little Muralikrishna prostrated in front of his Guru, who blessed him. This boosted Muralikrishna's confidence. Pattabhiramayya was already sitting on stage with the tambura, tension writ all over his face. Praying that his son wouldn't embarrass everyone, he closed his eyes and kept strumming the tambura.

Muralikrishna looked at his Guru from the stage and bowed once again. He closed his eyes and began the Varnam 'Vanajakshiro' in Ragam Kalyani. Singing it in all the three speeds, Muralikrishna impressed everyone. He finished and bowed to his Guru once again. This time he began a quick Aalapana in Ragam Jaganmohini and followed it with a Tyagaraja Kriti, 'Shobhillu Saptaswara'. His fast-paced swara patterns and clear diction in that high-pitched voice once again had the gathering eating out of his hands. Before anyone realized it, three hours had flown by. He sang the Mangalam and everyone saw the time. Pantulu got up from his seat and first of all apologized to Bhagavatulu. But mid-way through, his voice choked with emotion, he ran to the dais, picked up Muralikrishna in his arms and hugged him tight. He realized he had misjudged the talent and capabilities of this little boy.

Bhagavatulu, who was equally immersed, decided to change the contents of his performance. Instead of giving his regular Harikatha, he began analysing the concert Muralikrishna gave, much to everyone's amusement. He gave a passionate speech praising the boy and announced that his name should be 'Balamuralikrishna', with everyone's approval. Guru Pantulu, Pattabhiramayya and the august gathering had witnessed something extraordinary that morning. They all unanimously agreed to Bhagavatulu's suggestion. This name was to become the boy's permanent name and create history in the world of music.

His foster mother Subbamma was uncontrollable. She removed *drishti* or the evil eye by holding a fistful of rock salt and red chilies. Everyone had labelled him unlucky at birth! Today, he was the toast of the town. Everyone was talking about him. Pattabhiramayya, too, was excited and relieved that his son was on the right path. Pantulu realized he was in possession of a rather unusual and precious diamond. It was now his duty to polish it further and make sure it shone brighter. Truly, a star was born!

4

At the Threshold of Fame

Carnatic music is easily the one genre where the concept of child prodigies has been consistent, more than in any other. For several decades now, musicologists and researchers have been trying to understand the phenomenon. Many believe that this could be a carry-over from another birth. Though the idea might go against modern scientific rationality, it is not new to the Hindu traditional understanding of the theory of Karmic law.

Oliver Wolf Sacks (1933–2015), the author of *Musicophilia: Tales of Music and the Brain*, wrote: 'There are some people who can scarcely hold a tune in their heads and others who can hear entire symphonies in their minds with a detail and vividness little short of actual perception.' How else can one explain a young child, incapable of writing a simple sentence, rattling off the names of Ragams or melodic scales within five seconds of hearing them? How does one explain what brings about this detailed musical imagery in the mind of a child? Going by the ancient philosophy of 'rebirth' enshrined in Hindu, Buddhist, Jain and other parallel schools of thinking, some have forwarded the theory that many of these child prodigies might be carrying forward some unfinished business from another lifetime.

Indian classical music has had its share of child prodigies. In North Indian or Hindustani classical music, there was the vocalist Kumar

Gandharva. Born Shivaputra Siddharamayya Komkali (1924–92) in Karnataka, he was only twelve years old in 1936 when his debut at the All India Music Conference in Mumbai made headlines. He had begun performing in smaller villages across Karnataka from the age of five. Then, there was Rais Khan (1939–2017), who, again at age twelve, was recognized as a child prodigy on the sitar.

Tabla maestro Zakir Hussain also began early in life. Having trained under his father Ustad Allah Rakha Qureshi from childhood, Hussain debuted on stage before he was ten. In Dhrupad, we have the Rudra Veena maestro Bahauddin Dagar, who hails from a long and illustrious musical lineage. He began playing from a very young age.

Carnatic music has been a proverbial hotbed of young geniuses. The post-Trinity era of Carnatic music has stories of how twelve-year-old Vaidyanatha Iyer (1844–93) was given the title of Maha or great, after a concert. It is said that he was able to render a Ragam Aalapana and Pallavis in his seventh year and had begun giving concerts by the time he was ten. Thereafter he came to be known as Maha Vaidyanatha Iyer. In the twentieth century, the first name that comes to mind is the famous M.S. Subbulakshmi (1916–2004). Trained under her mother Shanmugavadivu, she was only ten when she cut her first LP record. If you listen to the song, now available on YouTube, it is clear that this was a musical genius in the making.

The list of prodigious instrumentalists is equally impressive. Among them is S. Balachander (1927–90), the veena maestro, who debuted at age six. Long before he took to performing on the veena, as a prodigious teenager, he had already mastered about half a dozen instruments, including the sitar and dilruba. Among the percussionists in Carnatic music, Palghat Mani Iyer (1912–81) made his debut when he was only eight years old. And then there is Umayalpuram K. Sivaraman (b. 1935), who began performing on the khanjira at a young age. Hailing from one of the principal *shishya-paramparas*, or musical lineages, of Saint Tyagaraja, Sivaraman grew up in a musically rich atmosphere at home. Having mastered the complicated art of Carnatic rhythm, he is today hailed as one of the finest exponents of the mridangam.

The trend of musical prodigies is not limited to the distant past. The 1970s and 1980s saw the rise of Uppalapu Shrinivas (1969–2014) on the mandolin. He not only mastered an instrument alien to Carnatic music but also grew to be an unparalleled genius on it. With the arrival of television in India, regular telecasts of concerts resulted in greater viewing and appreciation. A superstar by age ten, his demise at the age of forty-five was a great loss to the world of music.

His contemporary, gottuvadyam and chitra veena artiste N. Ravi Kiran (b. 1967) hails from a musical family. At the age of three, he is said to have been capable of identifying over 100 Ragams. The other name on the veena is E. Gayathri (b. 1959), who began performing as a teenager. The violinist duo of brothers Ganesh Rajagopalan and Kumaresh Rajagopalan, too, debuted before the age of ten. Shashank Subramanyam (b. 1978) from Karnataka began performing very early on the flute and was christened Master Shashank, a title that stayed with him till he was well into his twenties.

It is interesting to note that in the twenty-first century, there have been more prodigies in Carnatic music than in any other genre. Abhishek Raghuram (b. 1985) and Anantha Krishnan (b. 1983), both grandsons of Mridangam Vidwan Palghat Raghu (1928–2009), began performing before they were ten.

The list continues to grow by the day. At the time of Balamuralikrishna's debut, in the Andhra countryside, there was no other prodigy like him. The festival where he debuted made Balamuralikrishna the talk of the town. Back at his lessons with Pantulu, everything had changed. Pantulu recognized this was no ordinary student. He had barely taught him one Geetam and now decided to graduate to teaching him Keertanams. In addition to being a vocalist, Pantulu himself was an ace violinist. Balamuralikrishna found himself attracted to that as well. In no time, he managed to master the instrument.

The news of an eight-year-old Balamuralikrishna debuting at Susarla Memorial Festival spread across the region. Several music sabhas and organizers began writing letters to both Pantulu and Pattabhiramayya. The next concert came a few months later during the festival of Dussehra. In the Durga Malleshwara temple nearby, grand celebrations would be conducted on all the nine days of the festival. Every evening noted musicians would be invited to perform. On 9 October 1938, Balamuralikrishna was invited to sing. The festival was also a meeting point for all the great scholars of the city. The great poet Kashi Krishnacharyulu and the noted poet and Sanskrit scholar Chellapalli Venkata Sastri were in the audience. Having heard the little boy, both poets immediately wrote poems in praise of his music and read them out to the assembled gathering.

News of these eminent poets praising the little boy's concert spread across the music world. Harinagabhushanam Pantulu (1884–1959) was a renowned musician living in Machilipatnam. He ran an organization by the name of Gana Vidyabhivardhini Sabha. He would organize concerts to celebrate the festival of Karthika Pournami. He invited Balamuralikrishna to perform on 30 November 1938. Also present at the festival was Sri Vimalananda Bharati, the Vedanta teacher of Ramakrishnayya Pantulu. After the concert, the organizer, Pantulu and Bharati blessed the little boy with gold medals.

Slowly Balamuralikrishna began getting more concert bookings. At other times, he was busy in the company of his Guru. In the December 2010 issue of Telugu magazine *Surabhi*, Nookala Chinna Satyanarayana remembers his schedule.

I would ferry little Muralikrishna on my cycle from my Guru Pattabhiramayya's house to Pantulu Garu's house. I would wait there while his music lessons were taken. The classes were not every day but whenever Pantulu Garu informed him. The classes would last for a few hours where Murali would both sing and play the fiddle. After that I would bring him back on my cycle to my Guru's house. During free time we would play games. Since he was very puny, I would carry him on my back like a horse and sing songs. I called him 'Murali' from the beginning and he would treat me like an older brother and call me 'Sathyam' or 'Annayya'. Whatever Pantulu Garu taught him in his class would be repeated while sitting on my back! So I knew which day it was a new Varnam or a new Kriti!

He also remembers another fascinating incident.

Once I accompanied my Guru Pattabhiramayya and Murali to the Ansari Park in Vijayawada. Those days if any Radio program came, someone would put it on speaker and everyone could hear it. We sat in the park and overheard a whole recital by violinist Dwaram Venkataswamy Naidu Garu. My Guru Pattabhiramayya said there was no point in the life of a violinist if they couldn't play like this! All three of us were too stunned for words. We returned home. The same night after dinner, Murali took his fiddle and reproduced everything he had heard in the park! Just the same way we had heard it earlier!

It was this power of grasping and reproducing whatever he heard that made Balamuralikrishna special and different from the other children of his age, or for that matter, other students of music too.

While Balamuralikrishna was doing well with music, a new worry popped up in Pattabhiramayya's mind. Balamuralikrishna needed regular modern schooling as well. He approached the municipal school. The principal was the known scholar Puttaparthi Narayanacharyulu. After speaking to the boy and seeing his high aptitude and IQ, he decided to admit him directly into grade six. Many people in school knew he was a singer and requested him to sing the morning prayers. Gradually, these morning prayers began turning into morning concerts. No students were ready to go back to their classrooms to study after the prayer. This was turning out to be a big hindrance. Moreover, there were examinations round the corner. One teacher put this grievance in front of the principal. Narayanacharyulu called Pattabhiramayya and explained the situation. He said his son really didn't need modern school education. And so, Balamuralikrishna's schooling came to a halt in just three months. Years later in many interviews he was to laugh about it and comment about his 'lack of education' with sarcasm.

Pattabhiramayya went to his Guru Pantulu and narrated what had happened in school. It was decided that Balamuralikrishna would only focus on music. Moreover, he had become the pet of the Pantulu household. Pantulu's wife Venkataramanamma took care of him like her own son. She would patiently feed and take care of Pantulu's large contingent of disciples. Years later Balamuralikrishna gave an interview to Hyderabad Doordarshan that though he lost his own mother at an early age, god had been kind enough to bless him with many more mothers. At home,

Subbamma took care of him and in his Guru's home, Venkataramanamma. He never felt the lack of a mother's love while growing up.

As news spread of the young boy's performances, one of Pattabhiramayya's students, whose husband worked at the All India Radio station in Madras, sent them an invitation. Surya Narayana Murthy was a native of Vijayawada working in Madras as the programming executive at the All India Radio. He retired as the deputy director general, years later. He invited the father and son to Madras. Thus, the first All India Radio broadcast of Balamuralikrishna happened on 2 July 1941. It was heard by the music-loving audiences of Madras and became the talk of the town. Many musicians who got to know that he was a student of Pantulu dashed off telegrams congratulating him and praising his student's singing. Balamuralikrishna had made news in the 'Carnatic Capital' even before he had formally performed there.

Pantulu arrived in Madras to attend the December Music Festival like every year. This time, he had his protégé Balamuralikrishna and Pattabhiramayya with him. The Jagannatha Bhakta Sabha was hosting the festival of the Madras Andhra Mahasabha concerts. On 31 December 1941, Balamuralikrishna gave his first live performance for the audiences of Madras. During this time, Pattabhiramayya kept up a steady correspondence with Subbamma back home, giving details of their travels. Through these letters, we know a lot of what took place in December 1941.

Tryst in Thiruvaiyaru

Thiruvaiyaru on the banks of the River Kaveri on the outskirts of Thanjavur is a site of holy pilgrimage for all Carnatic musicians. The *Adhishtanam* or final resting place of Saint Tyagaraja near the Bhavaswami Agraharam is the most well-known area here. Also famous is the ancient temple of Lord Panchanadeeswara and his consort, Goddess Dharmasamvardhini. Every year on the traditional Hindu calendar of Pushya Bahula Panchami, which normally falls in January on the Gregorian calendar, all Carnatic musicians arrive in Thiruvaiyaru to pay homage to the saint.

The festival began in a small way till it came under the management and guidance of Bangalore Nagarathnamma, the famed courtesan of

Mysore who built a shrine over the Samadhi. She was the first woman artiste to break through the patriarchal boundaries that governed the arrangements and organizing of the Tyagaraja Aradhana.

Pantulu was a regular attendee from the 1920s. Being a part of the Tyagaraja Sishya Parampara, he deemed it his moral responsibility to travel to Thiruvaiyaru every year for the Aradhana. He would also take his students along. They would travel to Thanjavur together a week ahead of the Aradhana. They would camp at Thanjavur and spend their time visiting ancient temples. From the detailed notes of his student Nallan Chakravartula Krishnamacharyulu, we know that they visited Thiruvarur, Vaduvoor, Umayalpuram, Lalgudi, Tiruchirapalli, Srirangam, Rockfort, Kumbakonam, Ganapathy Agraharam, Swamimalai and other areas around there. As the day of the Aradhana neared, they would make their way to Thiruvaiyaru. In Thiruvaiyaru, they would stay in the Bhavaswami Agraharam, close to the Adhishtanam of Saint Tyagaraja. There they would spend the next three days before Pushya Bahula Panchami, in the company of stalwarts of music. Three warring factions of Tyagaraja's disciples were conducting the Tyagaraja Aradhana then. Pantulu and his students would go to all three. Several of Pantulu's friends lived in Thiruvaiyaru: Patnam Suramaniam Iyer, Mysore Vasudevacharya, Sabhesha Iyer, Mangudi Chidambara Bhagavatar, and the queen bee, Bangalore Nagarathnamma.

Over the years, the three factions merged into one major group led by Nagarathnamma. She was responsible for reviving the memory of the saint in more ways than one. Witnessing her devotion to Tyagaraja, Pantulu strongly supported all her activities from the beginning.

The Tyagaraja Aradhana of 1942 was historical. Like every year, Pantulu and his students arrived in Thiruvaiyaru. Camping at the Bhavaswamy Agraharam, they actively participated in the Aradhana festival. A large tent was erected outside the Adhishtanam of Saint Tyagaraja. In the centre of it was a smaller enclosure for musicians. Everyone was expected to be seated there. The common practice was that great stalwarts of music would sit in front of the Adhishtanam of Saint Tyagaraja and sing songs. Sometimes a musician would go on and on without a pause. On the auspicious morning of Pushya Bahula Panchami, Pantulu got into that cramped enclosure with little Balamuralikrishna.

Placing the boy on his lap, they sat and heard the proceedings for the day. Bangalore Nagarathnamma performed the Kumbha Aarati to the Adhishtanam all the while singing the Tyagaraja Ashtotharam.

The great flute artiste Palladam Sanjeeva Rao opened the morning's concerts with 'Chetulara Sringaaramu Chesi', a composition of Saint Tyagaraja in Ragam Bhairavi. The year 1942 was the first time when the singing of a Pancharatna Kriti, a set of five special compositions by Tyagaraja, was announced. A senior musician's concert would be followed by those of others. After the first musician finished his concert, there was a little gap before the second one began. And that's when the unexpected happened. Did Pantulu trigger his student or was the little boy inspired by the overpowering musical ambience surrounding him? Sitting on Pantulu's lap, Balamuralikrishna began singing 'Manasa Sri Ramachandruni', a composition of Saint Tyagaraja in Ragam Eesamanohari.

Pantulu himself was not sure when his turn would come in the long list of musicians lined up to sing that morning. This was totally unscheduled and absolutely unexpected. All the gathered musicians began to peep over each other's shoulders to see where this Kriti was coming from. The curiosity of the audience was equally palpable. The song ended and there were a few seconds of silence. It seemed as if the crowd was too stunned to respond immediately. Those in the front row kept looking back and finally everyone's eyes turned towards Pantulu. He silently picked up the little boy, stood up and held him aloft so that everyone could see his face. Little Murali kept grinning while looking around. A special souvenir on Pantulu mentions that one of the organizers who knew Pantulu immediately announced, 'The voice you just heard is from this boy. His name is Balamuralikrishna. He is the son of Mangalampalli Pattabhiramayya of Bezawada. He is here with his Guru, our very own Pantulu Garu. One of these days we will arrange his Kacheri to fulfil all of your curiosity.' This announcement brought the much-needed calm and helped the function to continue. But as per the announcement, the organizers now had to fulfil their promise.

Looking at the tightly packed schedule, they enquired with Pantulu where they could fit this boy. On the one hand, they were hesitant to fix this concert ad hoc. But on the other hand, they had made an announcement and several curious vidwans kept asking them about this programme. Pantulu had his own concert on 7 January. If the organizers agreed, he said, he would be happy to give that slot to his little shishya. They reached an agreement and announced the said program. The news spread around Thiruvaiyaru very soon. At 5 p.m. on 7 January, Murali walked in with his Guru and sat on the slightly elevated platform. The audience began to crowd in to get a closer look at this little wonder.

One of the organizers got a little wooden box for Murali to sit on so that everyone could have a clearer view of him. Balamuralikrishna bowed to his Guru, then turned in the other direction and bowed towards the Adhishtanam of Saint Tyagaraja. Pattabhiramayya, too, had arrived and was delighted to know that his son had already made news. He took the tambura and sat behind his son. Murali closed his eyes and began an Aalapana. What happened after that is a tale that has been narrated with awe for decades. The time allotted was thirty minutes. It was almost close to an hour before he ended the concert and nobody seemed to have realized it. The assembly of musicians and Rasikas was too stunned to react. Once the concert ended, everyone got up and began rushing towards the platform. Amidst the chaos that ensued, little Balamuralikrishna went missing. The crowds kept mobbing around, while both Pattabhiramayya and Pantulu frantically looked for him.

One of the organizers got a hold of Pantulu and whispered something into his ears. Pantulu grabbed Pattabhiramayya's hand and waded through the crowds, following the organizer. They reached a little room behind the Adhishtanam. There, they saw Murali seated on the lap of Nagarathnamma. Everyone heaved a sigh of relief!

Nagarathnamma had realized that once the concert ended, there would be a hysteria of sorts. Towards the last Kriti, she asked an organizer to be ready to pick up the little boy and bring him to her room. She wanted to be sure that the crowds wouldn't inadvertently harm him. While she was narrating this to Pantulu and Pattabhiramayya, a village mendicant was passing by the room. He looked at Nagarathnamma and did a Namaskaram. She promptly asked him if he had heard the boy sing. The mendicant pulled out a coconut from his bag, moved it in circles above the boy's head as if to remove Drishti and broke it by flinging it onto the ground. He then pulled out a little rosary of tulsi beads and put it around the boy's neck. He turned towards Nagarathnamma and announced that this was no normal boy. He was a *Kaarana-Janma,* having taken birth to fulfil a great purpose in the world of music. After this incident, Pantulu and Pattabhiramayya took the blessings of Nagarathnamma and immediately left for Thanjavur. The next morning, the whole of Thiruvaiyaru was abuzz with the news of little Balamuralikrishna. Everyone was frantically searching for him only to be told that he had gone back with his Guru. A rich merchant from Chettinad who had brought a big silver bowl to gift him sent it through Daliparti Pichahari, the Nagaswaram Vidwan who was also a student of Pantulu and was scheduled to return a couple of days later.

The Aradhana of 1942 was a historic one in Balamuralikrishna's life. He became a sensation in the music fraternity. Senior music critic Sri Srinivasan Venkataraman got me a precious newspaper clipping. Ananda Vikatan dated 18 January 1942, had published a photo feature 'Aradhanai Kaatchigal' (scenes from the Aradhana). The caption for his photo reads: 'Master Balamuralikrishnan: *Paththey vayadhaana indha payyan, pramaathamaaga paadi periya vidhwangalai ellam mookin mel viral vaikka seidhuvittaan* (Just ten years old, this young boy with his fantastic singing has astounded the Vidwans).' Years later in several interviews, including the documentary series made on him by ETV in the 1990s, Balamuralikrishna would laugh saying, 'My music made news in Tamil Nadu even before I migrated and settled here'.

Even as a boy, Balamuralikrishna had a fairly hectic concert schedule and he made a significant name for himself across music circles. The veteran violinist Prof. T.N. Krishnan (1928–2020), in an interview with me, said: 'It was in 1942 that I first saw Murali. I was a young boy and we both were present at a festival in Chettinad. He was already famous by then! I don't think I know of any other boys (of) that time who enjoyed the kind of fame and a busy concert schedule like he did at that age!"

Remembering another concert in 1942, veteran vocalist I. Kameswara Rao writes in the commemoration souvenir 'Madhura Murali':

I clearly remember this like it all happened yesterday! It was in Naguluppalapadu, a village six kilometres away from the suburban railway station of Ammanabrolu. We all travelled by a passenger train from Ongole. It was the festival of Sri Rama Navami and Balamuralikrishna was scheduled to perform on the 15th of March. A huge crowd had gathered there. Balamuralikrishna gave a concert for three and half hours nonstop! The highlight of this was the Kriti by Pallavi Gopala Iyer, 'Needu Charanamula Pankajamula' in Ragam Kalyani. The elaborate Raga Aalapana, the beautiful Neraval at 'O Jagadjanani Manonmani Omkara Roopini Kalyani' are still in front of my eyes. There were no microphones or electricity those days. And yet, this voice reached every corner of the place. Tadigadapa Seshayya, a great musician who came all the way from Bapatla, was moved to tears. He came and blessed little Balamuralikrishna and took out the gold chain from his neck and put it around the boy's neck. It became the talk of that festival! Couple of days later, Balamuralikrishna was again scheduled to sing at the Upanayanam (sacred thread) ceremony in an advocate's house in Ongole. All of us went for that too! We were not invited, as it was someone's family event. Despite that, we all gate-crashed. He gave a three hour long concert. The highlights were 'Rama Neevadhukondhuvo' in Kalyani and 'Nagumomu'. He also sang 'Kommaro Vaanikintha Biguve', a Javali composed by Thirupandal Pattabhiramayya in Ragam Khamas. The great Sanskrit scholar Kalluri Veerabhadra Sastry who was present at the function spoke at the end. He wondered how a kid of this age could bring out the complicated emotional value present in the Javali which was difficult for adult singers to do!

Decades later Balamuralikrishna was to write an elaborate foreword to Sastry's well-researched and exhaustive book on Tyagaraja Kritis.

Balamuralikrishna was now singing at countless local temples and festivals in addition to being invited to private home functions of affluent people. He was only twelve! 'I remember seeing him performing in the royal household of Nuzividu, at one of their family functions. Bangalore Nagarathnamma, who was present there, carried him in her arms throughout the evening,' recollected scholar and archivist V.A.K. Ranga Rao in an interview with me later.

Invitations began pouring in from all over. Pattabhiramayya's letters back home have elaborate details of some of the more important concerts. 'After the Tyagaraja Aradhana, several local senior Tamil Vidwans have shown interest to accompany Murali,' he writes. On 3 June 1942, Balamuralikrishna performed at the house of Lakshmanan Chettiar in Nattarasankottai in the Sivaganga district of Tamil Nadu. He was accompanied by Mayuram Govindaraja Pillai on the violin, Kuttalam Sivavadivelu Pillai on the mridangam and Aalangudi Ramachandran on the ghatam. Another concert in Kandaramanickam had K.C. Tyagarajan on the violin, Umayalpuram Ganesa Iyer on the mridangam, Alangudi Ramachandran on the ghatam, Karaikudi Natesa Iyer on the dholak and Nettakudi Harihara Sarma on the morsing. A full-bench concert like a veteran at the age of twelve. Balamuralikrishna recorded with the All India Radio Madras station in August. 'I was working as the first music composer in the All India Radio, in 1941 and '42. I remember Balamuralikrishna coming with his father Pattabhiramayya Garu to the studio. He was a loud and noisy kid, jumping all over the sofas and running all over the studio. He would run away in between the recording and purposely go and open the door of the studio. I remember him as an uncontrollable child, giving a lot of trouble to his father,' wrote Vinjamuri Anasuya Devi, the legendary folk song singer in her book *Endaro Mahanubhavulu*.

The same month, an issue of *Vaanoli*, the Tamil edition of the All India Radio journal, carried an image of Balamuralikrishna on the cover, where he is recording for the studios. On 25 September 1942, he was invited to perform at the house of Devakottai Annamalai Chettiar for a marriage function in their family. He was accompanied by Palakkad C.R. Mani Iyer on the violin and Karaikudi Muthu Iyer on the mridangam.

The year 1943, as Balamuralikrishna entered his teenage years, was a busy one for him. The first big concert on 4 January was in Ongole. The local Telugu press flashed as the image of the day the young Balamuralikrishna with the headline, '*Adhbutham! Ascharyam!* (Wonder!)'.

The Andhra Saraswata Parishad was founded as an organization in the service of promoting the arts, culture and literature in Andhra Pradesh. From the very beginning, they had the support of all the stalwarts of the era. They had so far honoured great writers, poets, Sanskrit scholars and veteran musicians. They broke protocol and decided to have a grand felicitation ceremony for Balamuralikrishna. It was the first time that a teenager was being honoured. On 15 January 1943, the Andhra Saraswata Parishad organized a huge event in Nuziveedu and conferred the title of 'Gana Sudhakara' on him. 'Sudhakara' is one of the many names of the moon god, meaning 'a receptacle of nectar'. It was indeed an apt title for the teenager whose nectarine music was going to rule the Carnatic world for decades to come.

In addition to his regular vocal concerts, Balamuralikrishna was also giving accompaniment on the violin. While his Guru Pantulu was a regular performer, several visiting stalwarts from the Tamil land also gave concerts in Andhra. On one such occasion, he accompanied the stalwart Carnatic vocalist G.N. Balasubramaniam (GNB) (1910–65) at a concert in Kakinada. GNB was thrilled. The following day he had another concert in Rajamundhry and took Balamuralikrishna along with him. GNB's music deeply influenced Balamuralikrishna's own ideas in later years. In addition to the violin, the boy also gradually mastered the art of percussion. That he was brilliant in maths was confirmed further through his mastery over the mridangam and khanjira. In a later interview to *Andhra Prabha* news magazine dated March 1991, he said: 'I learnt Mridangam by observing Sri Radhakrishna Raju. I didn't have any formal lessons but he guided me in understanding the fingering techniques. I practiced all the known Taalams on it. Same way, the Khanjira. I figured out both instruments were not difficult to play!'

The testimony for this comes from a review by one Donappa Bhagavatulu in the *Akhila Andhra Patrika*, a weekly published from Srikakulam, dated 4 October 1943. Bhagavatulu writes: 'I heard a performance where the versatile child Balamuralikrishna was accompanying a young Voleti Venkateshwarlu, a staff member of the All India Radio in Vijayawada, on the Mridangam. His mastery over the instrument came as a surprise to me. It would not be an exaggeration to call him a "Savyasachi" or ambidextrous person for his age!'

While it was normal practice for Brahmin boys to have their Upanayanam or sacred thread ceremony once they reached the age of seven, Balamuralikrishna's had somehow been missed earlier. It was only in his thirteenth year that he was initiated into the Brahmacharya Deeksha and Gayatri Mantra. In consultation with Bethapudi Sarabhayya, 14 February 1944 was fixed for this event. *Andhra Prabha* carried a detailed report of the festivities that lasted for four whole days. Nadaswaram recitals by the Daliparti Pichahari brothers, a Harikatha by Musanuri Sooryanarayana Bhagavatulu, a veena concert by Akkaji Rao, and finally Guru Pantulu gave a special concert for his Shishya's thread ceremony. The celebrations across the artistic fraternity were as grand as a wedding ceremony.

Concerts continued, and now Guru Pantulu too began to have his protégé accompany him on the violin. A concert notice dated 17 April 1945 announced the vocal concert of Pantulu, along with his 'Shishya Ratnamu', 'Gana Sudhakara' Mangalampalli Balamuralikrishna playing the fiddle, with vocal support by Vankadaari Venkatasubbayya Gupta and Kovvidi Hanumanta Rao on the mridangam. The notice shows a portrait of Pantulu and another of Murali with his fiddle. The very next day, on 18 April 1945, there was a vocal recital by Balamuralikrishna accompanied by Saride Subba Rao on the fiddle and Kovvidi Hanumanta Rao on the mridangam. This notice carries a portrait of Balamuralikrishna with a medal pinned to his coat. What is fascinating about these two concert notices is that, while Guru Pantulu's concert was not ticketed, Balamuralikrishna's vocal concert the next day had tickets priced at two paisa! This was a wonderful testimony to the popularity of the young musical genius.

The Beginnings of a Versatile Vaggeyakara

Meanwhile, something was brewing in the curious mind of the teenager. One day he sat down to write a poem. The same evening he showed it to his Guru, who was pleased and appreciated his efforts but didn't say anything else. The next day the boy returned with two more poems. The Guru took them and kept them aside; he never discouraged any of his students. A week later, Pantulu's Vedanta Guru, Sri Vimalananda Bharati Swami, asked the young boy to meet him. When Balamuralikrishna arrived at his home, the famous poet 'Shatavadhani' Kashi Krishnacharyulu was already present. In front of them were all the bits of paper on which Balamuralikrishna's poems were written. Pantulu had obviously given them to these veterans for feedback. After reading through them, they brought out a book titled *Kavita Lakshanamu*. They patiently explained to the boy the nuances of classical poetry, prosody, *Yati*, *Praasa* and so on.

In addition to that, they questioned Balamuralikrishna, asking him what music was like before Saint Tyagaraja. Not knowing the answers, he innocently said maybe Ramadasu, Annamayya and others who sang Bhajana Sampradaayam.

'So what is the big deal about Tyagaraja?' they prodded.

The boy sat there, clueless, overpowered by the presence of two big personalities who had just finished reading his work and were now interrogating him. 'Tyagaraja began a new era in music. Today, whatever he did, is sacred. We all ascribe a rebirth to the art form like never before. Similarly, you should also think new. Do something original so that the world will remember you for your contribution to this sacred art form,' said Vimalananda Bharati Swami.

By the end of that morning, Balamuralikrishna was intellectually charged, highly stimulated and thoroughly inspired. He ran back home and began writing more. What emerged from that moment of inspiration was totally different from what he had written earlier.

Until then very few composers had written songs in all the seventy-two Melakarta Ragams of the Carnatic music tradition. The first was Vaidyanatha Iyer (1844–1893), who was a child prodigy. He wrote under the pen name or Mudra of Guhadasa. His magnum opus was the long composition 'Pranatarthihara Prabho Purare'. Setting it to a Ragamalika or a garland of Ragams, he strung together all the seventy-two Melakarta Ragams into this composition. It was the first of its kind and many stalwarts like Musiri Subramania Iyer (1899–1975) and M.S. Subbulakshmi have recorded it. The second such composer was Koteeswara Iyer (1870–1936) who wrote in Tamil.

Balamuralikrishna was just fourteen years old when he began composing. Over the next couple of years, he wrote under the guidance of Pantulu and other Sanskrit scholars. He completed writing a composition in each of the seventy-two Melakarta Ragams by the time he was seventeen.

In a later interview to *India Today* news magazine dated October 1984, Balamuralikrishna mentions how and why he felt the need to compose. 'Vaidyanatha Iyer's composition is brilliant. But it doesn't give the complete Raga Swaroopam. You would have barely started Kanakangi when you realize it is already over in one line. It would give you a glimpse of that Ragam. But if you wanted to enjoy the Ragam completely, you couldn't get more as the composition didn't offer more. As for Koteeswara Iyer's compositions, they were hardly known. Even today many aren't sung. I felt the need to elaborate each Ragam. Bring the Raga Swaroopam and enjoy the composition in leisure. Hence I began composing one by one.'

'Janakaraga Kriti Manjari' was hailed as a pioneering effort. No other musician from the Telugu-speaking lands had attempted this earlier. The teenager was hailed as a *Vaggeyakara*. The word is not easy to translate and 'composer' is the closest meaning. But it is not 'composer' in the Western classical music sense of the word. In the Carnatic context, a Vaggeyakara is ascribed with more faculties. He is a master of several languages, he is a master of grammar and poetic expression, he is a master of the Carnatic genre of music, and he is a master of the vocabulary of percussion. A Vaggeyakara would encompass all these faculties with the precision and skill to craft his compositions.

According to the thirteenth century treatise on Indian music *Sangita Ratnakara* by the eminent Kashmiri poet and scholar Saranga Deva, a 'Vaggeyakara' is one with equal prowess in the written and spoken word and the musicality of it. He writes:

वाङ्गातुरुच्यते गेयं धातुरित्यभिधीयते।
वाचं गेयं च कुरुते यः स वाग्गेयकारकः।।

Balamuralikrishna fit this ancient description so perfectly, like it was written for him. The story of *Janakaraga Kriti Manjari* is equally exciting and inspiring. The final draft of the manuscript stayed with Pantulu for a few months. He went through each of the songs written, but didn't say anything. After that, it was given to the eminent poet Shatavadhani Kashi Krishnacharyulu, then living in Guntur, where it stayed for a few more months. Krishnacharyulu was a multifaceted genius who could play over half a dozen musical instruments, was a master of Sanskrit, Yoga, the traditional martial arts of wrestling, musicology theories and much more.

Balamuralikrishna began writing the book when he was fourteen and it was complete before he was seventeen. Browsing through the book, one is filled with a sense of wonder thinking of the possibilities of what a teenager could do.

The book is dedicated to Goddess Kanakadurga whose shrine on top of the Indrakiladri Hill in Vijayawada was an inspiration to his parents. The opening page shows a lovely teenage portrait of Balamuralikrishna wearing a black waistcoat crammed with medals. Printed at Welcome Press in Guntur, the hardbound book of 124 pages was priced at a princely sum of Rs 4.

Pantulu's old friend, the poet laureate Kavi Samrat Viswanatha Satyanarayana, then associated with the NRR and CVR College in Vijayawada, wrote an elaborate foreword to the book. 'I am not an expert of the Shastras related to music. My knowledge of music has been gained by listening to hundreds of concerts of many stalwarts over the years!' he wrote in Telugu. Going through the compositions he writes, 'Particularly in the eleventh Kriti, the usage of *Murali Gaana Sudhaa Rasaasvaada*, in the thirteenth Kriti the usage of Murali Krishnaadi Gaayaka Priyakaram give excellent insights into the mind of a brilliant composer.' He also praises the idea of including the Ragam names in a Kriti as a part of the Sahityam in various songs. He finished his foreword saying: 'Though young in age, but mature in knowledge, this book will fly high like a flag of triumph among the other stalwarts of Andhra in the years to come!'

In 1971, Viswanatha Satyanarayana was awarded the Bharatiya Jnanpith Award, the highest award for literature in India, for his book *Ramayana Kalpavrikshamu*. He was the first Telugu writer to receive this prestigious award. Balamuralikrishna, who was by then a superstar in the world of Carnatic music, visited him. He gave a surprise concert in his honour by singing some of his own poems. Viswanatha's grandson, named

Viswanatha Junior, recollected another occasion when Balamuralikrishna performed at the marriage of one of his cousins. Veteran Viswanatha who heard him requested him to sing something in Raga Gangeyabhooshani and Balamuralikrishna obliged. Decades later, for the birthday celebrations of Pattabhiramayya in Vijayawada, Viswanatha was one of the many eminent chief guests on the dais. In older family images shared by Balamuralikrishna's eldest son Abhiram, one can see the admiration Viswanatha Satyanarayana had for Pattabhiramayya. He admired Balamuralikrishna as a fellow poet who had the added talent to sing. If there was one thing Balamuralikrishna kept constant, it was his immense sense of gratitude to everyone who helped him when he was not as well known. He remembered old friendships and kept in touch with many of his old friends from Andhra long after he had moved out and settled in Madras.

There is a letter of blessing from spiritual Guru Sri Vimalananda Bharati Swami, dated 31 August 1948. Another letter titled 'Abhipraayamu' or opinion by Pingali Lakshmikantam, dated 7 September 1951 follows. In *Mangala Shaasanamu* by Kavi Kathaka Ratna Peddinti Suryanarayana Deekshitadas Bhagavatulu from Narsapuram writes: 'We can be proud that the womb of Telugu Talli (mother Telugu) is not barren! May she bless this little Balamuralikrishna with health and inspiration to keep writing further!'

In a letter from senior musicologist T.S. Parthasarathy, dated 8 August 1950, which is published in the book, he writes:

No further testimony of his musical precocity is necessary than his composing of Kritis in all the 72 Melakarta Ragams before he attained the age of eighteen. The music world may consider this rather ambitious attempt on the part of the young musician, as the feat has so far been performed only by a few eminent musicians like Maha Vaidyanatha Iyer and Koteeswara Iyer. I have personally heard Balamuralikrishna render several of these Kritis, notably those in Sucharitra and Ragavardhani and have no hesitation in saying that, difficult as the task is, the Vidwan has accomplished it with remarkable ability. His proficiency in Telugu and his acquaintance with Sanskrit have enabled him to compose suitable Sahityas on appropriate themes.

It is common knowledge that music is not having, in the Andhra Desa, the support and interest it so richly deserves and the publication of works like these will, therefore, be welcomed by all interested in the development of music.

Bethapoodi Veera Sarabhayya, associated with the Durga Malleshwara Devasthanamu, wrote on how and why he decided to 'sponsor' the making of this book. The music critic Kona Venkataraya Sarma, who was the biographer of Pantulu, wrote a letter of blessings to Balamuralikrishna.

In the 'Vinayanjali' (A Humble Offering), his piece in the book, Balamuralikrishna wrote: .

Earlier in the Janaka Ragaas only a few Kritis were in circulation. Though there are Kritis in all the 72 Ragas, they often materialise only in Ragamalikas or in other languages, hence they don't materialise in completeness. It is also my opinion that a singer cannot enjoy any of these Ragas entirely because the elaboration required for the Manodharma doesn't come through. Keeping that in mind, my Guru Gayaka Sarvabhowma Sri Parupaalli Ramakrishna Pantulu blessed these compositions like Kritis, Varnams with a fatherly love and concern. I place them with gratitude at his feet. I also express my gratitude to the authorities of the Sri Sri Durga Malleswara Devasthanam who from my childhood have been the channel through which I have received the blessings of Goddess Kanakadurga. I offer my salutations to Mahopadhyaya Madhwasri Kashi Krishnacharyulu who has been a great source of encouragement from the very beginning. I offer my Namaskarams to Bandagarbha Kavi Samraat Brahmasri Bhamidipati Appayya Sastri who showed me the knowledge of poetic nuances. I bow down to Kavi Samraat Brahmasri Viswanatha Satyanarayana who is known in the literary world as 'Andhra Tagore' and who was gracious to write the foreword to this book.

He further writes the details of his compositions:

The 72 Melakartas have been grouped into six each and formed into twelve Chakras. The twelve Chakras are 1. Indu, 2. Netra, 3. Agni, 4. Veda, 5. Baana, 6. Rutu, 7. Rishi, 8. Vasu, 9. Brahma, 10. Dishi, 11. Rudra, and 12. Aditya. The names of six Ragams encapsulated within the six Chakrams are 1. Paa, 2. Shri, 3. Go, 4. Bhu, 5. Ma, and 6. Sha. For example when it says Brahma Bhu, it would mean the 4th Ragam in the 9th Chakram (Ramapriya). This way one can know the Kritis through the symbols given on the top. He signs off his little note with the phrase 'Itlu Vidheyudu'.

The actual text of the book opens with five songs. The first one is 'Guru Smriti Kriti' set to Hamsavinodhini Ragam and Adi Taalam. The lyrics go 'Guruni Smarimpumu O Manasa', dedicated to his Guru Pantulu. The second one is a Geetamu set to Ragam Vijaya Saraswati, another Ghana Raga Geetam in Ragam Varali and two Taana Varnams in Ragams Ramapriya and Thodi.

The text of *Janaka Raga Kriti Manjari* opens with Ragam Kanakangi. The first Kriti 'Sri Shivaputraya Namostute' is dedicated to Lord Ganesha. All the songs display a scale of the ascending and descending notes in the beginning in a neat grid. All the seventy-two songs are notated. Out of the seventy-two compositions, only seven are in Telugu. The rest are in Sanskrit.

Though he wrote the book by 1948, it was only published and released in 1952. Nevertheless, it launched Balamuralikrishna in the world of music as a versatile Vaggeyakara. He had achieved what was until then considered to be an impossible height to reach for a musician his age. After that, composing over the years became an easier game for him. The same year, he was honoured with the titles 'Sahaja Vaggeyakara Ratnam' and 'Geeta Kala Bharathi'.

Since we will not be dealing with this in detail later, I have provided the list of compositions in the seventy-two Melakartha Ragams as they fit into the respective cycles along with the Taalams below.

Compositions in Seventy-Two Melakarta Ragas (Thirty-Six Shuddha Madhyama)

INDU:

SreeSaputrAya–kanakAngi-roopaka
SreGurum–ratnAngi-roopaka
pAhijagadeeSwara-gAnamoorti–Adi
eSvaree–vanaspati–Adi
Sri hanumantammAnavati–Adi
Sri rAmamsadA-tAnaroopi–Adi

NETRA:

JAlamEla–sEnApati–Adi
tyAgarAjaGurum–hanumatODi–KhanDatripuTa
AvayyarAmayya–dhEnuka-roopaka
paripAlayamAm–nATakapriya–roopaka
VAdamEla–kOkilapriya–Adi
pAlayamAm–roopavati–Adi

AGNI:

SreemahAvishNum–gAyakapriya–khanDajhumpa
kumArunivalenu–vakuLAbharaNam–Adi
SyAmalAmbike–mAyAmALavagaula–Adi
girijApatE - chakravAkam–chaturasraaTa
karuNincharA–sooryakAntam–Adi
rakshAsumAm–hATakAmbari–chApu

VEDA:

jhashakEtana–jhankAradhwani–miSrajhumpa
naLinanayani–naTabhairavi–roopaka
Sri dakshiNAmoortim–keeravANi–Adi
paramESwara–kharaharapriya-roopaka
smarEchitta–gaureemanOhari–chApu
samASrayAmi–varuNapriya–khanDaEka

BANA:

ramApatinA–mAraranjani–chApu
paradEvee-chArukESi–Adi
vandEham–sarasAngi–miSralaghu
smaramAnasmara–harikAmbhOji–Adi
Sri subrahmaNyam-dheeraSankarAbharaNam–Adi
dAkshAyaNee–nagAnandini–Adi

RUTU:

yaSOdEyam–yAgapriya-chaturasrajhumpa
gAnasudhArasamE–rAgavardhani–roopaka
pAlayAsumAm–gAngEyabhooshaNi–Adi
praNamAmyaham–vAgadheeSwari–khanDaEka
pAlayAsumAm–Soolini–roopaka
nagAtmaja–chalanATa–Adi

Compositions in Thirty-Six Prati Madhyama Ragas

RISHI:

vAraNa vadanam–sAlagam–Adi
mahESvaree–jalArNavam–Adi
mAdhava dayayA–jhAlavarALi–Adi
himAtmajE–navaneetam–Adi
jaya dhanada–pAvani–Adi
khatilaka vamSa–raghupriya–Adi

VASU:

vinati chEkona–gavAmbOdhi–roopaka
mAdhava mAmava–bhavapriya–Adi
karuNa nanu–Subha pantuvarALi–roopaka
haimavateem bhaja–shaDvidha mArgiNi–roopaka
Sri raghupatim–ragam–taalam
naumi tava–divyamaNi–Adi

BRAHMA:

Sri vANi–dhavaLAmbari–Adi

mahAdEva–nAma nArAyaNi-roopaka

SaraNam tava–kAmavardhani–Adi

mahAdEva maniSam–rAmapriya–jhumpa

enni mArulu–gamanaSrama–miSrachApu

bhO SambhO–viSvambhari–Adi

DISI:

SyAmalAngi–SyAmalAngi–chaturasra jhumpa

sadA tava pAda–ShaNmukha priya Adi

mAmava mAyE–simhEndra madhyamam–Adi

taruNamidE–hymavati–Adi

vaSamA–dharmavati–Adi

smaraNam–neetimati-roopaka

RUDRA:

bhuvanESvari kAntAmaNi triSra tripuTa

nandeeSam–rishabha priya-roopaka

tAmralOchani–latAngi–Adi

nutintu sadA–vAchaspati–Adi

gati neeve–mEcha kaLyANi–roopaka

SreerAma naumi–chitrAmbari–Adi

ADITYA:

chintayAmi–sucharitra–miSra chApu

Sree gAyatreem–jyOtisvaroopiNi–roopaka

mahESam–dhAtuvardhani–Adi

ambikAmupAsE–nAsikAbhooshaNi–Adi

Oh manasA–kOsala–roopaka

navanatanaya–rasikapriya-roopaka

A detailed study of these compositions reveals what a musical genius of a mind Balamuralikrishna had as a teenager. In fact, Carnatic vocalist

Saketaraman pointed out something interesting. Decades later, a famous mridangam maestro worked with leather research scientists to 'discover' the *Aadhara Shruti*, or the base tonal note, for the mridangam was Rishabham. Balamuralikrishna had already figured this out way back and inculcated it in his Kriti Nandeesham set to Rishabapriya Ragam and Roopaka Taalam. This is just one insight. But there are many more if one does a detailed analysis and study of these compositions. With this work itself, Balamuralikrishna's versatility as a Vaggeyakara was written in stone for posterity. Nobody understood the science of composing Kritis in the way he did. This was to be revealed in later years.

A Young Family Man

It was a common practice among various sects within the Brahmin community to marry off boys once they became teenagers. In keeping with that, Subbamma began telling Pattabhiramayya that they should start searching for a suitable bride for Balamuralikrishna. As the process began, several fathers came forward with the horoscopes of their daughters. Who didn't want such an accomplished son-in-law, after all?

Balamurali Vibhu, the grandson of Balamuralikrishna, who saved a copy of the marriage invitation, shared it with me. The pink paper invitation starts with a 'Jai Hind' on the top. The invitation was sent out by his uncle Mangalampalli Sitaramayya of Bezawada. It reads: 'Mangalampalli Sitaramayya, Bezawada, requests the pleasure of your company with family and friends on the occasion of the marriage of his Brother Mangalampalli Pattabhiramayya's son Chy. Bala Murali Krishna with Chy. Sow. Annapoorna (second daughter of Sri Prayaga Venkataratnam Garu) on Sunday the 14th March '48 at 10-30a.m. at the Bride's residence in Vissakoderu.' Below that are best compliments from Mangalampalli Jagannadham and Mangalampalli Pattabhiramayya.

The other side of the invitation is printed in Telugu. The transliteration of these auspicious words reads 'Srirastu' and 'Shubamastu'. It gives the traditional date '*Svasti Sri Sarvajit Nama Samvatsara Phalguna Shuddha 4 Adivaramu Udhayam 10-30 Laku Ashwini Nakshatra Yuktha Vrushabha Lagnamandu Naasodharudu Chiranjeevi Pattabhiramayya*

Kumarudu Chi. Balamuralikrishnaku Brahmasri Prayaga Venkata Ratnam Bhavagari Dvitiya Putrika Chi. Sow. Annapoornanu ichi Bhimavaram Taluku, Vissakoderu Gramamulo Kanyadaata Gaari Svagruhamandhu Paanigrahana Mahotsavamu Jarukutaku Daivajnyulu Shuba Muhurthamu Nishcayinchinaaru Gaana, Taamu Sakutumba Parivaramuto Vichesi Vadhu Varulanu Aasheervadhinchi Nache Nosangavadu Srakshandanathaambhooladityadhula Gaikuni Mammanandimpacheyu Veduchunnanu, Itlu Mangalampalli Seetaramayya 1st March 1948, Bezawada'.

Balamuralikrishna married Annapoorna. Life was no longer going to be like before. He was now a family man. As a young musician at the threshold of fame, a new life awaited him.

5

Trailing the Path of Tyagaraja

The fact that Balamuralikrishna hailed from the Shishya Parampara of Saint Tyagaraja was a matter of pride for him from an early age. In innumerable interviews to newspapers, magazines and television channels, Balamuralikrishna emphasized this. Rather, there is hardly an interview where he doesn't mention the name of the saint.

Throughout his twenties, Balamuralikrishna's busy concert schedule meant extensive travels across the Southern states. After his marriage, life changed drastically. He now had the responsibility of managing a household. Annapoorna was only fourteen when she married him. Her entry into 'Sooryakanta Bhavanamu' filled the house with good luck. True to her name, as everyone would say, she ushered in a sense of 'completeness' into his life. She knew she had married a famous musician. She had Subbamma and Pattabhiramayya for support, but handled everything gradually. Unlike her parents' house, her new home was buzzing with activity all through the year. Guests stayed for months on end. Fellow-musicians, event organizers, students and well-wishers showed up without notice, and she was always ready to handle any situation at home. She soon got used to the hectic schedule. As a busy musician, Balamuralikrishna would be away for weeks and sometimes months on concert tours with his father.

The late 1940s saw Balamuralikrishna fairly active on the Andhra cultural scene. Every month at least twenty public concerts were part of his schedule. In addition, there were private functions. When he was not performing, he would read books on music and music theory. In an interview to All India Radio, Vijayawada station, much later, he rattled off slokas from a range of Sanskrit and Telugu treatises effortlessly to augment his arguments on music. From Sangita Ratnakara of Saranga Deva to Brihaddesi of Matanga, from the Natya Shastra of Bharata Muni to Abhinaya Darpanam of Nandikeswara and from Sangita Sampradaya Pradarsini of Subbarama Dikshita to *Sangeeta Swaraprastara Sagaramu* of Nadamuni Pandita, Balamuralikrishna seemed to have read all these texts, and recalled them from memory on being asked any technical questions on Carnatic music.

Around that time, literary personality and Sanskrit scholar Veturi Prabhakara Sastri (1888–1950) discovered a few copper plates in the Tirumala temple of Lord Venkateswara. On further research, it was revealed that these plates had the compositions of the famous composer Tallapaka Annamacharya inscribed on them. These copper plates were one of the greatest literary discoveries of the century in the world of Telugu literature. With the permission of temple authorities, Sastri brought these plates to Balamuralikrishna. He went through the compositions and set them to tune. Many are popular even today, from 'Narayanathe Namo Namo', 'Brahmakadigina Paadamu' to 'Indhariki Abhayambulichu Cheyi'. These songs have also been sung by other musicians in the later years, often without due credit to Balamuralikrishna. A new episode in the musical life of Balamuralikrishna was to begin. It was a long-lasting relationship with the lord of the seven hills. In the decades to come, Balamuralikrishna tuned and sang hundreds of compositions in praise of Lord Venkateswara. He was also made the 'Asthana Vidwan' of the Tirumala Tirupati Devasthanams, the details of which we will come to later.

In 1949, another new chapter began in the life of Balamuralikrishna and Annapoorna. In November, Annapoorna gave birth to a baby girl in her mother's house in Vissakoderu. They named her Durga Suryakanti in honour of the goddess of Vijayawada of whom both Balamuralikrishna and his late mother Sooryakantamma had been firm believers. She came to be addressed fondly as 'Ammaji'. She studied at AKTP High School in Vijayawada till the sixth standard and later joined the Kesari High School in Mylapore in Madras after the family migrated there. Ammaji graduated with a degree in music, philosophy and psychology. 'My father was thrilled when I got first prize for music at Pachiappa's College,' she recollected.

Writer and scholar Kovala Suprasannacharya recollects a concert organized by P.V. Narasimha Rao as part of the annual festival conducted by the Kakatiya Kala Samithi in Warangal in 1951. Rao was a celebrated literary figure in his own right, way before he got into active politics. He was a prolific writer and translator who took active part in most of the literary gatherings in the Warangal region. He calls Balamuralikrishna a 'Rasatapasvi' in a later essay on him. That same year, though, Balamuralikrishna's voice suddenly broke. It is normal for singers to struggle through this phase of adolescence. But for Balamuralikrishna, this was tougher than usual. According to his student, the veteran musicologist and scholar Dr B.M. Sundaram, 'His original singing pitch was G, but now he found it difficult to even sing in C!'

He had accepted many concerts and they all had to be cancelled. Several advance payments had to be returned. A cloud of depression set on him. He had never faced this situation earlier. Nor had he known anyone who had faced this, whom he could seek help from. In addition to this, another sadness descended into his life. His Guru Pantulu passed away on the third day of the festival he conducted in the memory of his Guru Susarla. Balamuralikrishna felt orphaned. If there was one person he was attached to, it was his Guru Pantulu. With his physical absence, Balamuralikrishna felt at a loss. He decided to stop singing for the time being. But there were other pressures at home. He was now the father of a baby girl. As the sole bread earner of the family, how long could he sit at home jobless? He decided to seek out work that would cover monthly expenses at least. One morning without telling anyone at home he showed up at the house of Ayyagari Veerabhadra Rao (1908–90), the station director and one of the founders of the All India Radio in Vijayawada.

Rao hailed from an illustrious family of Sanskrit scholars and musicians. His father worked as a revenue officer in the British Government and his mother was a musician. 'He grew up with enough literature and music, and was fond of them all his life!' his octogenarian daughter Dr Lakshmi Ayyagari recollected. Rao was closely associated with scientist C.V. Raman as one of his research students, and worked briefly at the Indian Institute of Science in Bangalore. Later he got a doctorate from Andhra University.

His familiarity with Balamuralikrishna went back a long way. On that historic morning of 1942 at Thiruvaiyaru when Balamuralikrishna stunned everyone with his performance, it was Rao who was in-charge of arranging the microphone as the boy sat atop a box. He was then serving as a program assistant at the Madras station and was sent to Thiruvaiyaru to cover the Tyagaraja Aradhana. 'He and two others worked under Mr Victor Paranjoti, the first station director. Since all the three were Telugu people, Paranjoti had assigned them the task of covering the Thiruvaiyaru Aradhana,' Dr Ayyagari said. She remembers him returning home and telling her, 'A small boy from Bezawada stole the show. You don't know how beautifully he sang. He is Pantulu Garu's student. I must say I was feeling fortunate to have recorded it. He is going to go a long way. Wait and watch.' Ayyagiri, who is five years younger than Balamuralikrishna, became a close family friend for many decades.

'He came to our house one morning and asked my father for a job. But my father couldn't give him any immediately even if he wanted to. He was certainly fond of his music but that was not enough. Murali did not have a degree or a high school certificate. On what basis could he be given a job? Even my father was in a fix. For many days, both Balamuralikrishna and his father Pattabhiramayya would come home in the morning and talk to my father. One day Murali walked into my father's office in the Vijayawada station and told him he had nowhere else to go. He knew nobody else. "Babai Garu, you have to give me a job!" he said,' recollected Dr Ayyagari.

Rao finally managed a decent deal. He got Balamuralikrishna a job with the designation 'light classical music supervisor'. 'This role never existed earlier. It was a job on a contract basis and it was created for Balamuralikrishna. They couldn't put him under "classical" because that would require him having to show school certificates, going through a screen-test and so on. So "light classical" was just fine for him!' recollects Dr Ayyagari. According to records, on 26 March 1952, Balamuralikrishna assumed office. It was Ugadi, the Telugu New Year's day on the traditional calendar.

Bhakti Ranjani Overtakes Binaca Geetmala

According to Dr Ayyagari, her father and all the station directors from across India were invited to a special conference by the then minister for broadcasting B.V. Keskar. Keskar had just been appointed minister for information and broadcasting, a post he served for a decade from 1952 to 1962. He was clearly handling an office he knew very little about. Added to that, there were his eccentricities. He hated everything about cinema, so much so that he decided to levy a 10 per cent quota on any programming connected to cinema until he had film music totally banned on All India Radio. AIR's loss was Radio Ceylon's gain. Its Hindi service, launched in 1950, delivered hit programmes based on popular film music, such as *Binaca Geetmala, Purani Filmo Ke Geet* and *Aap Hi Ke Geet*. Gradually, All India Radio began to lose listeners and revenue, forcing it in 1957 to launch the 'Vividh Bharati' service. On the advice of Prime Minister Jawaharlal Nehru, Keskar also banned the harmonium on AIR. He also banned cricket commentary. Historian Ramachandra Guha in one of his columns titled 'Subcontinental Shift' in the TIME magazine dated 19 June 2008, cited Keskar's contempt for cricket. 'Will Cricket Quit India with the British?' Cricket, insisted B.V. Keskar, could 'only thrive in the atmosphere of English culture, English language and English rule.' The Indians who played the sport were brown in colour but white in spirit, said Keskar, such as 'the Maharajas, the rich and the snobs'. Cricket would 'never be able to survive the shock of the disappearance of British rule from our country,' he asserted. These were few of the eccentricities of a politician holding the wrong ministry. This was not the first or the last time such an incident would occur in Indian politics.

At the meeting of station directors, Keskar expressed his concern over the popularity of Binaca Geetmala. He wanted to promote light classical music. He wanted each director to think of programs that would outshine the film music program. Rao returned to Vijayawada and put the idea before his team, which included writer and composer Balantrapu Rajanikantha Rao, who previously worked at the Madras station. 'Balantrapu Garu', as he was fondly addressed, was a polymath, a scholar, researcher, dramatist, orator and director, and wore many more creative hats. His move to

Vijayawada added value to the new station. From the very beginning, he took a keen interest in developing new content.

A new program was conceived of and titled 'Bhakti Ranjani' in 1954. It would be broadcast from 10.00 p.m. to 10.30 p.m. in the Madras station. It would be broadcast from the Vijayawada and Hyderabad stations between 6.30 a.m. and 7 a.m. Rajanikantha Rao was in-charge of this program. The program became so popular in a short span of time, he began to be addressed as 'Bhakti Rajani'. The director in-charge of the same program in the Vijayawada station was Balamuralikrishna and in Hyderabad Palagummi Vishwanatham.

The idea of starting one's morning with devotional music caught on with the listeners. Until then radio programming was only limited to news and content that came from the film industry. However, there was a huge challenge in terms of planning and programming. To start with, the entire content had to be gathered from scratch. According to Dr Ayyagari, Balamuralikrishna would travel to little villages with a notepad and a pen and source songs from rural folk. When he was not travelling, he would consult scholars and wade through old manuscripts and books and collect songs, poems and other content suitable for the programme. Gradually, primary content was put together. Then came the challenge of recording the music. A lot of these were originally scored by Balamuralikrishna himself, and others by Rajanikantha Rao and a few other musicians. Of the folk songs, some were collected from primary sources in their original and some others tuned by musicians like Ogirala Veeraraghava Sarma, Vinjamuri Sitadevi and her sister Anasuya. Over some months, several hundred songs and poems were gathered and fresh content prepared to be programmed. This feat earned Balamuralikrishna the praise of all the seniors at the radio station and the music fraternity.

However, not everyone was equally pleased. With some hesitation, Dr Ayyagari recounted the story of a radio play on Saint Tyagaraja written by Dr Vinjamuri Sivarama Rao, a popular writer and lyricist. 'His relatives Vinjamuri Lakshmi and Saraswati were equally popular singers. He wanted them and Balamuralikrishna to render all the songs in the play and that I think is where exactly all the problems began. The script was ready, the singers were ready and my father was the programme director.'

Dr Ayyagari said. Dr Ayyagari's father was also a theatre artiste who had not only acted in a number of plays, but written radio plays under the pen name 'Koundinya'. Though he was a station director, he didn't limit his activity to administration, and created new programs as well.

'It was his idea to do this play as well, the first of its kind on Saint Tyagaraja. This selection of artistes didn't make everybody happy, especially one vocalist, Voleti Venkateshwarlu. He had already raised an issue that Balamuralikrishna was only working on a contract basis and moreover didn't have any educational qualifications,' recollected Dr Ayyagari. Someone reportedly wrote letters to Delhi to Keskar's office stating that a young boy who had not even completed his schooling had been given a job and made the supervisor of an important program while qualified artistes were being ignored. In addition to that he met a lot of important people in Vijayawada and before anybody knew it, a new rumour began.

The Telugu Brahmin community is divided into numerous factions. The Vaidikis and Niyogis were two such constantly at loggerheads with each other on a number of issues. Word went around that Rao, a Niyogi, had given an important assignment to Balamuralikrishna, a Vaidiki boy. This led to intense gossip across Vijayawada, asserted Dr Ayyagari, thanks to a bunch of locals and eminent people. In addition to this, Rao was also accused in the letters to the ministry of taking bribes. 'Because of these letters, my father got reverted from his job from Delhi. This was absolutely shocking to all of us at home,' recalled Dr Ayyagari. According to Dr Ayyagari, this was not the first run-in between Keskar and Rao. 'My father was one of those instrumental in opening the radio station at Shimla. Around that time, Keskar, who had visited the station for an inspection, also planned a private family trip to Kullu. He wanted to use the official vehicle of the station. To which my father objected, saying that the official vehicle could not be given for anybody's private trips, however important they were. My father was a man of strong principles who never compromised all his life and that earned him a lot of bad will. Keskar had issues with him. He could certainly not remove him from his job, but he could use his might in having him transferred from station to station. So these letters of allegations from Vijayawada station triggered Keskar to act,' recalled Dr Ayyagari.

Dr Ayyagari clearly remembers the day her father was demoted.

My father was an avid sportsman. After office hours, he would play cricket and badminton for an hour. The premises of the radio station had a huge ground for such activities for employees. On normal days, Murali and his father would come home in the evening and stay on till the night. There would be endless discussion about both Sangeetham and Sahityam. In fact, many of those connected to Bhakti Ranjani would be discussed. He would come up with tunes or content like Bhadrachala Ramadasu Suprabhatam and works of lesser-known Telugu poets. That particular day, my father returned home early and announced that 'I have become an assistant station director from a station director'. In fact all the employees felt very bad about this demotion except him. He would say, 'There is nothing for me to feel bad (about). If I have done anything wrong, I should feel bad. When I have been correct all along, I am not guilty of anything.' He was in this position for about six to eight months before he got transferred to Poona. Balamuralikrishna rushed to our house to express shock and grief on knowing what happened, but my father pacified him saying all these were a part of a government job.

This was the first instance of Balamuralikrishna seeing the dirty politics being played at such close quarters. He was shaken from within. But it was only the beginning of what he would encounter in the years to come.

Yet this chapter of his career was not forgotten. In 2011, in a feature on Balamuralikrishna carried in *Sruti* magazine, eminent musicologist N. Ramanathan dedicated a large section to the program. He wrote: 'The Bhakti Ranjani programme of All India Radio, Vijayawada, initiated by Balamuralikrishna, will form an important chapter, if ever a book comes to be written on the history of twentieth century music. Established purely for devotional music, this daily programme also included songs tuned and sung by Balamuralikrishna himself and which reflected a devotional spirit without attempting to pass off art music compositions as devotional songs. In the 1960s and '70s, this early morning programme was a great draw in the households of not only Tamil Nadu but wherever non-resident Tamils lived, like Mumbai, Delhi and Kolkata. I'm not sure if it was that popular in Andhra Pradesh, his home state. The musical memory of the song "Emi Setura Linga" rendered by Balamuralikrishna along with Srirangam Goapalaratnam, to the accompaniment of a single Tuntina-like instrument, still haunts us today. We can listen to it today in YouTube, with Balamuralikrishna rendering it in a concert, with the violin accompanist doing that Tuntina part using Pizzicato. "Ae Theeruga" and others of Badrachala Ramadas, tuned by him, came out during this time. Although set in seemingly simple tunes, the songs would make any serious student of art music sit up and listen every time it was broadcast.'

As mentioned by Ramanathan, Bhakti Ranjani was a rage with listeners, even in Andhra Pradesh. Even now, veterans recollect the programme with fondness. 'Bhakti Ranjani made exciting mornings when I was in my teens. Since we never had a television set, radio programmes were our only window into the world of art. His mastery of innumerable Kritis of the three greats (Carnatic Trinity) and also Janapada Geyalu at the same time! His imagination, gifts of fine renditions of Dasara Padagalu—I do not think any other Carnatic musician has been such a multi-faceted personality in the true sense of the term,' writes the erudite scholar Dr Prema Nandakumar to me. Her father, Dr K.R. Srinivasa Iyengar (1908–91), had served as the vice chancellor of Andhra University in Waltair, as a result of which Prema spent her teenage years in Andhra Pradesh around the same time that Bhakti Ranjani was taking over the airwaves.

In the meantime, Balamuralikrishna regained his voice and began performing. In addition to this, the launch of *Janaka Raga Kriti Manjari* in 1952 put Balamuralikrishna's name into the news and back on the concert circuit. At a function held in Vijayawada, the book was launched by the poet laureate Viswanatha Satyanarayana, followed by a concert by Balamuralikrishna. Then in December 1952, Annapoorna gave birth to their second child, in Bhimavaram, where her parents were staying then. Their son was named Abhiram in honour of Balamuralikrishna's father. The year had been a tumultuous one for Balamuralikrishna. He had lost his voice and his Guru. However, the birth of his second child also reminded him of his additional responsibility.

In 1953, Balamuralikrishna was selected for the President's award, making him the youngest classical singer in the state of Andhra Pradesh to receive this prestigious award. In a glittering ceremony in New Delhi, he was honoured by Dr Rajendra Prasad, the first President of India. Details of the award ceremony and the concert that followed are scant. But what remains is an image of a shy Balamuralikrishna sitting next to the President. The concert in Delhi was held at Rashtrapati Bhavan and in the audience was a Telugu couple, P.S.L. Sarma and P.S. Hymavathi and their son. Little did they realise their son, P. Subramanyam, who would later join the defence services and rise to the rank of colonel, would one day get married to Durga. After he returned from Delhi, a grand reception awaited Balamuralikrishna in Vijayawada. Going by his records, Balamuralikrishna was probably the only Carnatic musician to have met all the successive Presidents of India and receive an award from them. The same year, Annapoorna and he became parents for the third time, this time to a girl. They named her Lakshmi, as a herald of good luck into their lives.

According to Pattabhiramayya's letter back home, in 1954, Balamuralikrishna travelled to Barampur to participate in the music festival organized for Srirama Navami and gave two concerts on two consecutive days. On 15 April 1954, Balamuralikrishna gave a vocal recital accompanied by Dwaram Narasinga Rao Naidu on the violin. The next day he played the violin for the vocal recital of Palghat K.V. Narayaswamy accompanied by Palghat Mani Iyer on the mridangam. This was not the first time Balamuralikrishna was accompanying a musician on the violin. He had already accompanied greats like Ariyakudi Ramanuja Iyengar, Chittoor Subramanya Pillai and G.N. Balasubramaniam.

Radio programming continued and Balamuralikrishna made every effort to present new content. Devulapalli Krishnasastri (1897–1980) was then one of the greatest literary figures in Andhra. He was known as Andhra Shelly. He joined the All India Radio as one of the producers, and wrote a radio drama in the style of a traditional Telugu Yakshaganam based on the legend of 'Vipranarayana'. Krishnasastri wrote the lyrics and the music was set by Rajanikantha Rao and Balamuralikrishna. The programme was so successful that it became a rage with listeners.

The Vipranarayana story was also made into a movie starring Akkineni Nageshwara Rao and others, but the radio programme was more successful. Years later, the same was performed on stage to huge success. Balamuralikrishna was fond of Krishnasastri's literary works. Legend goes that it was Krishnasastri's collection of devotional poems titled *Mahati* that inspired Balamuralikrishna to create a new Ragam with the same name. A decade later, when he migrated and settled down in Madras in his new house, he named it 'Mahati'.

Krishnasastri's son, Devulapalli Subbaraya Sastri, who became famous as an illustrator and cartoonist under the name 'Bujjai', remembers a young Balamuralikrishna accompanying G.N. Balasubramaniam at the golden jubilee celebrations of the Saraswathi Gana Sabha in Kakinada in 1954. Bujjai also recollected how popular Balamuralikrishna was, even at that time. 'That year, my father was one of the chief guests at the ceremony. What was special that year was the performance of the Hindustani maestro Ustad Bade Ghulam Ali Khan, who was a guest of G.N.B.,' recollects Bujjai. That year, Balamuralikrishna accompanied G.N.B. on the violin and in the audience were Khan Saheb and a number of other stalwarts from the world of music and literature. It was only a decade or so ago that the great Harikatha scholar Srimad Ajjada Adibhatla Narayana Dasu had carried little Murali in his lap in the same Sabha and proclaimed '*Okka Roju Nuvvu Naakante Goppa Vadivi Avuthavu* (One day you will be more famous than I)'. A rare blessing from an unparalleled genius in the history of South Indian classical music and arts. Decades later, Balamuralikrishna was to recollect this in an interview to ETV with a tinge of emotion. In 1955, Annapoornamma gave birth to their fourth child and second son, Sudhakar.

In 1956, the music lovers of Vijayawada decided to organize a Gajaarohanam and Gandapendaram ceremony to honour Balamuralikrishna. He was taken around the town of Vijayawada in a special procession seated on an elephant. These are distinguished ceremonies usually conducted to honour great scholars and artistes in the Telugu-speaking regions. It is said that in the times of the Vijayanagara Empire, a similar ceremony was organized to honour the great poet Alasani Peddanna by emperor Krishnadevaraya.

A gandapendaram is a heavy gold anklet studded with precious diamonds, rubies and emeralds. The traditional ceremony involves either a king or a patron or somebody extremely senior in that field to be seated on the floor, while the awardee is seated on a throne above. The person on the floor takes the left foot of the awardee in his lap and adorns it with this precious anklet amidst auspicious chants. Usually a ceremony of this nature is conducted among various communities of artistes. For example, in a society of poets, the senior-most poet should agree to put this anklet on the foot of whoever he is awarding without any hesitation and be ready to equally proclaim the awardee's greatness in a public ceremony. In an era filled with numerous stalwarts, this was a tough act as several legends would not easily compromise to this sort of an arrangement. This ceremony was known to be common among the large community of Sanskrit scholars in the regions of East and West Godavari.

In the recent musical history of the Telugus over the last 200 years, there have been very few gandapendaram ceremonies. So when the music-loving audience of Vijayawada decided to host one in honour of Balamuralikrishna, it raised eyebrows. Here was a young boy who, according to some musicians, had barely begun his career. Others argued that this award was a recognition of the genius that was already evident. According to Annavarapu Ramaswamy, when some of the organizers approached existing senior musicians in Andhra, many of them refused and many others chose to stay away.

At that time, one of the senior-most leading musicians in the Carnatic fraternity was Chembai Vaidyanatha Bhagavatar. Hailing from Chembai, one of the ninety-six villages in the Palakkad district of Kerala, he belonged to an illustrious musical lineage that went back five generations. In addition to being a vocalist, he was also a violinist and a versatile genius. In the twentieth century, Bhagavatar's name was to stand out like the proverbial Dhruvatara of Carnatic music from Kerala. As historian V. Sriram writes in his book *Carnatic Summer*, 'By the early 1920s, Chembai had established himself in the top slot along with Ariyakudi Ramanuja Iyengar and Maharajapuram Viswanatha Iyer. The fast-rising violinist T. Chowdiah simply adored him and together they made a great combination. He was almost the only vocalist whose bell-like voice could drown the seven-stringed violin of Chowdiah.' Bhagavatar had kept an extremely busy concert schedule. In addition to this, he was popular for his generosity towards upcoming artistes, a rare quality in the music industry.

'Palghat Mani Iyer had his initial breaks as an accompanist to Chembai. Palani Subramania Pillai was rescued from the bleak future he faced owing to his being a left-handed mridangist by Chembai who engaged him for his concerts continuously. Violinist V.V. Subramaniam, the multi-faceted T.V. Gopalakrishnan and others such as T.N. Krishnan, Lalgudi G. Jayaraman, M.S. Gopalakrishnan, Vellore Ramabhadran were all encouraged by Chembai. It was no surprise that even artistes such as S. Balachander, who rarely got along with anyone else, worshipped Chembai. Mali, the eccentric but brilliant flautist, too, venerated Chembai and had the fortune of being accompanied by him on the violin once. He taught many and most notably pooh-poohed objections from the orthodox when he took on K.J. Yesudas as his student,' wrote Sriram in his profile of Bhagavatar.

Here was a great artiste who was humble and encouraging towards fellow artistes despite his stalwart stature. So when the festival committee in Vijayawada approached him, he readily agreed to honour the young Balamuralikrishna. Dr B.M. Sundaram, in his profile of Balamuralikrishna in *Sruti* magazine, quotes from Bhagavatar's speech at the ceremony: 'It is not possible to attain such a high pedestal without god's benign grace. Some of my colleagues tried to dissuade me from taking part in this function. They told me "after all, he is a young boy from a distant Telugu-speaking region." We have all earned fame and riches by singing the song of Tyagaraja. Was he not from that Telugu territory? I am a Malayalee, but Tamil Nadu welcomed me.'

The news of the gandapendaram ceremony spread far and wide. That same year, Balamuralikrishna got a brief transfer in All India Radio first to Madras and then to Hyderabad. In Madras, he began working with stalwarts like G.N.B. and other musicians who were associated with the radio. He even performed with G.N.B. for All India Radio. One of the memorable concerts still in the archives is G.N.B., accompanied by T.S. Balasubramaniam on vocal support, Thanjavur Ramamurthy on the mridangam and Balamuralikrishna on his viola. The concert begins with the Begada Varnam 'Inthachalamu' a composition of Veena Kuppaiyer. After that, come Tyagaraja's 'Kalala Nerchina' in Ragam Deepaka set to Deshadi Taalam and 'Raga Ratna Malikache' in Reetigowla, a Deekshithar's Kamalamba Navavarna Kriti in Kalyani, 'Kamalambam Bajare', another Tyagaraja Kriti, 'Kanulu Takini' in Kalyanavasantham, a grand Todi followed by Shyama Sastry's 'Ninne Namminanu' and a Ragamalika in the end. If you listen to the recording even now, you can see what a brilliant combination G.N.B. and Balamuralikrishna made as a musical duo. While in Madras, he also met well-known personalities in the film industry like A.V. Meiyappa Chettiar, director K.R. Subrahmanyam and other prominent figures.

The same year, on 1 November, to commemorate the Andhra Pradesh state formation day, a grand celebration was organized at the Parade Grounds in Hyderabad. Recollecting the concert, Palagummi Vishwanatham writes in a special souvenir, 'A huge dais was erected at the exhibition grounds. All the stalwarts from the various fields were present on the stage. That day, a special concert of veteran violinist Dwaram Venkataswamy Naidu Garu was organized. He played extraordinarily and everybody was going gaga. After his concert, was a concert by a young Balamuralikrishna. Everyone wondered why a youngster's concert was programmed after such a veteran's. They also doubted if audiences would stay. Balamuralikrishna began his concert and soon audiences almost forgot the first concert. He had the audiences eating out of his hands. They were intoxicated with his voice.' Viswanatham was working as the head of the Lalitha Sangeetham department of Aakashavani in Hyderabad. He was a long-time friend and associate of Balamuralikrishna, having worked with him in numerous capacities. 'For a few, music is like penance and for others it is like a play. For Balamuralikrishna it was the latter.' added Viswanatham in a feature he wrote in the souvenir on his association with Balamuralikrishna.

In 1957, Balamuralikrishna gave his first performance at the Sri Rama Seva Mandali in Bangalore, organized by Narayanaswamy Rao. The festival is one of the oldest and iconic ones conducted during the Srirama Navami festival. 'He performed every year after that up to 1984 and announced his retirement in 1984 on the same stage. Twenty years later, he performed again and a record crowd of nearly 20,000 people attended it at the Fort High School compound and another 5000 outside the compound, including the neighbouring Makkalakoota,' recollected Rama Prasad, the son of Narayanaswamy Rao, who continues to conduct this festival annually. Looking at the impressive collection of images from Balamuralikrishna's concerts given at the Mandali, one can say these were probably some of the finest concerts with a wide range of accompanying artistes. He would also thoroughly enjoy performing at this festival in particular as he could present a wide variety of Bhadrachala Ramadasu and Tyagaraja Kritis. In 1958, he was awarded a cash award by Dr Sarvepalli Radhakrishnan, the then President of India. Radhakrishnan was a fan of Balamuralikrishna and had attended several of his concerts in the past. When the suggestion to honour a young musician came up, the obvious choice was Balamuralikrishna.

Towards the end of the 1950s, the Andhra Pradesh state Sangeetha Nataka Akademi invited Balamuralikrishna to be a member of the general council. He was the youngest member then. In a group photo of the general council taken on 16 December 1960, a young Balamuralikrishna is seen seated in row one beside stalwart musicians like Chittoor Subrahmanyam and the legendary violinist Dwaram Venkataswamy Naidu. Others seated beside them are Vinjamuri Anasuya Devi, who worked with Balamuralikrishna in All India Radio, actress Uma Sashi, and Dr M. Chenna Reddy, who went on to become the Chief Minister of Andhra Pradesh. Standing behind them in the general council photograph are stalwart scholars like Dr Biruduraju Rama Raju, Vinjamuri Varadaraja Iyengar, Banda Kanakalingeshwara Rao, Nataraja Ramakrishna and D. Bhavaranarayana Rao. At the age of thirty, Balamuralikrishna was rubbing shoulders with stalwarts twice his age in the field of arts from his home state. This was also the year, in the summer of 1960, that Annapoorna had become a mother for the fifth time. A boy was born in Vijayawada. They named him Vamsi Mohan.

In Madras, the Music Academy would hold its music festival at PS High School in Mylapore, with concerts taking place at a special pandal. On 1 January 1960 at 9 p.m. at the special pandal, there was a Hindustani music concert by Pt Bhimsen Joshi, accompanied by Ghulam Rasool on the tabla. Balamuralikrishna attended that. His own concert was scheduled on 4 January at 9 p.m. He was accompanied by M.S. Gopalakrishnan on the violin, Palghat Raghu on the mridangam and Palghat Sundaram on the ghatam. He began his concert with his own composition 'Mangaladayaka' in Ragam Arabhi. He then sang Tyagaraja's 'Bhajanaseyarada' in Ragam Atana, Subbaraya Sastri's 'Ninuvina' in Ragam Kalyani and 'Kanikaramuchi', a composition of Tacchur Singaracharulu in Ragam Panchamam. He also presented a Ragam-Taanam-Pallavi in Divyamani, a rarely heard Ragam. That year, a new friendship began between Bhimsen and Balamuralikrishna that would last for a lifetime. At the 1960 season, on 27 December, at the special pandal in PS High School, he was accompanied by Govindaswamy Naicker on the violin, Umayalpuram K. Sivaraman on the mridangam and Bangalore Manjunath on the ghatam. He began his concert with 'Vande Nishamaham', a composition of Mysore Vasudevacharya in the Ragam Hamsadhwani. He continued with 'Nepogadakunte', a composition of Tyagaraja in Ragam Subhapantuvarali and 'Nagumomu' in Abheri for which he was already making a huge name for himself.

Radio programming continued. Balamuralikrishna always kept trying to think of newer programmes. In January 1959, All India Radio Vijayawada broadcast Tyagaraja's famous opera *Prahlada Bhakti Vijayamu* for the first time, produced and directed by Balamuralikrishna. Several artistes associated with All India Radio then participated. The role of the Sutradhara was by Voleti Venkateswarlu, Prahlada by A.P. Komala, Mahavishnu by M.V. Ramanamurthy and Goddess Mahalakshmi by Vinjamuri Lakshmi. Balamuralikrishna rendered the role of Samudra in his voice. In the vocal support chorus were artistes like Duluri Arundati, Srirangam Gopalaratnam, N.C.V. Jagannathacharyulu and D. Pandurangaraju. In the production's music, veena was by G.M. Dhandapani, clarinet by M. Radhakrishna Naidu, flute by K. Kannan, mridangam by Dhandamudi Rammohana Rao and ghatam by Annavarapu Gopal. The broadcast was a huge hit. Balamuralikrishna sang exactly two songs, 'Vinataasuta Rara' in Ragam Huseni and 'Vachhunu Hari' in Ragam Kalyani.

In 1961, the All India Radio, Madras, conducted his concert at the Bala Arangu auditorium. He was accompanied by T.N. Krishnan on the violin and Umayalpuram Sivaraman on the mridangam. He began the concert with 'Vande Nishamaham', a composition of Mysore Vasudevacharya in the Ragam Hamsadhwani. This was followed by Saint Tyagaraja's 'Tulasi Bilva' in Ragam Kedaragowla and further followed by 'Ninuvina Gati', a composition of Subbaraya Sastri in Ragam Kalyani. As Sreenivasa Murthy, an ardent fan and a meticulous archivist of Balamuralikrishna's music writes in an article, 'Three factors make this concert a memorable one. BMK's speed of delivery with accuracy and precision enveloped by his creative Manodharma, TNK's melody in raga development and UKS's impeccable and subtle playing of the nuances of both masters.'

There aren't many recordings of T.N. Krishnan accompanying Balamuralikrishna available in the public domain. 'Balamuralikrishna was working as the first Principal of the Vijayawada Music College. Around that time, I had given music for a Kannada movie titled *Mahatma Kabir*. This was my first stint as a music director. I wanted him to sing at least one song in the movie. He not only came by himself all the way from Vijayawada to record in Madras, but sang three songs in the movie. More than that, he was ready to sing totally free for me, but I gave him a very small remuneration within the budget. It felt like Krishna accepting the humble offerings made by Sudama,' recollected Vinjamuri Anasuya Devi.

As work went on in the radio on one side and a concert schedule on the other side, a new chapter was about to begin. The government of Andhra Pradesh, under the chief ministership of Damodaram Sanjivayya (1921–72), wanted to start a music college in Vijayawada. "Bezawada Gopala Reddy was a friend of my father and he called him up to express this idea and suggest someone suitable for the job of running the institution. My father immediately put in the name of Balamuralikrishna,' remembered Dr Ayyagari. Balamuralikrishna readily took up the assignment after a letter arrived from Bezawada Gopala Reddy, a minister who was known to be a great art lover. He was already a fan of Balamuralikrishna's music, having heard him on numerous radio programmes. Balamuralikrishna went to Vijayawada. He also made a request to have the college named after his Guru Pantulu, but that was not to happen. The college was called Government Music College and later got rechristened to Ghantasala Venkateswara Rao Government Music College after the famous Telugu film playback singer. Balamuralikrishna took office and for the first time designed a proper syllabus for music students. Several students enrolled from across Andhra Pradesh.

The college functioned smoothly for a while, but soon trouble began to brew. There were a few who thought they were better qualified to head the institution and a few others questioned Balamuralikrishna's capabilities as an administrator. This reached a peak with Chella Anantalakshmi, a student who was considered an 'outsider', being appointed as the head of the music section. According to Dr Ayyagari, 'Chella Anantalakshmi was a Telugu girl whose family lived in Madras while she was studying in the music college in Trivandrum. Her brother was in Vijayawada and had invited her to join the college. That is how she came armed with a degree and joined the college. Somehow the locals spread a rumour that she was a Tamil girl and this created a fuss. Balamuralikrishna's concern was that someone academically qualified would be of better use to this institute, which was only beginning to take wings. This obviously didn't go (down) well with many of the locals who felt they were better qualified for the job.'

Around the same time, Balamuralikrishna began getting a number of concert offers from across Tamil Nadu. Once, while returning from a concert in Rameshwaram, he stopped at Thiruvaiyaru and on finding out the dates of the Tyagaraja Aradhana, he expressed his desire to perform. One of the secretaries bluntly refused his request, stating that the schedule had been fixed, and he being a junior artiste should have applied a long time ago. Balamuralikrishna was shocked. Only two decades ago, at this very place he was the talk of the town, and now he was being refused a chance to sing. He went to Thirumanjana Veedhi, where the old house of the saint was. He decided that evening to sing there. Coming from the Shishya Parampara of Tyagaraja, it didn't matter if he did not perform at the Adhishtanam. Tyagaraja's blessings would reach him even otherwise. Soon the news of this concert spread all over Thiruvaiyaru. A huge crowd gathered and he gave a performance. He sang 'Evarito Ne Telpudu Rama' in Ragam Manavati. The sorrow in his heart poured out in the form of a new Kriti 'Samagana Sarvabhouma' in Ragam Amritavarshini. In the Charanam he writes, 'Oh Tyagaraja! You're the emperor of music. We have acquired all our name, fame and riches singing your songs so many times. Still there are a few, whose pride blinds them and they say Murali's music is not worth appreciating. Please bestow your grace and bless Murali.' He was visibly hurt and decided not to step into Thiruvaiyaru until better times came.

In the summer of 1962, Annapoorna bore a sixth child, a girl they named Mahati, after the Ragam Balamuralikrishna had created. In a later interview, he said that Mahati was the first Ragam that he had created. It was obviously one of his favourite creations. The following year, tiring of the politics that the music college was getting embroiled in, he decided to put in his papers. At the same time, he got a telegram that read: 'Appointed as music producer AIR Madras. Join duty forthwith- B Gopala Reddy'. The telegram had come from Bezawada Gopala Reddy, who was minister of information and broadcasting in the central cabinet during 1958–63. He was aware of the various problems Balamuralikrishna was facing at the college. Balamuralikrishna decided to migrate from Vijayawada and permanently settle down in Madras.

Chanakya in his writings mentions:

क: काल: कानि मित्राणि को देश: को व्ययागमौ ।
कस्याहं का च मे शक्ति: इति चिन्त्यं मुहुर्मुहु: ॥ - चाणक्यनीति: 4.18

'How is my surrounding?
Who are my friends?
How is the condition in the country?
What are the things for and against me?
Who do I belong to?
What are my strengths? –One should always think over these questions'

Balamuralikrishna was quick to understand the hostility in his own homeland. His decision to move away from a place that held so many fond memories of his childhood, family, gurus, friends and relatives was depressing. But for the sake of his music, this was a sacrifice he decided to make. It was Annapoorna who gave him strength and convinced him to make the move. She took on the entire domestic responsibility on her head so he could pursue his music without tension.

Balamuralikrishna joined duty at the All India Radio, Madras on 1 February 1963.

Initially the family lived in a rented apartment in Venkatachala Mudali Street, Mylapore. Ammaji, their oldest daughter, remembers the famous poet Dasarathi being their neighbour.

But living in a rented accommodation and managing such a large family in a constricted space was obviously uncomfortable. Annapoorna's discomfort and struggles with the children bothered him. One day he walked down the Cathedral Road and saw a bunch of houses in one corner. On enquiring, he found out that they belonged to the famous dancers Lalitha, Padmini and Ragini, who were popular as the 'Travancore sisters'. They were shifting and had put them up for sale. They had decided to purchase a house in Kanakasri Nagar, which was a lane away from the Music Academy. Balamuralikrishna named it 'Mahati'. The Gruha Pravesam ceremony was performed on 2 May 1964. Back in Vijayawada, Subbamma and Pattabhiramayya were not too happy with this decision. Subbamma refused to migrate to a new city in her advancing years. Pattabhiramayya reluctantly agreed to live with the rest of the family in Madras.

In 1964, Balamuralikrishna visited Vijayawada on his way back from a concert in Delhi. He went to his old house in Satyanarayanapuram to find a huge crowd assembled there. Subbamma was not keeping too well. He went inside and sat by her bedside. Subbamma, who had not eaten for several days, was lying unconscious. On hearing Balamuralikrishna's voice, she opened her eyes and signalled to him to bring her some water. He brought the water from the pooja room and poured it into her mouth. Pattabhiramayya was also present along with a few students. Balamuralikrishna advised them to take care of Subbamma and left for Madras. By the time he reached home, he got the news of Subbamma's demise. He was shattered. He had not seen his own mother and Subbamma was the only mother he had known all his life. With that bond gone, he didn't feel like returning to Vijayawada. As per Subbamma's wishes, her funeral was conducted on the banks of the Krishna river. The memory of Subbamma filled Sooryakanta Bhavanamu. All that survives of Subbamma is an image of her sitting on a deer skin in front of the holy tulsi plant, holding her Japamala and in prayer. Pattabhiramayya, who was reluctant to move to Madras earlier, came to live with the rest of the family. A big chapter in the life of Balamuralikrishna and the musical history of Vijayawada came to an end.

In 1967, Balamuralikrishna was invited to Sri Lanka for a concert tour. This was his first foreign visit. The tour was a huge success, with the music lovers of Sri Lanka honouring him with the title Gandharva Gana Vithakar. But there was a bit of a problem. Balamuralikrishna realized his lack of fluency in the Tamil language, especially when it came to rendering classical performances. Very soon, though, he overcame this handicap. Back in Madras, along with concerts, he also began actively teaching students through a Gurukulam system at home. Some of his students from Vijayawada like Chella too stayed at the house and learnt music. Dr Ayyagari remembers the twin singers Jaya and Vijaya who were students of Chembai, also living and learning in Balamuralikrishna's house then. In addition to that, there were students of other Gurus who began coming to him. One of the first students was P. Purnachandra Sekhar Rao. But his journey to Balamuralikrishna came through a different route:

> I still remember that Friday evening, that was August 29th,, 1959, I was in Hyderabad, when a radio broadcast of Balamuralikrishna's music accompanied by Lalgudi G. Jayaraman on the violin caught my attention. I was so fascinated by the violin that I decided, if I learnt it, it had to be only from him. I had never seen Lalgudi G. Jayaraman in my life. I would scout magazines to find any images. I remember the All India Radio's Vaani magazine carrying his images. I cut them out and pasted them in my violin box. Three years later, I got a chance to visit Madras and I went to his house. I just burst into tears with emotion. I requested him to come to my house when he was in Hyderabad next time. He obliged my request when he visited Hyderabad, while accompanying G.N.B. on a concert.

Jayaraman was thirty-two and Purnachandra just nineteen when this hero-worship began. When Jayaraman visited his house in Hyderabad, Purnachandra made preparations to perform Jayaraman's Paada Puja, requesting him to be his Guru. Jayaraman was pleasantly surprised and asked him to come to Madras. Purnachandra reached Madras and Jayaraman's house while he was away. Jayaraman's father, the great Lalgudi Gopala Iyer, was there. He asked Purnachandra to play something on his violin. Purnachandra played a Thodi. Gopala Iyer was pleasantly surprised seeing this young boy reproduce his son's music phrase to phrase. And thus, Lalgudi agreed to have Purnachandra onboard. 'I was the first student of violinist Lalgudi G. Jayaraman in 1965. I got an education scholarship from the ministry for advanced studies. That enabled me to pursue music while I also worked as an upper division clerk,' recollects Purnachandra. 'Lalgudi Jayaraman was a very sensitive musician. I remember once when music critic Seshadri, who wrote under the pen name 'Aeolus', wrote in Shankar's Weekly, "Lalgudi depends more on his fingers than his head", Lalgudi was so upset that he didn't eat for four days. This way I saw a different side of Lalgudi as a musician,' remembers Purnachandra.

By 1970, when Purnachandra performed in Madras, the *Indian Express* dated 13 June 1970, called him 'Lalgudi II'. As a tribute to his Guru, Purnachandra prefixed Lalgudi to his own name and began being called 'Lalgudi Purnachander'. This didn't please Lalgudi Jayaraman. Around the same time, he approached Balamuralikrishna, who began teaching him music from 1969 onwards. On being asked how he was different as a teacher and whether he learnt something new, Purnachandra said, 'Lalgudi taught me technique not music, Balamuralikrishna taught me musical imagination.' As a violinist, Purnachander accompanied Balamuralikrishna in over 3000 concerts.

The job at All India Radio was good for a while. But like many government organizations, there were delays due to bureaucratic processes and corrupt officials to deal with. For every little thing, a long list of letters seeking permission and 'no objection' had to be got. This was tedious and time-consuming, and Balamuralikrishna was not used to it. Soon he decided he had had enough of the job and quit All India Radio in 1964. He kept up a hectic concert schedule and continued playback singing for cinema. In 1965, his song 'Oru Naal Podhuma' for the movie *Thiruvilayadal* became a rage with both classical music lovers and cinema lovers. Several Sabhas in Chennai welcomed him. Krishna Gana Sabha run by Yagnyaraman offered him multiple *Kutcheris*, both for their Gokulashtami festival and for their December season. 'Looking back, I think, the only artiste who was consistently given the maximum number of concerts was Balamuralikrishna. In fact, he would be given a double bill, one for his vocal and another concert for his viola,' recollected Y. Prabhu, the son of Yagnyaraman who currently heads the Krishna Gana Sabha. This association was to last for over a decade.

By the mid-1960s, Balamuralikrishna had given his voice to several movies as a playback singer in Telugu, Kannada, Tamil and Malayalam. In the 1966 *Sandhya Raaga*, directed and produced by A.C. Narasimha Murthy was released in December. The plot was based on a novel by the famous Kannada writer A.N. Krishna Rao, popular as 'Aanakru'. The movie had a star cast of Raj Kumar, Udaykumar, K.S. Ashwath and others. The music was composed by G.K. Venkatesh. Balamuralikrishna sang two songs in the movie. 'Nambide Ninna Naada Devate', written by G.V. Iyer, and the Purandaradasa Kriti 'Ee Pariya Sobagu'. His old friend Bhimsen Joshi was also singing in the movie. In fact, 'Nambide Ninna Naada Devate' was sung by three singers in different versions in the movie, Balamuralikrishna, Bhimsen Joshi and S. Janaki. 'Ee Pariya Sobagu' was sung as a duet between Balamuralikrishna and Bhimsen Joshi. This rekindled their old friendship. The movie became a huge success. Soon, at his concerts, Balamuralikrishna began getting requests to sing both these songs. He cleverly stuck to singing the Purandaradasa Kriti, which did not breach the protocol of the Carnatic Sabha decorum. We will look at his contribution to cinema music in a later section.

The 1960s shot Balamuralikrishna into unprecedented fame with Bhakti Ranjani. Through that programme, there were numerous achievements. The first one was obviously the quality of a programme of that nature, but the bigger one was the expansion of Balamuralikrishna's repertoire of songs. In addition to the music of the classical trinity, the music of composers from post trinity eras, lesser-known composers like Tumu Narasimha Dasu, philosophical poetry like Tattavalu, folk songs of Nanduri Subba Rao that became popular as Yenki Patalu, songs of saints like Kaivaram Yogi Nareyena, classical Sanskrit and Telugu poetry and much more enriched his existing treasure of songs. In years to come he would often get requests at concerts to sing these. Even today Bhakti Ranjani is synonymous with the music of Balamuralikrishna for many of the Rasikas and audiences. No programme like it was ever produced before or after in the history of All India Radio.

It was around this time that he began extensively performing with the multi-faceted mridangam vidwan T.V. Gopalakrishnan and the violinist M.S. Gopalakrishnan. The trio would become popular on the concert circuit as 'Krishna-Trayam'. 'I was already aware of Murali's music and knew of his popularity among the audiences. I, M.S. Gopalakrishnan and Murali performed for the first time together at Narada Gana Sabha,' remembered T.V. Gopalakrishnan. This Krishna-Trayam also performed at the Music Academy in the December season of 1963 and again in 1965. The 1963 concert consisted of only four compositions. Balamuralikrishna opened his concert with a Varnam 'Enta Sudiname' in Ragam Shankarabharanam. After that he sang two Tyagaraja Kritis, 'Kanugonu Soukhyamu' in Nayaki and 'Nannu Palimpa' in Mohanam. He sang a Ragam-Taanam-Pallavi in a combination of Anandabhairavi and Amritavarshini. On enquiring further about how M.S. Gopalakrishnan fit into the trio, he replied in an interview with me, 'M.S. Gopalakrishnan had unfathomable dexterity and awareness as an accompanying violinist. If you gave him a free hand, he could go on and on and wander, but as an accompanist he was 100 per cent faithful.'

M.S. Gopalakrishnan's association with Balamuralikrishna went a long way. His brother M.S. Anantaraman and their father Parur Sundaram Iyer had known Balamuralikrishna from his very entry into Madras. Parur Sundaram Iyer was the founder of the Sri Tyagaraja Sangeetha Vidwat Samajam in Mylapore. He was one of the first violinists to perform with a young Balamuralikrishna on the radio and later presented him in his Samajam. 'Balamuralikrishna sir has been like a family member in our house. There has been almost no function at the Parur House without a concert of Balamuralikrishna sir. He sang at the Gruha Pravesham of this house, he sang at my sacred thread ceremony, at my wedding reception and at my son's sacred thread ceremony also. He is the only Carnatic vocalist, four generations of Parur Baani violinists have performed with. My grandfather Parur Sudaram Iyer, my father Anantaraman, my uncle M.S. Gopalakrishnan and his daughter Narmada, myself and my brother Krishnaswamy and my son Ananthakrishnan,' recalled M.A. Sundaresan, the current trustee of the Samajam. The Krishna-Trayam team gave several thousands of concerts and was a huge hit. They also did innumerable recordings for All India Radio. 'Murali was also an excellent Mridangam Vidwan. I remember recording a unique programme for the All India Radio where T.N. Krishnan played the flute, I played the violin and Murali played the mridangam,' remembered T.V. Gopalakrishnan.

In Carnatic music history, this sort of grouping of artistes was not uncommon. The great vocalist Ariyakudi Ramanuja Iyengar performed extensively with violinist Papa Venkatramaiah and Mridangam Vidwan Palghat Mani Iyer. Over a period of time, they came to be referred to as 'Ari-Papa-Mani'. Similarly, 'G.N.B. "Lalkudi" (Palghat) Raghu' was another famous trio. In the same way Krishna-Trayam became a huge hit among Rasikas.

Balamuralikrishna also released his first LP record with the Krishna-Trayam. It was a record of seven songs, out of which two were compositions of Tyagaraja, 'Nannu Kanna Thalli in Sindhu Kanada' and 'Nannu Palimpa in Mohanam', one composition of Sadashiva Brahmendra, 'Pibare Rama Rasam in Aahir Bhairav', and four of his own compositions, 'Saraguna in Thodi', 'Mahadevasutham in Arabhi', 'Sadatava Pada in Shanmukhapriya' and a 'Thillana in Brindavani'. It would have taken great courage to release one's first LP records in which one's own compositions occupied the major portion. This was a testimony to Balamuralikrishna's confidence. 'Swaraprastara is Murali's speciality. His flights apart from the melodic curves, often alternate either individual Swara or phrases, octaves apart that often works hard on the accompanists. Besides being a popular exponent, singing classical compositions of the Trinity and other composers, Murali is also well-known for his own compositions, which he has made very popular on the stage. Of late, Balamuralikrishna is also rapidly becoming popular as a film playback singer and a film star too,' reads the sleeve notes at the back of the LP record.

On 14 November 1969, Balamuralikrishna suddenly received a letter. It read:

Dear Shri Balamuralikrishna ji, Namaskar. Two or three years ago I chanced to listen to one of your records. I've never met you nor have I ever had the opportunity to hear you personally. But when I heard your record, I experienced deep joy and felt extremely happy. I must admit that god had not only bestowed upon you a voice, but has also gifted you with a rare knack and art to sing in different forms. This, I feel, is god's blessing. When I heard you sing, I also felt, as if I had been listening to good music after a long period. I pray that god may give you a long life and continued strength to sing. If at any time in the future, you are planning to visit Bombay, kindly let me have your intimation. With best wishes and kind regards – Sincerely yours, Lata Mangeshkar.

Two months later, another letter came from Lata Mangeshkar, inviting Balamuralikrishna to give a concert for the twenty-eighth anniversary of her late father Pt Dinanath Mangeshkar. Balamuralikrishna's music was spreading beyond the usual Sabha circuit, going to places where Carnatic music was not a common affair. In his mind, he had only one wish, to take forward the legacy of Saint Tyagaraja.

6

The Sensational '70s

In 1970, Balamuralikrishna visited the Tyagaraja Aradhana in Thiruvaiyaru. Here, he rendered 'Enta muddo Enta Sogaso' in Ragam Bindumalini. This created a rather unnecessary fuss. 'A huge criticism fell on him. Several people wondered what this Kriti was, several others joked what is this Bindumalini, it must be the name of one of his girlfriends,' recollected Thiruvaiyaru P. Sekar, one of the students who got drawn to Balamuralikrishna's music and had a lifelong association with him. Sekar's father, T.N. Pattabhishekam, was the headmaster of the Thiruvaiyaru School. The fact is, very few in Thiruvaiyaru and among the festival committee had the knowledge of the kind of repertoire of Tyagaraja Kritis that Balamuralikrishna had.

In 1971, the government of Tamil Nadu recommended Balamuralikrishna for the Padma Shri award. At a glittering ceremony in New Delhi, President Varahagiri Venkata Giri (1894–1980) honoured him. The Tyagabrahma Mahotsava Sabha in Thiruvaiyaru was scouting for someone who could assume office and head that organization. There was a problem with some of the older officials, and many of them had quit. After much deliberation, Balamuralikrishna's name was suggested by the then treasurer Thillaisthanam Vasudevan. Call it luck or fate, he was now being welcomed into the place that he hadn't entered for a decade. Saint Tyagaraja must have finally heard his prayerful appeal. His term in

Thiruvaiyaru brought about a huge set of changes. 'Balamurali sir would come to Thiruvaiyaru, and before the meeting, there would be a prayer song in the Sannidhi. I remember him singing "Sri Ganapathini". I had nothing to do with the meeting, but was there as an awestruck fan. I was waiting outside when Mr Panchanadham signalled for me to sing. I couldn't imagine singing in front of Balamuralikrishna sir. I was literally shivering with fear and excitement. I somehow mustered courage, closed my eyes and sang. He came out of the Sannidhi, I fell at his feet and took his blessings. He enquired who I was. Mr Panchanadham told him that I was a local boy. He then enquired where I was learning music from. I told him from my mother and immediately expressed my wish to be his student as well,' recollected Sekar, about his first encounter with Balamuralikrishna. 'His student Rajalakshmi Santhanam appreciated my singing and gifted me two of his books. I had an image of him with me which I asked him to autograph. He obliged. I was on cloud nine,' added Sekar.

Before that the Aradhana was a fairly unorganized affair. Artistes came and went and performed as they wished. 'Sometimes a senior artiste would perform nonstop for as long as he liked and there was no one to object, just in case it hurt the ego of the artiste. At other times, a scheduled event would be pushed ahead because some senior artiste showed up without prior announcement and demanded a slot to sing. Sometimes there were members in the committee who would silently sell a slot for money that they pocketed. Two veteran members, Sethuraman and Ramaswamy, had suggested pricing slots, the money from which would go into the festival fund,' recollected Sekar. Balamuralikrishna decided to put a stop to all of these things. He introduced a life membership scheme, wherein artistes who enrolled were given a chance to perform. After some initial hesitation, all artistes gladly supported this initiative. Some of the first to come on board were Semmangudi Srinivasa Iyer, M.S. Subbulakshmi and Sadasivam, Maharajapuram Santhanam, Brinda-Mukta, K.V. Narayanaswamy, D.K. Pattammal, T.N. Krishnan and others. In addition to Carnatic musicians, there were several from other fields who supported his initiatives, including film actors Bhanumathi Ramakrishnan and Vyjayanthimala Bali. 'I was a regular to the Thiruvaiyaru Aradhana every year along with my mother. In fact, I even learnt two Tyagaraja

Kritis from Balamuralikrishna sir,' recollected Vyjayanthimala about her association with the Aradhana and Balamuralkrishna.

Next, Balamuralikrishna spoke to the authorities at the Tirumala Tirupati Devasthanams to sponsor the building of a guest house that could accommodate artistes who visited the festival. He managed to convince the government of Andhra Pradesh to donate a sum of Rs 2,00,000 for the project. 'He changed the presentation format of the Kutcheris. He introduced the system of having two stages side by side. As one artiste would come to the end of the concert, the second artiste would ascend the other stage. This way there would be no time wasted and the concerts would go on smoothly,' recollected Vidhushi Rama Kausalya, a lifetime resident of the Thillaisthanam Agraharam who belongs to the Thillaisthanam Shishya Parampara of Saint Tyagaraja. Kausalya's grandmother was a disciple of Panchu Bhagavatar along with Narasimha Bhagavatar, who were called the 'Thillaisthanam Brothers'. They were Thillaisthanam Rama Iyengar's prime shishyas who kept the Thillaisthanam Shishya Parampara of Saint Tyagaraja going.

At the same time, he started familiarizing himself with everybody in and around Thiruvaiyaru who was associated with the Aradhana. Carnatic vocalist Sandeep Narayanan took me to his ancestral home in the Rayampettai Agraharam in Thiruvaiyaru. His grandfather, R. Varadarajan, and his grand uncle, R.R. Narayanan, were active members helping with the Aradhana. In fact, Narayanan's own ancestral house would host artistes like Ariyakudi Ramanuja Iyengar and Madurai Mani Iyer in the heydays. Narayanan's son N. Madhavan recollected Balamuralikrishna's visit to their house very fondly.

The other house he frequented was that of Vidhushi Rama Kausalya at Thillaisthanam Agraharam. Kausalya is a trained musician, student of legendary gurus like Karaikudi Samba Siva Iyer and Chittoor Subramanya Pillai. She had served as the principal of the Music College at Thiruvaiyaru. Her sister Meenakshi Rajamohan recollected several instances of Balamuralikrishna's visit to their home. He also taught her a few Kritis.

He knew everybody in the Bhavaswamy Agraharam and frequented the Panchanadeeswarar Temple, popular as Aiyarappar Kovil. At the temple he would find a peaceful corner to sit and sing to his heart's content.

His trips to Thiruvaiyaru and Thanjavur became more frequent. When not touring the various temple towns around Thanjavur like Swamimalai, Kumbakonam, Mayavaram, Mannargudi, Vaduvur, Thiruvarur, Lalgudi, Srirangam and Thiruvanaikovil, he would spend his free time reading and exploring the vast collection of books and manuscripts housed at the iconic Saraswati Mahal library in Thanjavur. He befriended several scholars of Telugu, Tamil, Marathi and Sanskrit and often invited them to his home. During his visits to the temples, he spent time studying their histories and singing the particular Kshetra Kritis of those places. All these trips would be of use in later decades.

In 1974, the Tamil edition of Balamuralikrishna's *Janaka Raga Kriti Manjari* was published. This is the same book which was published in Telugu in 1952. It was translated in Tamil with a foreword by the musicologist professor P. Sambamoorthy. He writes,

The 12 notes of the octave are universally known. But the number of heptatonic scales using these notes is very limited. The scale, of Vachaspathi (64th Mela), harmonic minor scale (21st Mela), the harmonic minor scale using the 'F' sharp in the place of 'F' natural and heard in Gypsy music (57th Mela), may be mentioned as examples. It was given to a genius in south India to point out that the 72 heptatonic scales, based with these 12 notes of Octave are possible. This scheme is logically perfect, mathematically accurate and aesthetically sound. Hence, this scheme should be of interest to musicologists of all countries claiming to possess a highly developed system of music. A scale can become a Raga when the various Raga Ranjaka Prayogas establish its melodic personalities and determine through a process of ratiocination.

Vidwan Bala Muralikrishna has remarkably succeeded in his 72 Kritis depicting the Mela Ragas. These Kritis were published in Telugu scripts and they were not easily accessible to those who do not know the Telugu script. It is a very fine idea to publish a transliterated version of Kritis in Tamil script. This will enable more people to learn his Kritis and popularize them. Thus in this edition where the music remains in fact, musicians have the benefit of easily learning these Kritis which are veritable gems in the 72 Mela Ragas. I heartily commend this publication.

I was desperately searching for a copy of this book, and finally found it with Sekar, who got it as a gift from Balamuralikrishna on the Aradhana day dated 12 January 1974. A fascinating aspect of the book is a detailed chart of Melakarta Ragas listed in their respective cycles in Tamil in the back flap of the book. The book also carries a portrait of Balamuralikrishna, and is specially autographed for Sekar in Tamil. Who would have thought that only a few years ago, Balamuralikrishna was doubting his own mastery over the language. The portrait also lists eight of the prominent awards that he had got by then. They include 'Gana Sudhakara', 'Gandharva Gana Vithakar', 'Sangita Kala Sagara', 'Geetha Kala Bharathi', 'Vaggeyakara Vachaspati', 'Gandharva Kalanidhi', 'Gayaka Sikamani' and the 'Padma Shri'. As a loyal disciple, Sekar has carefully saved a copy of this precious book for all these decades.

The same year, the Gramophone Company of India released an LP record of Sri Tallapaka Annamacharya's Samkirthanams. Balamuralikrishna was accompanied by Dwaram Mangathayaru on the violin, Guruvayur Dorai on the mridangam and Palghat Sundaram on the ghatam. He recorded eight Samkirthanams of Annamacharya. All of them were set to tune by him. Side 1 contains 'Narayanathe Namo Namo (Behag)', 'Brahma Kadigina Padhamu (Mukhari)', 'Deva Ee Thagavu (Malahari)' and 'Hari Rasama Vihari (Hindolam)'. Side 2 contains 'Tholli Kalave Iviyu (Padi)', 'Indharikinabhayambu Lichhu Cheyi (Mishra Harikambhoji)', 'Evvarulero (Varali)' and 'Kommathana Muthyala Kongu (Yadhukula Kambhoji)'. The sleeve notes for this record were written by V.A.K. Ranga Rao, while the famous illustrator Bapu did the artwork on the cover. The record was a huge hit. That year, on 3 August 1974, Andhra University honoured Balamuralikrishna with the honorary doctorate title of 'Kala-Prapurna'. This was an important academic recognition for his contribution to the field of music.

Many more awards were to come his way. He was nominated for the central Sangeet Natak Akademi award in 1975. Under the vice-presidentship of the famous Marathi playwright P.L. Deshpande (1919–

2000), he received the award in Delhi from the then Union minister for education, social welfare and culture, Saiyid Nurul Hasan. Along with him, the veteran Mridangam Vidwan C.S. Murugaboopathy (1914–98) too received the award. The award ceremony was followed by a series of concerts. Balamuralikrishna enthralled the audiences in Delhi with a wide selection of compositions, from Saint Tyagaraja's to his own. Murugaboopathy's style was not alien to Balamuralikrishna. His guru Palani Subramania Pillai (1908–62) had accompanied Balamuralikrishna for hundreds of concerts. The Palani Baani or style of mridangam was Balamuralikrishna's favourite too. His close friend the Hindustani vocalist Bhimsen Joshi, too, received the award that year. At the award ceremony in Delhi, both the friends got to catch up after a long time. The same year Balamuralikrishna won a national award for best music director and the best male playback singer for the Kannada movie *Hamsageethe*, directed by G.V. Iyer. Balamuralikrishna, had made musical contributions to the world of cinema too.

Silver Screen Songs

Carnatic music and musicians have had a long association with cinema. If you take the first 100 years of South Indian cinema, particularly Tamil, Telugu and Kannada, you will find a large number of actors and singers had great parallel lives as music concert artistes. However, there were very few Carnatic musicians who straddled all the four main South Indian film industries with as much ease as Balamuralikrishna. If Telugu was his mother tongue, his Karma Bhoomi was Madras (now Chennai) and the Tamil industry wasn't far from his reach. His impeccable Kannada and Malayalam saw him involved in the respective industries with equal ease.

In Tamil cinema, when the talkies made their way in after the silent era, the earliest movies such as *Kalidas* (1931) and *Galavarishi* (1932) featured singer–actors who came from the theatre traditions. These included T.P. Rajalakshmi (1911–64) and P.B. Rangachari. In 1933, *Seethakalyanam*, made by the famous Prabath Film Company in Kolhapur, had Carnatic musician S. Rajam (1919–2010) in the lead role. The same film also debuted his younger brother S. Balachander (1927–90), who rose to be another stalwart in the Carnatic music industry. Around the same time, the scholarly musician Papanasam Sivan (1890–1973) entered the film industry as a music composer. By the mid-1930s, the great stage star M.K. Tyagaraja Bhagavathar (1910–59) made his way into screen acting. He was one of the earliest stars to sing his own songs for all his movies. In 1937, the famous Carnatic vocalist Musiri Subramania Iyer was invited to act in a movie on the life of Saint Tukaram of Maharashtra. Though the film was not commercially successful, the songs sung by Musiri were well-received.

The year 1939 saw another classically trained stalwart make his way into Tamil cinema. M.M. Dhandapani Desikar (1908–72) was not only a great singer and music composer but also a fantastic actor. His role as Nandanar in the movie produced by Gemini's SS Vasan studios is a modern classic from 1942. The famous stage couple S.G. Kittappa (1906–33) and his wife K.B. Sundarambal (1908–80) were a rage with audiences of both the stage and the screen. One of the earliest singers who also acted later was N.C. Vasantha Kokilam (1919–51). Another Carnatic stalwart who acted in a few movies and later pursued a full-time singing profession was M.L. Vasanthakumari (1928–90). G.N. Balasubramaniam (1910–65) was another star who rose in the mid-1930s, but gave up his acting career to pursue Carnatic music. His contemporary M.S. Subbulakshmi, a child prodigy, began as an actor before giving up her career at the peak to pursue her first love, i.e., Carnatic music. Several others like T.M. Soundararajan (1922–2013) and Sirkazhi Govindarajan (1933–88) who were highly trained in Carnatic music had a flourishing career in the film industry.

The Telugu film industry began with actors hired from the famous Surabhi Nataka Mandali. A whole generation of actors in early Telugu cinema were well-trained musicians on the stage. Many of them also recorded a number of gramophone discs. By the 1940s, it was not uncommon in Telugu cinema to have actors who could also sing. Several of them also had active concert and performance lives outside of the screen. In an interview with me, the famous playback singer P. Susheela recalled a number of actors who gave music performances. 'I have personally attended the music concerts of actors like Chittoor V. Nagaiah, Pasupuleti Kannamba, Bhanumathi Ramakrishna, Rushyendra Mani, S. Varalakshmi and many others. All of them were greatly trained in classical music. Though they might not have given a large number of performances, they used their skills in their acting career to sing on the stage and on screen,' she said. Chittoor V. Nagaiah also turned into a producer and director and brought out a number of movies like *Bhakta Pothana* (1943), *Tyagayya* (1946), *Yogi Vemana* (1947) and others.

In Kannada, several stage actors from popular drama companies made their screen debuts in the talkies era. One of the early stars was Honnappa Bhagavatar (1915–92) who was a trained singer and a star actor, both on stage and on the screen. Among the famous ones were M.N. Gangadhara Rao, Malavalli Sundaramma, Bangalore Tripuramba, Ashwathamma, M.N. Vasudeva Rao, Pandari Bai and the heroines of the Gubbi Company like Jayamma and Sundaramma. Even Kannada cinema's greatest superstar Dr Rajkumar came from a background of stage and musical training. Under the patronage of the Mysore royalty, several great stalwarts of Carnatic music emerged: composers like Veene Sheshanna and Bidaram Krishnappa whose music was popular in theatre; the celebrated violinist T. Chowdiah (1894–1967) who made a film, *Vani* (1943), on the travails of a musician in which he played the lead role. Several classical musicians like Chembai Vaidyanatha Bhagavathar and Palghat Mani Iyer made a guest appearance in the movie.

It was not new for well-trained professional Carnatic musicians to venture into singing or acting for the silver screen. In many later interviews, Balamuralikrishna said he never approached the movie industry himself, but several prominent members of the industry sought him out. By the time he relocated to Madras, a large group of friends from Andhra were already residing there, among whom were several prominent actors, directors, poets, music directors, lyricists, and playback singers. It was not difficult for him to make his entry. By all accounts, his first ever playback assignment was to render a sloka in the movie *Sati Savitri* (1957), starring Akkineni Nageshwar Rao as Satyavan and S. Varalakshmi as Savitri. Though the film titles list D. Baburao, Master Venu, S. Rajeswara Rao, Mallik, J. Lakshminarayana and Balamuralikrishna together as music directors, in an interview given in 2008, Balamuralikrishna denied being the music director. He said he only sang one sloka. There is one Padyam or stanza from a poem rendered by Balamuralikrishna. The movie also had S.V. Ranga Rao in the role of Yama Dharmaraja, music composed by S.V. Venkataraman, dialogues by Ravuri Venkata Satyanarayana Rao, with screenplay and direction by K. Nagabhushanam. The choreography was by Kuchipudi dancer Vempati Chinna Satyam. The actor S. Varalakshmi produced the movie under her own banner, Varalakshmi Pictures. It was a super hit when it released.

In 1959, Sarada Productions released *Jayabheri*, starring Akkineni Nageshwara Rao, S.V. Ranga Rao, Anjali Devi and Gummadi, and directed by P. Pullaiah. Pendyala Nageswara Rao was the music director. Balamuralikrishna rendered a Sanskrit sloka 'Suklam Brahmavichara Saara Paramaam' in praise of Goddess Saraswati at the beginning of a song. The actual song that follows this sloka, 'Madi Sarada Devi Mandirame', sung by Ghantasala Venkateshwara Rao, became a huge hit too. The actor visualized as singing the sloka was Chittoor V. Nagaiah, a singer in his own right. He normally rendered his own songs in movies. The story goes that he insisted that the young Balamuralikrishna's voice be used here.

In 1963, Padmini Pictures released *Karna*, directed by B.R. Panthulu, with music by Viswanathan and Ramamurthy. Balamuralikrishna, along with his old friend P. Susheela, sang a duet 'Neevu Nenu Valachitimi'. The movie was originally made in Tamil titled *Karnan*, starring Sivaji Ganesan and Savithri, and later dubbed into Telugu.

The bigger break came in 1963 with the movie *Nartanasala*. Released on 11 October, this movie was one of the biggest hits in the history of Telugu cinema. It recounts a few significant episodes from the Viraata Parvam of the Mahabharatha. The Viraata Parvam has a long history of its own in the Andhra regions. Several movies had been made on this theme already. In the silent movie era, R. Nataraja Mudaliar produced *Keechaka Vadha* with the same story and released it in January 1918. In 1937, a movie in Telugu titled *Vijaya Dashami* was released; here, Surabhi Kamalabai played the role of Draupadi. Lakshmirajyam and her husband Sridhar Rao, under their banner Rajyam Pictures, produced the 1963 *Nartanasala*. They roped in Kamalakara Kameswara Rao. Lakshmirajyam was a stage and screen actress who turned towards producing movies. They had successfully produced several movies earlier.

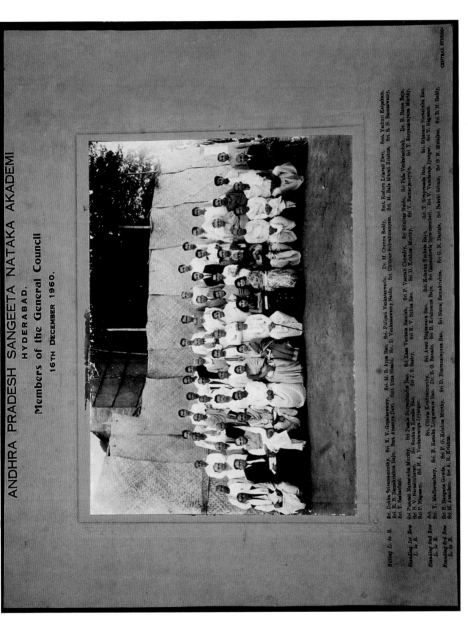

Balamuralikrishna, the youngest member of the Andhra Pradesh Sangeeta Nataka Akademi.

Balamuralikrishna accompanying G.M. Balasubramaniam on his viola for the All India Radio. Also seen here is Seerkazhi Govindarajan.

Balamuralikrishna performing a solo khanjira concert.

Sri Ayyagari Veerabhadra Rao of the All India Radio, who gave Balamuralikrishna his first job.

Balamuralikrishna in the role of Narada along with S.V. Ranga Rao and Anjali Devi in the Telugu movie *Bhakta Prahlada*.

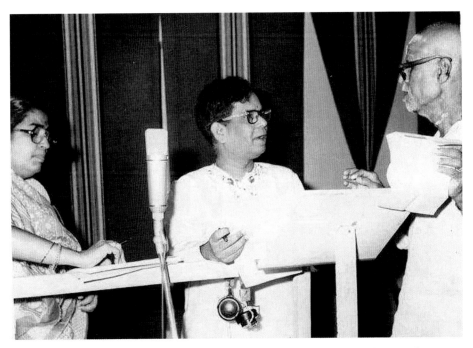

Balamuralikrishna with playback singer P. Susheela and music director Dakshinamurthy at a recording session.

Chembai Vaidyanatha Bhagavatar felicitating Balamuralikrishna.

The famous Jnanpith awardee Viswanatha Sathyanarayana (*extreme left*), an old friend of the Mangalampalli family, along with the noted writer Sripada Subrahmanya Sastry (*second from right*), listening to Pattabhiramayya.

Balamuralikrishna with the first President of India,
Dr Rajendra Prasad, in New Delhi, 1953.

An early concert poster flaunting the versatility of Balamuralikrishna
as a singer, percussionist and a violinist—basically a one-man concert
band. An example of great vintage photoshopping.

Balamuralikrishna with S.V. Narayanaswamy Rao, the founder of
Sri Rama Seva Mandali, and M.S. Ramachandra in Bangalore.

Balamuralikrishna with A.V. Meiyappa Chetti of AVM Studios.

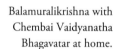

Balamuralikrishna with Chembai Vaidyanatha Bhagavatar at home.

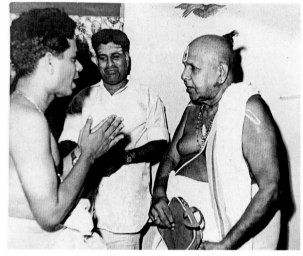

Balamuralikrishna and Annapoorna with the famous film director and Dadasaheb Phalke awardee B.N. Reddi at the sacred thread ceremony of their son Abhiram.

Balamuralikrishna as the youngest principal of the music college in Vijayawada, along with the staff.

Balamuralikrishna performing to a packed Sri Rama Seva Mandali at their annual Rama Navami festival at the Fort Highschool grounds in Bangalore in the 1960s.

Balamuralikrishna with the famous poet Devulapalli Krishnasastri, politician Bezawada Gopala Reddy, music director Palagummi Viswanatham and others during the All India Radio days.

The story revolves around the character of Arjuna who is in disguise as a eunuch and joins the queen's quarters as a dance teacher. The name of the character is Brihannala. In *Nartanasala*, the role of Arjuna was played by N.T. Rama Rao, and of Keechaka by S.V. Ranga Rao. Savithri played Draupadi. The main sequence where Brihannala teaches dance to Princess Uttara, daughter of the king of Virata, is shown in a song with music direction by Susarla Dakshinamurthy. This song, 'Salalita Raga Sudharasa Saaram', was sung by Balamuralikrishna. Picturized on N.T. Rama Rao as Brihannala and dancer L. Vijayalakshmi as Uttara, the song was one of the biggest hits of the movie. Long after the movie was forgotten, it remained evergreen. The movie went on to win several national and international awards. It was the second-best feature film in the eleventh National Film Awards. It received awards for best production design and best lead actor at the third Afro-Asian Film Festival held in Indonesia in 1964. S.V. Ranga Rao was given the award for the best actor. N.T. Rama Rao made another movie in 1979 called *Srimad Virata Parvam* in which he played five roles. However, that turned out to be a massive flop.

In 1964, actor-turned-director Chittoor V. Nagaiah produced and directed *Bhakta Ramadasu*, starring Akkineni Nageshwara Rao, Anjali Devi, N.T. Rama Rao, Sivaji Ganesan, Gummadi and Kannamba, among others. The playback singers included Mohammad Rafi. The choreography for the dance sequences was by Kuchipudi dancer and Guru Vempati Chinna Satyam. In this movie Balamuralikrishna rendered a few Padyams.

This was also the beginning of a new love for the compositions of Bhadrachala Ramadasu. Later Balamuralikrishna went on to tune, sing and popularize hundreds of Ramadasu Keertanams.

The same year the producer D.R. Naidu released *Navakoti Narayana*, a movie in Kannada directed by S.K. Ananthachari with music by Shivaprasad. Starring the Kannada superstar Raj Kumar along with actress Sowcar Janaki, the movie was based on the life story of the poet, saint and composer Purandaradasa (1484–1564). It turned out to be a big hit. Several songs sung by Balamuralikrishna—'Achutananda', 'Aadadella Olithe Aayithu', 'Bangaravidabare' along with P. Leela, 'Madhukara Vruthithi' with S. Janaki and 'Indina Dinave'—became huge hits with Kannada music lovers. This was the beginning of yet another long association with the Kannada movie industry.

That year also saw him make an entry into playback singing in Tamil cinema. The musical film *Kalai Kovil* directed by C.V. Sridhar was a rags-to-riches story of a musician, a veena player. Starring S.V. Subbaiah, R. Muthuraman and Rajashree, the movie had music direction by Viswanathan-Ramamurthy and lyrics penned by poet Kannadasan. Though the movie was not a commercial success, the song 'Thanga Ratham Vandhadhu' sung by Balamuralikrishna and P. Susheela became a huge hit. Years later, they performed it again on a television show. This was also the beginning of Balamuralikrishna's love affair with the Tamil cinema industry.

In 1965, D.L. Narayana Rao produced *Dorikithe Dongalu*, directed by P Subramanyam. Starring N.T. Rama Rao and Jamuna, the movie had lyrics written by the famous poet Dasarathi Krishnamacharya and music direction by Saluri Rajeswara Rao. Balamuralikrishna sang one song, 'Sri Venkatesa Eeesa', along with P. Susheela and Vasantha. This became another hit. Decades later, both Balamuralikrishna and Dasarathi were to receive honorary doctorates from the Sri Venkateswara University. The same year, in *Pandava Vanavasam*, directed by Kamalakar Kameswara Rao, starring N.T. Rama Rao, S.V. Ranga Rao and Savithri, with music direction by Ghantasala Venkateshwara Rao, Balamuralikrishna rendered a small Padyam on lord Surya. Then there was another song 'Sri Sati Manovihari' in the Kannada movie *Sati Savitri*, with music by G.K. Venkatesh and lyrics by R.N. Jayagopal. However, the biggest hit was yet to come!

Thiruvilayadal was directed and co-produced by A.P. Nagarajan. Featuring Sivaji Ganesan, Savithri, singer and actor K.B. Sundarambal, T.S. Balaiah, T.R. Mahalingam and others, the film had music composed by K.V. Mahadevan and lyrics penned by the famous poet Kannadasan. Balamuralikrishna sang only one song in the whole movie, 'Oru Naal Podhuma'. The story goes that the director approached another famous singer Srikazhi Govindarajan first. Govindarajan refused it for some reason, and when the offer came to Balamuralikrishna, he gladly took it up. The lyrics of the song are written such that each line mentions the name of the Ragam that it is sung in, as a part of the Sahityam. The song covers Ragas Kalyani, Darbar, Thodi, Maand, Kaanada and Mohanam. Released on 31 July 1965, the movie turned out to be a massive hit with audiences. It won numerous awards, including the Filmfare award for Best Film in Tamil.

A new phase had also begun in the life of Balamuralikrishna. In his usual Carnatic concerts, he began getting requests to sing this song. It was sacrilege to sing cinema songs on a classical platform. However, he would entertain the demand towards the end of the concert. At one such concert, Lalgudi G. Jayaraman accompanied him on the violin. As he traversed into the song, the line 'Enakinaiyaga Darbaril Evarum Undo' came. It means, 'Who else is there in this chamber who can compete with me?' As he sang, he gently turned towards Jayaraman. The audience burst into laughter. Jayaraman felt mighty offended. It might have been done as a passing joke but in a serious Carnatic concert with serious audiences, it could be pretty humiliating. Jayaraman had been a great accompanist for Balamuralikrishna through the 1950s. A student of both of them, P. Purnachander, recalled, 'Jayaraman sir and Palani Subramaniam Pillai were regular accompanists for Balamuralikrishna for hundreds of concerts. Jayaraman sir also recorded numerous gramophone records with him earlier.' This incident strained the relationship forever. Jayaraman decided to withdraw as an accompanying artiste. He was already in the process of establishing himself as a soloist. Incidents like these gave him enough scope to pursue his passion. That was the last time Lalgudi Jayaraman accompanied Balamuralikrishna. By the late 1960s, M.S. Gopalakrishnan began accompanying him to all the important concerts.

The same year, he sang 'Yeti Loni Keratalu' in the movie *Uyyala Jampala,* starring K. Jaggaiah and Krishna Kumari. The lyrics were by the famous Telugu poet Bhagavatula Sadasiva Sankara Sastry who wrote under the pen name 'Arudra'.

Palnati Yuddham was released on 18 February 1966. Directed and produced by Gutta Ramaneedu, the film had a star cast of N.T. Rama Rao, Bhanumati, Anjali Devi and others. With lyrics written by Malladi Ramakrishna Sastry and music by Saluri Rajeswara Rao, Balamuralikrishna sang a duet 'Seemalu Galavari' with P. Susheela. This was yet another hugely successful movie. The same year, in the Tamil crime-thriller *Sadhu*

Mirandal, Balamuralikrishna sang 'Arulvaye Nee Arulvayee' penned by Alangudi Somu.

Having successfully launched himself as a playback singer in Telugu, Kannada and Tamil cinema, it was as if Malayalam cinema was waiting to happen. In the movie *Anarkali,* directed and produced by Kunchacko in 1966, that was fulfilled. He sang a duet with P.B. Sreenivos, 'Sapta Swarasudha Sagarame'. The movie saw the screen debut of the famous playback singer K.J. Yesudas in the role of Tansen, a court musician wielding a sitar alongside another actor, L.P.R. Varma, Balamuralikrishna was singing for him while Sreenivos was singing for Varma. The film starring Prem Nazir and K.R. Vijaya was a hit at the box office and the music caught on with the film lovers of Kerala.

In the Telugu movie *Srikakula Andhra Mahavishnu Katha,* starring N.T. Rama Rao and Jamuna, with music by Pingali Nageswara Rao, Balamuralikrishna sang one track 'Vasanta Gaaliki' in a duet with playback singer S. Janaki. The same year, he sang 'Hanave Ninnaya Guna' in the Kannada movie *Dudde Duddappa,* directed by B.R. Panthulu, starring Panthulu and M.V. Rajamma, and with music by T.G. Lingappa.

The success of the music in *Sandhya Raga* in Kannada saw numerous offers coming his way. *Subba Shastry,* produced and directed by M.V. Krishnaswamy, was based on the novel *Aashadabhoothi* by A.N. Murthy Rao. The music direction was by the famous Carnatic veena artiste Mysore Doreswamy Iyengar and S. Krishnamurthy. Four out of the five songs in the movie were sung by Balamuralikrishna, and the last by his friend from Andhra, Srirangam Gopalarathnam. Out of the four songs, two were traditional Kritis, 'Yenu Madiddarenu' and 'Kararavindena' by Purandaradasa; the other two were 'Thanu Ninnadu' by Kanakadasa and 'Kala Beda Kola Beda', a Vachana by Basavanna. The Sanskrit scholar and writer Dr 'Shatavadhani' Ganesh, in a later tribute to Balamuralikrishna, recollected an incident from the making of *Subba Shastry.* He wrote:

The music directors for the film Subba Shastry were Doraiswamy Iyengar and S. Krishnamurthy (grandson of Mysore Vasudevacharya). I am reminded of an incident related to me by Krishnamurthy himself. When Balamurali was invited to sing for the movie and it was insisted that he should be around when the melody is being tuned, he landed up with his large family and seemed to be happy in meaningless time-pass. When the orchestra had been readied and the tune had been composed, Balamurali would take a quick look at the composition, write down the lyrics and the Ettugede Svaras, and see the name of the Raga. Then he would say in Telugu, 'Intena?' (Is that all?). He would go to the microphone and sing it. The amount of time the song would be shown on the silver screen was also the time taken for recording it. After the recording, he would be back with his family. His wit and humour mixed with general conversations and gossips went on. The harried music directors would take another two or three hours to compose the next song only for it to be met with the same treatment by Balamurali. In a single day, he recorded all his songs for the movie. But when another singer had to sing a song from that film, it took more than two days of toil for the recording.

The film was a huge success, to say the least. The music outdid the movie in popularity.

His success as a playback singer in all the four South Indian film industries saw other offers coming his way. In 1967, Balamuralikrishna gladly took up the role of Narada in the Telugu movie *Bhakta Prahlada* and debuted on the silver screen. Produced by A.V. Meiyappan's AVM Productions, *Bhakta Prahlada* was a large-scale film based on the mythological story of the devotee Prahlada, a character in the Shrimad Bhagavata Mahapuranam. It had a star cast of S.V. Ranga Rao in the leading role of demon king Hiranyakashipu, Anjali Devi as his wife Leelavathi, debutante Roja Ramani in the central role of Prahlada and Balamuralikrishna as sage Narada. D.V. Narasa Raju wrote the film's story and screenplay, while Saluri Rajeswara Rao composed the background score. In the title credits, Balamuralikrishna's name features immediately after S.V. Ranga Rao's. Balamuralikrishna makes his entry on the screen about half an hour into the movie. As sage Narada, he flies across the skies singing songs in glory of lord Vishnu. He encounters lord Indira kidnapping Leelavathi on the Pushpaka Vimana and a dialogue ensues. In an interview in *The Hindu* in 2008, Balamuralikrishna recollected his experience. 'When I acted as Narada, I had to stand on a stool without proper balancing, and I go up as someone raises it up on a jack. I precariously stand there with a fear that I'd fall off the stool, but I should not show it in my face—I should instead sing with a smiling face!'

Balamuralikrishna not only acted but also sang his own songs in the movie. The opening song was 'Aadi Aanadiyu Neeve Deva', an Annamacharya composition, which is a lullaby 'Siri Siri Lali', in a duet with P. Susheela. A joke on the set of the movie went *'Balamurali Padithe, Prahaladudu Enti, Hirnaryakashipu Inka Andaru Padutharu'* (if Balamurali sings, why just Prahalada, Hiranyakashipu and everybody in the movie will sing), a comment on his mastery. All the Padyams in the movie were from the classical works of the poet Bommera Pothena, a subject that Balamuralikrishna knew like the back of his hand. Legend goes that he would glance through the script once and render all the Padyams, in fairly literary and complicated Telugu, at one go. His co-actor, the great S.V. Ranga Rao, who had several Padyams in the film, had to refer to the script multiple times, despite being a seasoned stage actor. The movie was a super-hit, and celebrations were held when it crossed the 100-day mark in theatres. It also got dubbed into many other languages. This was among a handful of his screen appearances.

In an interview with me, his disciple Purnachander mentioned why he didn't act more. 'To be on the screen you need a strong personality. You need good height. And a screen presence. Balamuralikrishna had none of that and he was aware of it. He was short, not a very handsome face for the screen in comparison with the actors of his times and certainly no screen presence. Keeping all these in mind, he even told me, I am better off letting my voice be on screen. Those who want to see me can come and attend my Carnatic music Kutcheris!'

Bhakta Prahlada was his debut on screen as an actor and his last major acting gig. Though numerous offers, many with big money, came his way, he politely refused all of them. But he did make guest appearances in several other movies in later years.

In 1967, a full-length biopic was made on the poet composer 'Sangita Pitamaha' Purandaradasa. Directed by C.V. Raju and R. Ramamurthy, the movie had a star cast of K.S. Ashwath, R. Nagendra Rao and Pandhari

Bai. All the songs were original compositions of the poet composer. Under C.N. Panduranga's music direction, Balamuralikrishna sang a number of songs for the background score. The same movie was made in Telugu later.

In 1968, he sang in the Kannada movie *Amma*, the Malayalam movie *Kodungallooramma* and the Telugu movie *Pedarasi Peddamma Katha*. If we look at the movies in the early-1970s, several of the songs he sang became huge hits. The song 'Terateeyara', in the Telugu movie *Sri Venkateshwara Vaibhavam* would be played in temples well into the 1990s. Then came *Andala Ramudu* in 1973, *Sri Rama Anjaneya Yuddham* in 1974 and *Hamsageethe*, for which he got the national award in 1975. It is a difficult task to track every single song he sang. But most of the songs that he sang in the different south Indian languages were huge hits, sometimes even bigger than the movies.

In 1977, in the Tamil movie *Kavikuyil*, under the music direction of Ilaiyaraaja, he sang 'Chinna Kannan Azhaikkiran'. This song would again be a huge hit. Decades later, in a public function honouring Ilaiyaraaja's contribution to music, Balamuralikrishna sang it to huge applause. The musical camaraderie and love that the two icons shared on the stage during this event can be seen in a video available on YouTube even now.

The same year in the Telugu movie *Kurukshetram*, he rendered three Padyams, all from the traditional Pothana Bhagavatamu. In the 1979 Telugu movie *Guppedu Manasu*, he sang the famous 'Mouname Nee Bhaasha, Oo Mooga Manasa'. This song became a huge cult hit. Looking back, this was also the year in which Balamuralikrishna faced a lot of criticism and difficulties over the raga controversy. The Sahityam of the song was a reflection of his own mental condition at that point of time. In a later interview, when he was asked to comment on some of those criticisms, he replied to the interviewer: '*Mouname Nee Bhaasha, Oo Mooga Manasa* (Speechlessness is your language, Oo silenced mind).' The song, however, continues to be a huge hit.

In the 1980s, the major chunk of his cinema work was for the famous director G.V. Iyer. Though he wasn't very active after that, he never shied away from making an appearance at functions connected to film awards or TV shows. In fact, well into his eighties, he appeared on the TV talk show *Swarabhishekam*, conceived of by Ramoji Rao of ETV, and sang 'Mouname Nee Bhaasha, Oo Mooga Manasa' in honour of his old friend and music director M.S. Viswanathan. In many interviews later, he would say all genres of music were one for him, as long as they were enjoyable.

A Renaissance Man

In 1976, the Music Academy of Madras celebrated its golden jubilee year with much fanfare. The great Sanskrit scholar Dr V Raghavan was the secretary of the Academy. To commemorate the occasion, he composed a song in praise of the institution. The lyrics of the song go: '*Sangeeta Vidwatsabha Jayati Madhrapuri, Suvarnotsava Samaye Sakala Gayakanandamaye.*' The Charanam goes, '*Angeekrutha Shuddha Saampradaya Vidwatchartita Shastra Vishaya Desha Videsha Suvivadha Raghavadi Sevita Naadathanu Shankarasya Krupaya Vardhatham Vardhatham Vardhatham.*' This was set to tune in the fiftieth Melakarta Ragam 'Namanarayani' by Balamuralikrishna. He also sang the song in his concert that season on 27 December.

Balamuralikrishna continued experimenting with music whenever he could. For example, around that time he created his own tambura—a long rectangular box with an open top. On the reverse, four strings were attached, fastened by four screws on either side. He insisted on using this for a lot of his concerts. 'I don't think the Tumbi (the gourd) has anything to do with the production quality of music. I tried this and it is sounding fine,' said his student Thiruvaiyaru Sekar, who was one of the regular students who accompanied him and handled this new creation. 'It was very easy to carry, like a flute box. It was a bit tough to pluck, but it produced good *Nadam (*or resonance).' In a lot of his concert images from that time, we can see his students holding this unique tambura.

The Thiruvaiyaru Tyagaraja Aradhana had become a huge national event. 'I remember M.S. Subbulakshmi was scheduled to perform between 9.30 p.m. to 11 p.m. This was going to be aired on the national programme of music in a live relay all across India. It normally takes about ten to fifteen minutes for balancing the microphones of the All India Radio and the venue. Which means the person singing before must stop at 9.15 p.m. He was not sure other musicians would keep to time, so he asked me to sing. I performed and finished exactly at 9.14 p.m. and as I turned around, I found M.S. Subbulakshmi and party on the other stage. This was his sense of keeping time. Absolutely meticulous,' recollected Purnachander.

'Another year, Chitti Babu's veena concert was scheduled for twenty minutes. At 6.30 p.m., a telegram arrived that Chitti Babu wasn't able to make it to the venue. He simply asked me to perform in that slot and even supported my concert by playing kanjira,' added Purnachander. Balamuralikrishna looked into the needs of musicians and started a small dining hall facility where all the visiting musicians could have their meals on time. In addition, there were the accommodation facilities. They would stay at the Kalyan Mahal School building which would be vacant due to Pongal holidays. This way he took care of every little arrangement to make sure the Aradhana was a successful festival.

In 1977, trouble began brewing at Thiruvaiyaru. A few of the committee members wanted local politicians on board. Balamuralikrishna was against this. He believed that politicians had no business here. They would also bring in unnecessary politics and pollute the musical atmosphere. All committees should only have artistes, he believed. This view didn't go down well with a part of the committee, and members started taking sides. In addition to this, many of them began passing unnecessary remarks about Balamuralikrishna. Those in favour of having politicians onboard started a signature campaign. 'This reached a peak when during one of his Aradhana concerts, the power was disconnected and mysteriously got back once his concert ended. On enquiring, a blame game began,' recollected his student Sekar.

As an expert in Dvi-Raga Pallavis, he presented one in Sunadavinodini and Bhairavi, with Sahithyam paying tribute to the Carnatic composer Shyama Sastry, whose 150th death anniversary was being observed by the Academy. 'To add to the grandeur of the Pallavi, Balamuralikrishna set it to *Sankirnajati Tisra Jhampa Taalam*,' writes historian V. Sriram.

The Music Academy of Madras in 1978 announced the prestigious title of 'Sangita Kalanidhi' for Balamuralikrishna. This was received with a mixed response. There were those who thought it was well-deserved, while many others thought it was too early for this recognition. Several other fellow musicians said it was long due!

Balamuralikrishna was the president of the Music Academy's fifty-second conference. He also presided over the morning academic sessions from 22 December 1978 to 1 January 1979. The sessions began with his own special demonstrations of his musical creations. The special features for that season were the 125th birth anniversary of Veena Seshanna and the birth centenary of Kallidaikuruchi Vedanta Bhagavatar. A number of scholars presented research papers and lecture-demonstrations on numerous topics. Several of Balamuralikrishna's long-time friends presented some interesting papers. T.V. Gopalakrishnan presented a Pallavi in Mudrika Taalam, Nori Nagabhushanam Pantulu of Hyderabad presented a paper on the Tacchur Singaracharya brothers, A. Satyanarayana Murthy of Vijayawada presented on Purandaradasa, and Nookala Chinna Satyanarayana of Hyderabad spoke on the technique of teaching music.

The much-awaited Kalanidhi concert happened on 23 December 1978. He was accompanied by his childhood friend Annavarapu Ramaswamy on the violin and Umayalpuram Sivaraman on the mridangam. His student Thiruvaiyaru Sekar accompanied him. To everyone's surprise, he broke tradition and opened his concert with a chant from the Sama Veda:

पावुका नः सरंस्वती वाजेभिर्वािजिनीवती ।
यज्ञं वंष्ट धियावंसुः ॥ १.४.१० ॥

Listening to the chant even now, one can see how particular he was of the intonation, in keeping with the Samagana tradition. With prayers to the goddess of wisdom and knowledge, he began his concert with Tyagaraja's famous Pancharatna Kriti 'Saadinchane' set to Ragam Aarabhi. Legend goes that Subbudu, in his statement about the concert and in this Kriti, is supposed to have said:

'It was enjoyable listening to Balamurali singing "Saadinchane"' at the Academy, as he has achieved his will to join the elite group of Kalanidhis below the age of fifty, a rare phenomenon at the Music Academy.' Balamuralikrishna continued with Tyagaraja's 'Tatvameruga Tarama' in Ragam Garudadhwani, before launching into his own composition as a prayer to his Guru Parampara—'Bhavamay Mahabagyamura' set to Ragam Kaapi. After that it was a Deekshitar composition—'Neerajakshi Kamakshi'—in Ragam Hindolam. This was followed by a Ragam-Taanam-Pallavi in Kalyani. He announced the Ragam-Taanam, saying, 'I have done a Pallavi in a new Taalam which I have invented. I will explain that before the Pallavi.' After the Ragam-Taanam, he announced the new Taalam. This was yet another revelation and revealed what a mathematical genius Balamuralikrishna was. For the first time in the history of the Academy, a new Taalam system was being introduced. He patiently explained the details of the Taalam.

His announcement went thus: 'About this new Taalam, the principle and basis for thirty-five Taalam is Jaati Bheda—Laghu, Dhrutha and Anudrutha. There is Jaati Bheda for Laghu, but no Jaati Bheda for Dhrutha and Anudhrutha. Now the new principle is, there are Kriyas—Sashabdha Kriyas and Nishabdha Kriyas. There is Gathi Bheda. Gathi means Nadai. There is Gathi Bheda for the Shashabdha Kriyas but not for Nishabhda Kriyas. Just like how there is no Jathi Bheda for Dhrutha. Then there is only Jathi Bheda for Laghu. The Gathi Bheda is only for Sashabdha Kriyas and not for Nishabdha Kriyas. On that principle, a new Taalam which is named as Panchamukhi Adi Taalam. If it is Tisra Nadai, it is Trimukhi-Adi Tala, if it is Khanda Gathi it is Panchamukhi-Adi, if it is Misra Gathi, it will be Saptamukhi-Adi and if it is Sankeerna it is Navamukhi-Adi like this . . .' The audience sat gasping for breath as he went ahead and demonstrated the Taalam before he sang the Pallavi Sahithyam. The Sahithyam was fairly simple. It went: 'Sangeetha Layagyanamu Sakala Sowbhagyamu.' Later, his student Ragavan Manian pointed out that it was actually the first line of an entire Kriti that Balamuralikrishna had composed.

In the traditional Taalam system, there are thirty-five Taalams, based on various combinations of Laghu (beat + fingers), Dhrutham (beat + turn) and Anudhrutham (just a beat). There are five jathis, which are all based off the Laghu: Tisram, a count of three, or Beat - Little Finger - Ring Finger; Chatusram, a count of four; Khandam, a count of five Misram, a count of seven; and Sankeernam, a count of nine. Balamuralikrishna's new Taalam principle is based on the Kriyas, the manual act of 'putting' the Taalam. There is a Sashabda Kriya, where a sound is made (like the beat): and the Nishabda Kriya or the silent part of the Taalam action. In Balamuralikrishna's new Taalam system, he introduces Gathi Bhedam (changing of the Gathi, or Nadai, or 'gait' of the Taalam) into the Sashabda Kriya part of the Taalam.

In this particular Pallavi, the Gathi that is introduced into the Sashabda Kriya part of Adi Taalam is the Khanda (five count), hence the name Panchamukhi (five-faced) Adi Taalam. Adi Taalam goes thus:

Beat - little finger - ring finger - middle finger - beat - turn - beat - turn.
In this sequence, the Sashabda Kriyas are all the BEATS. So the Kriyas are:
Sashabda - nishabda - nishabda - nishabda - sashabda - nishabda - sashabda - nishabda

As per Balamuralikrishna's new system, the Sashabda Kriyas get a Khanda Gathi, or a count of five, while the Nishabda Kriyas get a count of two. That would give this Panchamukhi Adi Taalam a total count of 5 + 2 + 2 + 2 + 5 + 2 + 5 + 2 which equals twenty-five!

Or:

takatakita taka taka taka | takatakita taka | takatakita taka

Umayalpuram Sivaraman stepped up to the occasion and accompanied the Pallavi with equal mathematical brilliance. After this mind-boggling Pallavi, Balamuralikrishna sang a composition of the Tamil poet Thirugnanasambandhar 'Utrumai Servadu' set to Mohana Ragam. For those who doubted his fluency over the Tamil language, he gave them a beautiful surprise with his effortless rendering of a classical poem. He went further and presented his own composition in Tamil 'Endrum Thunai' in Ragam Charukesi in praise of lord Muruga. After that, came a composition of Purandaradasa 'Anugaalavu' set to Ragam Abhogi. And then he announced a new Thillana that he composed specially for the occasion. His announcement went: 'Now I'm going to sing a new Thillana. This is Priya Ragamalika in Pancha Gathi Bheda. This first opening Raga is Gurupriya, second is Rasikapriya, third is Gayikapriya, fourth is Sunadapriya and fifth is Karaharapriya.' He concluded with another *Rik* from the Sama Veda, and finally ended his concert with a Mangalam. For the Mangalam, too, he chose 'Ramachandraya' in Ragam Kurinji, a composition of Bhadrachala Ramadasu, yet another first, for a Kalanidhi concert at the Academy. This was a reminder of his phenomenal contribution in popularizing the compositions of Bhadrachala Ramadasu in the last three decades. 'This Sangita Kalanidhi concert was the talk of the town for a long time. It took a while before Rasikas could get out of the spell he cast,' recollected Sekar who accompanied him and remembered every little detail about the concert even four decades later.

The award was given on 1 January 1979, by Raja Sir Muthaiah Chettiar. The Music Academy journal recorded the proceedings of the *Sadas* (convocation).

The Sadas (convocation) of the fifty-second conference of the Music Academy was held at the auditorium of the Academy at 4 p.m., on the 1st January, 1979, with Raja Sir Muthaiah Chettiar in the chair. There was a distinguished gathering of members of the Academy, music lovers and musicians and scholars. The proceedings commenced with a prayer by Smt. R. Vedavalli. The Sadas was convoked by Sri S. Natarajan, secretary, Sri R. Ranganathan, another secretary of the Academy, read out messages received for the success of the functions. Sri K.R. Sundaram Iyer, President of the Academy, welcomed the guests and gave a resume of features of the fifty-second conference and the steps taken by the Academy to wean away the younger generation from the influence of pop music. Sri T.V. Rajagoplan, secretary of the Academy, presented Dr M. Balamuralikrishna with the following citation.

The Music Academy's souvenir, which gave a brief biographical sketch, also mentioned Balamuralikrishna having created new Ragams. The souvenir read, 'Besides, he has invented many new Ragas like Mahati, Sumukham (containing only four notes), Sarvashri, Omkari (containing only three notes) . . . call for special mention—Ragas like Hamsavinodini, Revathi,

Rohini, Pratimadhyamavathi, Janasammodini, Manorama, Vallabhi, etc., are his personal creations.'

The 1979 journal of the Music Academy carried a detailed report of the 1978 conference that was presided over by Dr Balamuralikrishna. The then chief minister of Tamil Nadu, M.G. Ramachandran (M.G.R.), inaugurated it. In his inaugural speech, M.G.R. said,

> I offer my respect to all the Vidwans, Vidushis and music lovers assembled here for the inauguration of the fifty-second conference of the Madras Music Academy. The Academy has invited me to inaugurate this conference and music festival, but it is really you, who will be inaugurating this function. This is like inviting a minister to inaugurate the pulling of a temple car. The minister will merely touch the heavy ropes and the devotees present there will then pull the car and bring it to its destination. Similarly, I take part in this function as a mere music lover.

Further in his inaugural speech, M.G.R. said, 'Dr Balamuralikrishna, who is being honoured this year, is a prodigy who acquired fame even in his boyhood. He has rendered yeoman service to the conduct of the Tyagaraja festival at Thiruvaiyaru. I commend his anxiety to encourage promising young musicians.'

It quotes excerpts from Balamuralikrishna's presidential address:

> I deem it a great honour to have been considered worthy by the experts committee to be chosen as the president of this, the fifty-second Conference of the Music Academy. I am deeply conscious of the awe-inspiring line-up of great exponents of Carnatic music on whom this unique honour has been conferred in yester years. I myself have been undoubtedly, along with several of you, a reverent and keen listener to the eloquent words of sagacity and wisdom that have marked the presidential addresses of my worthy predecessors. Most of them had been conferred this great honour in the twilight of their long and illustrious career. This had enabled them to recount the glories of the golden age of Carnatic music, which, in the opinion

of many, is fading, and to extoll the glories of ancient systems of
learning and tradition in musical performance. I have the dubious
honour of being a relatively young recipient of the honour, even
though I'm in a position to look back over forty years of my career
as a performing artiste and to share with you the lessons that I feel
worthy of learning from this long experience.

He further said,

No doubt, tradition is the basis of all human achievements but
the music should not become a museum piece by rigidly adhering
to tradition alone. Tradition is the very substance from which
one creates and progresses: but traditionalism is a barrier placed
on progress in the name of what is obsolete. Change is, however,
inevitable whether one likes it or not. Without invention, there
cannot be progress, and therefore a judicious interplay of tradition
and invention is necessary to develop good music. It is well-
known that the existing tradition of our Carnatic music is only the
Sampradaya of the recent past. One cannot sing or play as it was
sung or played some hundred years ago or even fifty years back.
Thus the concept of tradition is a dynamic factor.

He presented what seemed to be a lot of thoughts running through his
mind at that time. 'The general audience for classical music has greatly
increased which is a welcome change but this has brought with it a number
of problems and responsibilities for the performing artistes. The integrity
of the art should be well guarded by the artistes.' He added,

The creation and innovation of the artistes should never be at the
cost of abandoning our great musical tradition: they should be within
the framework of the style of Carnatic music . . . The merits of the
time-honoured Gurukula system can never be challenged, but since
the times are changing, it finds (it) difficult to meet the demands of
the public and so music conservatories have a great responsibility to
train the students of music in a proper way. The syllabus, methods

of teaching, examination and evaluation systems of the present day need modification . . . new experiments may be conducted in Carnatic music by musicologists as well as by musicians, provided the experiments neither change nor affect the nature of Carnatic music. . . I took some initiatives in this, like: it is followed today by both south Indian and north Indian artistes in their performances. Pallavis in complicated Talas and, last but not least, the orchestral musician Carnatic music, can be experimented successfully. Here I wish to express my sincere thanks to our hon'ble chief minister of Tamil Nadu Sri M.G. Ramachandran for having instituted awards for talent promotion in musicians for creating new Ragas and new musical forms and I also wish that the awards should be given wherever talent is found.

He also made suggestions about the responsibilities of the media:

The music Sabhas, press, radio and TV play a major role in maintaining the standard of music. The Sabhas should encourage the deserving young artistes but not by degrading the art by getting monetary help from them. Biased reviews with destructive criticism from the press, and sub-standard musical broadcasts from the radio and TV should be averted.

He concluded his speech saying, 'A few suggestions have been made for improving one's talent but apart from all human efforts, the grace of the almighty is the vital factor for any achievements. I conclude by praying to Sadguru Sri Tyagaraja for the welfare of all musicians and Rasikas, and I dedicate this distinguished honour you have done me to my Guru Parampara, to Sri Sadguru Tyagaraja, Manambuchavady Sri Venkatasubbiah, Sri Dakshinamoorthy Sastri and revered Guru Parupalli Sri Ramakrishnayya Pantulu.'

His presidential address was received with a huge applause. The Academy's journal also records under its resolutions, 'On behalf of the Tiruvarur Music Trinity Commemoration Sabha, Sri K. Chandrasekaran, trustee of that body made an appeal to the Academy, Rasikas, Vidwans and Vidushis and Vidwan Balamuralikrishna as Secretary of the Tyagaraja Aradhana Sabha at Thiruvaiyaru, to take special efforts to collect subscriptions and to renovate Tyagaraja's birthplace at Tiruvarur which had suffered serious damages during the recent cyclone.'

A copy of this souvenir reached the Veena Vidwan S. Balachander. What was to follow was one of the greatest controversies in the modern history of Carnatic music. This came to be known as the 'Raga Controversy'. Balachander wrote a letter on 18 January 1979, to the president and committee members of the Music Academy that read:

In the latest souvenir of the Music Academy released recently, in the biographical-sketch pertaining to Shri Balamuralikrishna, it has been clearly mentioned that Ragas Hamsavinodini, Revathi, Pratimadhyamavathi are personal creations of Balamurali. It is a pity that it has now fallen upon me to spot and point out the fact that these Ragas are already there and happily existing, duly found in music-works printed long long ago before both Balamuralikrishna and Balachander were born!!! Under the very same name of Hamsavinodini this Ragam is found as Janya of Shankarabharanam in the Tamil book titled 'Sangeetha Chandrikai'. Under the very same name Revathi, this Ragam is found as the Janya of Melakarta Ratnangi in the Telugu book titled *Sangeetha Swaraprasthaara Sagaramu*. Featuring the same Aroha-Avaroha, Pratimadhyamavathi is found under the name of Yogini and under the name of Brindavansaranga in the above mentioned Telugu and Tamil book respectively . . . in the former, duly mentioned as a Janya of Hemavathi and the latter as a Janya of Vachaspati.

In the above article, a few other Ragas are accredited to Balamurali. The sources of those could have easily been traced, had been only known their Aroha and Avaroha. Kindly note that I am not concerning myself with his unethical and unaesthetic 4-note and 3-note Ragas which is bound to finally end in a single note!

In spite of having a big library and a bunch of experts under the Academy, how sad that such a gross blasphemous lie has been sown fraudulently perpetuated by a single individual, whose sole aim has been to boost his personal image with an inflated ego. In future at least before printing any such tall claims by any person, the Academy should check upon the bonafides and authenticity of such vital issues, as is expected of a responsible institution serving the cause of Indian music with an international impact.

Balachander also wrote numerous 'Open-Letters' to several newspapers and magazines stating this issue and emphasizing that nobody could create Ragams. The *Indian Express*, dated 26 January 1979, published a letter by Semmangudi Srinivasa Iyer in support of Balachander that stated:

I duly checked up and verified the points quoted by him in some books on musicology and have found them correct. I wish to congratulate Balachander for his courage to bringing out the truth.

As the war brewed, Balamuralikrishna was not one to sit silent. In a letter dated 27 January, he wrote back to the Music Academy saying:

I'm extremely unhappy to point out the stupidity of a Veena player which has now become unavoidable. It is rather a shame on the part of Mr. Balachander to indulge in writing this kind of letters without having proper knowledge of music, misquoting references too. I pity Mr. Balachander who calls himself 'Veena Virtuoso' for not being aware of the demarcation lined between a 'Scale' and a 'Raga'. The theoretical possibilities of scales are many and they have now become innumerable in the present age of computers. A scale is converted into a Raga only through a composition by a Vaggeyakara. It is here that the science of music becomes an art. Well, I feel below my integrity to stand par with Mr. Balachander and comment about his remarks on the bonafide aspect of my creation of new Ragas. I will explain to my beloved Rasikas, when necessary.

It is unfortunate that an esteemed institution like the Music Academy has paid serious attention to this sort of cheap letters and I came forward to reply for his remarks only because I have great regards for the Music Academy, Madras. I request you not to drag me in future in this kind of dirty politics which is unwarranted in the field of music.

This letter aggravated Balachander further, whose ego was wounded with Balamuralikrishna's caustic language. Further letters flew, with each expressing their view on the subject. The press made the most of this controversy. The Music Academy decided to convene an initial meeting on 3 March to discuss this issue. In the meantime Balachander continued his tirade. At his own expense he printed pamphlets and personally handed them out at the gate of the Academy to everyone who walked in. The Academy committee, which consisted of eminent musicians like flute player N. Ramani, veterans like Titte Krishna Iyengar, Prof. S. Ramanathan, Sandhyavandanam Srinivasa Rao, Semmangudi Srinivasa Iyer, Veena Vidwan K.P. Sivanandam and others, once again met on 21 April. The whole Carnatic fraternity eagerly awaited the verdict of this meeting. It was 'unanimously resolved that when a Raga, whose name and Arohana-Avarohana are found in old books, is sung by a musician, even for the first time giving it a Swaroopa, he cannot be said to have created it. He can only be "Popularising the Raga".' Balamuralikrishna himself was not aware of this meeting, though by virtue of being the Sangita Kalanidhi, he was already a member of the experts committee. Overjoyed by the resolution of the Academy, Balachander organized a tea party at the New Woodlands hotel for all the mediapersons he had interacted with. The *Swarajya* magazine, dated 13 May, summed up this war in its edit.

In addition to this, Semmangudi Srinivasa Iyer threw a fit against Balamuralikrishna, using colourful expletives in public. Someone recorded the whole speech and that cassette reached Balamuralikrishna. He was outraged. He decided to file a defamation suit against Semmangudi Srinivasa Iyer and with the help of a legal expert, sued him for the sum of Rs 2,00,000. Semmangudi was shocked on knowing that a copy of his speech had reached Balamuralikrishna. He was defenceless and sent word through a few common committee members who visited Balamuralikrishna seeking pardon. Balamuralikrishna was flustered and said it was not fair for such a senior vidwan to use language that was damaging to his professional career. He also accused Semmangudi of being jealous because of his successful career. A long battle began between Semmangudi and Balamuralikrishna that would go on for many years.

In his essay titled 'Creator's note on creations', Balamuralikrishna wrote: 'The word create literally means "bring into existence", and the noun creation is defined as "a production of human intelligence or power, especially of the imagination".' Further in his essay he added 'it can never be said that a musician or a composer invents a Raga but a new Raga is "discovered" by him. The finished product is the Raga, while the scale is the raw material. But it is very different from the raw material . . . A Raga can be described in other words as an aesthetic projection of the composers "inner spirit". . . the bare notes in a scale vibrate, pulsate and come alive through varied Gamakas, subtle Shrutis, range of Sancharas, Vishesha Prayogas (peculiar musical phrases) and through the movement of notes. Here it becomes a Raga in the hands of a composer. He is the creator of a Raga who converts a scale through his creation of a song into a Raga and fortunately who happens to be the first person to compose a number on the particular scale'. The longer essay deals with Balamuralikrishna's thoughts on music.

Looking back at his career in the 1960s and 1970s, which by many is considered the peak of his professional career, one can say he was unconventional, a rebel of sorts, a constant innovator who operated within the large framework of 'tradition', often expanding its horizons.

Abhayambika

While writing this book, I was asked by almost everyone associated with Balamuralikrishna and the world of Carnatic music, if I would mention Abhayambika. As I was going through several hundreds of images of Balamuralikrishna, I found her present in many of them. So I began digging further into the archives. 'I think she came from somewhere around Mayavaram. She became popular in Madras sometime in the '60s for a rather unique reason. She was an excellent kolam artist. She had won several kolam competitions and had hit upon a new plan. She would collaborate with musicians, and as they would sing, she would put kolam designs and this would be a performance in its own way. This idea was unusual and unique in the concert circuit in those days. This way she would go from artiste to artiste,' recollected Dr Lakshmi Ayyagari, who knew a bit of her history.

And this is how she chanced upon Balamuralikrishna. 'Initially, he didn't entertain any of this. He found it a bit of an unnecessary nuisance and distraction in the middle of a concert. Then she began following him everywhere asking him to try out an experiment at least. Guruji was one who easily got excited about experiments. She had in fact, come all the way to my house asking me to introduce her to Guruji. I don't know how and when she managed to meet him. One day, I was at home talking with Annapoornamma, when Guruji emerged from the car and behind him I saw her. I was shocked, she looked at me and gave me a wicked smile. I requested Guruji to stand with Poornamma. I quickly did a Pradakshinam around them and took their blessings and left thinking something was not okay,' said Dr B.M. Sundaram in his interview recollecting the initial days.

Abhayambika soon endeared herself and found a way into his coterie. She would accompany him in concerts as a tambura artiste, and in later years, on concert tours. Rumour mills began to churn. Soon Abhayambika began telling everyone that she was his manager. At that time in his life, Balamuralikrishna had a hectic schedule and a lot of pressure in his professional life. He probably needed someone to handle his schedules and the clerical work, and found she fit the bill.

The problem began when a foolish organizer in Bangalore once announced Abhayambika as Mrs Balamuralikrishna in his vote of thanks after a Kutcheri. He was reprimanded for the same, but this was much talked of. Meanwhile, Abhayambika started asserting herself more. She began coordinating his concert schedule, dealing with organizers, corresponding with the press and more. She even began taking control of his recording schedule. V.A.K. Ranga Rao recollected an incident: 'Once we had recorded Tyagaraja's famous opera *Nauka Charitamu*. The recording was over and I was sent a copy to write the sleeve notes. I saw the recording and sent it back to Balamuralikrishna. He promptly called me, asking "Ranga Rao Garu why have you not written the sleeve notes? The recording is waiting to be released." I told him, I refused to write the sleeve notes because it says music by Abhayambika. How can she provide the music? It is already a classic opera with music by Saint Tyagaraja himself.

You can say orchestration by Abhayambika and I will write the notes." He agreed to my point and so we went ahead.'

By the end of the 1960s and the beginning of the 1970s, she had complete control over his schedule and professional life. There were both good and bad things about her. 'In Thiruvaiyaru, she was made one of the four joint secretaries of the Aradhana committee. One must commend her for her administrative capabilities,' recollected Dr Rama Kausalya. 'I don't know about her capabilities, but at that time, Balamurali sir was short staffed and required a helping hand, especially to run around with the organizing. She was happy to do all that running around, all the while giving an impression that she was given the powers to take all decisions,' added Purnachander. In those years Balamuralikrishna began the practice of giving an interval between his concerts. 'In one of those concerts during the interval, Semmangudi Mama was standing in the lobby of the Academy, talking to important people. It was a breezy winter and in his signature style, Mama had wrapped a muffler around his head wearing a winter cap to keep himself warm. Abhayambika popped in from nowhere, butted into his conversation asking him if he had covered his head because he was scared of the Pallavis and Taalams Balamurali sir was singing. Mama was obviously furious with such mockery. He left for home and didn't attend the second half of the concert. She had no business doing these things,' recollected Sekar about one such incident.

Balamuralikrishna got an account of such incidents much later. For example, in the above instance, Balamuralikrishna was under the impression that Semmangudi left because he didn't like his concert. It was only much later that he got to know what had happened in the interval. According to Sekar, he was outraged and reprimanded her, asking her to seek pardon from the senior vidwan.

'Even during the Raga controversy, Balamurali sir wanted to end it long back. It was Abhayam who insisted that he should not give up and kept pulling him to continue the controversy. At some point when he realized it, he had enough,' added Sekar. However, Balamuralikrishna's public image suffered from such instances. By then, Balamuralikrishna had bought her an apartment on Bharathidasan Road. She would live there and sometimes, it would also be the venue of Balamuralikrishna's music class. A lot of students remember visiting this place.

'Things came to a halt on the issue of making the film titled *Vecha Kaalu Sariya*, which means 'is this a right step?'. The irony of it, it was obviously not the right step. The film was on schedule and almost (a) small percentage of it was under production and then the financial demands began to grow. She wanted Balamuralikrishna to fund the production of the movie further. She also supposedly mortgaged her house, the one he bought for her, and apparently took some big bank loans. He said he was happy to give music but not waste money in the production. Who was to bear the loss, if the film flops?' recollected Dr Pappu Venugopala Rao, who was a writer, scholar and a close friend cum student of Balamuralikrishna from the early years. This created a lot of unnecessary tension for Balamuralikrishna. He had sung in countless films and knew enough people in the industry. He was also intelligent enough to know his limitations and recognize where he was capable of contributing. Music was his only deal and nothing else. He certainly didn't have the kind of money she was seeking. Moreover, he had a large family and responsibility back home. He told her she could sell the Bharathidasan apartment and put that money into the film, if she wanted. A number of arguments began. Enough people had complained to him about her, but he had kept quiet all along. But the film controversy went overboard, with her trying to constantly trigger a spat in public. Several people recollected the kind of fights she would launch into at the drop of a hat.

At around the same time, the child prodigy Mandolin U. Shrinivas was making waves in the world of music. His parents had brought him to Balamuralikrishna's notice seeking blessings for the boy. This was a normal practice for the parents of young musicians. Abhayambika took a great liking to him, and asked the parents to give him to her in adoption. This shocked the parents. She also started pressurizing Balamuralikrishna to persuade the parents. If she didn't have her way, she would throw tantrums and create an embarrassing situation for everyone, including Balamuralikrishna, often in public view.

Finally, by the late 1980s, Balamuralikrishna decided to distance himself from her. He had secured her a job in Annamalai University's arts department. His student recalled the harm she was doing to his image. 'She would even go around using his name, suffixing it to hers later. But by then the public knew and she couldn't fool anyone easily,' said Purnachander. Not much was heard of her till she died. In her will, she had declared that her obituary, that appeared in *The Hindu*, be carried in the name of 'Abhayambika Balamuralikrishna', rekindling the long-lasting gossip about her. Balamuralikrishna became a bit more vigilant about the ways of the world.

* * *

In September 1979, Balamuralikrishna went on his debut concert tour to the USA. This was organized by V.V. Sundaram, who was also instrumental in founding the Tyagaraja Aradhana in Cleveland. Over a period of time he came to be known as 'Cleveland Sundaram'. Balamuralikrishna's debut in the USA was a grand entry. He performed at the Carnegie Hall in New York, accompanied by Annavarapu Ramaswamy on the violin and Thanjavur Upendran on the Mridangam. 'I clearly remember that concert like it happened yesterday. I had flown in from Cleveland with an expensive tape recorder. I was more concerned about the recorder than anything else,' said Sundaram in an interview with me. 'We were only getting to know each other then. He was not like any of the musicians I had interacted with earlier. Venakataraman who is now in Toronto was responsible for all the logistics. Later we did a coast-to-coast concert tour of about twenty-six or twenty-seven concerts. He was brilliant in all of them. The audiences were eating out of his hands. I have never come across another musician with a more remarkable imagination,' Sundaram recollected. The US tour was a huge success, and he was invited on many more tours in the decades to come.

Back in India, despite all the controversies, Balamuralikrishna kept a calm face and continued with work. In November 1979, Balamuralikrishna's daughter Lakshmi and son-in-law Devarakonda Ramachandra Rao had a son. He named the child Deepak Himan. Once again a little bit of his own creativity in naming the child. His reasoning was that if 'Deepak' stood for fire, 'Himan' balanced out the heat with the coolness of snow.

One of the things that he never forgot was to encourage talented youngsters. Several of them are big names today in the world of Carnatic music. Bombay Jayashri recollected her first meeting with him back in the mid-1970s when he went to perform at the Rasika Priya Sabha in a concert organized by her uncle Sethuraman. 'I clearly remember that concert. He sang his famous "Nagumomu" and after that, made an announcement that he would sing a composition in Ragam Rasikapriya to mark that occasion specially and in honour of my uncle. I was a little girl completely in awe of him. By then, we had both the books that he published and would go through them meticulously, trying to learn new compositions. We were presented before him to seek blessings. He was extremely gracious and blessed us after enquiring about where we were learning music and encouraged us. We were on such a high after that. We went back home and continued to devour his books,' recollected Jayashri.

Chitraveena N. Ravikiran was hailed as a child prodigy at a very early age. He began performing in Sabhas even before he was ten. 'I was twelve maybe. I was performing at the Music Academy in the season. Balamuralikrishna was sitting in the front. In between my concert, he got up and left. For a second, I thought he didn't like the concert or worse, I might have made some mistake while performing. As I continued my concert, about ten minutes later, I saw him walking back into the Academy. After the concert, he met me and my father and gifted me a silver medal. saying, "I got this medal when I was ten years old", and he presented it to me. This was the nature of his generosity and large heartedness,' recollected Ravikiran.

In addition to that Balamuralikrishna also asked Ravikiran to accompany him for one of his cassette recordings. Years later, they even performed a Jugalbandi together. One of the other artistes who received immense encouragement was Veena E. Gayathri. Gayathri was yet another child prodigy who began performing before adolescence. For a stalwart of his stature, he didn't have to go beyond a few encouraging words for the child. But he not only encouraged her greatly, he went ahead and recorded a video with him on the viola and Gayathri performing on the veena. Balamuralikrishna never hesitated to appreciate talent or beauty whenever he spotted something worthy. This characteristic stayed on well into his old age. He silently encouraged and nurtured children a fourth his age with equal enthusiasm as they came to him.

7

'M for Murali, M for Music, M for Money'

'M for Murali, M for music, M for money,' Balamuralikrishna says nonchalantly in a documentary produced in the 1980s, while sitting across a desk from ghazal singer Penaz Masani who was anchoring the show. 'And M for Masani,' he adds before they shake hands and burst out laughing. In the same documentary, produced by the Hindustani Bansuri Vidwan Pt Hariprasad Chaurasiya's Vrindavan Gurukul, one can see different shades of Balamuralikrishna. In fact, just before the quote above, he says, 'Since I have retired from active performances, I decided I should do something for other musicians.' The story behind that is a long one.

The early 1980s saw a lot of adulation and criticism coming his way. He was now a 'Sangita Kalanidhi', the prestigious title bestowed upon him by the Music Academy, Madras. Even that came wading through the waters of controversy stirred by his contemporary veena artiste S. Balachander. After that, something within him seems to have snapped.

But the 1980s saw a lot more of Balamuralikrishna on screen than before. He voluntarily took part in a lot of television programmes, interviews, documentaries and even a cameo in a movie after a long gap. It was also a decade that saw a fairly political side to him, unknown earlier.

The famous Mysore Dasara festival saw a grand concert by Balamuralikrishna on 12 October 1980. He was accompanied by H.K. Narasimha Murthy on the violin, Thanjavur Upendran on the mridangam, Bangalore Venkataram on the ghatam and Sosale Sheshagiri Das on the khanjira. The Durbar hall of the Mysore palace was crammed with Rasikas. He opened his concert with Tyagaraja's 'Sri Ganapathini' in Saurashtram and followed it up with Dikshithar's 'Sri Saraswati Namostute'. The brilliance of Balamuralikrishna's concert planning was seen in this. He presented his own composition 'Nee Saati Neeve Ranga' in Ragam Chandrika, as a prayer to lord Ranganatha enshrined in the temple at Srirangapattinam near Mysore. Then came his signature 'Nagumomu' followed by a grand Ragam-Taanam-Pallavi in Sunadavinodini, as a tribute to the creator of the Ragam, the great Mysore Vasudevachar. Then came a Dasarapada in Abhogi followed by the famous 'Oru Naal Podhuma', just to let the Rasikas enjoy the context of him performing in the 'Durbar' hall. Excellent place and timing to play around musically. The audience and the royal family of Mysore couldn't have gotten a better musical gift for Navaratri. He was one of the earliest masters of good concert planning. To sing music suitable for any occasion became his forte.

In addition to his usual performances, he had also set up a small institute to propagate music education. Murali Ravali Art Centre was an organization which he began very ambitiously in the 1970s. Through this organization, he wanted to do a lot in the field of music: from academic research to music concerts, from honouring artistes to producing high-quality content in the field of music and so forth. In 1980, the Sri Raja Lakshmi Foundation decided to honour Balamuralikrishna with its annual award. The foundation was formed in 1979 and the first award was given to the famous Telugu literary figure Srirangam Srinivasa Rao (1910–83) who wrote under the pen name 'Sri Sri'. Balamuralikrishna was the second awardee. The invitation of the award ceremony listed the merits of his Murali Ravali Art Centre, saying 'The only organization which has no barrier irrespective of age, caste and creed, lights the candle of eminence is Murali Ravali honour services to humanity, talents in any field of art and literature is: Murali Ravali transmits, to the deserved, music and dance, nobly and generously is: Murali Ravali first to produce the light and sound of honouring fifty great personalities in various walks of life within a span of eight years is: Murali Ravali ever ready to render its yeoman services to the society of art and literature is: Murali Ravali Art Centre.' At a grand function organized by Sri P.V. Ramanaiah Raja, the award was given by Rukmini Devi Arundale, the founder president of Kalakshetra in Madras, on 19 November.

On 14 February 1981, the chancellor, vice-chancellor and the members of the senate of the Sri Venkateswara University honoured Balamuralikrishna with another doctorate. This was his third doctorate. Along with him was his old neighbour and friend, the famous poet Dasarathi Krishnamacharyulu, who received the same honour on the occasion. That year, his oldest son Abhiram and daughter-in-law Krishnaveni gave birth to their first son. Balamuralikrishna named him Sadagati.

The same year, the *Times of India* dated 22 December, announced in its headline, 'Balamurali appointed AP state musician.' This also led to him becoming the head of the Andhra Pradesh Sangeeta Nataka Akademi. This was the time Doordarshan made several recordings of his, and he gave numerous interviews. One of his favourite topics was 'voice culture'. A part of that series continues to be viewed regularly on YouTube even today. In the video, he explains his idea of producing a voice and demonstrates a wide range of techniques in bringing about a great voice. One of the fascinating things about this video, and the entire series, is how effortlessly he manages to traverse three octaves. It shows his incredible command and control over breath and demonstrates what he thinks are issues bothering the music world. The only catch is that few other musicians had the grand dexterity and voice that he had. There were several musicians who used nasal voices, several others who distorted Sahityam and many others who compromised on their music, sometimes consciously and other times out of ignorance. Till today this series continues to be a greatly educational one.

In September 1982, Balamuralikrishna's second son Sudhakar and daughter-in-law Pushpa gave birth to a daughter. Balamuralikrishna named her 'Lavangi', after a Ragam that he had created. A busy concert life continued with rave reviews. Sulochana Rajendran, in her review in the *Free Press Journal* dated 19 October 1982, wrote, 'Among the neo-classicists who have blazed a new trail, enlarging the vistas of improvisatory Carnatic music, Mangalampalli Balamuralikrishna is a name to reckon with. He has given a turn and twist to concert craft by voice power and musical vision. Even when past fifty, Balamurali's voice retains its resonance and resources, power and pliance. Nevertheless, playing with pyro-techniques in music has been his second nature.'

In November 1982, the Bangalore Gayana Samaja was conducting its annual festival. It was presided over by the veena maestro Doraiswamy Iyengar. Balamuralikrishna was invited to give a lecture-demonstration. On 6 November, the discussion was about Ragams and scales. 'Please give me the Aarohana and Avarohana of any scale and specify the name of the Melakarta Raga,' said Balamuralikrishna. For a while, there was silence in the hall and then Veena Doraiswamy Iyengar got up and said, 'The Aarohana is "S G3 P M1 D2 S" and the Avarohana is "S N2 D2 P M1 G3 R2 S" and this is a Janya Raga of the twenty-eighth Melakarta Ragam Harikhamboji.' Balamuralikrishna looked at the audience, hummed around for a while and came up with a Sahityam, 'Manaku Vochenu Swatanthramu'. He then created a new Taalam, calling it 'Tri-Mukhi', and sang this new composition. Dedicating it to Doraiswamy Iyengar, he said the new Ragam would be called Ragam 'Dorai'. He was accompanied by M. Chandrasekharan on the violin and Thanjavur Upendran on the mridangam. Before the concert, he announced cheekily, 'This scale is given by Dr Doraiswamy Iyengar. Maybe it might be found in some books. But that does not mean that he has not created the scale. He thought over something and created this scale. There are five lakh informed ragas, excluding the Baashanga ragas, Nishadanta and Dhaivatanta. So you can find out how many more ragas are there and how many we know. Even if we know, how many are we hearing? Simply because you find something in a book, you cannot say that somebody has not created. Just I wanted to demonstrate how it is possible to create something on the spot. I wrote the Sahityam in Telugu, which Dr Lakshmi Naryana Bhatta immediately translated into Kannada.' He goes on to sing the Aarohana and Avarohana and then dedicates it to Doraiswamy Iyengar. 'Gentlemen and ladies, you have all witnessed the creation, I have not bought any book nor have I consulted any as you saw,' he added before going ahead and singing this new creation.

On 6 December 1982, Balamuralikrishna's father Pattabhiramayya breathed his last. Having lived a long and illustrious life with excellent contribution to the world of music by training some great disciples, having seen his son being celebrated as a superstar, having spent time with his grandchildren and great grandchildren, Pattabhiramayya made his final exit. He may have gone up to heaven and told stories of his son's successful musical conquests to Sooryakantamma whose wish was to see Balamuralikrishna blossom into a great musician. With the demise of his father, Balamuralikrishna was now the patriarch of the large household.

In a concert review of a performance at the Bhatiawadi auditorium, under the aegis of Rasika Ranjani Sabha of Ghatkopar in Bombay (now Mumbai), N. Hariharan wrote in the *Times of India* on 4 April 1983, 'While the earlier half was accented on classical idiom, the post-interval fair was largely lyrical fair with a novelty of appeal.' This was another format Balamuralikrishna was presenting in a few of his concerts. The first half would be full of pure classical, traditional pieces, and after the interval, he would sing Bhajans, Ashtapadis, Tarangams, Tattavalus and sometimes even take audience requests.

Until then, Balamuralikrishna had done a number of recordings, mostly for record labels like HMV and others. In 1981, Bangalore-based cassette company Sangeetha Records approached him. Sangeetha was the first licenced company to manufacture pre-recorded audio cassettes in south India. They explored a market that was neglected by everyone else: spiritual and devotional music. The first year they released 200 titles and were instantly successful in the market. They recorded Balamuralikrishna's Dasara Padagalu in Kannada. They assumed this would be like any of their other recordings, but the success of that cassette was overwhelming. 'We first recorded two albums with him at Tarangini studios at Saligramam in Madras and they were a hit,' recollected H.M. Mahesh, the founder of the record label. This association was to create a new history in the modern culture of recorded music. Over time, Balamuralikrishna recorded over 1,200 songs for them. Looking at their catalogue, one can see he released about 105 cassettes of vocal music, two instrumental, thirty-five Telugu albums, twenty-eight Kannada devotional albums, seventeen Sanskrit albums, six Tamil albums, two Malayalam albums, ten albums of Dasara

Padagalu, one dance solo album and one Tamil film (Thodi Ragam) album. In addition to that were 160 solo albums and thirty albums with co-singers. A large repertoire of his music was recorded by Sangeetha. This included Bhadrachala Ramadasu Kritis, Sadasiva Brahmendra Kritis, Narayana Theertha Tarangams, Ragaanga Ravali—his own compositions in the seventy-two Melakarta Ragams, eighteen chapters of the Bhagavad Gita, self-composed Thillanas, Telugu patriotic songs, Telugu Tattavalus, songs of saints like Mantralayam Raghavendra Swami, Kaivaram Amara Nareyana, Kannada Bhava Geethegalu, instrumental music with him playing the viola and khanjira, and so on. This achieved for him a mention in the Limca Book of Records for the highest recordings done by a single artiste for a music company. 'One very special quality of all the recordings of Dr Balamuralikrishna is that every recording was done in a single take, meaning there were no repeat takes, or any editing required,' said Mahesh.

One of the other long-term associations that Sangeetha Records rekindled was with the multifaceted Hari Achutarama Sastry. He was the son of the well-known Vaggeyakara Hari Nagabhushanam (1884–1959) whose association with Balamuralikrishna went back to his childhood days in Vijayawada. He was a violinist, a singer and a prolific composer. He learnt music from the likes of Konerirajapuram Vaidyanatha Iyer and violin from Thirukodikaval Krishna Iyer and Malaikottai Govindaswamy Pillai. He was also a qualified lawyer. Among his compositions were the entire Ramayana rewritten into seven parts containing 132 slokas, a Harikatha in three parts on Saint Tyagaraja, Harikatha in seven parts on Jagadguru Adi Shankaracharya and other Harikathas. He would himself give Harikatha recitals on Tyagaraja Aradhana day. He had mastery over both Telugu and Sanskrit. He also wrote a number of Taana-Varnams and Kirtanams under the mudra of Tyaga. He was adorned with the title of 'Vaggeyakara Ratna'. Introducing him in a CD released much later, Balamuralikrishna recollected attending his concerts. He also recollected that it was Hari Nagabhushanam who had given the violin the name 'Vayuleenam', meaning something that has merged with air, giving it a different perspective and understanding. He says how in the earlier days there were no solo violin concerts and that a violinist had to sing along and play the instrument so that the violin would embellish the singing. He goes ahead to add, '*Sangeethamu, Sahityamu Lenide, Paripoornatha Chandhadhu* (music does not gain completeness without the backing of Sahityam).'

His son Hari Achutarama Sastry was an equally versatile musician and composer. As a violinist, he had accompanied Balamuralikrishna in hundreds of concerts in the 1960s and 1970s. Along with being a performer, he was also a music director and composer of great merit. Further, he was a Sanskrit scholar, an authority on a number of Upanishads, scriptures and pooja rituals. He set to tune a number of devotional songs of various poets. He also recorded a large amount of pooja rituals and made them accessible to the world at large, at a time when it was getting increasingly difficult to find priests who would perform these rituals authentically. Balamuralikrishna and he worked together on some of the most popular cassettes in the devotional music category for Sangeetha Records. One of the more popular cassettes was the *Bhadradri Seetaramula Ekanta Seva*, composed by Tumu Narasimhadasu. This was set to tune by Hari Achutarama Sastry and sung by Balamuralikrishna and P. Susheela. They also worked on the album *Bhadradri Seetaramula Prabhata Seva* and a number of devotional songs.

'He was feeling very homely in our studio, and he has mentioned in many of his public speeches that this music company was like his home. We remain indebted to him forever,' added Mahesh.

For those who were fed on a diet of his music from the Bhakti Ranjani era, this was a blessing. There was something for everyone in the Sangeetha cassettes that Balamuralikrishna recorded. For classical musicians and music lovers, in addition to recording the compositions of the Trinity and other Vaggeyakaras, he also recorded Ragam-based cassettes where the many shades of a single Ragam would be explored through a number of compositions. This was a first in the history of recording Carnatic music! For those interested in devotional music, there were songs of Bhadrachala Ramadasu, Annamacharya, Raghavendra Swamy and more.

In 1986, another significant project began: a thirteen-episode television series titled *Swara Raga Sudha*, directed by Murali Nallappa. This was a first of its kind where a Carnatic artiste would explain thirteen different compositions in different Ragams—the series would be shot at thirteen different locations. Balamuralikrishna was chosen for this. He normally never cared much for the press or their opinions and writings about him, though he was constantly in the news since his childhood. In October 1986, the *Economic Times* carried a four-part profile of Balamuralikrishna by a columnist who wrote under the pen name 'Naarada'. The column was in the light of Balamuralikrishna's regular statements that he would be retiring soon. That column was titled 'Balamurali Krishna—An enigma'. No other Carnatic classical musician had received this kind of attention in the national press. This, of course, set the ball rolling for a lot of other musicians to flaunt their jealousy, mostly born of insecurity.

Scoring Art over Politics with N.T. Rama Rao

The general election in Andhra saw the Telugu superstar Nandamuri Taraka Rama Rao (1923–1996), famous as NTR, win with an overwhelming majority. He overthrew the Congress government with his Telugu Desam Party that promoted the idea of 'Telugu pride'. According to Mohan, 'NTR was a superstar no doubt, but he had zero political experience and was surrounded by the wrong advisers. He was as impulsive as artistes can get!' True to this, one of NTR's advisers was Narla Venkateshwar Rao (1908–85). Popular as 'Narla', he was an accomplished writer, poet, a senior journalist writing for numerous newspapers and a fairly controversial literary figure. He was appointed as cultural adviser to the newly formed government. 'It was on the random advice of Narla that NTR acted very impulsively,' said veteran journalist Puttur Venkateshwar Rao to me.

What happened was that NTR decided to dissolve the Andhra Pradesh State Sangeet Natak Akademi. He wanted to form a unified body that included all the performing and visual arts, literature and allied arts under one large umbrella. He later established the Telugu University in 1985.

But this sudden dissolution of the Akademi upset everyone connected with the art field. 'What is shocking is almost nobody protested. One would assume NTR being an artiste himself would be more sympathetic and understanding of the needs of his community. Instead, he took a vague coffee-table conversation so seriously to take this step. The only person who came out and made any noise was Dr Balamuralikrishna,' Rao recollected.

Balamuralikrishna, then the head of the Akademi, was shocked with this ad-hoc decision. An article in the *Free Press Journal* dated 20 May 1983 read:

> President of the Andhra Sangeeta Akademy, M. Balamuralikrishna, renowned composer and musician, and 17 others have reportedly resigned from the Akademy in protest against the "unsympathetic and crude" attitude of the state government towards fine arts, music and musicians. The government had recently abolished the honorary posts of "Asthana Vidwans" without consulting those appointed by the erstwhile Congress-I government. With the exit of Balamuralikrishna, according to many cultural organisations, the stature of both the Akademy and the state would diminish to a large extent. In their joint letter of resignation, the members have expressed indications at the government's move to bring about changes in the Akademy, according to authoritative sources here. Secretary of the Akademy M. Anandham, is also likely to resign in a couple of days.

This was going to be a long-run tussle between an artiste and a state. 'When N.T. Rama Rao became the chief minister, he wanted to save money for the state treasury. There were Asthana Vidwans of the state like M.S. Subbulakshmi, Dwaram Venakataswamy Naidu, Balamuralikrishna and others who were paid an honorarium of Rs 5000 per month. NTR removed that Asthana Vidwan through a gazette notification. Balamuralikrishna gave a press statement saying, "We are not living on this 5000. The chief minister should have asked us to forgo the honorarium. Instead he has unilaterally dismissed all appointments. Being an artiste he doesn't know how to behave with his own artiste community." Balamuralikrishna got a lot of support from many people, but no one protested like this in public,' recollected Purnachander. Balamuralikrishna also made an announcement that he would no longer sing in Andhra Pradesh. 'To add to their irritation, he began draping his dhoti in the Tamil style, like a Veshti. Until then he would mostly be seen wearing the traditional Telugu drape of Pancha-Kacham. This angered the Telugus even more,' added Purnachander, bursting into laughter.

The press of the day had a heyday. Editorials across papers took sides. Many of them were in support of Balamuralikrishna's stance, and others wrote against him. 'An editorial appeared in *Andhra Prabha*, titled "Aththa Meeda Kopam Dutta Meeda" meaning misplacing one's anger. This editorial mentioned that NTR shut the Academy. For that, why should Balamuralikrishna punish the audiences and music lovers of the entire state? Haven't we all been regularly attending his concerts and loving his music and so on? I got a call from him showing me this editorial. To this I wrote a retort saying when an auto driver is attacked, the entire auto union joins hands to protest. When a factory worker is attacked, the entire union comes together. Here the biggest face of Carnatic music in Andhra is being humiliated and not one person stood for him. People like Balamurali are not born every day. This editorial got published,' recollected scholar and musicologist Dr Pappu Venugopala Rao. Dr Rao migrated to Madras in 1980 and was working at the American Institute of Indian Studies. His friendship with and admiration of Balamuralikrishna was an old one. 'I joined office in 1980, and on the first evening, I came to Guru Garu's house. Our first meeting was as if we had known each other for many Janmas (lives),' recollected Dr Rao.

The spate of newspaper editorials on the subject continued unabated. 'One day, the editor in chief, Sri Nanduri Rammohan Rao Garu called me and said "let us put an end to this, instead of dragging it". Everybody was getting tired of this and there seemed to be no immediate solution in sight,' added Dr Rao. Balamuralikrishna was firm in his stance. He didn't perform in Andhra Pradesh for the next decade. One can only imagine how pained he must have felt at the way in which the state and establishment treated artistes. In many public functions even when invited to speak he would pass scathing remarks like, '*Telugu Vallaki Pourusham Ekkuva, Pani Thakkuva* (Telugus have all attitude but no ambition)'. In another public function he announced, 'Today Tyagaraaja is alive because the Tamils remember him. They sing his songs every day, they pray to him religiously and revere him to no end. The Telugus have long forgotten him. They are only obsessed with cinema and politics.' Once again the press of the day ran riot with long columns analysing his statements. In retrospect, there is nothing wrong with his statements, even though they might have been made in the mood of the moment.

In an article written as an open letter titled 'AP and Telangana, where are your artistes?!', journalist Vikram Venkateswaran writes in the Quint in 2018, 'For decades now, there has been a mass exodus of artistes of different fields from your states. I don't think you understand the gravity of the situation which is quite surprising, considering your innate love for your language and art forms.' He goes on to list the number of Telugu artistes who opted to live outside of Andhra Pradesh, from classical musicians like Balamuralikrishna to dance gurus like Vempati Chinna Satyam, poets and writers like Arudra and Devulapalli Krishnasastri, film personalities like director, illustrator and cartoonist Bapu (Sattiraju Lakshminarayana), playback singers like Ghantasala, P. Susheela and S. Janaki, directors like K. Vishwanath, actors like Anjali Devi, Raja Sulochana, Gollapudi Maruthi Rao and others. The fact is that a large community of Telugu artistes chose to live wherever they found better patronage and respect for their art forms.

In 1989, the Congress came into power in Andhra Pradesh very briefly. The then chief minister Vijaya Bhasker Reddy invited Balamuralikrishna to perform, which he accepted. He was also made the pro-chancellor of Telugu University. However, within days, the Telugu Desam Party came back to power. Keeping his word, Balamuralikrishna resigned from the university position. He had said that he would never perform as long as N.T. Rama Rao ruled the state and he stuck to his words. This generated negative press for NTR, who was already amidst political chaos. It was around that time that his wife Lakshmi Parvathi and the state's special information commissioner, K.V. Ramanachari, managed to calm Balamuralikrishna down by apologizing on behalf of the state. Lakshmi Parvathi also spoke to N.T. Rama Rao, and soon things were looking better.

In the summer of 1995, a grand welcome and reception for Balamuralikrishna was organized personally by N.T. Rama Rao at the famous Ravindra Bharathi in Hyderabad. He not only apologized for his earlier erratic behaviour, but also conducted a 'Kanakabhishekam' (showering gold flowers on him) in honour of Balamuralikrishna. Also present at the function were Jnanpith awardee C. Narayana Reddy, veteran Telugu film actor Akkineni Nageshwara Rao, Lakshmi Parvathi, K.V. Ramanachari and other dignitaries. Ravindra Bharathi was spilling out of its seams. The music and art lovers of Hyderabad showed up in large numbers.

'All these years, politics completely controlled my life and I totally ignored art. I'm extremely embarrassed for my behaviour. Balamuralikrishna is an asset to the Telugu cultural scene. He is a treasure to this country and we as Telugus should be extremely proud of his music. I have heard him and have been moved within my heart,' said N.T. Rama Rao in his grand felicitation speech. NTR also announced the establishment of a Balamurali Peetham at Telugu University and reinstated Balamuralikrishna as pro-chancellor. After the ceremony, Balamuralikrishna enthralled the audience in Hyderabad with a huge musical feast. Among the selection of songs he chose to present was 'Salalita Raga Sudha Rasa Saaram', the famous track from *Nartanasala* which he had sung for NTR decades ago. The audience went berserk. The press had a field day extolling the virtues of the 'son of the soil' who had returned home. This was probably the last major cultural event NTR organized on his own. A few months later, he passed away. The music lovers of Andhra felt he had redeemed himself from the odd situation he created with a world famous vidwan like Balamuralikrishna. It was much later, after the Chandrababu Naidu government came to power, that Balamuralikrishna received due state honours. Naidu, an avid fan of his, gave him the rank of a cabinet minister and all the paraphernalia associated with it. Balamuralikrishna too enjoyed the attention he received, with escorts around him and the state finally giving him the love they were supposed to all along.

* * *

The big clash with N.T. Rama Rao was national news, but Balamuralikrishna behaved like it was just another part of his daily life. Concerts continued, reviews and interviews continued. He would sometimes choose to comment on the NTR fiasco, and other times couldn't be bothered. A review in the *Indian Express* dated 26 October 1983, by 'Vivadhi', of a concert held at the Shanmukhananda Sabha in Bombay, said, 'It was the Balamurali of old that we saw, in a perfectly disciplined recital in which all his best points were to fore.' He was accompanied by Annavarapu Ramaswamy on the violin and Palghat Raghu on the mridangam. 'The uncanny anticipation with which he played, coupled with a highly didactic Thani added lustre to an already great performance,' continues Vivadhi's review. He kept a busy concert schedule, but something seemed to have snapped from within. He began saying 'I'm retiring from music' very often. In an interview with Geetha Aravamudan, published in the *Sunday Observer* on 6 November 1983, he said, 'For the next two years, I will play for anyone who pays. After that I retire; I will sing only when I want. Not for money.' He was obviously frustrated with all the politics surrounding the world of music.

The G.V. Iyer Trilogy

In the early 1980s, Ganapathy Venkataramana Iyer (1917–2003), popularly known as G.V. Iyer, embarked on a new idea that was unlike anything in the history of Indian cinema: taking complicated philosophical ideas and turning them into visuals suitable for celluloid. Iyer's work was a pioneering effort. Till then, Iyer had made and acted in several movies, but this trilogy was his calling. The first of the three episodes of *Adi Shankaracharya* (1983) was India's first movie to be made in Sanskrit. Produced by the National Film Development Corporation of India (NFDC) with cinematography by Madhu Ambat, the film starred the Bengali actor Sarvadaman Banerjee in the lead role of Adi Shankaracharya. Director G.V. Iyer himself appeared in the role of Veda Vyasa. The music direction for this movie was given by Balamuralikrishna. One can hear his voice throughout the movie, be it chanting different slokas or the works of Adi Shankara or excerpts from various Upanishads. He also roped in several of his musician friends and students to give various soundtracks for the movie. These included P.B. Sreenivos, Rajkumar Bharati, Nookala Chinna Satyanarayana, Vedavathi Prabhakar, Purnachander Rao, and the famous Dhrupad maestros Zia Moinuddin Dagar and Zia Fariduddin Dagar, who performed the rudra veena in the movie. The film won several national awards, for best feature film, best screenplay, best cinematography and for best music.

In 1986, G.V. Iyer directed *Madhwacharya*, the second film in the trilogy, based on the life of the famous philosopher of the Dwaita tradition. Produced by Ananthalakshmi Films, the cinematographer was again Madhu Ambat, and the music composition and direction was by Balamuralikrishna. He was assisted by the Hindustani vocalist Vidushi Shyamala Bhave of Bangalore. Bhave and Balamuralikrishna got along very well. In fact, Bhave's institution Saraswati Sangeet Vidyalaya, near the Shivananda circle in Bangalore, became a regular *adda* for Balamuralikrishna where he would meet a number of artistes and friends. In addition to that, he and Bhave also performed together at several venues, including the famous Rama Seva Mandali at Fort High School. All the lyrics were based on the original works of the philosopher saint Madhwacharya. The film was screened at the eleventh IFFI panorama. It also won Balamuralikrishna the national award for best music director. The film became a rage in Karnataka among the large followers of the Madhwa Sampradhaya. Balamuralikrishna's music was heard in every nook and corner of the state. He would get repeated requests to sing these songs in his concerts.

In 1989, Iyer wrote and directed *Ramanujacharya*. Once again, the music direction was by Balamuralikrishna. The film credits open with Balamuralikrishna's voice reciting:

Punyāmbhoja Vikasāya Pāpadhvānta Kśayāyaca I
Srīmānāvirabhūdbhūmou Rāmānuja Divākarah II

Accompanying him, the orchestra had veena maestro K.S. Narayaswamy, P.B. Sreenivos, Rajkumar Bharati, G.S. Mani Ambili Kutty, M.G. Venkataraghavan, Kalyani Menon and others. Shyamala Bhave assisted him in this too. In the movie, Balamuralikrishna sings several songs, including the Pasuram for Thiruppanazhwar, and scores a whole range of classical Ragams in every other scene throughout the movie.

After this trilogy, Iyer also directed *Bhagavad Gita* in 1993. Starring Neena Gupta, it was written by the famous Sanskrit scholar and commentator Sri Bannanje Govindacharya (1936 -2020), based on the Bhagavad Gita. The music was given by Balamuralikrishna. 'I was pleasantly surprised to know that Balamuralikrishna Avaru had read the entire Sarvamoola Granthas of Sri Madhwa, though he himself didn't belong to our Sampradaya. He rattled off several complicated Slokas along with their Tatparyas with ease, all through sporting a cheeky smile on his face. We became very good friends after this,' recollected Govindacharya in an interview with me. The film went to win a national award for the best feature film.

Iyer brought about a new sense of aesthetics with his cinema, exploring content that was Indic through India's spiritual legacies. Alongside Iyer's movies, one got to listen to a wide range of music and musical ideas executed extremely well by Balamuralikrishna. In the several interviews that Iyer gave, he never failed to mention the genius of Balamuralikrishna as music director. There were stories about how he would read the script or lyrics just once and reproduce everything effortlessly from his memory in the recording studios.

* * *

But there were a lot of things bothering Balamuralikrishna about the music field, and he hadn't spoken much in public about these after the 'Raga controversy'.

In January 1984, Balamuralikrishna gave an interview to the assistant editor V.S. Sundararajan and correspondent V.S. Kumar of *Sruti* magazine. This was one of the more interesting interviews he gave, expressing a lot of his thoughts openly to the press for the first time. A few excerpts:

'Q: What is the importance of preserving tradition in Carnatic music and to what extent should breaking tradition be allowed?

A: What do you mean by tradition?

Tradition is a method of singing established by the musicians and musicologists. It is exemplified in the concert Paddhati, for instance . . .

Is it? Platform singing—concert-giving—you call that tradition? Tyagarajaswami has said that those who sing for others are unpardonable sinners. *Paluku bojina sabhalu ani patitamana vana kosage khalulu.* He never sang for others, he never sang someone else's songs too. The practice of singing on the platform is of recent origin, maybe the last seventy-five years. So how can that be tradition? If anything, it's most untraditional. Indeed, we are all sinners, we who sing for others.

Tradition is something fundamental—it's like the foundation for a building, or a construction plan. Let's say you built a house thirty years ago, and now you have it repainted, change the windows and doors, add two storeys. You don't alter the foundation, of course—that can never change. But you don't stop at the foundation, you have to build further, if you want to live in the house. That should be the outlook for any fine art too—especially music. You have to keep improvising, embellishing, developing the music.

Change is an integral part of life and the musician is no exception—he should keep with the times. I don't say this. The Sastras say that change is inevitable: *mrugaihi khagaihi nagaha sailaha siddha devaha maharishyaha kalam samana vartante yadha vahava yuge yuge.* Those who harp on 'tradition' (and tradition the way they understand it) should either go along with the traditional musicians to heaven or understand what tradition really is.

By making music so broad-based, aren't you inviting trouble in the form of musicians performing any way they like and making a mockery of the great art?

Don't allow such people to perform then. Don't listen to them, that's all. They'll automatically disappear. But for God's sake don't throttle innovations—not all innovations are gimmicks, you know.

How would you define tradition?

Tradition to me is merely the grammar of music—the seven swaras and the laya systems. I don't want to impose any further limits and constraints on interpreting music (in the name of tradition). Our music is the music of the world. Our foundation, our system is the greatest and the best. We have allowed it to degenerate, to become stilted because of our narrow outlook, our severely inhibiting views. That is why enough people aren't listening to our music, that is why our music is losing its appeal. On the other hand, other countries and other people have taken some part of our music and expanded it into a different type of music. They consider it now to be 'their' music, and they've made it popular. Only the way of singing, the accent and the emphasis are different. They have become great and people flock to listen to them—but it is only a spark of our music.

After all, what is Western music, Arabian music, Jazz music? It's all our music only. I can show you the sangatis of any music in our old Tyagaraja and Dikshitar compositions.

But does that mean that you can add Western tunes in your singing?

Where is the question of adding? It is there in our music. Just highlighting it here and there neither makes you great nor is it bad music. I'm criticized just for adding a sangati in Hindustani style in my exposition of a raga. That criticism is totally unwarranted—what I'm showing is only a different facet of our own music, a different colour.

With such unbounded powers to improvise, would you still call it classical?

There goes another word that has been disastrously misdefined. What do you mean by 'classical'? How will you define classical music? Whatever stands the test of time, whatever lives, is classical. Anything that gets out or becomes a casualty of time is light, is trivia. Even if a film song has retained its freshness, its appeal, after three decades, I would call it classical. So Carnatic music can remain classical music only if it continues to pull audiences, to make successive generations of people come and listen. To do that you must inject Carnatic music into the present generation, you must win them over. This is a fairly difficult proposition with today's listeners, you know. The listening public today is a motley crowd—some who come only to relax, some who are interested in the technicalities, some who come only to compare, and a few who are there to pray, to contemplate the Divine. If you want your music to be classical, you must carry all these listeners with you.

And you do that by making your concert a mixture of compositions of all kinds?

What is wrong? I recently composed a song in Khamboji which portrays the different natures of the people of our four southern states. It has become so popular that I have been asked to translate it into the other southern languages too. It has caught the fancy of the younger set, the students, those who listen only to pop and jazz—I have injected Khamboji raga into them through this medium. Isn't that what will make Carnatic music stay? All I'm asking you to do is, give a song that touches the heart, that touches the mind, that makes the listeners ask for it again. By this you will improve their minds, make classical music acceptable.

Times have changed, you see. And values have changed rapidly with the times. You tell the youngster today that it is sinful to have more wives than one, you sing to him praises of the God who has a thousand wives. This contradiction is unacceptable to him. Something's wrong somewhere, he tells you.

Again, you din into him that sex is bad, is sinful—but want him to extol sex among the Gods as divine. These wrong notions make them lose faith in God, in elders, in good systems. Instead, you tell them that the Gods could cope with a thousand wives and so they had them. By all means you can do it too, if you are capable, if you can take the responsibility. He will find this logic much more agreeable.

Likewise he is not content with just one rasa in music. Why is cinema such a popular medium? Only because it depicts all the different rasas. Try infusing similar variety into our classical music, you'll find its popularity scaling dizzy heights. Such licence will admittedly result in some bad music but the listening public will soon throw that out and retain only the good music, classical music.

What role should the government play in the promotion of classical music?

Government should recognize and help the promotion of the art and artistes. Recognition is a must—without a postage stamp, for instance, how can your letter reach? There is a great deal that (the) government can do, and only the government, to foster classical music. You may have money, you may be willing to spend it for music, you may also have the ideas for the development of the fine art. But over and above all these, you require the authority, the power, to implement your ideas and do what you want. And for that kind of authority, you need (the) government behind you.

Does music get this kind of backing today from our present governments? What has been your own experience?

Music today gets none of the support that it so badly needs. The reason is very simple: no government can do anything without polluting it politically. Politics is a predominant feature in all governmental decisions, especially when it comes to subjects like the fine arts. Any government today believes only in undoing all that a previous government has done. In Andhra Pradesh, for instance, state musicians were appointed and academies of music established by the previous regime. And all these have been removed by the present government for no better reason than mere politics.

But weren't budgetary constraints the reason for these measures?

I agree that budget constraint plays a crucial role in an economy like ours. But with all the cutting and pruning, you do set aside a certain amount every year for the promotion of music. All I ask is: Can't that money be spent more usefully, more effectively, without bringing in political colours? For instance, you honour me as the Asthana Vidwan, the state musician.

You give me an honorarium. But is that enough? I want you to listen to my ideas, take my advice and implement it. Otherwise the money you have spent appointing and paying me as Asthana Vidwan is a waste.

Let me illustrate my point. During my tenure as president of the Andhra Pradesh Sangeet Akademi, I had originated the proposal for a research-oriented University of Music. This university was not intended for conferring degrees, diplomas and certificates (that make no sense to me anyway) but for carrying out research. So much research can be done in music, has to be done in fact if classical music is to stay alive. My plan was accepted and I was asked to be the vice-chancellor of the university at least for the first two years. But then the government changed and everything has been washed out.

What were your specific plans in establishing such a university and running it?

My commitment in the field of classical music is to four objectives which I consider to be of paramount importance. One, a good singer shouldn't complain that he has been denied a platform; two, a retired, old musician shouldn't die of penury; three, a youngster who is keen on learning music shouldn't be thwarted either by lack of finance or the absence of a guru; and four, a dedicated teacher shouldn't lack good students. We did quite a bit towards achieving these ends during the time the Sangeet Akademi functioned. During my tenure, eminent musicians were honoured, hundreds of music concerts were arranged at the regional and some even the national level. In every one of these concerts, we took pains to ensure that the gentry of the place attended and listened to the concert. I also ensured that the younger, lesser-known musicians were received and honoured in the same manner that the top-flight musicians were. The performing artistes were suitably remunerated too. Above all, our main job was to give opportunities to the musicians. We would select performers in each category and give them ten concerts per year over a stretch of two years all over Andhra. So a musician had as many as twenty chances to prove himself and if he couldn't do it in that period, even God couldn't help him. We even had plans to send them to other states . . .

Do you think you could have achieved these objectives as vice-chancellor of the University for Music, if there had been one?

No, I don't think it would have helped. As a vice-chancellor, I would probably have been eternally bogged down in administrative details and I would have had no time to think, to create. I would have been spending all my time getting sanctions and approvals. So I told the government I'd have to be positioned above the vice-chancellor, even the chancellor. I should be given access to every department in that university and carte blanche to do what I wanted in the pursuit of my goals. I should have the power even to remove the vice-chancellor if I felt he was hindering the progress of the university. I sincerely believe I needed that kind of authority to realise my cherished dream of the upliftment of our music.

As things stand today, what is being done by the governments to promote music and the other fine arts?

Nothing at all. The present educational system cannot produce even a single artiste of whom we can be proud. The teaching methods that are prevalent will only kill talent by crushing innovativeness and imagination. The good old gurukula system is of course the best; and if our music is to recapture its glory, a system on the lines of the old gurukula method is the only answer. And it can be done. I have all the answers, but I don't want to publicise them now. My advice shouldn't go to waste; I need that assurance. If my ideas are accepted, I should be given the authority to implement them. I would take the responsibility to produce results, to create first-rate musicians within five years. And any punishment can be meted out to me if I don't live up to my commitments. I say to the governments: don't ask me to give out my plans and allow you to distort them anyway you like. Try me, and you will not find me wanting.

* * *

One can sense the agitation in his mind and the vision he had for developing the future of classical music. Neither did that university happen nor did he manage to implement a lot of the ideas he discussed, thanks to an unfriendly system that rarely thinks of arts and artistes as a priority.

Despite all these hurdles, Balamuralikrishna was not one who let his angst harm his art and continued giving concerts. At the annual festival of the Fine Arts Society, Chembur, Bombay, Balamuralikrishna was accompanied by Palghat Raghu on the mridangam and Annavarapu Ramaswamy on the violin. 'Palghat Raghu was in rare form during this concert. His playing had so much "Ranjakam" this was particularly true of the Thani which was one of the most inspired ones that one has heard from him. Balamurali is a great artiste on his own, but when he is provided with first-rate accompanists and when he produces the right admixture of tradition and innovation, such concerts tend to scale truly dazzling heights.' wrote Vivadhi in his review in the *Indian Express* dated 3 February 1984.

The following year was momentous for him for two reasons. His son Abhiram and daughter-in-law Krishnaveni had a second son. Balamuralikrishna named him Tejas. And on 14 May 1985, the chief minister of Kerala K. Karunakaran issued a certificate of honour in appreciation of Balamuralikrishna's contribution to the growth and development of Malayalam cinema.

However, whoever he met that year, he kept telling them he was going to retire. One of his concerts in Bombay was announced to be the final one. 'Balamurali to Quit Professional Stage' screamed the headline of an article written by V. Sridhar in the *National Herald* dated 23 September 1985. 'The stormy petrel of Carnatic music, Balamuralikrishna, has thrown another bombshell. He is retiring from the public professional concert stage. His last Sabha performances in Bombay were on Sunday (Aegis: Shanmukhananda Fine Arts and Sangeetha Sabha) and on Monday at Dombivili. His farewell appearance in Madras will be on September 24th and at Trivandrum on the last day of this month.'

It seemed like Balamuralikrishna was on a farewell tour of sorts. Sridhar wrote:

'Disgusted and disillusioned at the current crass commercial trends, Balamurali looked a little bitter (though he denied this at the interview). He said he was quitting to uphold the dignity of music. He bemoaned the infighting among artistes and his own court battle with a revered vidwan, for which he said he was not responsible. According to him, there was lack of unity among musicians and a lot of back biting. He listed seven reasons for his drastic action of retirement:

1. The dignity of music had deteriorated. Music has become mainly commercial, communal and political with groupism.
2. Sabha secretaries and critics have become more important than artistes.
3. Musicians are more interested in talking than singing.
4. There is no unity, understanding and right thinking among Carnatic musicians.
5. Creative talents and innovations are criticized and forbidden.
6. Some institutions are encouraging the above points.
7. Young and promising artistes have come to the level of applying for chances and paying money to Sabhas to get these chances.

There were multiple reasons for this outrage. Several musicians and Sabha secretaries had started rumours that Balamuralikrishna's voice was not doing well, that he was incapable of singing a full concert and hence began giving an interval in the middle. Several others created a fuss that this interval was breaking tradition. Yet many others were unhappy with Balamuralikrishna singing his own compositions. Balamuralikrishna seemed to be running out of patience in dealing with these things.

'Balamurali Evolves a New Style' read the headline of an article in the *Statesman* dated 30 September 1985, by the famous music critic 'Subbudu'. He wrote,

It is difficult to imagine the Carnatic music scene without the ever controversial figure, Balamurali. He has now decided to spend his future in research and giving concerts for the benefit of deserving institutions. However his concert at Pilani on September 30 would be the last public 'Sabha' concert. Balamurali singing should not be judged by the normal accepted, so-called traditional pattern. He bid farewell to it long, long ago and in a judicious mixture of voice culture and new variations, of course within the framework of grammar, he has successfully evolved a new style which has attracted attention. In Alapanas, he has emphasised the beauty of the modes rather than the stereotyped methodical style that has been in vogue. Likewise, in Swaraprastharas he has masterminded a technique in which tricky pauses, operating contra octaves, exploring Mandrasthayee passages and the like which have been greatly admired by his Rasikas. So much so, his concerts have always drawn the largest clientele. It is unnecessary to detail all the Kritis he rendered on Friday evening and it would suffice if an attempt is made to evaluate his superb Mohanam, which he rendered in extenso. There is a proverb in Tamil which says, 'It is not necessary to dip one's hand in the boiling pot to find out if the rice has boiled; it would do if one particle is pinched with a finger.' With this mellifluous wide-ranging voice, Balamurali handled this Raga in majestic fashion, digging pearls embedded therein. Now lingering on a note, now traversing an octave or two, now operating on double or trouble shifts in alternate octaves and finally investing the Alapana with wide sweeps, he made the mode glow. It was difficult to believe that human voice could be capable of such manoeuvres. It was Mohanam par excellence. The Kriti of Tyagaraja, Baaga Teliya Ledu was sung with gusto. As could be expected the Swaraprastharas were inter-laced with quicksilver shifts and teasing pauses. M. Chandrasekharan on the violin rose admirably to the occasion and reproduced every phrase presented by the vocalist. If some of the faster manipulations of Balamurali were beyond the reach of Chandrasekharan, well it was not the fault of the violin.

It was around this time that a young Ragavan Manian encountered Balamuralikrishna. 'I was already learning music from Pallavi Narasimhachari. The Rama Bhakta Sabha in Selaiyur would conduct the Rama Navami festival every year and Guruji (Balamuralikrishna) would be a regular performer there. Narasimhachari would conduct the annual Tyagaraja Aradhana at the Selaiyur Sabha. Whenever he needed to showcase a student of his, the Sabha would let him. I had sung there in '83 first. That year my concert was followed by a concert of Madurai Somu. The next year in 1984, my concert was followed by a concert of Balamuralikrishna's. There is an old Sabha tradition where a senior artiste would come and garland the junior who sang before him and speak a few words of encouragement. So my Guru Narasimhachari came and told me that they would be the senior artiste who would come and put a Mala around you and so forth. My Appa was very excited,' recollects Ragavan Manian about his first meeting with Balamuralikrishna. His father T.K.S. Manian was a huge fan of Balamuralikrishna by then. He had migrated from Tirunelveli to Madras around the same time that Balamuralikrishna had moved to the city from Vijayawada. 'The entire Madras city was bitten by the Balamuralikrishna bug by 1965. Appa was a huge admirer of Balamuralikrishna. For close to a decade he would check the morning newspaper and see the cultural programmes and religiously attend every single concert that Balamuralikrishna gave. He would buy his ticket for a rupee or two and keep a track of all his concerts. Naturally I was fed on a diet of Balamuralikrishna's music from the day I was born,' said Ragavan.

However, at that particular function, nine-year-old Ragavan had no clue about who Balamuralikrishna was or his greatness. 'Guruji came 15 minutes earlier. He heard a bit of my concert, after that he put the Mala around me and blessed me and gave a brilliant concert. I was sitting very close to him on the stage and listening. I still remember what he sang. He began the concert with "Sriramam Sadaa Bhajeham", his own composition in Ragam Tanarupi. After that a beautiful "Aparama Bhakti" of Saint Tyagaraja and then he announced an intermission,' recollects Ragavan as though it had happened just the day before.

And it was in that intermission that Ragavan's life changed. 'During the intermission, he walked to somebody's house down the lane and was accepting Thamboolam. I must say my Guru Narasimhachari had a big role to play here. While this *Upacharam* (service) was going on, he sneaked me into the house somehow and presented me before him.

He said that I was his *Abhimani* (admirer) and requested him to bless me. Balamuralikrishnaji blessed and after the concert, my Appa had a brainwave. He suddenly asked Balamuralikrishnaji if he could teach me. "I'm going to retire next year. After I am 60, I will think about it, said Balamuralikrishnaji to my father,' adds Ragavan.

His father's persistence paid off, and Ragavan formally became a student in 1986. 'Looking back now, I can only say it was serendipity. We have no musical history in the family. Nor do we have any political connections. And suddenly, I landed at his feet. Here was a little kid performing and here was a genius who kept a rather busy life and he could have said "no". He could have refused or anything could have been possible,' adds Ragavan, talking about the large-heartedness of his 'Guruji'. Ragavan was his disciple for close to a decade from 1986–96. 'After 1992, I was less regular with my studies at IIT. It became a bit hard to juggle. But 1986–92 were my best years. My music was strengthened and reinforced because of those years with Guruji,' he adds. Ragavan's classmate from IIT, Balachandran was another student who joined Balamuralikrishna around the same time. More about him later.

In October, the Kerala government appointed Balamuralikrishna as Professor Emeritus in the three music colleges in the Kerala, Calicut and Gandhiji universities. This was announced by the state education minister, T.M. Jacob. The *India Today* magazine dated 31 October 1985 announced Balamuralikrishna's 'Stormy Exit'. The *Illustrated Weekly of India* dated 13 November 1985, carried an interview titled 'Swan song?'. Excerpts from the interview he gave to K.P. Sunil:

Why did you suddenly decide to quit singing?

It was not such a sudden decision. Way back in the sixties V.V.K. Sastry, if I remember right, (he) used to write under the pen name Murali, interviewed me and wrote an article in the Weekly, where I had stated that a musician should retire after he completes 55 years. I am 55 now. And I have retired. I kept to my word.

What does retirement mean? Will you quit singing altogether?

My retirement is from my job as a professional singer. All these years I have been living off this profession. Now I shall no longer sing for money. But I shall continue doing so for AIR and Doordarshan. I shall continue to record cassettes. You see, those are the media through which I can make known, or spread, my creations. I shall also continue to sing in films. In other words, the only difference between then and now is that I shall no longer be giving professional concerts. Some concerts for charity, maybe, but I shall not live off them.

There must have been some precipitating factors that forced you to take this step?

You see, it is only if old men like us retire, that talented youngsters will get a chance to come up and make their presence felt. This should not be the case. Any talent should be recognised and encouraged. But unfortunately, there is too much groupism, too much of politics to ensure such a state of affairs. There is no unity amongst musicians. The situation is such that a person can come up only politically.

Unless you know some Minister, you don't get an opportunity to perform at any function organised by the government. In the past 47 years since I began singing, I have never been included in a single government-sponsored cultural delegation. If that is the treatment received by a person of my standing, just imagine what it must be like for a newcomer.

Would you say that you have been deliberately victimised by the government?

No. Not victimised. But deliberately ignored. If I had made my rounds of the secretariat and Ministerial bungalows calling them 'Sar, Sar', I too would have been on such cultural delegation. I came up on my own, without any political sponsorship, and in the face of considerable opposition and jealousy from some of my fellow musicians.

How was that?

Well, a group of well-known musicians met in my absence on one occasion, and discussed some of my own creations. They passed some wrong and unhealthy resolutions which they thought that they could fool the public. But they failed, because they were not right.

Was that the controversy some time back involving veena virtuoso S. Balachander?

Yes, but Balachander was not the main man in the controversy. He was a mere tool used by others because he had the money and clout to discredit me. The main man behind it was a musician whose name I do not wish to mention now. What saddens me most is the loss of dignity.

What are your post-retirement plans?

I have been thinking about this for the last five years and have some nebulous ideas in mind. Maybe in another two months I could give you a more firm answer. Music is, I think, something more divine than a mere product for commerce. I feel guilty about selling my music and making a living off it. I now intend devoting my time and resources to cure them with music. I also want to do some research on vibration. Sometimes, when we sing, we perform very well even without our own knowledge. Sometimes, even if we strive hard for it, we don't get the perfection we desire. Why? What goes wrong? These are some of the subjects I would like to study.

There is another reason for my retirement. I do not wish to be equated with the other South Indian classical musicians. I would like to be different from them—in my views, my style of singing, my research. In every one of my concerts you will find something new. I render even the most well-known compositions differently. I never practise at home. No one has even heard me hum there. I just go and sit on the stage and sing whatever comes to mind. I innovate on the spot. I improvise, improve. I don't want to be remembered by future generations as just one among several musicians. I am a creator, a composer. In future I should be listed amongst great composers like Thiagaraja, Dikshitar, Swati Tirunal and Purandara Dasa, and not with some Narasimhan, M.L. Vasantha Kumari or M.S. Subbulakshmi. So, unless I stop appearing along with them, I may not achieve my ambition.

I think it was this ambition of yours that ran into heavy weather in the hands of the die-hards of the Madras Music Academy . . .

Partly, yes. You see, they were jealous of me. They may all be authorities on the existing ragas and compositions. But their vision is limited to those. They do not see beyond the limitations of conventional classical tradition. But I create new ragas. It was this that they discussed, and passed resolutions about. I have also created a new taal system. I am the only person in India to receive the President's Award both for classical and film music. These people were jealous of my achievements. They wanted to discredit me. They claimed that only the Lord Brahma was the Creator and that no one else can create new ragas or taals. They claimed that one or two of the names I had given my own creations were already there in ancient books of music. What you find in books are called scales. They are merely skeletons. They are not ragas. Thiagaraja composed songs in many ragas based on these scales. We know the raga only because of his compositions. This fact is accepted by musicologists.

One of my discreditors questioned me on one occasion. He said 'Only God can create. How can a mere human being create anything?' I asked him how many children he had. 'Four,' he said. I told him, 'How can you call them your children? You cannot create them. Only God can. Yet you call them your creation.' I then went on to tell him:

"God created man and he vested in him the power of further creation. Everything you see around you, your car, your air conditioner, everything is man's creation. In the very same way I created my own ragas and take credit for that. What is wrong with that?" He kept quiet. I came out of the controversy unscathed. They thought they would give me adverse publicity, but what happened was that they ended up giving me free publicity.

A controversy that gripped music circles about the same time was one concerning Swati Tirunal's compositions. It was alleged that the works have been wrongly attributed to him and that they are actually the works of Thiagaraja. What was your contribution to that controversy?

It was a totally unnecessary controversy. I did not partake in it because I felt that it was unnecessary. You see, some individuals claimed that Swati Tirunal was not a composer at all and that he was no poet either. And that because of his influence and position as a rajah, he got someone else to compose in his name. That there was no proof that the compositions attributed to him were indeed his. Now, let me ask you this. Is there any proof that Thiagaraja wrote or composed any of the songs attributed to him? Is there any proof that Valmiki wrote the Ramayana? Then why isolate Swati Tirunal alone and lampoon him? The controversy was set in motion by some vested interests who badly wanted some publicity to prop up their sagging images as authorities of music. I don't approve of such doings. And that too of the works of a person long dead and gone. This sort of discredition behind the back just isn't the done thing. I don't go with it. And in any case what purpose does it all serve? Whether Swati Tirunal wrote poems or not, they are there. They are good. People are enjoying them, and singing them. That is all that matters. Why all this unnecessary and pointless probing? Obviously, it is for publicity. But it is unethical.

What do you feel about various festivals of India being conducted abroad? Are they, in your opinion, of any use at all to Indian art and culture?

I don't really know. As I told you earlier, I'm never invited to any government-sponsored festival or delegation. I have not visited these festivals of India. They may be good only to the extent of increasing foreign awareness of things that are Indian. But then, the problem is that we do not tend to present things properly. When trying to popularise Indian music for example, we tend to first acquaint them with the grammar of music. And only then the art. You see, this puts them off. When a child grows up, he first picks up a language. Only later you teach him the grammar.

If it is the other way round, the child will never learn to speak. This is exactly the case with our art and culture also abroad. Another unhealthy consequence of this festival fever is that everyone who has some talent wants to represent India abroad. There is unhealthy competition between artistes here to somehow wrangle foreign trip at any cost. This can be detrimental to the growth of art in our own country. The foreigners may catch on to Indian art, music or dance but these will die in India.

From your present position, looking back on life, what have been your most rewarding experiences?

Mine has been a uniformly happy life right through. When my creations or efforts gain recognition, naturally I feel happy. My most thrilling moment was perhaps when I got my first doctorate. You see, I have never had any formal education. I never went to school. When I was appointed principal of the College of Music in Andhra Pradesh, they had to relax the basic rules of the institution. After all, they were appointing me to a gazetted post. I felt very bad at the time. So when I got my first doctorate from Andhra University, I felt very happy. Now I could put it down as Dr Balamuralikrishna PhD in my letter pad.

* * *

The December 1985 issue of *Sruti* magazine listed the twenty-two top Carnatic musicians of 1985. In the vocal category, Balamuralikrishna's name stood first. They listed four categories for their selection: frequency of performance, that is, the musician must have been performing frequently in India during 1985; popularity with listeners; devotion to the art; and technical plusses and minuses of the musicians grasp and display of the Lakshana and Lakshaya aspects of Carnatic music.

In the meantime, a new controversy was brewing in the Carnatic world. Balachander, who had attacked Balamuralikrishna, now found himself in yet another controversy. The National Book Trust had published a book on Swati Tirunal, the erstwhile Maharaja of Travancore, who was also a Carnatic composer. The book was authored by Semmangudi Srinivasa

Iyer. Balachander asked the National Book Trust to withdraw the book and ban its translation into other languages. 'I hold nothing against the ruler-prince,' thundered Balachander at a press conference. 'But I must state that Swati Tirunal is an exaggerated fake, a boosted fraud, a manipulated hoax, a deliberate humbug, a bloated bogus.' To prove his point, Balachander even prepared a booklet of 158 pages putting down his reasons. The Carnatic music world was exploding with the excitement of this new controversy. Amidst this chaos was Semmangudi Srinivasa Iyer, who was the target of Balachander's tirade.

It was around this time that Balamuralikrishna began touring and taking on other assignments extensively. The film critic Baradwaj Rangan writes on his blog how the famous south Indian film star Kamal Haasan became his student.

> Kamal is a very busy actor. It's been some ten years since he sat in Madurai Venkatesan's class. It's been ten years since he learnt any new music. He's shooting in Bombay for Karishma, the Hindi remake of Tik Tik Tik. He has an accident. He breaks a leg. He has to buy two tickets to fly to Chennai, the extra one for the seat in front that has to be folded down so he can stretch that broken leg. The man in the adjacent seat observes his plight and asks him: 'What are you going to do in the months it's going to take for this to heal?'
>
> That was M. Balamuralikrishna. Kamal said he didn't know. Balamuralikrishna asked Kamal if he liked music. Kamal nodded. Balamuralikrishna said, 'Instead of wasting time, why don't you learn something from me?' Kamal thought he was joking—until Balamuralikrishna landed up at Kamal's house the next day. Classes began with the shishya's foot in the air. 'My guru found me,' Kamal Haasan said.
>
> Balamuralikrishna asked Kamal what he'd learnt. Kamal said he knew some 30-odd Keerthanais. Balamuralikrishna asked him to sing. Kamal sang. Balamuralikrishna said, gently, 'Let's start at the beginning, with a Geetham.' Kamal Haasan laughed at the memory. 'So I knew what he thought of me. He wanted me to be good enough to give a public performance, but I wasn't there yet. He still keeps

asking me when I am going to sing on stage.' When Kamal's leg got better, Balamuralikrishna said, 'We can shift the classes to my house.' Kamal began to hobble over to his guru's house, where he'd sit on a sofa and learn music. Eventually, Balamuralikrishna asked him, 'Is your leg okay? Can you walk?' Kamal said yes. Balamuralikrishna said, 'Then you can sit on the floor and continue.'

Classes went on for about one-and-a-half years. I asked Kamal Haasan to name something he learnt. He thought for a minute and then launched into the Karnataka Kapi Geetham, Shree Raghurama samara bheema. I thought he'd stop there, with this opening line of the pallavi, but he continued . . . Sasi mouli vinuta seeta ramana . . . mukendu lalitha hasa pariyathi . . . And then he sang the swarams . . . pa dha ni pa ma ri ri ga ma ri sa / pa dha pa sa ni pa dha ni pa ma ri ga ma . . . He stopped dramatically, after negotiating the sharp, colourful turn at ramana . . . ri ga ma.

Kamal Haasan said he still remembered the song because he learnt it when he was going to New Delhi to receive the National Award for Best Actor for Moondram Pirai. "My guru asked me to learn a new Geetham for the occasion." When the leg healed and Kamal resumed shooting, he continued with classes whenever he found the time. He'd call Balamuralikrishna and go over. Then, during a shooting, Kamal misplaced a notebook filled with song notations. 'I think he was a little upset about this. Then I got busy, and we gradually lost touch—otherwise, I would have been his student for 22 years now.' I asked him about his guru's dream, which Kamal Haasan should sing on stage. He laughed. Balamuralikrishna saying that I can do this is like 'Sivaji', Ganesan saying, 'Nadippu romba easy pa.' You shouldn't take it seriously.

'Mile Sur Mera Tumhara'

On 31 October 1984, Prime Minister Indira Gandhi was assassinated in Delhi. Soon after, massive riots began all over the country. There were efforts by the state to control them in many ways. Rajiv Gandhi was made the prime minister. He formed a body called Lok Seva Sanchar Parishad.

One of the main aims of the organization was to bring in a flavour of patriotism into a society that was being divided by various political conflicts. He met Kailash Surendranath, the famous ad film maker. Surendranath thought up a brilliant campaign.

'This was somewhere back in 1984–85, a time when an Indian wasn't actually in the progressive space; it was a closed economy. Back then, the unanimous feeling that clutched the nation was that Indians were not proud being Indians; they were a restricted, self-doubting lot. Thus, Rajiv Gandhi told us to do something which should make the Indian population proud. It was a rather simple brief. Based on this, Suresh Mallick from O&M and I sat at my work-pad in Walkeshwar. We began brainstorming on the next moves. Something that would evoke the "Mera Bharat Mahan" feel. One thing which we both loved and were passionate about was sports. Suresh being older than me knew all the legendary sportsmen of India, while I was more aware of the contemporaries. So we decided to create an ad with all the famous sports people passing on the torch. We were also influenced by the "Chariots of fire" and this is how we zeroed onto the idea,' recollected Surendranath in an interview he gave K.V. Sridhar in his book *Thirty Second Thriller*.

Sridhar is one of India's most celebrated ad makers and the founder and chief executive officer of Hyper Collective. This ad was called 'The Torch of Freedom'. It would be aired on Doordarshan at prime time, particularly on Sundays. It took the nation by storm. 'The very next year after 'Torch of Freedom', Lok Seva Sanchar Parishad and Rajiv Gandhi called us for yet another spectacle. Who knew that would get etched in the history of advertising and the minds of audiences forever! 'Mile Sur' was an enigma. Piyush Pandey who penned the lyrics, narrated the history of working with that.' Writes Sridhar: 'Piyush narrates his experience: 1987 was when Suresh Mallick asked me to write Mile Sur. He had tried out many eminent writers, but somehow, he wasn't finding anything that touched his soul. He wanted something very simple and hence, approached me to write. I asked, "Are you sure you want me to write it?" and to this, he simply replied, "Yes! I think you can do it."'

'So I began. After many attempts, I got what he wanted. He approved the lyrics at the eighteenth instance. This was the end product: "Mile Sur

Mera Tumhara, Toh Sur Bane Humara. Sur Ki Nadiyan Har Disha Mein Behke Sagar Mein Mile. Badalon Ka Roop Leke, Barse Halke Halke." This culminated into an icon which is greater than any advertisement that we have seen till date. Hats off to Suresh Mallick for thinking of an idea like this. I was purely a lyricist for him. It was Suresh who had the entire ad, frame by frame in his mind,' Piyush tells Sridhar.

'Once we got the lyrics, the first thing we did was to send it to Pt Bhimsen Joshi. He pondered over it for two weeks and then visited us at Louis' studio. As soon as he came, he said, 'I have decided on Raag Bhairavi'. Saying this, he started singing with his harmonium and tanpura; giving us an half an hour recording. He was in a trance and one could not stop him at a stipulated twenty seconds. His recording became the foundation of the track. We cut the recording into two parts and extracted forty seconds, which we decided to use; at the beginning and at the end of the ad. Then we simply gave his recording to varied people like M. Balamuralikrishna, Kavita Krishnamurthy and Vaidyanathan to follow,' narrates Surendranath to Sridhar.

Narrating a few more stories from that shoot, Surendranath adds, 'Yet again, it was an act of improvisation, although Suresh had everything clear in his head. However, we kept adding bits and pieces, as and when they were required. One fine day, we decided that we have to shoot Kerala. So we went to Periyar Lake and there we found a Mahout (elephant rider). We caught hold of him and asked him to sing the line in his native language, to which he happily obliged. Then we caught an actual newly married couple, who were sailing in a basket-boat in Kerala. In the Punjab shor, Suresh's sister and my brother too, were seated on the tractor and were a part of the frame.

As for the celebrities, we contacted actresses and television personalities. It is noteworthy that all of them obliged without any monetary involvement. One of the key things at the celeb-front was to get Amitabh Bachchan, Jitendra and Mithun Chakraborty together. It took quite a long time to co-ordinate and set a common date for all three to be present. Each came in their own attire. We shot the scene in fifteen minutes at the Mehboob studio; after which all three went their ways.

One person we could not miss out on, was Lata Mangeshkar. We wanted Lataji but during the entire schedule, she wasn't available since she was travelling. Thus, until then, we had Kavita Krishnamurthy do her part. Fortunately, at the last moment, we were able to get some time of hers and she featured.

The presence of Kamal Hassan was purely coincidental. The Telugu part of the ad was being taken care of by Balamuralikrishna. He arrived at the studio and performed his part. Along with him Kamal Hassan had come, as Balamuralikrishna was his guru. We decided to shoot Balamuralikrishna's part at the Juhu Beach the morning after. Kamal simply requested if he could be present, for all that he wanted to do was just be there. We agreed. All the featured celebs became a part of the ad out of honour. Well, some of them who had asked for money were refused candidly.'

'Mile Sur Mera Tumhara' became an even bigger rage. It caught on with the viewers very fast. Looking back at the video even now creates a sense of awe-inspiring patriotism in you. As the camera pans over Balamuralikrishna on the Juhu beach, you can hear him singing and a star audience listening to him on the beach. They include his old friend, the famous Bharatanatyam dancer Sudharani Raghupathi, film actors K.R. Vijaya, Revathy and Prathap Pothen, tennis player Ramanathan Krishnan, cricketer S. Venkataraghavan and others. This video was regularly broadcast on the national public service network, so much so that Indians all across began to hum the entire track, despite not knowing the lyrics in all the languages. However, there were rumours that the Balamuralikrishna bit upset several musicians both in Tamil Nadu and Andhra Pradesh. The Tamilians were not happy that a Telugu singer was representing and singing Tamil. The Telugus were not happy that a Telugu singer was singing in Tamil, ignoring his own mother tongue. None of this made any difference to Balamuralikrishna. In fact, the same team of ad-men made a third video titled 'Raag Desh' which was a bigger hit. 'Raag Desh' featured all celebrated Indian classical musicians of that era, like sitar maestro Pt Ravishankar, santur maestro Pt Shivkumar Sharma, sarangi maestro Pt Ramnarayan, flute maestro Pt Hariprasad Chaurasiya, tabla maestro Ustad Allah Rakha and his son Zakir Hussain, sarod maestro Ustad Amjad Ali Khan, violin Vidwan Lalgudi G. Jayaraman, veena Vidwan S. Balachander and last but not the least Balamuralikrishna. In this video, he not only sings in Telugu and in Malayalam for the Mohiniyattam dancer Kanak Rele, he also plays his signature viola.

In November 1984, the Malayalam movie *Sandyakkenthinu Sindhooram*, directed by P.G. Vishwambharan and produced by Soja Abraham, was released. It had Mammootty, Seema, Nedumudi Venu and Venu Nagavally in the lead roles. In this film, Balamuralikrishna made an on-screen appearance, acting in the role of a veteran music teacher. In addition to that, he sang two songs, both penned by the dramatist Kavalam Naryana Panicker. 'Manassin Aarohanam' in a duet with S. Janaki and 'Raaga Vistharam', a solo. This was the last screen appearance of Balamuralikrishna. Though he got many offers after this, he never showed any interest in acting.

The Silent Spiritual Quest

That Carnatic music came from the temple tradition to the royal courts before it reached the proscenium is a well-known fact. One of the long traditions associated with Carnatic musicians is their spiritual life. We have seen in the past how musicians of the older generation were known to be highly religious in their personal life and that religiosity also reflected in their music. There were others like GNB who practised at home and kept it a private affair. Balamuralikrishna belonged to that category of artistes. Over the period of writing this, I asked almost all his older associates, friends and relatives about his spiritual and religious life. All of them agreed that he was a blessed person from birth itself. The history might go back to his ancestors who were Vaidikas, who must have certainly been active in their spiritual quest. Then there were the major influences in his growing years, starting with Guru Pantulu, who was a deeply religious person. Pantulu was an old-timer whose spiritual belief reflected in his music. He was an ardent devotee of the Dakshinamnaya Sharada Peetham in Sringeri, the first Peetham established by Jagadguru Adi Shankaracharya in the eighth century.

Then there were Guru Vimalananda Bharati and Pantulu's own music teacher Susarla. By the time it came to Balamuralikrishna, it was also the upbringing and atmosphere at home. As we saw earlier, his mother and foster mother Subbamma were deeply spiritual. One of the earlier spiritual influences came from the multifaceted Kashi Krishnacharyulu, a staunch Madhwa and a host of great stalwarts and scholars, all of whom were deeply religious. No wonder that his first book, *Janaka Raga Kriti Manjari*, was dedicated to goddess Kanakadurga enshrined on the Indrakiladri hill at Vijayawada.

There is another fascinating episode from his childhood, when he was barely thirteen or fourteen, as a student of Pantulu. He had just returned from a long meeting and discussion with Sri Vimalananda Bharati and was lying down at home, contemplating the advice he had been given. He suddenly observed that the light that was hanging from the ceiling was flickering. So he decided to go and turn it off. All that he remembered was that he put his hand on the switchboard and a tremendous amount of electricity ran through his body, causing a shock. He collapsed on the floor and stayed there for a while. When he gained consciousness, he observed something strange. There was a huge monkey sitting in front of him. It ran up to him and extended its palm on to his forehead. The frightened little Murali closed his eyes tightly. He only remembered a strange sensation on his forehead. When he opened his eyes, there was nobody around. He sat, silenced in fear for some time. It was only when he met the venerable Kashi Krishnacharyulu that he got an insight into what might have happened. Krishnacharyulu was an ardent devotee of lord Hanuman. He explained to little Murali in detail how lord Hanuman was indeed a great exponent of music and that he was a *Nadayogi*. He also told the frightened kid that it was lord Hanuman who had blessed him that day and that he need not worry. In fact, it was after this incident that Balamuralikrishna began writing the *Janaka Raga Kriti Manjari*.

Growing up with religious people around him, one would have assumed that Balamuralikrishna would have been a deeply religious person in his adult life. But that was not the case. For the longest time he didn't believe in making a public display of his spiritual life. As Purnachander mentioned to me in an interview, he was an 'Antarmukhi', as in one who had internalized his spiritual feelings as opposed to being a 'Bahirmukhi', one who is constantly required to affirm from outside. No wonder

Balamuralikrishna receives the Padma Shri award from the President of India V.V. Giri, at Rashtrapati Bhavan, New Delhi, 1971.

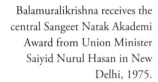

Balamuralikrishna receives the central Sangeet Natak Akademi Award from Union Minister Saiyid Nurul Hasan in New Delhi, 1975.

Balamuralikrishna after the Sangita Kalanidhi function with Tamil Nadu chief minister M.G. Ramachandran and members of the Music Academy.

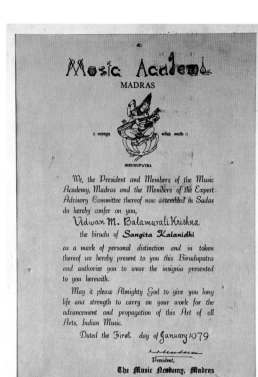

The Birudu Patra of the Sangita Kalanidhi award.

M.G. Ramachandran honouring Balamuralikrishna as a Tamil Nadu State Artiste.

Balamuralikrishna with Carnatic stalwart Semmangudi Srinivasa Iyer and T.T. Vasu, the president of the Music Academy.

Balamuralikrishna being felicitated by Mother Teresa.

The famous jugalbandi between Balamuralikrishna and Bharatanrityam
dancer Padma Subrahmanyam at the Music Academy.

The Mangalampalli couple with the Sadasivams.

Balamuralikrishna with D.K. Pattammal, her husband,
Easwaran, K.V. Narayanaswamy and actor Gemini Ganesan.

Balamuralikrishna and Annapoorna with their entire family of sons, daughters, sons-in-law and daughters-in-law.

Balamuralikrishna shows a mirror to a blushing Annapoorna in the middle of a ritual during his 60th birthday celebrations.

Balamuralikrishna and Annapoorna with their six children—a happy houseful.

Balamuralikrishna receiving the blessings of Jagadguru Sri Bharati Tirtha Mahasannidhanam, the 36th Jagadguru of the Dakshinamnaya Sri Sharada Peetham, at Sringeri.

Balamuralikrishna with Lata Mangeshkar and Asha Bhosle at the
Dinanath Mangeshkar Award ceremony.

Balamuralikrishna with Yagnyaraman of the Krishna Gana Sabha.

Balamuralikrishna with Ustad Allah Rakha, Ustad Ali Akbar Khan, Pt Ravishankar, E. Gayathri, Lalgudi Jayaraman and T.V. Gopalakrishnan.

Balamuralikrishna playing the role of a musician in the Malayalam film *Sandhyakkenthinu Sindooram*, directed by P.G. Viswambharam in 1984.

Balamuralikrishna and his father, Pattabhiramayya, with musicologist Prof. Sambamurthy and the then chief minister of Tamil Nadu Nedunchezhiyan.

everybody around believed he was neither religious nor spiritual in his life. But that was untrue. At home he did have a pooja room and did worship his Ishta Devatas. How else can one explain the divinity that manifested in his music in the countless songs he sang to all the gods in Bhakti Ranjani? How else would one justify his passion for restoring, reinvigorating and reinventing the compositions of saints Bhadrachala Ramadasu, Tallapaka Annamacharya, Sadasiva Brahmendra, Kaivaram Amara Nareyana and Mantralayam Raghavendra Swamy? How else will you understand his passion for the philosophy encapsulated in the Bhakti of Tyagaraja Kritis? He manifested his own spiritual thought process in his music without much ado. It was this softer side of him that opened his heart towards many charitable causes.

In the mid-1980s, Balamuralikrishna did a number of fund-raising concerts in aid of several religious charities and endowments. In addition to these were a number of records that he released in aid of numerous ongoing projects in different religious institutions. One charming episode is the story of the construction of the 'Vidya Theertha Sethu', the bridge in the Sringeri Peetham. The Peethaam was already planning to have this and the then Jagadguru Sri Sri Abhinava Vidyatheertha Maha Sannidhanam, the thirty-fifth Jagadguru in the lineage, had expressed his Sankalpam at a public gathering on his visit to Bangalore. One of the ardent devotees of the Peetham was Sri Harikere Srikanta Iyer Tyagaraja, whose large family were associated with the Peetham for a long time. He is a trained musician and hit upon the idea of releasing a cassette of hymns composed by the earlier Jagadgurus of the Peetham.

On approaching the Mahaswamiji, he got blessings and a special audience with the then Sri Sannidhanam, his holiness Sri Sri Bharati Tirtha Mahaswamiji. Swamiji patiently gave a selection of hymns and Slokas composed by Jagadguru Saccidananda Sivabhinava Nrsimha Bharati Maha Swamiji, the thirty-third Jagadguru of the Peetham and Sri Chandrashekhara Bharati Mahaswamiji, the thirty-fourth Jagadguru of the Peetham. Tyagaraja took those songs and visited the house of Balamuralikrishna in Madras. 'I clearly remember going there. When we had arrived, Balamuralikrishnaji was at home, watching *Tom and Jerry* and eating ice cream. He received us with great courtesy and patiently heard the whole project. He went through the papers which I left with him for about a month and a half. I had suggested the Ragams in which these should be sung,' recollects Tyagaraja. Having gone through the papers, Balamuralikrishna contacted his favourite label Sangeetha Records and at his own expense, hired the studio, recorded everything and finished it within a short time. This recording was named 'Bhakthi Kusuma' (blossoms of devotion) by Bharati Tirtha Mahaswamiji. The cassette cover showed an image of the famous Vidyashankara temple at Sringeri, an image of Balamuralikrishna on the cover, and it announced 'with the blessings of their Holinesses of Sringeri Jagadgurus Shankaracharyas'. The cassette was priced at Rs 34. Through the cassette sales, an amount of Rs 3 lakh was raised and contributed towards the construction of the Sethu in Sringeri.

A little after this, Balamuralikrishna visited Sringeri and sought the blessings of the then Maha Sannidham, who blessed him with a Rudraksha. Listening to the cassette even now, it is an extraordinary spiritual experience. The cassette opens with a small speech by Sri Bharati Theertha Mahaswamiji in beautiful Tamil, 'I went to Sringeri to seek the blessing of Swamiji. I had a small recorder with me. That day, it was pouring heavily in Sringeri. Swamiji gave a short Anugraha Bhashanam in Tamil, which I recorded. This was the first time and the last time that Swamiji blessed the recording of any classical musician this way!' recollects Tyagaraja about the making of the cassette.

After the little speech are three slokas, the first to lord Rathnagarbha Ganapathy enshrined in Sringeri, the second to Abhinava Vidyatheertha Mahaswamiji and the third to Bharati Tirtha Mahaswamiji. After that is a beautiful composition in praise of Rathnagarbha Ganapathy. This way the whole cassette is filled with Slokas and compositions of the Gurus. The cassette was not the last of Balamuralikrishna's association with the Peetham. He was made the Asthana Vidwan of the Peetham in 1993. In addition to that he travelled a number of times and gave concerts in Sringeri. When the Guru Nivas opened in Sringeri, Balamuralikrishna performed once again. In addition to *Bhakthi Kusuma*, Balamuralikrishna also released another album titled *Sringeri Sharada*, a selection of hymns in Kannada set to various Ragams, many years later. He was honoured with the Bharathi Thyagaraja Samman in 2015, by Jagadguru Sri Sri Bharati Theertha Maha Sannidhanam and Jagadguru Sri Sri Vidhushekhara Bharati Srisannidhanam in Bangalore. Besides the Sharada Peetham, he was also affiliated with other religious institutions.

Way back in the 1950s, when Sathya Sai Baba of Puttaparthi began his new Ashram called Prashanthi Nilayam, the inaugural concert was given by Balamuralikrishna. In a later interview that he gave to Radio Sai, the radio channel of the Sai Baba Ashram, he recollected how he and Sai Baba wrote letters to each other and Sai Baba's advice to him to never go and perform if he was not called to any place. He says he took that advice very seriously for the rest of his life. He performed in the Sai Baba Ashram at Prashanthi Nilayam towards the end of his life. In the 1970s, Balamuralikrishna visited the Ashram of Matrusri Anasuya Devi, popular as 'Jillellamudi Amma'. He was also associated with the Chinmaya mission. 'It is not frequent that a nation discovers a Balamuralikrishna in her history,' declared Swami Chinmayananda in one of his speeches. His association with the Ashram of Kaivaram Yogi Amaranareyana, too, went a long way. He was the Asthana Vidwan of the Sri Kalahasti Devasthanam in Sri Kalahasti, Srisailam Devasthanam, in Srisailam, the Kanakadurga Devasthanam in Vijayawada and the Anjaneya Devasthanam in Nanganallur in Chennai. He was given the title of 'Sangeetha Sudhakara' by the pontiff of Kanchi Mutt.

The Dharmadhikari of the Kaivaram Amara Nareyana Sri M.R. Jayaram recollected how Balamuralikrishna got drawn into the works of Amara Nareyana.

'In 1984, I had taken all the books of Kaivara Thathayya to Balamuralikrishnaji and visited him in Madras. He asked me to leave everything there, saying that he wouldn't promise anything. That he would take time to go through all the material, and if he was convinced, he would let me know. When I returned, he asked me to give him three assurances in written, 1) that he should be allowed to sing the songs wherever he wanted to, 2) that he wouldn't sing a mangalam in this cassette, 3) even if he made some cassettes, he should be given the permission to do it. I agreed to all these three and gave it to him in written as he wanted. He recorded four cassettes by himself and sang the Mangalam at the end of the fourth cassette. Out of those four, one cassette is Kaivara Yogi's "Kala Gnanam". This was the first time any Kala Gnanam was being recorded. He eventually became a great admirer and devotee of Amara Nareyana.'

An officer at the Kaivaram Ashram, Anand narrated another incident. One day he had a call from Dr Balamuralikrishna, who was then in London. He had called saying that he had a dream in which the saint had appeared and blessed him. Those days he was also suffering from a sore throat regularly and wasn't able to sing the way he wanted to. He had called seeking permission if he could come and pay his respects at the Ashram. They were more than overjoyed. Balamuralikrishna not only came all by himself and performed in the Ashram but also set to tune and released several cassettes and CDs of the songs of the saint of Kaivaram.

When the 44th pontiff of Sri Ahobila Mutt Srimad Azhagiya Singar Jeeyar Swami decided to take on the massive task of reconstructing the Rajagopuram of the temple of Lord Ranganatha in Srirangam, one of the first people to send a handsome donation was Balamuralikirshna. It is the tallest temple tower in the world's largest living temple complex. Several other friends of Balamuralikrishna, like M.S. Subbulakshmi, film music director Ilayaraja and a host of generous philanthropists donated and realized this dream. The Rajagopuram was consecrated on 25 March 1985.

After seeing all these instances in his life, could anyone say that he wasn't a spiritual person? His compositions reveal yet another side of his spiritual thinking and we will see that later. He didn't believe in the religious exhibitionism common to the music world. And that was easily misunderstood. He didn't bother correcting that image either. Those who knew him up close and personal, could vouch for his spiritual nature.

* * *

'Jealousy Has Killed Many a Genius' announced the headline in the *Times of India*, dated 5 July 1986. 'I've been considered controversial since childhood. I've been a rebel ever since I can remember. To be controversial means to be great, unless you're important, why should people bother to counter what you are saying and regard you as a force to reckon with? Anyone trying to do something always finds himself opposed and thwarted. I do research into music, I bring to light certain unknown and little known facts, I correct certain prevalent wrong notions. All this may seem awkward and unacceptable to orthodox people, so they hit out at me, even at times when they know I am in the right, they criticize me,' said Balamuralikrishna in the interview. Despite all his angst, he never allowed his music to be affected. In the *Economic Times* dated 28 September 1986, Naarada writes, 'His voice can freely traverse three octaves without any difficulty and it retains both its power and Shruthi-Shuddha right from the lowest Shadjam to the highest Shadjam three octaves later. His mastery over the Lakshana and Lakshaya of Carnatic music is unparalleled. With all these attributes, he combines an unmatched ability to render light songs in Carnatic music with a clarity and seeming ease that can be quite breath-taking. His hold over Laya and his ability to sing beautiful solfa passages in Swaraprastharam are other hallmarks of Balamurali's music.'

These were turbulent times for Balamuralikrishna. He was agitated with a lot of things going on. One controversy barely ended when another began. The only thing that remained was his music. He continued performing and giving concerts all over. Rave reviews kept pouring in. About his concert at the Ravindra Bhavan lawns organized by the central Sangeet Natak Akademi in March 1987, Subbudu writes, 'Balamurali is a "show-biz" man and knows the pulse of the audience. The crowd being cosmopolitan, he chose to (add) a large dose of Hindustani colouring to the Ragas and Krithis he negotiated. Both Nattai and Vasantha have their Hindustani counterparts in Jog and Basant, and he did not fail to invest those touches in his delineations. His voice has a fantastic range, capable of touching the Anumandarasthayee (sub-bass register) and before you can say cheese, traverse three and a half octaves and touch Daivath in the fourth octave. He did, and the magic worked. The audience was swayed. Not only that, he could hop octaves in negotiating phrases—identical ones—in all these octaves and land back on cats paws precisely . . . Balamurali is unpredictable to the core.'

In 1987, Balamuralikrishna also launched his own film banner Balamurali Creations under which the first movie, *Thaliavanukkor Thalaivi*, was directed by Vittal T. Gnanam. The movie starred Mohan,

Rajiv, Nilalgal Ravi, Rekha and Vaishnavi. The music direction was by Balamuralikrishna. He also sang three songs in the movie, one in a duet with Vani Jayaram and the other with ghazal singer Penaz Masani. Balamuralikrishna's earlier suspicions were right. The film was not a profitable venture and he knew that he was best at dealing with music, not cinema. This was the last of his involvement with making mainstream films. However, he was happy to participate in several documentaries made on Indian classical music in general and on him in specific.

It was around this time that the Vrindaban Gurukul of Pt Hariprasad Chaurasiya produced a series of documentaries titled *Sadhana*, on the legends of Indian classical music. The one on Balamuralikrishna was directed by Ambrish Sangal and anchored by the late film actor Vinod Khanna. In this documentary, one can see Balamuralikrishna interacting with Penaz Masani, where he takes her to his house and narrates a number of incidents in his musical journey. The documentary is fascinating to watch even today. One can see the various faces of a multi-faceted genius. His versatility in effortlessly handling several musical instruments was something that very few Carnatic musicians excelled in. The documentary also showed a different side to him. He was then the chairman of Chrompet Saswatha Nidhi Ltd, a small bank. One may wonder what this was about. In the documentary, Masani probes him about it. 'Well Masani ji, you see I have been singing and receiving currency notes along with musical notes. Since I'm retired from professional music, I want to still deal with currency notes to help artistes to encourage them, to improve their musical notes,' he says nonchalantly.

On 4 September 1987, Malayalam film director Lenin Rajendran (1951–2019) released a biographical movie on Maharaja Swati Tirunal, the famous Carnatic composer who was embroiled in a controversy. The film cast had Ananth Nag in the role of Swati Tirunal, Srividya in the role of Gowri Parvati Bayi, Nedumudi Venu as Irayimman Thampi, Murali as Shatkala Govinda Marar and others. The cinematography was by Madhu Ambat and the music was by M.B. Sreenivasan. The film had numerous original tracks of legendary Carnatic composers like Saint Tyagaraja, Irayimman Thampi and Maharaja Swati Tirunal. Balamuralikrishna sang five songs in the movie. Tyagaraja's 'Mokshamu Galada' in Ragam

Saramathi, and Swati Tirunal's 'Jamuna Kinare' in Ragam Mishra Pilu. He also sang Swati Tirunal's 'Ragamalika Kriti', 'Pannagendra Sayana', along with Carnatic musicians Neyyattinkara Vasudevan and K.J. Yesudas. The movie had two additional tracks by Balamuralikrishna. Swati Tirunal's 'Bhaja Bhaja Manasa' in Ragam Sindhubhairavi and Saint Tyagaraja's Pancharatna Kriti 'Endaro Mahanubhavulu' in Ragam Sri. The movie won several Kerala state film awards. Balamuralikrishna was honoured with the 'best male playback singer' award for this movie. 'Balamurali was like a voice from Kerala. When I went and met him with the script in his house in Chennai, he readily agreed to sing. He asked what were the songs and when music director Sreenivasan told him, he sounded extremely happy. While recording, he finished everything in one take. Finally, it was as if this award was waiting to be at his disposal,' recollected director Lenin Rajendran.

In December 1987, the Mylapore Fine Arts Club honoured Balamuralikrishna with the title of 'Sangita Kala Nipuna'. The award and the citation were presented to Balamuralikrishna by Semmangudi Srinivasa Iyer and Lalgudi G. Jayaraman.

In another review in the *Statesman* dated 17 January 1989, Subbudu wrote, 'To Mr Lalit Mansingh goes the credit for making Dr Balamuralikrishna, the musician in exile from the concert platform for some time now, yield to his persuasion and give a memorable concert. Under the auspices of the ICCR at the FICCI hall . . . it would be difficult to describe adequately the terrific impact the concert had as it was indeed a musical experience . . . Balamurali has evolved a unique style of rendering Swaraprastharas. They are not mere mathematics, but melody coated ones. Not that alone, they contain quicksilver changes, mercurial shifts and encompass fraction-oriented bits that keep the accompanists guessing, where the next turn would occur.'

On 26 January, the Tyagaraja Sangeetha Vidwat Samajam in Mylapore conducted a ten-day Aradhana festival, under the presidency of Balamuralikrishna. It was presided over by M.L. Vasanthakumari. The Pancharatna Goshti group singing saw the participation of all the stalwarts, including Semmangudi Srinivasa Iyer, M.S. Subbulakshmi, K.V. Narayanaswamy and others. In addition to that, Balamuralikrishna also accompanied M.S. Subbulakshmi's singing on the viola. *Sruti* magazine, issue 55, carried a little report and didn't forget to mention that only two years earlier, Semmangudi had condemned the Samajam.

By the end of the year, Balamuralikrishna had resolved his differences with Semmangudi Srinivasa Iyer, whom he had sued earlier for defamation. Semmangudi consulted the lawyers he knew and the case had been dragging on for many years without anything favourable towards him. Semmangudi's legal experts told him he was fighting a losing battle. Taking the advice of everyone around, one day, Semmangudi walked up to Balamuralikrishna's house seeking pardon. Balamuralikrishna was pleasantly surprised and ran out to welcome him. He also said a simple phone call would have sorted out everything and such a senior Vidwan like Semmangudi ought not to have taken this trouble to come personally all the way. 'It was easier to come here and apologise to you, otherwise I would have had to run to the Saidapet court,' replied Semmangudi. Legend goes that Balamuralikrishna not only gave him the best hospitality, but sent him back with a message saying, 'Next time if you want to insult me, do it in private and keep the praise for public.' The September/October issue of the *Sruti* magazine was a special tribute to Semmangudi, titled 'A Mosaic-Portrait'. For that V.S. Sundara Rajan interviewed Balamuralikrishna. Here are a few excerpts:

> Semmangudi Srinivasa Iyer and I have cordial relations now. I have great respect and reverence for him.
>
> This was the case in the past too. I will give a couple of instances.
>
> Many years ago, Semmangudi gave a performance at, I think, Sri Krishna Gana Sabha. I don't exactly remember the place or the year. On the next day he was slated to sing at the Music Academy. The morning of the Academy concert, an English daily carried a scathing attack on Semmangudi's concert of the previous evening and the critic, Subbudu, had gone to the extent of suggesting that the veteran retire forthwith. Surprisingly, Semmangudi sent a note to the Academy informing that his programme fixed for that evening should be cancelled and that he would sing no more. The officials of the Academy approached me and sought my help in persuading the veteran to withdraw his note.

At an Experts' Advisory Committee meeting that afternoon, I expressed the view that Semmangudi should not mind a critic's opinion, that it was an individual's opinion and should not be taken as public opinion. In any event, I said, criticism should be taken in stride. I requested the Academy officials to convey my opinion to Semmangudi and kindly ask him to reverse his decision and agree again to sing that evening. I added that if Semmangudi did not sing, neither would I. A few other musicians also took this stand. Accordingly the officials went to Semmangudi to convey my remarks and request.

At first, he was reported to be unwilling to change his decision, but when he was informed that I and some others who were yet to perform at the Academy that year would pull out too if he persisted, he yielded. He gave a fine concert that evening.

During another music season, Tamil Nadu was in the grip of a severe drought and the Academy had announced that it would match the receipts of the concert which had the biggest gate collection and donate the total amount for drought relief. My concert netted the maximum collection and the Academy was to announce the same before making over the donation. But I informed the officials that, in order to avoid any ill-feeling that might be caused by such an announcement, they should give the honour to the Semmangudi concert (which had the second best gate collection) though they might donate the amount resulting from my concert. My suggestion was accepted and acted upon.

Semmangudi and I had happy relations when he was the All India Radio's Chief Producer of Carnatic Music, stationed in Madras. I was a producer of Light Music then at the station level. He had come to my house many times to praise some of my tillanas which were set to intricate talas.

Now to the controversy.

After I was awarded the title of Sangeetha Kalanidhi by the Music Academy, Veena Vidwan S. Balachander started a controversy saying it could not be accepted that I had invented a few ragas as mentioned in an article on me published in the souvenir of the

Academy. Though I did not bother about Balachander's statement, some of my well-wishers did contest his contention.

I was painfully surprised to learn that Semmangudi supported Balachander's view. (Balachander had publicised his objection in a letter sent to the Indian Express, and Semmangudi too had a letter published in the Indian Express voicing his support of the Balachander position). Later, he went to the extent of getting an extraordinary meeting of the Experts' Advisory Committee of the Academy convened during the off-season—an unheard of thing—and got a resolution passed which, in effect, said that Balamurali could not have invented any raga, and the ragas mentioned as his creations, already existed. (Balachander has claimed that it was he who asked for the meeting). Strangely all this was done behind my back. I was not even invited to the meeting though I was one of the members of the Committee. Nor was I given any chance to have my say in the matter.

I also came to know that Semmangudi had, in his speech on the resolution, made damaging and unparliamentary remarks about me. He was reported to have induced even the members hailing from Andhra to vote for the resolution.

All these provoked me to sue him for defamation to the tune of two lakhs of rupees; I felt that his action had damaged my professional career. If at all Semmangudi was serious about whether I had really invented the ragas or not, he could have called me to his house or visited my house and had a frank and healthy discussion. For reasons best known to him, he had taken an antagonistic stand on the issue and left me no option but to go to court.

For a few months, Semmangudi did not even answer the Court's summons, but he was reportedly consulting legal luminaries. I also came to know that the legal pundits were not giving him any hope.

Then mediators entered the scene. Well-wishers on both sides suggested that we two should come to some settlement. Semmangudi and I met and he expressed regret for his action and said he was sorry if it had hurt my feelings. He put it all in writing. I insisted that he should do the same before the presiding judge hearing the case. He came to the Court and gave a written apology and I withdrew my case with the permission of the Court.

The controversy behind us, we have been on good terms. He has even presided over a function at which I was awarded a title.

I would like to mention a funny sequel in this connection. The late Dr S. Ramanathan, who had earlier supported Balachander's views on the issue, later wrote an article in 'Shanmukha' that Muthiah Bhagavatar and I (Balamurali) had created a few ragas and listed all the ragas invented by me.

This patch-up made the news in the Carnatic world. The result of the patch-up was the famous concert held at the Thyagaraja Vidwat Samajam, where Dr Balamuralikrishna accompanied Semmangudi Srinivasa Iyer on the viola.

In the meantime, Balamuralikrishna was also working on a new idea, one that he had been trying to develop for the last few years. This was the concept of 'music therapy'. This had been running through his mind for almost a decade. In fact, in 1984, when M.G. Ramachandran was hospitalised due to kidney failure, Balamuralikrishna met him at the Apollo Hospitals where he was admitted. He was in bed for months. He had even made statements in the press that he would win the election 'lying down'. At that time, Balamuralikrishna went to him with a bunch of recordings and presented them, prescribing ways to listen. MGR was his old friend and believed that one of the reasons he managed to get cured from his ailment was the music. Balamuralikrishna strongly believed in the healing properties of music. He spoke about it at some length in a few interviews in those years. In 1989, the Cultural Centre of Performing Arts in Madras honoured him with the title 'Sangeeta Sagaram'.

8

The Magic of Murali Gaanam

It is important to study Balamuralikrishna's music from various perspectives. He was many things at one time, the most popular faces of him being that of a singer and a Vaggeyakara. Beyond these were his facets as a music director, musical thinker and visionary. In an older interview he said, 'I'm living many lives in this one!' He couldn't have been more accurate about himself.

It is a challenge for a writer to fathom where to begin, going by the humongous body of work Balamuralikrishna has done as a musician. To make it easy and find a method in this madness, I've tracked him as a Vaggeyakara and a music director first. We have seen his aptitude as a curious teenager experimenting with confidence in the book *Janaka Raga Kriti Manjari* that he authored. As seen earlier, he divided the Ragams into different Chakrams. While he was at it, he was also thrown into a job due to unforeseen circumstances.

The beginning of the 1990s saw Balamuralikrishna much more at peace with himself and willing to perform a wide variety of music for his audiences. In one of the concerts that he gave at the Rasika Ranjani Sabha in 1990, he performed his viola accompanied by Purnachander on the violin, Thanjavur Upendran on the mridangam and Harishankar on the khanjira. Listening to the record even today keeps you in awe of his versatility and mastery over an instrument like the viola. The same year, he travelled to Doha along with his old colleagues from Vijayawada, Annavarapu Ramaswamy on the violin and Dhandamudi Ramamohan Rao on the mridangam. He also travelled to the US on a concert tour, accompanied by Purnachander on the violin and M.L.N. Raju on the mridangam. In the summer of 1990, the audio cassette of the *Swara Raga Sudha* series was released. It contained thirteen tracks including the compositions of Saint Tyagaraja, Purandaradasa, Jayadeva, Shyama Sastry and others. The same year he was conferred the title of 'Isai Chelvam' by Muthamizh Peravai

There were constant references to music therapy in several interviews he gave to the mainstream press on his concert tours that were intriguing everybody, but this was not new to him. He had been working on the idea that music had curative properties for a long time. He began experimenting with this in the 1970s itself. He would spend time with various scholars of Ayurveda and Siddha Vaidya. He would also consult a number of astrologers and physicists who had worked on sound and vibration theories and how they affect the human mind, and conduct small experiments trying to analyse how Carnatic music applied properly had great curative and therapeutic properties. He continued this work on the side without making much fuss about it and applied it as and when he felt it was necessary. As seen earlier, he took a couple of his recordings and visited Chief Minister M.G. Ramachandran, who was then bed-ridden, and had a strong conviction that a part of his cure was also because of the power of classical music.

In an article published in the *Free Press Journal*, dated 3 July 1990, he voiced several of his thoughts on the subject:

It is a myth, it is impossible. He has put his might to make the impossible, possible, the unachievable task a reality. His search for healing ailments through music has raised more incredible eyebrows than acknowledging smiles and nods. Dr M. Balamuralikrishna's brain child, 'music therapy' will be the latest and most prestigious crown for the versatile musician, when the child starts to breathe.

The magnanimity of this task demands education leading to sincere efforts and finance in tons. Music schools must be started to train voices. A lot of research work must be conducted to come up with the right kind of punch—to prescribe music at a particular dosage to heal the ailment.

Sensing its seriousness, Balamurali is not to be counted among those who are struck with the mania of over-optimism about their projects. He is honest enough to express his own reservations about his brainchild. 'First of all, in India it becomes a time-consuming process. It may turn out to be reality or may remain a myth forever. I will not be disillusioned if the latter happens.' This indicates his belief in the saying 'Man proposes and God disposes.'

The laurels and recognition kept coming. In October, Balamuralikrishna participated in the Akashvani Sangeet Sammelan, the prestigious music festival of the All India Radio and performed before an invited audience in Bombay (now Mumbai). He was accompanied by Hampolu Muralikrishna on the violin and Guruvayur Dorai on the mridangam. The Vamsee Arts organization based in Hyderabad honoured him with the title of 'Thyagaraja Vamsee' on 23 October. That year the government of India announced India's second highest civilian award, the Padma Vibhushan, for him.

Then the Hindu temple of Greater Chicago and the Telugu Association of Greater Chicago presented an award to him on 21 September 1991. On 20 December, the Indian Fine Arts Society (IFAS) honoured Balamuralikrishna with the title of 'Sangeetha Kala Sikhamani'. IFAS is one of the oldest cultural organizations, founded by violin maestro T. Chowdiah and Gopalakrishna Rao in 1932. Ever since, it has been serving music and honouring musicians every year. The IFAS festival was inaugurated by S. Viswanathan and the award was given to both Semmangudi Srinivasa Iyer and Balamuralikrishna. But the bigger award was the prestigious Padma Vibhushan award, given by the President of India to various personalities for public service in different fields. Balamuralikrishna received this at the Rashtrapati Bhavan in New Delhi from President R. Venkataraman, who was his old friend and a seasoned rasika of Carnatic music.

The press continued writing about him in a number of columns. An excerpt from one column in the *Indian Express* titled 'The Maverick Musician', written by Jaya Ramanathan, reads:

Conventional Carnatic musicians almost always begin their concerts well before or after rahu kalam (the inauspicious 1-1/2 hours) . . . The singers begin with a varnam and a few light numbers and then, when they are sure the audience has settled down, they swing into the piece de resistance the ragam tanam pallavi followed by the musical duet between the mridangam and the ghatam and then on to a climactic jugglery before a totally enraptured audience which then breaks into thunderous applause. The concert would thus go on continuously for three to four hours, with the listeners entreating encores and the singer often obliging. Balamurali Krishna broke this set pattern—at the end of two hours, just when the listeners were warming up to the artiste, he would declare an intermission! An interval in paatu katcheri? The audience would be aghast—what did Balamurali think this was, show biz?

'What is wrong with having an interval?' asks Balamurali, warming up for yet another fight.

He claimed the break was 'for the convenience of the audience'. Instead of walking in and out of the hall, a dedicated time for the break so that they 'sit quietly through the rest of the recital'. 'What is a music performance after all if not entertainment? Do you not have intervals in all kinds of entertainment programmes? If you feel Carnatic music is sacrosanct, well then keep it in the confines of the pooja room, do not bring it on stage,' he is quoted as saying. The article also carried a portrait of Balamuralikrishna singing which was captioned 'Black Sheep'.

So much for speaking his mind! Why just 'Black Sheep'? The press referred to him in a number of negative ways, but none of that seemed to bother him or stop him from pursuing what he strongly believed in.

In April 1991, Balamuralikrishna was awarded the Dinanath Mangeshkar Award instituted by the Dinanath Smruti Pratishtan in Bombay. In a grand ceremony, the award was given to him by the famous

Hindi playback singer Lata Mangeshkar, her sister Asha Bhosle and the other members of the large Mangeshkar family. Balamuralikrishna was the first Carnatic vocalist to receive this honour. As usual, Bombay music lovers were excited and eulogized him in a number of articles across mainstream media.

Balamuralikrishna's sixtieth birthday celebrations were announced in all the newspapers in Bombay. 'Sweet 60 – A giant turns the corner, and the music world pauses to cheer him on' announced the *Mid-Day* dated 3 July. The sixtieth birthday celebration was grand, with a festival to commemorate it. VST Industries Ltd, in association with the Nehru Centre, put together a two-day function titled 'The Spirit of Freedom Concerts'. The first day had a felicitation ceremony for Balamuralikrishna, followed by a vocal recital by his friend Pt Bhimsen Joshi. The second day had a Bharatanatyam recital by the famous Vidushi Alarmel Valli, a veena concert by Chitti Babu and a grand finale by another of Balamuralikrishna's friends, Vidushi Kishori Amonkar. The press was agog, with many articles and interviews appearing in the media.

In an article titled 'Tinged with Brilliance', Vimala Sarma wrote in the *Economic Times*,

> Young avant-garde audiences are completely won over by Balamurali's music. The orthodox admit the talent, but have some reserves about the style. Natural perhaps, for in the traditionally oriented Carnatic music system each composition is a prayer and music only a means to attain the Godhead. Even on the concert platform, a certain distance may be perceived between audience and performer, who seems to strive to reach the head rather than the heart of listeners. Balamurali's music has a very personal appeal, an implicit sensuousness, with its emotion or bhava-predominant approach . . .
>
> With his undisputed command over the complex grammar of Carnatic music and the limitless potential of his voice, he has been able to imbue the classical idioms with colour and brilliance; even in the scholarly Kamalamba Navavarana kritis, rich in tantric concepts and usually rendered to emphasise majesty and dignity, he has been able to capture the note of awe and prayer with great sensitivity,

without losing the intellectual and grammatical contents. Needless to say, in the compositions of Tyagaraja, Bhadrachala Ramadas and Purandaradasa, his ability to distil the bhava content is at its best.

The article goes on to mention the reservations many felt against him—'flamboyant, theatrical, even arrogant. Sometimes in the higher registers his voice becomes screech'. But unreservedly, it mentions that the acclaim he has received is solely because 'the music is flawless'.

The celebrations made major news for two reasons. One was the involvement of all the great legends of music, most importantly those who came forward as friends. The other was because several newspapers equated it to the Wimbledon final that was being telecast at that time. Balamuralikrishna spoke his mind during the event, and in the interviews that he gave.

The *Illustrated Weekly of India* called him 'a controversial genius'. In an interview he gave, he said, 'Music is not just a profession for me, it is my life. Music has been the vehicle that allowed me to express the innermost feelings of my soul. Therefore, when I look back at these 60 years of my music career, I feel very contented and successful. I am absolutely satisfied and I can humbly claim that there have been no regrets whatsoever. Moreover, I don't see myself as having committed a mistake at any point of time.'

One can sense the disillusionment and frustration in his voice when he speaks of the criticism from critics and in the press.

They blamed me for changing the traditional style of Carnatic music. According to them, I was breaking conventions. But tell me, can't a person be innovative? Why is it that people find it so difficult to accept someone who has made improvements? . . .

Secondly, musicology states that tradition is fundamental and hence it must remain that way forever. If anything changes, it then takes place in the acharam, which loosely means the performance, because it is this aspect in music which can be improvised upon. I still sing with the basic swaras sa, ri, ga, ma, pa, da, ni, sa even if I have changed the pattern. A more simple way to explain this would be: when tradition says that we have to perform certain necessary chores every day, how you perform them is your choice.

He is forthright about the choices that he made, as well as the kind of opportunities Hindustani musicians receive to promote their arts over their Carnatic counterparts:

I have also been branded as a rebel musician by the press . . . Individual critics have also found my style quite unpalatable. It is mainly because I revealed certain previously ignored areas of Carnatic music, and made compositions more expressive for people to understand their meaning. This I achieved by introducing a suitable sthayi system, which invokes the wrath of these critics. I think critics should realise that mine was merely an act to create more awareness of music among the listeners. Fortunately, today, all criticisms have ceased to exist simply because my kind of music has become a well-established style . . .

People have often asked me about the fusion of Carnatic and Hindustani music. My opinion is that music is basically the same. Only, the reasons for and ways of performing differ. Musicians from the North give importance to aspects like the raga-alaapana while their counterparts from the South stress equally on the composition as well as the raga-alaapana. Frankly, I see no difference between the two, only the styles in expressing them vary.

In the past, in one of my interviews when I came down heavily on the northern domination in music, that was not what I literally meant. It was just that I found it quite disagreeable when I saw more opportunities being given to the Hindustani musicians. Of course, Carnatic musicians are also to be blamed. They simply do not make use of the opportunities that come their way, which I feel becomes a drawback in this profession. It is rather sad that they cannot promote their art nor are there any godfathers to project them.

However, with my musician-siblings from the North, it is different. As the government officials are mostly North Indians, they get the maximum preference. Nevertheless, it is upto the

Carnatic musicians to exploit the opportunities in order to excel in communicating their form of music to the world.

Sadly, both these forms of music are not perceived as being equals. At one point, people all over interpreted Indian classical music as Hindustani music alone, which was a grave misconception. This was also because the northerners had an excellent promoter in the sitar maestro Pandit Ravi Shankar, who during his frequent trips abroad, took it upon himself to encourage and promote Hindustani music.

But, today, I can proudly say that I am making positive attempts towards giving Carnatic music its rightful place in the world of Indian classical music.

Though he kept saying he was tired of controversies, the fact is that controversies never left him. His idea of music therapy or 'Sangeeta Chikitsa' was going to be the tip of another controversy. There was wide consensus across the world that music has therapeutic values, but without any confirmation based on facts or examples. Balamuralikrishna kept trying to convince people, though he probably wasn't articulate about his idea. The press had a field day. Here is one joke that was written by P.K. Doraiswamy in *Sruti*:

Melody for Malady

'Many diseases can be cured by music therapy', a well-known musician said the other day.

Here at last is a pill-less, painless panacea for all our illnesses, thought the Health Minister and decided to introduce it throughout the State in all government hospitals. After a couple of months, the Minister contacted the Director of Medical Services and asked, 'How's the scheme working?'

'Well, Sir, our experience is mixed, somewhat like a rogamalika, I mean a ragamalika,' replied the Director.

'Doesn't matter. After all, the scheme is new and we have to play it by ear,' said the Minister unable to resist the temptation to show off his capacity for musical metaphor.

'Give me some details.'

'Previously doctors used to quarrel about whether to administer penicillin or streptomycin to a patient. Now they are quarrelling about whether to play Kalyani or Kharaharapriya.'

'You mean finally it has turned out to be kalahapriya,' laughed the Minister enjoying his own joke immensely.

'That's nothing. In some cases it has ended up in our having to play Mukhari when the patient's body was being removed.'

'Well, tell me how the patients are responding to the therapy.'

'They're proving to be equally difficult, Sir. One patient was adamant. He wanted only Balamurali Todi. When we played Semmangudi Todi, the patient developed severe allergy. Immediately we had to play some pop music.'

'But why pop? I want only typically Indian music,' said the Minister. 'It makes patients temporarily deaf and partially dazed, you know,' replied the Director.

'What happened to our scheme of introducing music therapy on call on telephones?' asked the Minister.

'We did it, Sir, but you know how our telephones work. One blood pressure patient dialled for Anandabhairavi but got Ahir Bhairav and his BP shot up and he had to be rushed to the hospital.'

'What about our scheme for improving industrial relations in factories through music therapy?' asked the Minister.

'We tried it, Sir,' replied the Labour Commissioner.

'According to the latest reports, hand-to-hand fighting has broken out in many factories between workers belonging to rival unions.'

'Why?' asked the Minister in surprise.

'One workers' union wanted songs only from MGR films and the rival union insisted on songs from Sivaji films.'

'Whatever the problems, at least the music therapists do not have to pay heavy capitation fees and join a medical college,' said the Minister.

'I am not so sure, Sir. I am told that now all the music colleges have started collecting capitation fees.'

Besides this, the November 1991 issue of *Sruti* created a storm in the world of Carnatic music. The reason for that was a PhD thesis that was going to be published by Delhi University. The thesis was by Radha Venkatachalam, who was a student of T.R. Subramanyam. *Sruti* got a hold of it and published excerpts. It contained a section about musical luminaries and their contribution to art. Along with the composers of the Carnatic trinity, there were opinions on just about every famous post-trinity composer and twenty-first-century performing stalwarts. The comments on Balamuralikrishna read, 'After G.N. Balasubramaniam and Madurai Mani Iyer, Balamuralikrishna was the only vocalist whom people thronged to hear *voluntarily* . . . credit must be given for his sharpest intelligence, which is freely applied and seen in his music. His extraordinary brain can grasp any subject in music and put it into practice in a jiffy . . . Balamurali's voice is one of mysterious charm. To people used to rustic heaviness of Ariyakudi Ramanuja Iyengar's voice or the captivating manliness of G.N. Balasubramaniam's, Balamurali's voice might sound like a feeble voice of a frivolous female. But he is somehow able to work magic with that voice in which he is able to show samples of the world's best (European) bass musician and also that of a sopronist . . . He knows whom to contact when and is ever alert in the job of boosting his image higher and higher.'

To this, *Sruti*'s editor's comment: 'The question arises: is the author's contention in the case of other musicians, that compulsion was (is) used to bring listeners into the recital hall? . . . The thesis earlier complimented G.N.B. as a musician who applied his brain. Balamurali receives a similar compliment... His voice receives praise too... If a saxophonist is one who plays on the sax, is a sopronist someone who plays with the soprano? What? The thesis, regrettably is full of such solecisms . . . Apparently, brain power is not enough to "sing traditional Ragas touchingly." Balamurali, says the author, fails to project "live images of the Ragas" to which a musician can gain access only through a proper exposure to classical renditions right from childhood. Again, Balamurali, "in perfect Laya while singing light music," is seen as "shaking and uneven in Kalapramanam" in rendering classical music, especially Kalpanaswaras.'

The excerpts published in *Sruti* sent a tremor through the Carnatic world. The accusations were that these opinions were of T.R. Subramanyam's and were being passed off as his student's. However, none of that was confirmed and the controversy died down soon. In fact, T.R. Subramanyam was a great fan of Balamuralikrishna and his Pallavis. In later years, he openly praised Balamuralikrishna's music for originality and imagination.

Many Moods of Murali Gaanam

For a layman's understanding of Balamuralikrishna's music, the most important factors that stood out were his adherence to Sahityam and clear diction. His mastery over Telugu and Sanskrit aided in this. For those interested in the technical aspects of his music, there were other factors such as his sense of rhythm, his *Pada-Vinyaasam* or 'intelligent word play', and the unique aesthetics of his presentation that he developed from a very early age. There are very few known video recordings of his concerts before the 1980s, but what we do have are a number of audio recordings. Even within those, there are two varieties. The Balamuralikrishna who was famous for his single-take studio recordings was clearly a very different Balamuralikrishna from the one during a live concert.

Writing about his commercial recordings, musicologist N. Ramanathan says, 'Balamurali must have been the youngest artist at the time he started cutting discs. One notices two 78 rpm discs of HMV, listed in the Catalogues. The first disc has the song 'Tatvamerua' in raga Garudadhwani on one side and the keertana 'Needu charanamule' on the reverse. In the second one, there is Thillana (with an additional note - Tamil) in Hindolam raga and a Jayadeva ashtapadi 'Yamihe' rendered along with Lalgudi Jayaraman on the violin and Thanjavur Upendran on the mridanga.'

He further writes,

Balamurali's disc (Of Nagumomu) erased the memories of all the previous ones and pasted his version. Accompanied by Lalgudi Jayaraman and Umayalpuram Sivaraman (who were his standard accompanists in the early years), this rendering had the song in a relatively slow tempo. One surprising element is the singing of the niraval for the passage Jegamele paramatma and taking up the pallavi passage Nagumomu for the kalpanaswara passage, Balamurali makes his mark on the song by prefixing a swarakshara 'ni' to the refrain part Nagumomu, thus modifying the refrain to 'Ni nagumomu' (your smiling face). The swara passages have been intelligently organised and concluded to return to this refrain. Lalgudi's contribution too has been extremely creditable bringing back memories of the GNB-Lalgudi team, with of course a different style of music.

He looks at some of his EP and rpm records and writes,

The second EP was a sensation because it was a musico-technological feat with Balamurali singing, and playing the viola and the mridanga too. The disc contained his own varnam in Amritavarshini raga, Adamodigalada in Charukesi raga and finally his own ragamalika Amba mamava based on four ragas all ending with 'ranjani'. A lot of preparation must have gone into it for at no moment does one get a feeling that each role has been separately recorded, super-imposed and synthesised. Especially in the ragamalika, a swara passage is sung and then repeated on the viola. Just before the swara passage is about to conclude, the singer joins in with the last few syllables of the swaras, creating the feeling of spontaneity. A very imaginative and brilliant production indeed. The novelty in the varnam then was that, after the four swara passages in the charanam were rendered separately, all the four come again together without a return to the refrain in the middle.

This was the first time that a disc was released where an artiste was singing, accompanying himself on the viola and mridangam. This was an unthinkable feat in the recording world. The cover of the album shows Balamuralikrishna sitting in the middle, frozen in a singing pose, to his right side is Balamuralikrishna playing the mridangam, and to the left of singing Balamuralikrishna is another Balamuralikrishna playing the viola.

Not surprisingly, the disc was a huge hit, not just with Balamuralikrishna's fans but also with record collectors all over.

Ramanathan further writes, 'The third EP had the song Devadi deva of Mysore Vasudevachar in the raga Sunadavinodini. Among the many songs that owe their popularity to Balamurali, this certainly is one. In the 1960s and '70s this song must certainly have been in the Top-10.' This record was indeed one of the most famous ones.

In his childhood, his interactions with the scholarly Kasi Krishnacharyulu reflected in *Janaka Raga Kriti Manjari*. It is not going to be possible to go through the entire list of seventy-two compositions. A superficial study reveals his phenomenal grasp over Sanskrit and Telugu, as most of these are in Sanskrit. Then come the little nuances within the compositions. It is common for composers to inculcate their name into their compositions to leave a Mudra, or a signature of sorts, behind. But going through this book, he has used his Mudra in several smart ways.

In the seventh Kriti, in Ragam Senavati, he concludes the Kriti with 'Murali Bhaktha Rakshaka'.

In the thirteenth Kriti, set to Ragam Gayakapriya, he concludes the Kriti with

'Murali Krishnaadi Gayaka Priyakaram', putting both his Mudra and the name of the Ragam into one line.

In the fourteenth Kriti in Ragam Vakulabharanam, dedicated to Goddess Kanakadurga, he ends the Kriti with the Charanam:

Sharvaani Mahishasura Madhahaarini
Sada, Murali, Gaana Sudhamodhini,
Sadaananda Hrudaye, Sadashive
Vijayapuri Nilaye, Vakulabharane.

In the seventeenth Kriti, in Ragam Suryakantam, he cleverly uses 'Bhakta Sarasija Surya, Kantaguna/Vara Murali Gaana Madhupriya'.

In the sixty-second Kriti, in Ragam Rishabhapriya, another facet of his genius is revealed. The whole Kriti is indeed an invocation to lord Nandeeshwara. In the Charanam, he writes:

Parashiva Tandavakale, Murajarava Sammodam
Murali, Gaanamruta Pulakitha Kaayam Varadam
Sa Ri Ga Ma Pa Da Ni Saptasvara Rishabhapriyam
Karadhruta Vethram, Svethasu Gaathram Parama Pavitram.

What is interesting about this composition is that at that age, with the limited resources and whatever education he received from his Guru, he composed and confirmed the base note for the mridangam is Ri or Rishabham. Vrishabham or Rishabham is another name for Nandi, the vehicle of Lord Shiva. Decades later, several mridangam vidwans who supposedly conducted a great deal of research with scientists of leather technology and acoustical engineering declared Rishabham to be the Aadhara Sruti of the mridangam. Balamuralikrishna had cracked it long ago. But he never made a hue and cry about it. 'We need such slow thinkers also to show what a genius Guruji was. If you look at that composition, it starts with the Sarvalaghu and when we reach the Charanam "Parashiva Tandava", it reaches *Atheetham*. He loved playing with such things. What is beautiful is that I don't know if the system has made provisions and Balamuralikrishna could see them which others could not. Muthuswamy Dikshitar could see them and we find a lot of instances in his compositions. But Balamuralikrishna sir, coming from the Tyagaraja's Parampara, and integrating Dikshitar's ideas in these modern times was a feat in itself,' says Ragavan Manian. 'He would often say "Tyagaraja's Kritis are filled with Bhakti-Rasa, whereas my compositions have all the *Navarasa*,"' adds Manian, laughing.

Ragavan Manian, one of Balamuralikrishna's students, points to the composition in 'Sucharitra', the sixty-seventh Melakarta. His Kriti 'Chintayami Santhatham' is an ode to the composer Muthuswamy Dikshithar. 'I cannot imagine how a 14-15-year-old can write like this," says Manian. The Anupallavi Sahityam goes "*Apaara Raaga Layabhigyam Ramaswamy Suputhram Parama Pavitram Sucharitram*", cleverly using the wordplay of Sucharitra meaning "one with a good history". Each of these songs is a revelation and the book is a collection of priceless gems. It would be of great value to students of music if musicologists could analyse the technical aspects of each of these compositions. It would also give great insights into the mind of an original teenage composer.

In the Bhakti Ranjani era, Balamuralikrishna was increasingly exposed to several other styles, genres and forms of music, more than before. As a programmer in the light music genre, Balamuralikrishna travelled into a number of villages collecting original songs and tunes from the countryside. In addition to working with folklore scholars like Acharya Biruduraju Rama Raju, Vinjamuri Sitadevi and the Anasuya sisters, he picked up a lot of authentic Telugu folk poetry and tuned it suitably. One remembers his renderings of Nanduri Subba Rao's poetry, popular as 'Yenki Patalu', along with his colleague Vidushi Srirangam Gopalaratnam. The other side of Bhakti Ranjani contained his rendering of a number of Sanskrit Stotrams of philosopher saints like Adi Shankaracharya in extremely hummable tunes. There were also a whole host of patriotic songs like Sankarambadi Sundaraachari's 'Maa Telugu Talliki', which was the official song of the state of Andhra Pradesh.

While he was working on this, the compositions of the poet saint Tallapaka Annamacharya too came to him via Veturi Prabhakara Sastry. As mentioned earlier, several of the tunes popular now were composed by Balamuralikrishna and broadcast on Bhakti Ranjani. He worked with scholars like Rallapalli Ananthakrishna Sarma and Upanyaasa Kartas or traditional commentators like Malladi Chandrasekhara Sastry to get a better understanding of traditional treatises on music.

After the Bhakti Ranjani era, one sees Balamuralikrishna utilizing his vast knowledge of classical music in playback singing for cinema. Most of the songs that he sang were Ragam-based. It was one of his own creations, Ragam Mahati, which inspired the music director M.S. Viswanathan to compose the song 'Athisaya Ragam' for the movie *Apoorva Raagangal*, directed by K. Balachander. In an interview, Balamuralikrishna recollected how Viswanathan narrated to him the plot of the movie, which was based on 'strange relationships'. Viswanathan wanted something unique and requested Balamuralikrishna for the tune of Mahati. The song opens in the Ragam Mahati and was rendered by K.J. Yesudas.

Beyond all the usual odes to him for the music in the public domain, such as in films and radio, what is worth studying is his actual genius, which came through in his Carnatic music. It would be interesting to take a look at his compositions. There are hundreds of them, and it is a huge challenge to focus on just a few. But to find a method in the musical madness, a start would be to look at his *Varnams*. Speaking about these with his student Pappu Venugopala Rao in a televised series titled 'Murali Ravam', he mentions why he felt the need to compose new Varnams. 'All the traditional Varnams till then like Viriboni, Jalajakshi and others were of the amorous sentiment. When you open the concert itself, you don't need Shringara Bhavam. That can come in later into the concert. Once you as a performer and the audience have soaked into the mood of your music. Hence I began composing on the subjects of nature and other abstract aspects,' he said. Looking at some of the Varnams in well-known Ragams like Thodi, his composition 'Saraguna Gaavumu' is a beautiful example of how Thodi can be exposed in different facets. Thodi is a Ragam with all the seven notes, but in this version, Balamuralikrishna cleverly removes the Panchamam. In addition to this, the Charanam is filled with Swaraksharams '*Garimaganineedharinije/ritini sadaasaa . . .*', the lyric is strung in such a way that the syllables fall on the same notes in the scale.

In the *Muktayi Swara*, he sings, '*Bhaavamunanu Raagaalaapanamu Chesi Layamunu Manasunanu Nilpi Svaramunu Srutilo Nilpi . . .*' meaning elaborate on the bhaava in Raga Alaapana, instil the laya or rhythm in the mind and align the swaras in sruti, giving us a small glimpse into his own musical thinking. 'Balamurali sir's varnams sound very easy, but they are extremely complicated. Singing them is pretty challenging,' said Abhishek Raghuram. 'Two of my favourites are varnams that he used to sing in the early years. One is in Ragam Ramapriya, 'Chalamu Jesina' set to Adi Taalam. The beauty of this is in the Chittaswarams, the Nadai changes. The other Varnam that I like is 'Enta Sudhiname' in Ragam Sankarabharanam. Of course the other Varnams like "Omkara Pranava" in Shanmukhapriya, "Ae Nadamulo" in Nattai and "Amma Ananda Dhayini" in Gambeera Natta became much more popular,' he added.

Speaking about the Shanmukhapriya Varnam, Balamuralikrishna himself said in the interview with Pappu Venugopala Rao how he went about composing it: 'I always compose the Swarams first and then put the Sahityam, which is far more difficult. The composition should not sound or feel like the Sahityam has been force-fitted into the Swarams,' said Balamuralikrishna. The lyrics of the composition go: '*Omkara Pranava Naadodbhava Srutilaya Svara Sanketika Tribhuvanasakthi Murali Gaana Swaroopi*'. This whole line has to be sung at a single go and is a challenging task. 'After the Pallavi and Anupallavi, there is a Muktayi Swaram and that was the tricky part. I had already written the Swarams. *Ga Ga Ma Ma Pa Pa Da Da*. The challenge is, you can sing the Pallavi only after the Muktayi Swaram and after that you can sing the Ettugada. Which means the Sahityam of the Muktayi Swaram has to join back into the Sahityam of the Pallavi and it has to make sense according to the musical structure. So I wrote, "Pralayajalavalaya . . ." as the Sahityam.' The Sahityam means 'from the primordial waters emerged a banyan leaf, on that was lord Varada from whose Naabhi or abdomen emerged a lotus atop which was lord Brahma from whose voice was born Omkara.'

After that comes the Ettugada or Charanam which begins with 'Padaneerajamule' in Swaraaksharam. This is a small glimpse into the brilliantly mysterious ways Balamuralikrishna's mind as a Vaggeyakara worked. This Shanmukhapriya Varnam continues to be a challenge, as Abhishek mentioned, for many singers even today. Amongst the other Varnams are 'Aabaalagopaalamu' set to Amritavarshini Ragam and 'Saakarasadguna' set to Saurashtram.

One of the people who was inspired by Balamuralikrishna's Varnams was the late Vidushi Suguna Purushottaman (1941–2015), who learnt a few of his Varnams from him. 'These Varnams that your Guru created are like a big treasure for Carnatic music. In fact, it has given an impetus to many of us to think on those lines and venture into composing. He really opened new vistas with this,' Ragavan Manian remembered Suguna Purushottaman saying. 'What Guruji did was something unthinkable for all the light, glare and negativity that was focused on him always. Anybody else in that place would have thought twice about singing their own compositions. Many musicians would have worried about if they would even get another kacheri. He had no such insecurities. He would give a beautiful example and say: "If you went to a temple, you will see only the front of the deity. If you ask me, I will describe the same to you in a hundred ways. Similarly if you give me a Ragam, I will show you things which nobody else will show you." To say something like this, what kind of conviction one must have!' said Ragavan.

The other end of Balamuralikrishna's imagination comes forward in Pallavis.

In the early years, he was deeply influenced by the music of G.N. Balasubramaniam. He had accompanied him on the viola in his childhood. But GNB's musical ideas seem to have influenced his singing too. That they met quite often and discussed music is well-known. GNB's regular accompanying artistes like Palani Subramaniam Pillai and his students, Palghat Raghu, Lalgudi G. Jayaraman and others found an ease in accompanying Balamuralikrishna through the 1950s and well into the 1960s. The result of one of these many musical discussions with GNB was reflected in an early concert. It was the Carnatic vocalist Abhishek Raghuram who pointed this out to me in a conversation. The recording of it is a Ragam Taanam Pallavi in Thodi, accompanied by M.S. Gopalakrishnan on the violin. The Pallavi is 'Neeraja Dala Lochani, Nikhila Loka Janani'. If you listen to this with a keen ear, you can find how much of GNB's influence is there in it. Balamuralikrishna was obviously a great fan and follower of GNB's style of music. 'Through the late '50s and early '60s, nobody sang these Brikas with the same chastity that GNB did. He had a mix of both orthodoxy and romanticism in his singing,' said Ragavan Manian about the influence of GNB on Balamuralikrishna. 'When GN Sir passed away, things were in a terrible shape and it was Balamurali sir who was one of the people who paid Rs 50 or 100, that time a big amount, towards the funeral,' recollected Thiruvaiyaru P. Sekar.

There are hardly any recordings of the concerts Palghat Mani Iyer and Balamuralikrishna performed together. However, an old group image from a concert shows Mani Iyer flanked on either side by M.S. Gopalakrishnan and Balamuralikrishna. 'Yes, they did perform together. Not too many. I have been a witness to a few of them. But this didn't work for long because of a small incident. You know mridangam artistes generally keep a small blade with them, which they use while tuning the instrument. During one concert, Mani Iyer kept scratching the mridangam with his blade even as Balamurali was singing an elaborate Alaapana. That sound would have irritated anybody. Balamuralikrishna continued the concert without any complaint and decided never to have Mani Iyer for an accompanist again. That was probably the last occasion,' Sekar recollected. For Balamuralikrishna, it didn't matter if the artiste was a celebrated veteran, if he didn't adhere to Sabha-Maryada. After that, most of the mridangam accompaniment came from the Palani Baani. The artiste was either Palani Subramaniam himself or one of his many illustrious disciples like senior C.S. Murugabhoopathy, or Balamuralikrishna's old colleague from Vijayawada, Dandamudi Ramamohana Rao, or Trichy Sankaran in later years. Of course, there were other mridangam artistes who accompanied him through the 1960s, '70s and '80s like T.V. Gopalakrishnan, T.K. Murthy, Umayalpuram Sivaraman, Palghat Raghu, Karaikudi Mani, Vellore G. Ramabhadran, Vankayala Narasimham, Kamalakara Rao and Guruvayur Dorai. Then there was a whole generation of younger mridangam vidwans like Tiruvarur Bhaktavatsalam, Mannargudi Easwaran, Srimushnam Raja Rao, Trichur C. Narendran, Yella Venkateshwara Rao, Neyveli R. Narayanan, V.V. Ramanamurthy, K.V. Prasad, H.S. Sudhindra, Anoor Ananthakrishna Sharma, Pathri Satish Kumar, Arjun Kumar, B.C. Manjunath and many others.

In concerts in places like Karnataka, Kerala, Maharashtra and others, he was also accompanied by some local artistes. In Karnataka, there was Tumkur T.K. Bhadrachar, M.L. Veerabhadraiah, A.V. Anand and others. Among the ghatam vidwans, in addition to the iconic Vikku Vinayakaram, who accompanied him in hundreds of concerts, there were many others who accompanied him on the ghatam. In his younger days, he had Alangudi Ramachandran, Vilvadhri Iyer, Ghatam Manjunath, younger generation artistes like T.V. Vasan, Sukanya Ramgopal, V. Suresh, Ghatam S. Karthick and Giridhar Udupa. Balamuralikrishna was himself an excellent khanjira artiste. He knew the value of the instrument and encouraged a whole lot of youngsters. One of his regular accompanying artistes was G. Harishankar. He was the staff artiste of the All India Radio in Chennai. He even worked in Delhi. Anitha Kumar, an organizer of music events in Delhi, recollected a brilliant private session where Harishankar and Balamuralikrishna had an entire percussive conversation and Sawal-Jawab with both of them playing the khanjira.

There were also other morsing artistes like Ghantasala Sathya Sai and Bangalore Rajashekar who were encouraged to perform with him.

Writing about his Ragam Tanam Pallavi, musicologist N. Ramanathan detailed,

Endowed with a rich melodic conception and an incredible sense of laya, Balamurali was an ideal musician for the ragam-tanam-pallavi (RTP) suite. Apart from the ragamalika setup, sometimes using the graha bheda feature, he also used unconventional ragas and also swarakshara text. I remember a concert at the Music Academy, in which he took up the raga Hamsavinodini for RTP. The rasika sitting next to me kept patting my thigh enquiring which raga it was. I too was ignorant then, and said, 'Take it Sankarabharanam without the pa.' He shot back, 'How can there be Sankarabharanam without a pa?' I immediately answered, 'Take it Vasantha with higher ri instead of the lower one.' The neighbour left the hall. It was also a phase when Balamurali was notorious for singing unfamiliar ragas and his own compositions and his concerts were criticised as being 'by', 'of' and 'for' Balamurali. The pallavi sahitya in this case was Ni garima gani ni cheritini sadaa saama nigama modini. The problem with such texts is the prospect of doing niraval since we cannot do a melodic variation for the text reads Sa ri ga ma pa dha ni paadeda – gaanamuto tariyincheda in which the niraval has to be done for the latter part of sahitya.

Even in his early years he had cut an Extended Play [EP] disc of ragam-tanam-pallavi lasting just twelve minutes. It was an extremely compact and crisp presentation in which he had beautifully organised (not squeezing) a leisurely alapana, with opportunity for violin response (Lalgudi Jayaraman); a tanam; pallavi set in a two-kalai Adi tala, with niraval by him and Lalgudi; trikalam and tisram; a tani on the mridanga (T.V. Gopalakrishnan); kalpanaswara with korvai; swaram in ragamalika format – Todi, Mahati, Sahana and finally Sindhubhairavi sung in madhyama sruti. Only the final Sindhubhairavi has no violin response (although it is known that the violin response was recorded but had to be edited out because of constraint of time). The twelve-minute piece does create the illusion of a long and elaborate ragam-tanam-pallavi.

Balamurali's rendering of a pallavi can be mesmerising but never intimidating. He has the knack of making complex music sound like a nursery rhyme, like Shara shara samaraika dhira (Kunthalavaraali raga) and Raminchuva revarura (Suposhini raga), with breathtaking intricacies. In his interviews in the media, he has often ridiculed the early practice of conducting ragam-tanam-pallavi contests (a la Syama Sastra versus Bobbili Kesavayya) and compared them to cock fights and goat fights organised by rich landlords. One cannot agree more. But he himself betrays a kind of feudal attitude when he starts 'throwing challenge' at the rasikas to suggest the raga, tala and text and then present a pallavi impromptu.

Balamuralikrishna's Dvi-Raga Pallavis became extremely sought after. He would do several, like the combinations of Anandabhairavi-Amritavarshini, or the one in Ragam Hamsavinodhini. Being a master of wordplay, he would often do Swaraksharams. These Pallavis demanded sophistication of technical virtuosity. At one level, there were the calculations of the Taalam to adhere to, which was difficult in itself. For example, he would fit lyrics into a Sankeerna Chapu, which was challenging for his accompanying musicians. On the second level, there was the wordplay within the Sahityam where he would do Niraval with clever pauses. Sometimes you felt he was purposely giving his accompanists a challenge. Many decades later, Abhishek Raghuram took up the Pallavi in Hamsavinodini, the Sahityam of which went '*Nigama Sudha Vinodini Hamsavinodini*'. Executing it successfully was a huge task even decades later. Most of the Pallavi Sahityam that Balamuralikrishna presented sounded simple. Or rather, he made it sound simple. Some of the early Pallavis that he presented included:

- Sree Raghuvara Mamava Srutajanapalaka – Kambhoji Ragam – Sankeerna Jhampa Taalam;
- Anandamrutavarshini Jananee Pahimam Apara Karunakari Sachidanandabhairavi – Ragamalika, consisting of the Ragams

   Amrutavarshini and Anandabhairavi – Tisra Jhampa (Sankeerna
   Gati);
-   Mamava Sankara Umadhava – Begada Ragam – Adi Taalam;
-   Paramapavani Pahimam Varade Haimavati Lalite – Hemavati Ragam
    – Lalita taalam (rare one). In this Sahitya itself, the names of the raga
    and tala have been incorporated;
-   Mohanangi Kalyani Pahi Mam – Ragamalika. Consisting of the
    Ragams Mohanam, Kalyani and Anandabhairavi;
-   Amba Kalyani Sambhu Rani – Kalyani Ragam – Tisra Jhampa Taalam
-   Neeraja Dala Lochani, Nikhila Loka Janani – Shanmukhapriya
    Ragam - Tisra Jhampa Taalam

'I knew I reached a third stage of learning from him, when he would
ask me what I wanted to learn, as opposed to prescribing a song for the
day or for the class. I would tell him, I wanted to learn some Pallavi. To
which he would reply "You cannot teach Pallavis. They have to come on
their own and you have to perform them at that moment,"' recollected
Ragavan Manian. The fact that Pallavis had to be impromptu and suitably
delivered, irrespective of who was accompanying him, was another side
to Balamuralikrishna's silent mathematical genius. In fact, rarely did he
beat the Taalam on his thigh like Carnatic vocalists normally do. The
calculations happened in the mind and he would deliver them with his
signature grin. 'There is this Pallavi in Ragam Kalyani that he would sing.
"Sangeeta Layagnanamu", which was set to the Taalam that he devised. It
was only later that he told me that this was actually a whole Kriti that he
composed,' added Ragavan.

   Balamuralikrishna's sense of Sahityam was rooted in his knowledge of
Sanskrit, Telugu and the art of writing poetry. Having spent his childhood
in the company of great poets, compositions came to him with ease.
Sometimes the Sahityam outshone the Ragam, and other times it was the
other way around. There are compositions where the Sahityam and the
Ragam are equally brilliant. But there are a few where the Sahityam does
feel forced.

Some Thoughts on New Ragams

We have seen a bit of the 'raga controversy' earlier. What exactly were these new Ragams, and why they bothered the musicians requires a detailed study. Balamuralikrishna created or invented Ragams and named them Lavangi, Mahati, Manorama, Mohanangi, Pratimadhyamavati, Rohini, Sarvasree, Sumukham, Sushama and Vallabhi, amongst others. The stories behind the creation of each of these Ragams is fascinating. But before we go there, we need to deal with the accusation that some of these Ragams already existed in different music treatises and he had merely renamed them. Looking into the history of Carnatic music, it is not uncommon to find a Ragam having multiple names. For example, the Muthuswamy Dikshitar tradition has a number of Ragams which have names different from the way they are named in the other Paramparas. Though some of the criticism of Balamuralikrishna might have been technically valid, his own reasoning, pointing towards the nuances, had far more conviction. Aaron Copland (1900–90), the Pulitzer Prize-winning composer, in his seminal collection of essays titled *Music and Imagination*, writes on the nature of creativity:

> It is very difficult to describe the creative experience in such a way that it would cover all cases. One of the essentials is the variety with which one approaches any kind of artistic creation. It doesn't start in any one particular way and it is not always easy to say what gets you going. In music, it's more likely to be an emotion rather than a specific idea or thought that leads to a composition. It's comparable to a person who starts to sing to himself, though he is not even aware he's begun to sing. Then, if he suddenly begins to become aware that he's singing something with a sad sound to it, he wonders what he's feeling so sad about . . . Music is a language of the emotions. You can practice it either on a very plain and elementary basis, or you can practice it on a highly complex one . . . the reason for the compulsion to renewed creativity, it seems to me, is that each added work brings with it an element of self-discovery, I must create in order to know myself, and since self-knowledge is a never-ending search, each new

work is only part-answer to the question 'who am I?' and brings with it the need to go on to other and different part-answers.

In his note written to The Music Academy, Balamuralikrishna argues how a Ragam in a book remains a lifeless scale of notes. It only gets a lease of life when a musician performs it with his unique temperament. In several interviews, he mentioned how Mahati was the first Ragam he created when he was a child. He was inspired by the instrument which had four strings and was played around by sage Narada, was the other thing he said. The eminent scholar Kudavayil Balasaubramanian, points to a sculpture of Narada holding the 'Mahati Veena' in the ancient Brihadeeswara temple at Thanjvaur in his seminal work 'Rajarajecharam'. According to the Shastras, that instrument is called 'Mahati Veena'. So based on the four strings, he designed a Ragam which has only four notes, both in the Aarohanam (ascent) and Avarohanam (descent). It is a Janyaraga of the Harikambhoji Melakarta. The notes are Shadjam, Antara Gandharam, Panchamam and Kaisiki Nishadam. According to several music treatises, a Ragam must have at least five notes to fulfil its aesthetic requirement. Balamuralikrishna challenged this with Mahati. 'What is wrong with Mahati? It is an extraordinary idea and works fantastically. If you perform it, you realise the possibilities of aesthetics that are present in it,' said mridangam vidwan and long-time accompanist T.V. Gopalakrishnan.

Then came another creation which he called 'Lavangi'. It is derived from Kanakangi, the first Melakarta Ragam. It has Shuddha Rishabham, Shuddha Madhyamam and Shuddha Dhaivatham. This Ragam also has only four notes. His own composition 'Omkaraakarini' became one of his favourites in his concerts with Rasikas constantly demanding him to sing it.

Another four-note Ragam that he created, which he called 'Sumukham', was born out of the sixty-ninth Melakarta Ragam Dhaatuvardhani. This Ragam contains Shadjam, Shatsruti Rishabham, Prati Madhyamam and Kakali Nishadham. His composition 'Mahaniya Namassulive' set to Rupaka Taalam, is in praise of lord Ganesha. In fact, he even performed it for All India Radio, New Delhi, way back on 26 June 1962. He was accompanied by Lalgudi Jayaraman on the violin, T.K. Murthy on the mridangam and Alangudi Ramachandran on the ghatam.

Balamuralikrishna was greatly criticized and attacked for this. 'They said it was not possible to create a Ragam with four notes. But I proved them wrong. They could not give a suitable reply, so they attacked me. This encouraged me to create another Ragam, this time using only three notes. If you can find fault with the musical composition, you may challenge me,' said Balamuralikrishna in response to the criticism. The three-note Ragams that he created was 'Sarvasree', born out of Kanakangi—the first Melakarta. The Ragam contains Shadjam, Shuddha Madhyamam and Panchamam. While in theory this sounds impossible, listening to the composition 'Umasutam' you realize how excellent the execution by Balamuralikrishna was.

In the other Ragam 'Omkari', he uses Shadjam, Prati Madhyamam and Panchamam. This scale has been mentioned in older treatises, but it wasn't until Balamuralikrishna performed it that you could create emotional content out of singing just three notes.

His other Ragams include 'Vallabhi', born out of Dheera Sankarabharanam—the twenty-ninth Melakarta Ragam. This has both Madhyamams and both Nishadhams. The Aarohanam is normal, while the Avarohanam contains a Vakra Prayogam. The scale has Chatusruti Rishabham, Antara Gandharam, Shuddha Madhyamam, Chatusruti Dhaivatham and Kakali Nishadham with Shadjamam and Panchamam in the Aarohanam. The Avarohanam is the tricky part where he puts Kakali Nishadham followed by Kaisiki Nishadham, Prati Madhyamam followed by Shuddha Madhyamam. Balamuralikrishna took the composition of saint Tulasidas and set it to this Ragam. The lines go, '*Gopala Gokula Vallabhi Priya Gopa Gosuta Vallabham*'. This was yet another masterstroke. If you listen to the recording, it feels like Tulasidas himself would have composed and sung it, leaving a Ragamudra behind. This song was extremely popular in many of his All India Radio concert recordings. Many decades later it regained popularity with young Carnatic vocalist Sandeep Narayanan singing it in concerts and recording it for Madrasana.

The story goes that one evening, on the day of the lunar eclipse, he was on his terrace. It is believed that the star Rohini is dear to the Moon god. Inspired by that thought, he created a Ragam calling it 'Rohini'. It is born out of the seventeenth Melakarta Ragam—Suryakantam. The scale has Shadjam, Shuddha Rishabham, Antara Gandharam, Shuddha Madhyamam, Prati Madhyamam, Chatusruti Dhaivatham and Kakali Nishadham. Balamuralikrishna's own composition 'Mamava Gana Lola' became very popular, both in concerts and in radio recitals. He even gave a lecture-demonstration at the Bangalore Gayana Samaj in 1977, describing this Ragam and its notes. In fact, the late Thanjavur S. Kalyanaraman, a disciple of GNB, was one of the early musicians to rekindle an interest in Ragams which had both the Madhyamams sans a Panchamam. He had even given lectures at The Music Academy in his time and was heavily criticised for the same. However, the Ragam stays and is there for posterity.

Another Ragam that he created out of the twentieth Melakarta Ragam Natabhairavi is named 'Sushama'. He employs Shadjam, Chatusruti Rishabham, Shuddha Madhyamam and Shuddha Dhaivatham. His composition 'Ayya Guruvarya' is an ode to his beloved Guru Pantulu. When Balamuralikrishna was fifty years old, he sang it. The Sahityam goes 'Ayya Guruvarya Neeyanati Tho Paaduchuntimayya' and the Charanam goes 'Nee Mrudupallava Vacho Vilasamu Pallaviga Nee Anubandhamu Anupallaviga, Nee Charnamule Charanamuga, Neeyakrutiye Maakrutiga…' In fact, when Balamuralikrishna turned fifty, he gave a concert where he added another impromptu Charanam which reads 'Padulaidainadi Naa Vayasu Padipadilaina Naa Vayasu/ Padilamuga Neekai Naamanasu Padamulu Paadunu Pongunu Sogasu'. 'Padi' in Telugu means ten. He used this word to construct a whole new Charanam meaning 'Oh my beloved Guru, I seek your blessings in this fiftieth (ten times five) year, I pray that I will continue thinking about you and singing with gratitude even in my 100th (ten times ten) year'.

Ragam 'Manorama' was created out of the fifty-first Melakarta Kamavardhini. Balamuralikrishna utilised both the Madhyamams in this. The other notes were Shadjam Shuddha Rishabham, Antara Gandharam, Panchamam, Shuddha Dhaivatham and Kakali Nishadham. His own composition 'Nava Mohana Murari' sounds very close to a few Ragams in the Basant and Bahaar of Hindustani Ragams.

Ragam 'Mohanangi' is very close to Mohanam with the use of Chatusruti Rishabham and Shuddha Dhaivatham in the Aarohanam. In fact, when he sang this for the first time with M.S. Gopalakrishnan accompanying him on the violin, he began the Aalapana and as he gently glided over the notes, he abruptly stopped and made an announcement, saying: 'Excuse me for singing a rare Ragam', and continued the Alaapana as M.S.G. trailed along, loyally standing up to the occasion. Then he announced the name of the Ragam is Mohanangi and continued with the Kriti 'Ni Namamu Na Jeevamu Sudha Madhuramu'. Mohnangi is the Janyaraga of the thirty-fourth Melakarta Vagadishwari.

Another Ragam that came about was what he called 'Pratimadhyamavati'. There have been several theories and criticisms around this. The scale has the fifty-eighth Melakarta Hemavati in the Aarohanam and the twenty-second Melakarta Karaharapriya in the Avarohanam. The notes in the Aarohanam are Shadjam, Chatusruti Rishabham, Prati Madhyamam, Panchamam and Kaisiki Nishadham. The notes in the Avarohanam are Shadjam, Kaisiki Nishadham, Panchamam, Shuddha Madhyamam and Chatusruti Rishabham. The Ragam does away with the Gandharam and Dhaivatham notes. There were several stories of how Balamuralikrishna once began singing Madhyamavati and got carried away and added an extra note, a Prati Madhyamam and continued singing, giving birth to this new Ragam.

In addition to these Ragams which became popular, there were several others which he composed in later years on the spot or to commemorate an occasion. He composed a Ragam in honour of the veena maestro V. Doraiswamy Iyengar and called it 'Dorai'. On the 125th birth anniversary celebrations of Mahatma Gandhi, he created another Ragam and called it 'Mohana Gandhi'. The scale of this Ragam is derived from the thirty-sixth Melakarta Ragam Chalanatta. For that occasion Narayan Agarwal had penned a Bhajan 'Satya Sanatana'.

In the first week of December, at a seminar of national integration that was inaugurated by the then Prime Minister P.V. Narasimha Rao at the Ravindra Bharati, he created a new Ragam in his honour and called it 'Nrusimhabharanam' and performed it for him.

The idea of creating Ragams did not begin with Balamuralikrishna, for all the criticism heaped on him. Prior to him, several composers had created new Ragams. Harikesanallur Muthaiah Bhagavatar created Niroshta, Pasupatipriya, Hamsanandi, Karnaranjini and Vijayasaraswati;

Patnam Subramanya Iyer created Kadanakuthuhalam; Lalgudi Gopala Iyer created Uthari; GNB created Amruta Behag and Chaaya Ranjani; Lalgudi G. Jayaraman invented a Ragam that he named Jayadeep, and so on. The same musicians who readily performed all these Ragams, though they were all new, had criticized Balamuralikrishna. Balamuralikrishna was musically misunderstood and perhaps ahead of his times in his musical thinking.

The beauty of Balamuralikrishna's compositions lay in his poetry. He had a different understanding of Sahityam and how it should be expressed in his Sangeetam. Anandavardhana in his famous treatise, the *Dhvanyaloka*, writes:

प्रतीयमानं पुनरन्यदेव वस्त्वस्ति वाणीषु महाकवीनाम् ।
यत्तत्प्रसिद्धावयवातिरिक्तं विभाति लावण्यमिवांगनासु ॥

'The words of great poets are never explicit. Never following conventions. They speak in metaphors. It is like the idea of beauty in a woman. Underneath the striking externality, lies the subtle and suggestive.'

It was this intrinsic quality of suggestiveness that triumphed in the compositions of Balamuralikrishna. Each line and word could mean multiple things in different contexts. Within those words was wordplay with musical notes when he tired of Swaraksharams. A sound knowledge of Sanskrit and Telugu helped his cause.

Balamuralikrishna also composed a lot of Mangalams. Mangalams are usually sung at the end of a concert, to signify the conclusion. The most popular Mangalam is Tyagaraja's 'Nee Nama Roopamulaku' in Ragam Saurashtram, from his opera *Prahalada Bhakti Vijayam*. Balamuralikrishna made popular the Managalam of Bhadrachala Ramadasu, which goes 'Ramachandraaya Janakarajaja Manoharaaya Mamakaabhishtadaya Mahitha Mangalam'. There are hardly any Mangalams dedicated to lord Ganesha, as it is assumed that one only prays to him in the beginning. But going by the ancient Shastras, which prescribe 'Mangaladheen, Mangalamadhyani and Mangalantaani', where Mangalams are offered in the beginning, middle and end, Balamuralikrishna composed a Mangalam in honour of lord Ganesha in Ragam Surati. 'Heera Ganapatiki Haarati' is an unusual Mangalam. In addition to these three, he composed a Mangalam in honour of his beloved Guru Parupalli Ramakrishnaiah Pantulu, which went '*Saamagaana Saarvabhouma Sangeeta Jaladisoma Ramakrishnanama Neeku Neerajanam*'. The Mangalam describes all the qualities of his Guru Pantulu.

He composed a Mangalam in honour of Raghavendraswamy, the saint of Mantralayam. '*Mangalam Gururaja Mangalam Surapuja Mangalamu Shri Raghavendra*', the lyrics are about the greatness of the saint. Then he composed a verse in praise of Shyama Sastry, one of the Carnatic Trinity, the lines of which go: '*Brahamateja Prabhasaya Brahma Jnana Svaroopine, Devee Dhyana Nimagnaya Syamakrishnaya Mangalam,*' extolling the divine virtues of the composer. Then he composed a Mangalam in praise of the lord of the seven hills that went '*Venkatesaya Sankataagha Mochanaaya Vara Sasaanka Koti Sundaraaya Subhramangalam.*' This is set to Ragam Navroj. He composed another Mangalam to lord Shiva that went, '*Tripura Dharpa Bhanjanaaya Trailokya Poojitaaya Tuhinagirisuta Varaaya Sarvamangalam.*' After Shiva, Shakti couldn't be left behind, so he composed a Mangalam in praise of the divine goddess set to Ragam Madhyamavati. That went 'Mangala Giritanaye'. Who would have thought these many Mangalams were possible? Until Balamuralikrishna made the Ramadasu Mangalam popular, it was totally unknown within the Carnatic concert scene. Just like many of the Ramadasu compositions, this Mangalam too gained a life of its own.

In his childhood, Balamuralikrishna had veena as an accompanying instrument performed by Khambampati Akkaji Rao. If you look at his violin accompanists over the years, you'll find almost every possible violinist worth his salt accompanied him in his career. First, there were his childhood colleagues Annavarapu Ramaswamy and Nookala Chinna Satyanarayana. In the 1950s, there were Kumbakonam Rajamanickam Pillai, K.C. Tyagarajan, Palakkadu C.R. Mani Iyer, Mayavaram Govindaraja Pillai, Lalgudi G. Jayaraman, T.N. Krishnan, M. Chandrasekharan, V.V. Subramanyam, Kunnakudi Vaidyanathan and women artistes such as Dwaram Managathayaru, T. Rukmini and in later years Kanyakumari and M.S.G. Narmada. In fact, Rajamanickam Pillai was such a fan of Balamuralikrishna that he attended his concerts regularly. On one occasion, he heard his Thillana and requested an encore; Balamuralikrishna obliged. Breaking the protocol of a kacheri, he sang the Thillana all over again. This incident was news for many days in the Carnatic fraternity. He wasn't too stuck up about who his accompanying violinists were. Eventually, M.S. Gopalakrishnan and he made a brilliant pair. MSG, as he was fondly called, had a great sense of Hindustani music as well. His flexibility with the violin was far different from those of the other accompanists. Among the younger generation, some of the earliest violinists who played with him were L. Subramaniam and his brother L. Shankar, and the Mysore Brothers, Vidwan Nagaraj and Vidwan Manjunath.

There were also several others like Vitthal Ramamurthy, Bangalore H.K. Venkatram, H.K. Narasimha Murthy, R.R. Keshava Murthy and Sikkil Baskaran. There was a time when Mysore Nagaraj's playing technique and music was greatly influenced by M.S.G.'s. This is probably one reason the Mysore Brothers were among Balamuralikrishna's favourite violin accompanists. In Andhra, other than the seniors, he also had several others like Dwaram Bhavanarayana Rao, Hari Achutarama Sastry, Akella Mallikarjuna Sarma, Ivaturi Vijayeswara Rao, Peri Subba Rao and his son Peri Srirama Murthy, P. Purnachander and a few others. In addition to the regular violin, he has also had harmonium as an accompanying instrument. Once in a concert at Bangalore, Lalgudi was billed but was unable to come due to ill-health. The organizers struggled to find another violinist, because very few had the musical instincts to accompany Balamuralikrishna. At that time, the harmonium Vidwan Arunachalappa volunteered and the concert was a huge success. In Delhi, he also had the Hindustani harmonium artiste Mahmood Dholpuri, among others.

In an interview with me, Carnatic vocalist Abhishek Raghuram played a song from YouTube. If you listen to it, you would be shocked that a classical genius of the stature of Balamuralikrishna would indulge in such an act. The song was from a movie titled *Navarathinam* (1977), with music direction given by the violin maestro Kunnakudi Vaidyanathan. The song is titled 'High on the Hills' and is a duet with the singer Vani Jayaram. The song is an amusing remix of the famous 'The Lonely Goatherd' from *The Sound of Music* (1965). Vani Jayaram begins singing 'High on a hill was a lonely goatherd Lay ee odl lay ee odl lay hee hoo' with a chorus, and Balamuralikrishna joins in with Carnatic swarams in between before launching into a Carnatic composition. The entire song is an amusing medley. And one would certainly not think he would sing such stuff. But he did! 'If he wouldn't, who else would?,' summed up Abhishek to me. This too was a facet of Murali Gaanam. There was no genre of music he didn't enjoy singing if he wanted to indulge himself.

The IFAS in Madras conferred the title of 'Sangeetha Kala Sikamani' at the inauguration of its fifty-ninth music festival in December 1991. The award was conferred on him by S. Viswanathan, the chairman of Enfield India Ltd. At the function D.K. Pattammal and Rajam Iyer, two veteran Carnatic musicians, praised the versatility of Balamuralikrishna.

This was followed on 18 April 1992 by the Swati Tirunal Sangita Sabha in Tirvandrum honouring Balamuralikrishna with the title of 'Gayaka Ratnam'. In September, Sri Thyagaraja Swami Trust and the festival committee at Tirupati conferred the title of 'Sapthagiri Sangeeta Vidwan Mani' to Balamuralikrishna. On 23 November, he was honoured with the 'Haridasa Prasasthi Award' in Mysore.

It is a myth that Balamuralikrishna's public controversies with musicians was because of some kind of enmity amongst them. Rumours of musicians not liking each other are common in the classical music world, sometimes due to jealousy and insecurity, and at other times due to random gossip created by a third party. However in the case of Balamuralikrishna, things were extremely different. The Carnatic music world had acknowledged him as a child prodigy long ago. Musicologists like Prof. Sambamurthy and T.S. Parthasarathy had hailed his genius in the past. Veterans like Chembai Vaidhyanatha Bhagavatar, Ariyakudi Ramanuja Iyengar and Chittoor Subramania Pillai had attested to Balamuralikrishna's genius. His seniors like M.S. Subbulakshmi and the iconic Bharatanatyam diva Thanjavur Balasaraswati openly praised him. Subbulakshmi and Sadasivam were regulars at Balamuralikrishna's family functions. So were other musicians like D.K. Pattammal and her husband Easwaran, Palghat K.V. Narayanaswamy, M.L. Vasanthakumari, veena vidwans like K.P. Sivanandam, K.S. Narayanaswami, Veena Doraiswamy Iyengar, flute Vidwan N. Ramani and many others with whom he shared a wonderful camaraderie. Telugu musicians like the veteran violinist Dwaram Venkataswamy Naidu, the scholarly Rallapalli Ananthakrishna Sarma, Sripada Pinakapani, Balamuralikrishna's own contemporaries like Veena Chitti Babu, Nedunuri Krishnamurthi and several others acknowledged his genius time and again. Even his arguments with Semmangudi Srinivasa Iyer were limited to a couple of issues at one point of time. Semmangudi was well aware of him from the time of his Guru Pantulu who was a part of The Music Academy committee. In fact, Semmangudi even worked with Balamuralikrishna in the All India Radio days while recording Maharaja Swati Tirunal's 'Ajamilopakhyanam'. When they patched up, Balamuralikrishna announced him as the 'Sangeeta Paramacharya' and Semmangudi equally acknowledged him as 'Maha Medhavi'.

The same was true of the violinist Lalgudi G. Jayaraman. It was rumoured that the two never got along. In fact, for Jayaraman's eightieth birthday celebrations, Balamuralikrishna was one of the chief guests. 'He is a very capable singer, too. Good he did not take up vocal music, or musicians like me would have had a difficult time,' said Balamuralikrishna, speaking on that occasion. Balamuralikrishna never held a long grudge with any musicians. The arguments or disagreements might have been loud and pronounced, but he was quick to put them behind him and move ahead.

In addition to classical musicians, there were film personalities. Directors like B.N. Reddy and A.V. Meiyappa Chetti, actors like M.G. Ramachandran, Gemini Ganesan, Dr Rajkumar of Karnataka, and a large host of Telugu stalwarts were great friends and fans. Playback singers, from Chittoor V. Nagaiah and Ghantasala to contemporaries like P.B. Sreenivos, P. Susheela, S. Janaki and younger generation artistes like K.J. Yesudas, S.P. Balasubramaniam, Vedavathi Prabhakar, Vani Jayaram and others, sought inspiration from him. Among the music directors those he worked with, from veterans like Saluri Rajeshwar Rao, and K.S. Mahadevan, M.S. Viswanathan and later Ilaiyaraja, found a brilliant artistic collaborator in him. The music they created together remains historic and evergreen. So whatever rumours were circulated about artistes hating each other certainly weren't true in the case of Balamuralikrishna.

If the Carnatic and film fraternity were on one side, on the other side was the large Hindustani music fraternity that took a great liking to him and his music. He was the only Carnatic vocalist who performed jugalbandis with a host of Hindustani stalwarts like Pt Bhimsen Joshi, Pt Jasraj, Vidushi Kishori Amonkar, Pt Hariprasad Chaurasia, Ustad Amjad Ali Khan, Pt Ajoy Chakrabarty, Ronu Majumdar, and even ghazal singers like Penaz Masani and Pankaj Udhas.

'It is such a joy to know a person with a combination of great Panditya, humility and immense creative genius,' said Pt Ravishankar. Both these artistes had been friends for many decades.

'He is a rare combination of great inborn gift from the almighty. He has tremendous knowledge of not only Carnatic music but various traditions of music in India and also has an uncanny sense of the intricacies of rhythm,' said santoor maestro Pt Shivkumar Sharma. A number of his contemporaries were drawn to him only because of his music.

Building Musical Bridges with Jugalbandis

The concept of jugalbandis is not an ancient one within the classical music tradition. 'Yugala Gaanam' or two singers performing together was popular in all the three genres of Hindustani, Carnatic and Dhrupad. The word 'Jugalbandi' itself is a later invention. The coming together of Hindustani and Carnatic artistes to explore a particular Ragam or make music together is fairly recent. In the initial years it was looked upon as an exercise to build bridges between the artiste communities of the South and North Indian systems. Eminent writer Sheila Dhar in her book *Raga 'n' Josh*, wrote, 'listeners steeped in Hindustani music cannot relate to Carnatic music. To them, Carnatic music sounds like a staccato gunfire volley. The same applies to Carnatic listeners, who find Hindustani music too free-form and slow. It is like swimming in dark muddy waters. The gradual build-up of a Hindustani raga makes us want to snap, "Get on with it already."'

Some of the initial jugalbandis that happened might have been at the early gathering of musicians at various musical conferences. Ustad Bismillah Khan (1916–2006), in an interview, referred to his meeting with Musiri Surbamania Iyer and discussing Ragam Kalyani. Similarly, there are stories of Ustad Bade Ghulam Ali Khan's (1902–68) visit to the city of Madras and his friendship with GNB and their famed picnic to Mahabalipuram along with veena artiste S. Balachander. It is exciting to think they might have jammed over their respective forms of music.

However, performing both the genres together in public was unheard of then. In 1986, on the eve of Republic day, Pt Bhimsen Joshi and Balamuralikrishna performed together for the first time. This was yet a historic moment. The concert happened at Shanmukhananda Hall in Bombay. It was aired on TV and audiences were left wanting for more. This was fulfilled on the eve of Independence Day the same year. This time the venue of the musical feast was the iconic Chowdiah Memorial Hall in Bangalore. They presented Kalyani, Hindolam, Darbari Kaanada, Gamanashrama, and Sindhubhairavi.

The then governor of Maharashtra, Chidambaram Subramaniam (1910–2000), later known as one of the pioneers who ushered in the Indian Green Revolution, was a great connoisseur of Carnatic music. He was awarded India's highest civilian award, the Bharat Ratna, later. He was also an ardent fan of Balamuralikrishna. He organized this grand concert in December 1991 at Shivaji Park in Bombay. The show was compèred by the film actors Ashok Kumar and Jaya Bachchan. Televised on Doordarshan, it was a roaring success with music lovers across both the genres.

But this was not the first time these two legends were coming together. They had been friends since the early 1960s, since they heard each other performing at PS High School for the Music Academy, Madras, during the December music festival. Later they came together recording a song, a Purandaradasa Kriti, for the Kannada movie *Sandhya Raga*, based on a novel by 'AaNaKru'. Bhimsen was forty-four years old and Balamuralikrishna was thirty-six when they recorded this. It continues to be a hit with Kannada cinema lovers.

However, writing about the series, Bhimsen's biographer and eminent music critic Mohan Nadkarni wrote, 'But his teaming up with the eminent Carnatic vocalist, Balamurali Krishna, and the celebrated painter, M.F. Husain, in two separate extravaganzas, brought him more brickbats than bouquets. His jugalbandi with Krishna was a state-sponsored show, and it formed part of a series of similar duets partnered by noted exponents of the two sister sangeet paramparas. Here, too, as in the Doordarshan's show, the object of staging such a presentation was to promote the much-vaunted theme of national integration. In the eyes of the serious and ardent fan, however, the jugalbandi was a purely commercial gimmick.'

This might have been true. But it was certainly a great exercise in getting Rasikas interested in both genres of music by bringing these two titans together. Writer Hema Iyer Ramani from Chennai who responded to one of these jugalbandis wrote:

Much before jugalbandis came of age, here he was in a beautiful space sharing it with yet another monarch—Bhimsen Joshi. It was symbolic of two mighty rivers each rushing and gushing along its own course and then standing to gaze in wonderment of the grandeur of the other—teasing, dialoguing, conversing, exploring, until they together created the mighty waterfall in their sangamam. It was the first time I heard a jugalbandi of this kind, where each artiste had tremendous respect not only for the other artiste, but more importantly for the music—the innocence, the eagerness, the enthusiasm, the joy was infectious and there was no stopping them when there was the unleashing of the waters of the two distinct streams. It then seemed to me, the dam had been knocked to allow the free flow of one water into another—to understand that water has no form and that it can only take the shape of the container that it is poured into. It is a truth everyone is aware of, but to find practitioners of it is a rarity. To me the Bhimsen–Balamurali jugalbandi shall always be reminiscent of the mighty bond between Bhima and Murali of the Mahabharat where these two giants created their own epic in their merging—to actually unveil the grand reservoir they had created.

If the early years of the jugalbandi were about respect, generosity and sharing of space, the jugalbandis in the later years carried an extra ingredient: the deep affection and love that they shared. The way they treat the kriti 'Sangeetame vara sukha daayi' is a classic example of how the bond between them undergoes evolution, and hence, the concert too, which took place after nearly a decade. In the earlier concert, when Balamurali and Bhimsen sing the kritis—each sings a line, they delineate the swaras and Ragams taking care to give each other the same amount of time, respect for each other's art and the artiste being the key factor. It is touching to see Balamurali lift Joshi's hand and touch his eyes and Bhimsen in turn acknowledge the respect with the same admiration. But, in the succeeding years, when personal friendship between the two giants of music grew, their musical bond too became deeper and stronger. And so, when we listen to them rendering the same kriti (Sangeetame vara sukha daayi), we begin to see the subtle changes—the respect for the art and the person is the same, but when the affection is evident, this time, there are no boundaries drawn and there is a free flow of music that is unbridled, wild, pure and ecstatic. That is akin to witnessing the pristine glory of nature without the interference of man. The comfort level between the artistes is so good that their music comes in a single continuous flow. There is no pressure, no boundaries, no restrictions—there is only admiration and that is the phase when one singer becomes the rasika when he stops to listen to the concert of the other. It is a concert that is devoid of rivalry and one-upmanship! And, this time too, when the concert ends, Balamurali lifts the hand of Bhimsen respectfully and affectionately, a gesture that is once again reciprocated by Bhimsen!

This Jugalbandi became a huge hit, and they performed across the country at various occasions. From the birthday celebrations of Ganapati Sachidananda Swami in Mysore to the Ravindra Bharati in Hyderabad. Every time the duo sang, it was a different experience. In fact, the only jugalbandi Pt Bhimsen Ji ever performed was with Balamuralikrishna.

After that came another jugalbandi with Pt Jasraj, the scion of the Mewati Gharana. If you listen to the old recording, in one of the tracks Pt Jasraj begins 'Shaam Kunwar More Ghar Aye' in Drut. A little later, Balamuralikrishna starts 'Neela Mohana Bala Rara' set to Hamsanandi. You can listen to Pt Jasraj being drawn to the Hamsanandi until he is completely consumed by it. The bigger feature was Balamuralikrishna getting Pt Jasraj to sing Tyagaraja's famous composition 'Nadatanum Anisham' in Ragam Chittaranjani. The artistes shared a wonderful friendship and camaraderie. Balamuralikrishna was a special guest at Pt Jasraj's sixtieth birthday celebrations in Pune, and years later, a backstage video from the Sawai Gandharva festival in Pune shows Pt Jasraj rushing to hug Balamuralikrishna, telling everyone that if there was any voice in Carnatic music after Tyagaraja, it was Balamuralikrishna's. Though it sounds like a grand declaration, one can see the admiration Pt Jasraj has for him in the video.

This was only the beginning. The next big musical association was with the famous Hindustani vocalist of the Jaipur–Atrauli Gharana Vidushi Kishori Amonkar. This was yet another beautiful lifelong friendship of two great musical minds. Everyone in the world of Hindustani music kept a respectful distance from Kishori Amonkar. A number of rumours and anecdotes floated that she was a moody and eccentric artiste who tolerated no nonsense. But when it came to Balamuralikrishna, it was completely different. There was a warmth and camaraderie of two friends, both were considered to be rebels and misfits who disobeyed existing structures within the classical music world. When they met, it was like the meeting of two long-lost friends. The jugalbandi by itself is a fascinating recording to listen to. In fact there are several versions of it. The first time it happened, it was a different experience. In one of his later interviews, Balamuralikrishna mentions how Kishori was an extremely devoted person. One was the devotion towards her gods and Gurus and the second was to music. And that is how their wavelength matched. Balamuralikrishna also took the liberty to tell Kishori Amonkar that all the music she'd learnt and sung till then was incomplete because she did not know or sing Tyagaraja. This gave her sleepless nights. When they finally met again, he taught her Tyagaraja's famous Kriti 'Nadatanum Anisham Shankaram' on the condition that she would not only learn it but perform it. She was hesitant at first. In their next jugabandi, he got her to perform it. It was around the same time that Balamuralikrishna had completed recording the Ashtapadis of Jayadeva's *Gita Govindam*. He not only taught her a few Ashtapadis, but they performed them together in one of their jugalbandis.

Listening to the recording of 'Nadatanum Anisham' one is amazed and struck with a sense of awe, just thinking of what Balamuralikrishna persuaded Kishori to do. The recording of 'Nadatanum Anisham' begins with him slowly humming the tune before opening out to the Sahityam. One can hear the hesitant Kishori joining in. At this point, you should know that Kishori is alien to both the Ragam and the Sahityam, let alone understand the depth of philosophy embedded in it by the composer Saint Tyagaraja. However, as the song proceeds, she slowly but gently opens up and follows Balamuralikrishna as if he were holding her hands and walking her through the maze. As they reach 'Sadyojataadi' and 'Sa Ri Ga Ma Pa Da Ni', you can see Kishori is more confident and has opened up as she treads gently over the octave. You can find her comfort levels increasing till she finally reaches 'Vimala Hrudaya Tyagaraja Paalam' along with Balamuralikrishna with a complete sense of soulful achievement. It is in her voice that you find this deep sense of spiritual involvement with the song. Kishori Amonkar became a staunch devotee of Saint Tyagaraja. In the Ashtapadis that they performed together, you can find a playful camaraderie between two friends. Kishori starts with 'Yahi Madhava, Yahi Keshava' taking on the role of Radha as a Khandita Nayika as portrayed by Jayadeva. In response is Balamuralikrishna's 'Priye Charusheele', with Krishna trying to convince Radha in Jayadeva's portrayal. Towards the end, the singers join and complete the Ashtapadi with a sense of lovely reunion among the protagonists of *Gita Govindam*. Kishori Amonkar would later advise her students to listen to Balamuralikrishna's music if they wanted to develop their voice and sense of aesthetics.

Balamuralikrishna's jugalbandis were not limited to vocal music. Among his jugalbandis with instrumentalists are the ones with Hindustani flute players like Pt Hariprasad Chaurasiya and Ronu Majumdar, sarangi players like Pt Ramnarayan, sarod players like Ustad Amjad Ali Khan, younger generation Hindustani vocalists like Pt Ajoy Chakrabarty and his daughter Kaushiki, ghazal singers like Penaz Masani and Pankaj Udhas, tabla maestros like Ustad Zakir Hussain and more. Even among Carnatic musicians he has given performances of his viola with vocalists like the great GNB, flute Vidwan N. Ramani,

Veena E. Gayathri, Chitraveena N. Ravikiran and flute player Shashank
and others.

In the concert with Pt Hariprasad Chaurasiya, he was accompanied
by Raghavendra Rao on the violin, while Ustad Zakir Hussain
accompanied them on the tabla. They performed a beautiful jugalbandi
with Ragams common to both the systems like Yaman/Kalyani and
Bhoopali/Mohanam. This was not the last time that Pt Hariprasad
Chaurasiya and Balamuralikrishna performed together. Decades later,
they performed along with violin maestro L. Subramaniam as a trio in
Bangalore, accompanied by Pt Anindo Chatterji on the tabla. 'I am left
gaping when I watch them perform. I feel I should only watch them.
I am in the company of legends. It is a great feeling to be with them,'
announced Pt Chaurasiya on the occasion. To which Balamuralikrishna
replied, 'I have not written any examination for a long time in my
life. I wonder if I will pass the test with these legends.' Subramaniam
promptly took the mike and said, 'He is the one with the most number
of doctorates. So naturally he has studied more than both of us.' The
Koramangala indoor stadium resounded with applause. Subramaniam
was yet another old accompanist to Balamuralikrishna. In a later festival
called 'Legends of India' that he organized, he recollected his association
with Balamuralikrishna. 'Years ago, Tanjore Upendran told my father,
"There is a great singer called Balamuralikrishna—why don't you ask
Subramaniam to accompany him?" So we all went to some part of
Andhra for the concert. I hadn't heard of Balamurali Ji and didn't know
what to expect. He started singing and he sang a Raga Aalapana. Then he
sang another Raga and then a third. After three Raga Aalapanas, I began
wondering where the concert was going. He hadn't sung Varnam or Kriti
yet. He then sang a Tanam in each of these ragas and then sang a Three-
Raga Pallavi. This is my first memory of him. Such a versatile, brilliant
creative genius! I was a young boy and it was an exciting experience for
me as I had never played with someone who sang Ragam Tanam Pallavi
in three ragas. Later when I came back to Madras, someone told me that
Balamurali Ji was playing the viola in a concert. At first, I thought that as
a singer, he was also able to play the viola but he showed such virtuosity
on the instrument that I was amazed. He is the kind of person who

contributes to everything that he lays his hand on. When I wanted to do that 'Visions of India' series of concerts, the first name that came to my mind to represent Carnatic music was Balamurali Ji. When I spoke to him, he readily accepted my invitation. Also, I requested him to sing my composition in Abhogi, "Sadaa Manadil Vaazhum", and gave him a tape of the song. He sang the song so wonderfully that one would think he has sung this song for years. He put so much feeling into the song. I was deeply moved.' Subramaniam himself is an internationally acclaimed genius of the violin whose concerts with legends like Yehudi Menuhin and Stephen Grappelli have been landmarks in global music history. Subramaniam invited Balamuralikrishna along with his viola to perform at the 'Visions of India' festival, where several other artistes like Gangubai Hangal, Baul singer Puran Das Baul, the qawwali singers Wadali brothers and others participated.

Among the vocalists of the younger generation, Balamuralikrishna's jugalbandi with Pt Ajoy Chakrabarty stands out as a unique one. Pt Chakrabarty counts Balamuralikrishna as one of his Gurus. Their performance at the United Nations in 1997 was greatly acclaimed. The event was in celebration of representing India at the UN. It was compèred by the dancer Anita Ratnam. Later the two performed extensively in numerous festivals across India, right from the 'Spirit of Unity' concerts to several others. Pt Chakrabarty's daughter Kaushiki also performed a jugalbandi with Balamuralikrishna in later years.

A funny incident at this point is a story of how a Coimbatore-based organizer requested a jugalbandi performance between Balamuralikrishna and a well-known Hindustani maestro. Balamuralikrishna quite willingly took it up whereas the other musician began creating a fuss. He asked the organizer what Balamuralikrishna was being paid for the concert. On knowing the fee, he demanded to be paid Re 1 more than that amount. The organizer agreed. The concert happened, and towards the end, Balamuralikrishna took the mike and thanked everyone and gently made an announcement. That the hardworking organizer was an old friend and hence he was not going to charge any remuneration for that particular concert. The entire venue resounded with applause. As a result, the other artiste was given Re 1.

Music Therapy

In 1993, sarod maestro Ustad Amjad Ali Khan announced that the Ustad Hafiz Alikhan Award, instituted in memory of his father, would be given to Balamuralikrishna and sitar maestro Ustad Abdul Halim Jaffer Khan. In a grand ceremony in New Delhi, the Vice President of India, K.R. Narayanan gave the awards in the first week of March. Amjad Ali Khan and Balamuralikrishna shared a great bond of friendship and admiration. This award further strengthened their bond. It was on that trip that Balamuralikrishna stayed with his old friends P. Prabhakara Rao and his wife Vedavathi Prabhakar. Rao was the former director general of police. Vedavathi was an accomplished singer whose association with Balamuralikrishna went back to the Bhakti Ranjani days. She also sang for the 'G.V. Iyer trilogy' and recorded devotional songs of Saint Kaivaram Amara Nareyana along with Balamuralikrishna. He took a chance and requested Balamuralikrishna to give a concert at the Andhra Bhavan auditorium in Delhi. '*Naa Pelliki Vochi, Nene Mantralu Cheppukovala!* (Do I have to chant Mantras at my own wedding!)' Balamuralikrishna retorted jokingly and went ahead to give a wonderful concert attended by Chief Minister Kotla Vijayabhaskar Reddy.

'In the beginning of the concert, he looked at the Chief Minister and said, "*Meeru Adigina Padevanni Kaadu! Kaani Prabhakar Adigite Ledana Lenu* (I would have not sung even if you asked me. But I couldn't refuse when Prabhakar asked)." How gracious and affectionate he was towards someone like me, who did nothing for him. That concert, he readily agreed to sing all our favourite keertanams. It is the most treasured recording we have,' wrote Rao. He also shared one of his older memories of Balamuralikrishna: 'The fifty-year-old Thyagaraja Sangeetha Sabha in my native place Anantapur was unable to complete the planned auditorium and had virtually stopped functioning for some time. I advised them to seek the blessings of Balamuralikrishna Garu and Sadguru Sivananda Murthy Garu. After that, it got completed very soon. All the local leaders desired that the auditorium be named Sri Mangalampalli Balamuralikrishna auditorium. I hesitantly sought his permission. He agreed and suggested naming the entrance after Sandhyavandanam Srinivasa Rao, who was the former principal of the Madras College of Carnatic music, and a native of Anantapur. Balamurali Garu also inaugurated the auditorium, rendered a concert,' added Rao.

The same year, on 11 April, the government of Andhra Pradesh honoured Balamuralikrishna with the Nandi Award for his contribution to the movie *Bhagawad Gita*. On 22 April, the University of Hyderabad conferred the degree of doctor of literature on Balamuralikrishna. In the first week of May, Balamuralikrishna was made the 'Asthana Vidwan' of the Dakshinamnaya Sharada Peetham in Sringeri. He was honoured with the title of 'Sangeetha Samrat' by the blessings of His Holiness Sri Bharati Tirtha Mahasannidhanam at Sringeri. It was a homecoming of sorts, because Balamuralikrishna's Guru Pantulu, who was an ardent devotee of the Sharada Peetham, would have been delighted with this one blessing that came disguised as an award.

Balamuralikrishna was still continuing with his 'music therapy'. Whenever he came across somebody suffering, he tried to help them with his music therapy sessions. One of the people who experienced this was the Hindi poet and writer Sunita Budhiraja (d. April 2021), who was a long-time music connoisseur. She had several anecdotes to share about him:

I had been a long-term Rasika of classical music. I had always heard Balamurali Ji from a distance or attended a few concerts in festivals. I had zero knowledge about music, but I thoroughly enjoyed classical music. It was in 1993, I was working at the Vizag Steel Plant and we had decided to do a special souvenir about Andhra Pradesh, which I was editing. The souvenir eventually turned out to be a coffee table book of sorts. In that I had written one article on Balamurali Ji. So I called him up in Madras and took an appointment and went and visited him in his house. His daughter-in-law welcomed me with a wonderful lunch. After that, I went and interviewed him. I must say that, from the very beginning, we had fallen in love with each other. He felt here was somebody genuine wanting to know about him without asking the usual questions like who was his Guru and his other musical life details. My focus for the interview was about the feel of his music and how his music impacted me. A question came about the timing of Ragams, and his answer took me by surprise when he said all Ragams can be sung at all times. As a listener of Hindustani music, I was under the impression of Ragams for morning and evening and different seasons and so forth. He told me about how his mother had visited traditional Jyotishyacharyas who had told her that a musician would be born in the family. So here he was! That is how our friendship started and we kept in touch. Whenever he visited Hyderabad or any parts of Andhra Pradesh, he would call or at other times I would call to check where he was performing. We would have lunch or dinner or a drink together. That coffee table book was released by the then Chief Minister Vijayabhaskar Reddy. After which I sent a copy of it to Balamurali Ji in Madras. The book was bilingual and my article on him was in Hindi. He called me back and said, 'I got the book. But it is in Hindi and I don't know how to read this kind of Hindi. So I had somebody else read it for me.' Whoever was the person who read it for him, went gaga about the article and told him that there has never been this kind of a write-up about him. He was extremely happy. He called and said, 'I got to know all the details. I am coming tomorrow to meet you.' After that he actually took a flight and came to Visakhapatnam to meet me. He spent the whole day at my house. There were also a couple of my other colleagues who were thrilled to meet him. After that I was organizing a festival at the Gangavaram beach in Visakhapatnam. Our steel plant had a small captive beach. So I planned a three-day festival called Sagar Utsav. I had invited Balamurali Ji for the festival. By then N.T. Rama Rao had become the Chief Minister and Balamurali Ji refused to perform. 'I will not perform as long as that man is ruling,' he told me on the phone. He said he will come to my house and spend time with me but will not perform in Andhra Pradesh. And so he didn't come! As promised, when he came to Vizag on another occasion later, he told me he would come home for dinner. So I was making arrangements. Those days in my house, I had fixed air-conditioning only in the bedroom. He would normally come and go straight in the room and sit cross-legged on the bed. Those years I had a maid who used to cook for me. So I had told her that I have an important guest coming and so she should make the best of Andhra food. She was also quite happy. When he would come, I would normally play some of his music from his cassettes. So he came as usual and I told my maid to arrange the dining table for dinner, then introduced himself saying he is a great singer and the song you are listening to right now is his. My maid went in and returned in two minutes, looking totally clueless and asked me, 'Ma'am, you just now said he is a great singer and the music playing is his. But this is the music of Mangalampalli Balamuralikrishna?' So I said 'yes'. She continued looking at me clueless and asked, 'You mean this man is Mangalampalli Balamuralikrishna?' When I told her 'yes' again, she fell flat on the floor, doing a Shashtanga Namaskar. I was shocked! I asked how she knew his full name and she said she heard him on the radio every day and was familiar with his voice. Just that she hadn't seen him in real ever.

Another time, Balamurali Ji said he was coming home for dinner. I was making all the preparations, when I developed a severe stomach pain. It was so severe that I rushed to the hospital. On doing all the tests and check up, the doctor said that it was an inflammation of the appendix and that I needed to undergo a surgery the very same day. I told the doctor that this was not possible, because I was expecting an important guest at home and if he could postpone the surgery to the next day. The doctor said okay and gave me medicine with an advice not to eat anything the night before. I was in a dilemma, as I had invited Balamurali Ji for dinner. It was an odd situation. That evening Balamurali Ji came as usual. He was totally unaware of my situation. Those days there were no mobile phones to convey any messages immediately. So he observed why I was not eating and slowly learnt about my condition. He immediately held my hands and began singing Krishna Bhajans. And for a brief time I was completely lost in them. After that, he dropped me at the hospital and I went in for surgery immediately. I still think it was his music that helped me recover from my ailment. I can never forget this in my life, she recollected, choking with emotion.

Another time, I was doing a coffee table book on Andhra Pradesh. I suggested that we have a special chapter on the contribution of Hindustani musicians who lived in Andhra. There were several of them. One of the committee members bluntly refused and so the matter kept getting debated. The person went to Balamurali Ji and asked his opinion. Balamurali Ji looked at him and said, 'What is all this Hindustani and Carnatic? There is only one Indian music. Stop dividing us, musicians as Hindustani and Carnatic. Of course, there should be a chapter on the contribution of Hindustani musicians in Andhra Pradesh. Their contribution is as much as mine, if not more than mine. These people live there. I left Andhra Pradesh long ago. I don't live there anymore. So, they are the people keeping the art and culture alive.' That committee member was stunned into silence. Now this thought and attitude can occur only to somebody who is an open-hearted and forward-looking person. Balamurali Ji was such. I cherish every memory with him.

Budhiraja has penned her experiences with various classical musicians like Ustad Bismillah Khan, Pt Kishan Maharaj, Pt Hariprasad Chaurasiya and Pt Jasraj in her book titled *Saath Suron Ke Beech*. The only Carnatic musician featured in that book is Balamuralikrishna. She also took special messages from each of these musicians which she published in her book. The message from Balamuralikrishna reads: 'Music is god for me. It is like Prana. Every living being has "Swara" and "Laya" which are two ingredients of music or "Sangeetam". It is only a dead body that has neither "Swara" nor "Laya". If music is, I am, otherwise what is left?'

Music therapy might have or might not have worked. But what certainly worked was the overwhelming charisma of Balamuralikrishna. 'I don't subscribe to anything that is not scientifically proven. However, I think he cured because he was simply superb as a musician and things were possible with him. Just because Jesus could cure a leper, it doesn't mean everybody can do the same. Maybe the Navagraha Kritis did have their properties, but it is also about the person receiving them. It might have been a placebo effect. There 50 per cent of the battle is won, other fifty is by Balamuralikrishna himself, his presence and his voice. If that will not cure, I don't know what will. I set aside my scientific scepticism later and saw there is some serious work that is going on elsewhere in the world. There are research institutes in Switzerland, and in Germany and France. What they do is they try to customize it to the patient. They have a few interviews with the patient to try and understand their ailment and do a psychoanalysis on what kind of music they respond to and take that as a data point. It is like going to a Yoga class and figuring out what Asanas you require. I don't think so it works like popping a pill at a clinical level. M.G. Ramachandran was a beneficiary of this music therapy. MGR was not well during the '82 elections. He had even made statements to the press saying that "I will win lying down". A part of that palliative care was Balamuralikrishna's music. Neurologically speaking, music lights up more centres in your brain than anything else. It is like lighting up a 1000 watt bulb in your head. Secondly, certain kind of music has an effect on your brain, in terms of palliative care. Certain repetitive phrases have been demonstrated to relieve pain. In the last decade, more work has been done on this. Even sceptical people like me are beginning to be more convinced. Balamuralikrishna was so ahead of his times that he was very intuitive. Just that nobody seemed to understand him then,' said Ragavan Manian, looking back at the entire concept of music therapy.

* * *

The national citizen's award for 1992 was presented to Balamuralikrishna in the first week of March 1994, by the vice-president of India, K.R. Narayanan (1921–2005). That summer, on 19 June, the Ganapati Sachidananda Swami's Ashram in Mysore conferred upon Balamuralikrishna the title of 'Nada Nidhi'. The godman Ganapati Sachidananda himself was a music enthusiast, and had been dabbling with the idea of music therapy. As Balamuralikrishna gathered more accolades, All India Radio embarked on a major project, recording all the Utsava Sampradaya Kritis and Divyanama Sankeertanams of Saint Tyagaraja. 'It came from the main directorate in Delhi from N.S. Krishnamurthy. The station director in Chennai then was Mr Thiruvengadam. I had to document the Utsava Sampradaya Kritis and Divyanama Sankeertanams under the guidance of Dr Balamuralikrishna and the resource person for it was musicologist T.S. Parthasarathy. To assist Dr Balamuralikrishna, we had L. Krishnan. I had to coordinate everything. That time we didn't have the AIR studios that we have now. So the entire recording was conducted in the studios of Sangeetha Records. The entire project took about one-and-a-half years. We did not use any of the staff artistes. We had all artistes from everywhere. For each song, we had a detailed commentary and announcement by T.S. Parthasarathy and the music interlude was by Balamurali sir. We recorded about 110 songs. We also recorded the narration in all the four southern languages and in Hindi, just in case the All India Radio wanted to do a national broadcast. T.S. Parthasarathy did the narration for all the Kritis and then we got hold of scholars to translate them into other languages. At that time, there was a lot of farsight on the part of the radio. I didn't know we had stereophonic (at) that time. We had edited just two sets of copies at that time, one was stereo and one was mono,' recollected the Carnatic vocalist Vijayalakshmi Subramanyam, who was the producer of the entire series.

The project was a mammoth task in many ways. The series consisted of half-an-hour episodes that would be played every week. Vijayalakshmi Subramanyam also had to handle a whole lot of other issues that dealt with the All India Radio. 'It was outstanding working with Dr Balamuralikrishna. This series is one of the highlights of my musical career. He was so knowledgeable and was so sure of his knowledge. From the guy who got the coffee at the studio to the sound recordist, they would all converse with him and he would affectionately have conversations with all of them equally. It was a delight to work with him. We used to have our lunches together. He would also bring homemade food, made by Annapoorna Mami, for us. In this big-budget project, All India Radio had a fees of Rs 50 per day for hospitality! You can't even buy decent chai with that. So he would bring food for me and L. Krishnan. One day it would be a Dibba Rotti or some Telugus speciality food which Mami would send. Otherwise for the artistes, either me or L. Krishnan would be buying tea and snacks. One day, he asked me how much the All India Radio was paying for hospitality. I was hesitant and I hummed and hawed. "Come on, I know everything. I have worked with the government and with the radio!" he quipped. After I told him we all laughed about it,' added Vijayalakshmi Subramanyam. The series consists of thirty half-an-hour episodes and is an extraordinary project in the recording history of All India Radio. Even today when you listen to all the meticulously documented songs, you thank someone like Balamuralikrishna for this massive endeavour.

In 1995, the Narada Gana Sabha honoured him with the title of 'Nada Brahmam'. Things had become normal with N.T. Rama Rao in Andhra Pradesh and as we had seen earlier, N.T.R. had apologized and invited him back to the state. It was around that time that Prince Rama Varma joined him as a student. Varma hails from the royal family of Travancore and was learning music elsewhere. His family had known Balamuralikrishna from an earlier occasion when he sang at the Navaratri Mandapam. 'The thing is, that my exposure to music was so utterly restricted to the concert at the Navaratri Mandapam that I had never heard of this great man properly till then, and believed that Dr M. Balamuralikrishna, G.N. Balasubramaniam and S.P. Balasubramaniam were the same person whose name seem to metamorphose Kafkaesquely from one to the other in various situations,' wrote Varma in a later article about Balamuralikrishna. Varma till then was learning music under Vechoor N. Harihara Subramania Iyer in Thiruvananthapuram. The demise of his Guru led to him seeking another. That's when he chanced upon the cassette of Thillanas by Balamuralikrishna, which moved him tremendously. He decided to learn a few pieces and took an appointment and visited him in Madras. That was the beginning of a close relationship that would last the rest of their lives.

Balamuralikrishna was handling many things at that point. There was the music therapy that he was increasingly focused on, teaching his disciples, and then dealing with all the controversies surrounding him. 'I became very big and very old too fast. When I was young, I was already old. Now that I am old, I feel very young,' he told Shilpa Kagal, who interviewed him for the *Sunday Observer*, dated 23 April 1995. This was a comment on his state of mind and he couldn't have put it any better.

The Thyagaraja Sangeeta Vidwath Samajam, with whom Balamuralikrishna had a lifelong association, honoured him with the title of 'Kala Seva Nirata' on 6 May. Around that time, Dr Pappu Venugopala

Rao, who was working with the American Institute of Indian Studies, had visited Calcutta (now Kolkata). Rao recollected, 'Mr Pabitra Sarkar was on the advisory board of our institute and I met him in Calcutta. He knew that I was a student and a fan of Balamurali Garu's music. We got into a casual conversation and I asked him if anybody outside of Bengal had sung Rabindra Sangeet? He said there was nobody who could do it except Balamurali Garu with the kind of voice that suited the genre.' What followed was Balamuralikrishna recording an album of the poetry of Rabindranath Tagore. In a later interview, Balamuralikrishan mentioned how he did it. 'I am a great fan of Rabindranath Tagore. He was a poet, a philosopher and many things rolled into one. He created his own genre of poetry and music. While it is common to write on gods and goddesses, he wrote on more abstract things like nature. I have a great fascination for that kind of abstraction. So I read the poetry, understood its meaning and sang, instead of forcibly fitting all kinds of our Sangatis and making it sound like a bad Carnatic mix,' recollected Balamuralikrishna in a televised interview for the series *Muraliravam*. The result was a beautiful series of songs like 'Aakashbhora' and others.

But this wasn't the first time he was singing Tagore's poetry. Way back in his Bhakti Ranjani days, he sang Tagore's poetry translated into Telugu by Balantrapu Rajanikantha Rao. Even today when you listen to the songs, you can easily be mistaken since the voice sounds just like that of any professional Bengali singer. Years later, he even sang them in a live concert in Bangladesh. The music lovers of Bengal fell in love with Balamuralikrishna's voice. Very soon, the Rabindra Bharati University convened a special meeting and conferred upon him an honorary doctorate on 7 May 1997. 'Those were the days of fax. So the university faxed me the confirmation letter of honouring the doctorate to him. I had a staff member called Perumal, through whom I sent with the fax copies to Guru Garu's house,' recollected Pappu Venugopala Rao. Soon after, the Vishwa Bharati University, set up by Rabindranath Tagore, conferred on him the honorary doctorate title of 'Desikottama'. 'I was in America when they announced this. The Prime Minister of India was to give it away at a function. I could not attend that. So after I came back, I asked them to send it to me, but they refused. They said that there are hundreds of fans who were eagerly waiting to see me. So they organized another function, this time it was in the very room that Tagore (had) stayed. They arranged a chair beside his chair and conferred this title. After that, I even gave a short concert,' recollected Balamuralikrishna in an interview.

Balamuralikrishna's love for Rabindra Sangeet and Tagore's ode to nature won him unprecedented laurels from the music lovers of Bengal. 'The Bengalis are very territorial when it comes to Tagore. They don't accept anybody singing or any other version of Tagore's music. I am the only non-Bengali selected to record thirty songs in a project to preserve Tagore's compositions,' he would say in many interviews with a great deal of pride. Balamuralikrishna was also invited as a soloist to perform the 'Gitanjali Suite' with an award-winning British choir led by Dr Joel, the UK-based Goan composer.

He began another project of recording all the Tyagaraja compositions with authentic notations. This was a project with which he was entrusted by the ministry of information and broadcasting. While this was going on, at the end of August 1996, the famous spiritual centre of Mantralayam, where the Brindavan of the Holi Saint Raghavendraswamy is situated, honoured Balamuralikrishna with the title of 'Sangeeta Rathanakara'. Balamurali was a devotee of the saint for multiple reasons. The main one being the saint himself was a musician and a great devotee of lord Hanuman. In the past, Balamuralikrishna had recorded several songs for Bhakti Ranjani and later released cassettes in praise of Raghavendraswamy. His Hindustani musician friends Pt Bhimsen Joshi and Kishori Amonkar were also ardent devotees of the saint. When they met, on several occasions, they discussed performing together in Mantralayam, but that didn't materialise.

Balamuralikrishna never failed to perform for any charitable cause which he deemed worthy. In February 1997, he gave a special benefit concert at The Music Academy in aid of the Sri Phavaman Annadhanam Trust, run by the Maruthi Bhaktha Samajam of the famous Anjaneya temple at Nanganallur in Madras. The kacheri was a presentation of veterans who came together for the cause. He was accompanied by T.N. Krishnan on the violin, Umayalpuram Sivaraman on the mridangam, Vikku Vinayakaram on the ghatam and Harishankar on the khanjira. He presented some of his old favourites, including 'Nagumomu', 'Endaro

Mahanubhavulu' and 'Devadideva'. The concert was a huge hit, to say the least. For Independence Day, Doordarshan broadcast a special concert of the 'Krishna-Trayam'. Balamuralikrishna presented his composition 'Vande Mataram Andi Maa Taram' in Ragam Ranjani. Once again, the composition was a clever Swaraksharam for the occasion. As an 'Asthana Vidwan' of the Nanganallur Anjaneyar temple, in December, he sang in the grand finale concert of the Hanumanth Jayanthi festival conducted at the Samajam. He was accompanied by M.S. Gopalakrishnan on the violin, Umayalpuram Sivaraman on the mridangam, Nagaraja Rao on the ghatam and Harishankar on the khanjira.

The same year, the MBK Trust released a book titled *Suryakanthi*, a collection of 128 compositions of Balamuralikrishna in several Ragams, including the ones he created. The book was released by the former President of India, R. Venkataraman (1910–2009) at a function held at the Kalakshetra auditorium in Madras. The first copy of the book was received by S. Rajaram, the then director of Kalakshetra. On that occasion, a video cassette titled *Janaka Raga Kriti Manjari* was also released by Semmangudi Srinivasa Iyer and the copy was received by the former President. This had all the compositions of Balamuralikrishna in the seventy-two Melakarta Ragams. On that occasion, the president of The Music Academy, T.T. Vasu, and the secretary Sangita Kalaacharya T.S. Parthasarathy, who had been tracking Balamuralikrishna as a child prodigy, A. Natarajan, the director of Chennai Doordarshan and the veteran Semmangudi Srinivasa Iyer spoke about their association and showered praises. *Suryakanthi* also carried a foreword by T.S. Parthasarathy. The speciality of the book is that you find Balamuralikrishna's impeccable handwriting in Telugu, Tamil, Sanskrit and English in the entire book. It also has beautiful illustrations by Gita Ananthakrishnan. *Suryakanthi* is a priceless gift to the world of Carnatic music. In September, Balamuralikrishna participated in the Ganesh Utsav in Mangalore. He was accompanied by H.K. Narasimha Murthy on the violin, Mangalore Sainath on the mridangam, Srimati Sukanya Ramgopal on the ghatam and Vyasa Vittala on the khanjira.

The Thyagaraja Vidwat Samajam conducted their 150th Tyagaraja Aradhana in 1997, with a special concert by Semmangudi Srinivasa Iyer accompanied by Balamuralikrishna on the viola. They were accompanied by T.K. Murthy on the mridangam and G. Harishankar on the khanjira. Semmangudi had the vocal support of his disciples V. Subramanian, Palai Ramachandran and Kadiyanallur Venkataraman. Before the concert, Balamuralikrishna went to the microphone and announced, 'You all call him Semmangudi Mama, but I call him Snageetha Paramacharya.' Later in the concert, Semmangudi announces mid-way that Balamuralikrishna was a big 'Medhavi'. The concert made a big splash in the Carnatic world for many days. Even today you can watch it on YouTube and see the kind of energy and dynamics these veterans shared on stage. Sanjay Subramanyam recollected meeting Balamuralikrishna after the concert to express his appreciation. To which Balamurali replied, 'I hardly touched the instrument.'

In an interview with Meera Srinivasan of *The Hindu* dated 27 July 2008, the famous neuroscientist V.S. Ramachandran spoke about his interaction with Semmangudi Srinivasa Iyer.

Ramachandran asks, 'What is your opinion on Dr. Balamuralikrishna?'

Semmangudi: 'Buddhisali.'

Ramachandran: 'Oh, he can't sing like you, sir.'

Semmangudi: 'Neither can I sing like him.'

Balamuralikrishna presented a jugalbandi with his friend Pt Bhimsen Joshi on 5 January 1998, at the Nanganallur Anjaneyar temple. They were accompanied by Tiruvarur Bhakthavatsalam on the mridangam, Raghavendra Rao on the violin, Ravindra Yavagal on the tabla and others. In the summer of 1998, Balamuralikrishna performed in Mumbai at the Pochakanwala Auditorium. He was accompanied by V.V. Subramaniam on the violin, Sivaraman on mridangam and Harishankar on the khanjira.

Anything connected to Saint Tyagaraja was an emotional point for Balamuralikrishna. He never thought twice about venturing or expressing himself if it was connected to Tyagaraja. The same year, he was invited to Toronto, where he conducted the Tyagaraja Aradhana by leading the Pancharatna Ghoshti Gaanam at the Bharati Kala Manram. He was accompanied by Trichy Sankaran on that tour. The same year in December, the MBK Trust presented a special concert of Annamacharya compositions, tuned and sung by Balamuralikrishna at The Music Academy. He was accompanied by Usha Rajagopalan on the violin,

Rajesh Vaidya on the veena, V. Govindarajan on the mridangam and V. Gopalakrishnan on the ghatam.

We've only seen a small part of Balamuralikrishna's mind as a musician. One of the interesting sets of compositions that gained extreme popularity were his Thillanas. While the music world was already aware of them, the world of Indian classical dance lapped them up like never before, making them extremely popular. In addition to these were his light music songs or *Lalita Geetalu* and other semi classical songs. The Balamuralikrishna who was entering into the millennium was not just a Carnatic vocalist anymore. He had transcended those confines and become more universal, with his music appealing to a wide range of audiences across the globe.

Balamuralikrishna receives the Padma
Vibhushan award from the President of
India R. Venkataraman at Rashtrapati
Bhavan in New Delhi in 1991.

An informal session
of discussing music at
Rashtrapati Bhavan with
the then President Dr
A.P.J. Abdul Kalam.

Balamuralikrishna with Pranab
Mukherjee, who invited him to
perform at Rashtrapati Bhavan
in New Delhi.

Balamuralikrishna being honoured
by the President of India Giani
Zail Singh at the Talkatora
Stadium, New Delhi, 1984.

Balamuralikrishna with his disciple, the famous actress Vyjayanthimala Bali.

Balamuralikrishna with his student, the famous actor Kamal Hassan.

Balamuralikrishna, T.V. Gopalakrishnan and K.J. Yesudas.

Balamuralikrishna with the eminent violinist Kunnakudi Vaidyanathan, who went on to head the Tyagaraja Aradhana in Thiruvaiyaru after his term.

Andhra Pradesh chief minister N.T. Rama Rao welcoming Balamuralikrishna with a shower of pure gold flowers. Also seen here are Jnanpith awardee C. Narayan Reddy, Dadasaheb Phalke awardee Akkineni Nageshwar Rao, Lakshmi Parvati and Ramanachari, adviser to the government.

Balamuralikrishna with music director M.S. Viswanathan, lyricist Vaali and playback singer S.P. Balasubramaniam.

Balamuralikrishna with music director Ilayaraja.

Balamuralikrishna with
Gangubai Hangal, Purandas Baul
and violinist L. Subramaniam
at the Legends of India Festival,
Bangalore.

Balamuralikrishna with sarod
maestro Ustad Amjad Ali Khan.

Balamuralikrishna with Hindustani
vocalist Pt Ajoy Chakrabarty.

Balamuralikrishna with Bharat Ratna
Pt Bhimsen Joshi—a lifetime of
friendship and music together.

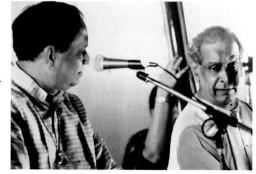

Balamuralikrishna with the stalwarts of Indian music, including Pandit Jasraj, Lata Mangeshkar, Asha Bhosle, Bhupen Hazarika, Jagjit Singh, Hariharan and A.R. Rahman, in the famous 'Jana Gana Mana' video.

Balamuralikrishna's statue in the famous Tummalapalli Kalakshetram in the heart of Vijayawada.

Balamuralikrishna's statue on the Rajagopuram of the Durga temple Seevalaperi near Tirunelveli.

The street in Satyanarayanapuram, Vijayawada, named after Dr Mangalampalli Balamuralikrishna.

Balamuralikrishna felicitating Bharatanatyam dancer Alarmel Valli, who performed for his 60th birthday celebrations in Bombay.

Balamuralikrishna with the famous film director G.V. Iyer, for whose iconic films he was the music director.

Balamuralikrishna with Palghat Mani Iyer, M.S. Gopalakrishnan, Kamalakara Rao and other artistes.

Balamuralikrishna and his old friend Vidushi Kishori Amonkar.

Author Veejay Sai with Dr Mangalampalli Balamuralikrishna.

9

The Twilight Years

On 1 January 2000, Balamuralikrishna was honoured with the first 'Vaggeyakara' award by the Music Academy at their annual Sadas. The award couldn't have been given to a better person in the world of Carnatic classical music. With his prolific output as a versatile composer, his in-depth knowledge of musicology, the complicated nuances of rhythm structures and more, Balamuralikrishna was indeed one of the greatest Vaggeyakaras of the century in the history of Carnatic music.

It was Republic Day, the fiftieth anniversary of the adoption of the Constitution of India. The President of India K.R. Narayanan released a special video in the Central Hall of Parliament to commemorate the occasion. It was the national anthem 'Jana Gana Mana' rendered by the best Indian classical musicians, arranged and orchestrated by music director A.R. Rahman and produced by Bharat Bala and Kanika Myer. The artistes included D.K. Pattammal, Pt Bhimsen Joshi, Lata Mangeshkar, Pt Jasraj, Begum Parveen Sultana, Bhupen Hazarika, S.P. Balasubramaniam, Asha Bhosle, Sudha Raghunathan, Unnikrishnan, Ajoy Chakrabarty, Hariharan, Nithyasree Mahadevan, Dr Balamuralikrishna and others. There were also instrumentalists like Pt Hariprasad Chaurasiya, Pt Shivkumar Sharma, Ustad Amjad Ali Khan, Pt Kartick Kumar and Ustad Sultan Khan. Among the Carnatic instrumentalists were Vikku Vinayakaram, Kadri Gopalnath, Chitraveena N. Ravikiran, Veena E. Gayathri, and violinist duo Ganesh and Kumaresh. The album has all of these artistes rendering their individual versions of the anthem before they come together, in a grand finale. It became a rage overnight and continues to be one that inspires a sense of patriotism in Indians living across the world. If the older 'Mile Sur Mera Tumhara' had created a sensation two decades ago, this new video brought in added nationalist sentiment with the involvement of all the musical stalwarts.

The same year, Balamuralikrishna was honoured with the title of 'Asthana Vidwan' of Srisaila Devasthanam, the famous Jyotirlinga Kshetram in Andhra Pradesh. It was here that Jagadguru Adi Shankaracharya composed his famous 'Sivananda Lahari' in the eighth century and dedicated it to lord Shiva and his consort, worshipped as Mallikarjuna Swamy and Bhramarambika Devi. Balamuralikrishna had recorded the entire Sivananda Lahari on an earlier occasion. At the ceremony organized for his felicitation, he recollected his wonderful association with the Devasthanam. Balamurali was also the first to record a series of compositions about this ancient temple and broadcast them in his years with the All India Radio. The Andhra Association also honoured Balamuralikrishna with the title of 'Sangeeta Kala Ratna'.

From his childhood, Balamuralikrishna had studied Sanskrit and spent time in the company of great scholars, poets and writers. A large percentage of his *Janaka Raga Kriti Manjari* is in Sanskrit. In addition to this, his renderings of Jayadeva's *Gita Govinda*, Narayana Theertha's *Sri Krishna Leela Tarangini* and the compositions of Sadasiva Brahmendra reflected his mastery over the language. So it was no surprise when the prestigious 'Kalidas Samman' was announced for him by the government of Madhya Pradesh. The award was conferred upon him on 12 February, by the then chief minister. In the concert that followed, Balamuralikrishna created a new Ragam and named it 'Kalidasa'. That summer, he visited the United States and gave a series of concerts. He was also honoured by the Tamil Sangam of Michigan on 6 May.

The central Sangeet Natak Akademi gave the fellowship award for 2001 to Balamuralikrishna. He was honoured in a glittering ceremony in Delhi. Later, he was made a member of the executive council. He later resigned from this post in protest, citing the autocratic behaviour of some of the then office bearers. Several other artistes followed him in this protest. Balamuralikrishna had had numerous bad experiences in dealing with government officials in the past. He was always against government interference in the arts. This was yet another instance. That year, the Bharatiya Vidya Bhavan chapter of New York honoured him with the title of 'Bharatha Jyothi'. Back home in India, the Andhra Pradesh Music Academy honoured him with the title of 'Sangeetha Vidhya Nidhi'.

In the summer of 2002, Balamuralikrishna was honoured with the title of 'Sangeeta Kala Visharada' by the then governor of Karnataka, V.S. Rama Devi. For somebody who didn't know a word of Tamil when he migrated to Madras, Balamuralikrishna became a master of the language in a very short time. He could not only read, write and speak Tamil, but even wrote a few compositions in Tamil. He gave a number of concerts at the Tamil Isai Sangam. In addition, he gave a number of golden hits in Tamil cinema, having worked with several legendary music directors like M.S. Viswanathan and Ilaiyaaraja. So it was no surprise that he was honoured with the title of 'Isai Perarignar' by the Tamil Isai Sangam on 14 December. The award was conferred upon him by the then President of India Dr A.P.J. Abdul Kalam. That December season, he was also honoured with the title of 'Sangeeta Kala Sarathy' by the Parthasarathy Swamy Sabha in Triplicane (in Chennai). Balamuralikrishna had a long association with Odisha and the literature and poetry of the state. He knew Jayadeva's *Gita Govinda* by heart, and had recorded and released a gramophone record earlier and tuned the entire work with orchestration later. He also had a close friendship with the dancer Sanjukta Panigrahi, her music director husband Raghunath Panigrahi and Hindustani flute maestro Pt Hariprasad Chaurasiya. They worked together on many earlier occasions. So it came as no surprise when the government of Odisha honoured him with their highest state award, Desh Ratna.

The Sarvasree Foundation was established in Dhaka, Bangladesh, in August 2002 and formally inaugurated by Balamuralikrishna on 10 July 2003. It was started by Meghna Ameen, who studied music from him. She was inspired by the three-note Ragam Sarvasree, created by Balamuralikrishna. He visited the foundation and spent time with the students of music there. This is probably the only foundation in honour of a Carnatic musician in Bangladesh. Later on in 2008, the foundation also opened branches in Iowa in the USA. The ancient temple of Sri Kalahasteeswara and goddess Gnana Prasoonambika, situated in the Chittoor district of Andhra Pradesh is one of the famous Panchabhoota Sthalams. It was a great centre for scholars and musicians under the rule of the Chola and Vijayanagara kings. From his younger days, Balamuralikrishna was a frequent visitor to this Kshetram. In his days of Bhakti Ranjani, he recorded a number of songs in Sanskrit and Telugu and broadcast them. Even later, he toured this place as part of his travels to the Panchabhoota Sthalams and recorded Muthuswamy Dikshitar's compositions on the same. In 2003, he was honoured with the title of the 'Asthana Vidwan' of this temple. The Chennai Fine Arts founded by P.N. Muralidharan presented the Gotuvadyam Narayana Iyengar Award for Excellence to Balamuralikrishna in its inaugural year 2003 that was also the birth centenary of Narayana Iyengar. The award was also given to Semmangudi Srinivasa Iyer, D.K. Pattammal, Madras A. Kannan and critic Subbudu at the same time. Years later, Chennai Fine Arts also instituted an award called the 'Balamurali Pavitra Patra' on the eightieth birth anniversary of Balamuralikrishna.

There has always been a question about who were Balamuralikrishna's actual and worthy disciples. There were many who affiliated themselves with him in his later years. But very few understood or inherited his musical thought process and approach. In many interviews, when Balamuralikrishna was asked to name his students, he cleverly dodged that question giving indirect answers. Two things could be made of this. One is he probably didn't want to be seen as indulging in favouritism. The other is he probably didn't think anyone was his worthy successor. But there were a whole lot of talented and promising youngsters whom he encouraged, and was also very close to.

In 2000, for instance, Balamuralikrishna got news that really shattered him. His disciple Ragavan Manian was diagnosed with a severe heart problem. 'I got busy with my IIT studies and after that I went abroad and got back. I was not in regular touch, but on and off (we had) an odd phone call or met in public spaces. I had developed a life-threatening ailment and the doctors had advised heart surgery. Somehow the word got around to

Guruji and on the third day that I was admitted into Stanford Hospital, I got a call. I wasn't expecting it. I picked up the phone and on the other side, I just heard his voice asking *"Idhu Enna, Raghava?"* He was crying inconsolably. And then he hung up! I was extremely moved. Though I was not learning from him by then, he took this effort to reach out to me. That itself was a big deal. Here was an emotional man with a heart,' recollected Ragavan, choking with emotion.

One of the earliest people who got attracted to his music and began learning from him in the 1960s itself was Prema Ramamurthy. Prema was also a member of his orchestral music and worked closely with him. She then began giving music for dance, and composed a lot of music for dancers like Alarmel Valli. Prema was one of the few disciples who learnt his entire *Janaka Raga Kriti Manjari* and other repertoire. A lot of her musical sensibilities, even while composing, came from her training with Balamuralikrishna.

Venkataraghavan from Mysore was one of the earlier students who joined him. 'I was performing at the Maha Shivaratri festival celebrations held at the Nanjangud temple. The chief guest, B.V. Balasubramanyam, thought my voice matched Balamurali sir's and advised my parents to send me to Madras. The following year, at the same festival, Balamurali sir was scheduled to perform after me. But he had arrived late owing to heavy rains. I could not even meet him, let alone have him hear me sing. I wrote a letter to him, expressing my desire to learn, and surprisingly got a reply asking me to visit him in Madras the following week,' recollected Venkataraghavan. As per instructions, Venkataraghavan landed up in Madras, to be faced with a huge flood. He somehow found his way to his relative's place before he managed to track down Balamurali's house. 'When I went and met him, he was surrounded by several musicians like Nookala Chinna Satyanarayana and Thanjavur Upendran. He said he didn't have time and asked me to sing something quick. I sang one piece, and after that he asked me to sing Ragam Shadvidamargini and Naganandini. He looked pleased and enquired about where I would stay and my source of livelihood. He told me that he was happy to teach, but the future clearly was not in anybody's hands. The next day, we began classes with him teaching me Girirajasuta.'

Around that time, Balamuralikrishna was going on a trip to Italy. 'He asked me to do some research and give him details about Italian music. I was aware of many things about Italy, but nothing about its music. So I went to the British Library and dug out some material and gave him. He took that and went to Europe and the trip was successful.' This way, Venkataraghavan started assisting him even outside of the stage. After joining as a student, Venkataraghavan eventually moved into the rooftop room of Balamuralikrishna's house. He would help with errands and office work. 'One day I had finished practising three hours of music and had fallen asleep in the room, without realising that the door was half open. I was severely sweating and I myself didn't realise it. Guruji suddenly gave a surprise visit to my room and saw me and returned without saying anything. In the evening, he called and asked if I had come to Madras to serve him and be his errand boy or learn music seriously. He said he would be doing injustice to my parents who had trusted me in his care. I didn't say much except that, along with learning music, I was willing to serve my Guru in every way. That night Poornamma came to my room with a table fan, saying there was an extra one lying around the house and that I should sleep comfortably. This was the kind of parental warmth I received in the house of my Guru.' Venkataraghavan spent many years with Balamuralikrishna, even through the 'Raga Controversy'. When Balamuralikrishna slapped a defamation case on Semmangudi Srinivasa Iyer, it was Venkataraghavan who was with him and did a lot of running around to the courts as well. Of course, he accompanied Balamuralikrishna in a number of concerts all along.

Another student was Mohanakrishna, who was visually challenged and over the years, won a great deal of critical appreciation for his music. 'I joined Guruji in 1980. My father took me to one of his concerts in Bhimavaram, where I was totally attracted by his voice. I decided if I had to learn music it has to be from him. So we went to Madras and I joined him as a student,' recollected Mohanakrishna. 'I used to stay in Alwarpet and take a bus and visit Guruji. After a few weeks, one day Guruji said he had a room in the house and that me being a blind boy, should not be travelling around. After that I shifted to his house and he took care of me like a son. I was just another member in his family. How can I ever forget Annapoornamma's love and care?' he added. Over the years, Mohanakrishna accompanied Balamuralikrishna in countless concerts. He recollected another moving incident. 'Those years there was another student by the name Ambili. She was a Malayali, who was physically challenged. She would come every day with a lot of difficulty and learn music. After a few days, Guruji called her house and told her family to stop sending her to his house. He told them to send him the empty car and that henceforth he would visit her house and teach her. Tell me, how many Gurus do this for their students? This was the kind of man Guruji was, with a golden heart, always full of care and love for his disciples.'

For many, it was Balamuralikrishna's music that had a huge impact on them and led them towards him. 'I was studying in IIT Madras. I had come from Madurai. I had learnt some amount of music, but I had a great interest in Carnatic music. One of my friends, who knew that I was a fan of Balamurali sir, introduced me to Ragavan. We were staying in two different hostels and when I met Ragavan finally, I told him what a great fan I was of Balamurali sir's Manodharma Sangeetham from the '60s and '70s,' recollected Balachandran about his initial exposure to Balamuralikrishna's music. Balachandran was from Madurai and had grown up on a staple diet of Madurai Mani Iyer's music. He learnt from four different Gurus, the last being Sivasailam Iyer, who was a retired tehsildar. In Madurai, he heard the music of Shankara Sivam and Madurai T.N. Seshagopalan.

'Those years, Shankara Sivam used to be charging Rs 100 a month for teaching music. That was a very big amount for me. Compared to that Sailam Iyer charged only Rs 30. Once in a class, he remarked about Balamuralikrishna saying *"Avar Periya Gnanasthar, Aana Oru Madhiri* Eccentric (He is a greatly knowledgeable and wise person, but a little bit eccentric)". I had really not listened to the technical aspects of Balamurali sir's music at that time. It was mostly the mellifluousness of his voice. I didn't have access to any of his other music. I must have been thirteen or fourteen when I got access to this cassette from a friend's brother. The cassette had Aarabhi (Ramana Vibho) on one side and Jaganmohini (Shobhillu) on the other side. One of the things that struck me about the Aarabhi was the musical imagination. I was flabbergasted. It was in that Jaganmohini that I first heard the sounds of silence. The way he would gently pause between the Swarams and gradually build them. I heard that cassette back-to-back for two days, and when my friend began demanding it back, I was so sad that I had to return it. I didn't have much access to any music. There was the All India Radio national programme broadcast. I think he sang a Latangi (Taamra Lochani). I was listening to it on a transistor while travelling. Till today I don't know what hit me, the Swaraprastarams and the Cheshte like a child, the freestyle Manodharmam . . . This freestyle Swaraprastarams on the go, it really touched me. I was very moved that one could have this kind of approach also to music. Not only the fact that I was touched by this, but also it lifted me. This left a huge impression on my mind. If you look at the Swaraprastarams, it is very natural for a musician to repeat a phrase. Sometimes they would have created something very profound and reiterated it several times. But in the case of Balamurali sir, there were no such repetitions. Each and every phrase was absolutely fresh,' said Balanchandran.

Thereafter, he met Balamuralikrishna, and a beautiful Guru-Shishya bond started. 'I joined him as a disciple. I would go cycling from IIT to his house in Kanakasri Nagar every day. I would call him in the morning and check if there is a class. I still remember the thrill of putting a Re 1 coin into the telephone machine and dialling his house and he would pick up the phone himself and say if there was a class, or on that day if he had any other engagement,' added Balachandran, reeling off his Guru's old landline number. Balachandran learned a number of traditional Kritis as well as Balamuralikrishna's own compositions. That Balamuralikrishna's music was influenced by G.N.B.'s was another point reiterated by Balachandran. He mentioned a quote in which G.N.B. once said that 'Ariyakudi is absolutely classical, I'm a neo-classical and Balamurali is a romantic.' Balachandran, being a student at IIT, was able to easily grasp the technical nuances of Balamuralikrishna's Manodharma. Balachandran's great love for music was transferred to his son Ramana too, who is an acclaimed child prodigy who plays the Saraswati veena exceptionally well.

Rajkumar Bharati, a musical genius who suffered at the peak of his performing career, was, the great-grandson of the iconic Tamil poet Mahakavi Subramania Bharati (1882–1921). Rajkumar was a student of his mother and later learnt music under T.V. Gopalakrishnan. Rajkumar had sung for Balamuralikrishna in the 'G.V. Iyer trilogy' earlier. Sharing his experiences of learning from Balamuralikrishna, Rajkumar said, 'I first heard Balamurali sir in the late '60s. He had sung "Oru Naal Podhuma", it was a rage. After that we would regularly hear him on the radio. And of course, there were the Thiruvaiyaru Tyagaraja Aradhana broadcasts. Once I had a criticism in one of my concert reviews that I imitated him,' he recollected. Rajkumar, who was already learning music and performing, was attracted to Balamuralikrishna's musical ideas. 'I was fascinated by his Thillanas and wanted to learn them. So I went to him and expressed my desire. He began teaching me his Tamil compositions. What impeccable Tamil! It didn't sound like they were written by a non-Tamilian at all.' I was curious to find out if Balamuralikrishna had sung any of the poems of Bharatiyar. 'Yes, he has tuned and sung. There is a beautiful poem of Bharatiyar titled "Naan". It goes:

வானில் பறக்கின்ற புள்ளெல்லாம் நான்,
மண்ணில் திரியும் விலங்கெல்லாம் நான்;
காணில் வளரும் மரமெல்லாம் நான்,
காற்றும் புனலும் கடலுமாய் நான்.

Vaanil parakkindra pullelaam naan
mannil thiriyum vilangkelaam naan
kaanil valarum maramelaam naan
kaattrum punalum kadalum naan . . .

'They say that Bharatiyar wrote this after he had the darshan of Bhagavan Ramana Maharishi, the sage of Tiruvannamali. This was tuned by Balamurali sir and he would emphasize the word "Naan". My mother heard this and was very happy. When I told him, he was absolutely delighted that Bharatiyar's grand-daughter liked his work,' recollected Rajkumar.

In addition to learning from him, Rajkumar also worked with him extensively in the recording studios. He saw Balamuralikrishna as a performer, as a music director and as a composer at close quarters. 'He was a Vaggeyakara in the true sense. I have done a number of recordings with him and attended countless concerts. In the recordings I observed how he really meant his music. Bharatiyar has written an essay titled "Sangita Vishayam", where he mentions that the lyric and the tune must have a relation with each other. This is found in the music of Tyagaraja. Tyagaraja was a Rasa-Kadal, an ocean of Rasa. And then he writes that the Sangita Vidwans nowadays, neither know Telugu nor know Sanskrit. Unless the Vaggeyakara knows the situation and accordingly the tune comes, he cannot do justice to the song. I remember while orchestrating the music of the film *Ramanuja*, how Balamurali sir studied the situation in the movie. In that scene, somebody has lost his wife. That lady was cremated or buried and this person is returning back from the funeral. It's a highly philosophical realization that everything is impermanent, everything fades away and so on. The artiste who was hired earlier could not understand this and so he could not do it. But Balamurali sir figured it out very easily. Another time during the shooting of *Adi Shankaracharya* film, the director wanted a bit of a change in the music connected to a particular scene. He changed it within minutes. He never had these airs that "who is this director to tell me to change what I have created?" Once I was doing the music for Vijay Nirman Constructions, the company that constructed all the flyovers. He came to Sai Saravanan's studio, so I complimented him saying his kurta was very good. He promptly said, "I came dressed well for you." He was an extremely jolly person, who had no airs about being a great Vidwan. In fact, when he saw youngsters, many times he would say "Hi". It would shock a lot of them. They never expected such a great Vidwan to do such casual talk. He would insist on saying a "Hi". This way he found how to easily connect with youngsters,' recollected Rajkumar about his long association with Balamuralikrishna and the unassuming attitude of the maestro.

Very true that anybody could easily connect to him, from a seasoned vidwan to an absolute novice. Balamuralikrishna carried his genius very lightly on his shoulders. There were times when you could look back and wonder if this was indeed the same man who had accomplished so much in his lifetime. In a later interview, he mentioned, 'I am living many lives at one time and none of them seem to be connected with the other. They all are independent of each other.' So while he wore many hats, he could also be many people at different times. But all that was easily condensed when you spoke to him. He was absolutely child-like. He would crack raunchy jokes, if you understood Telugu. Or otherwise say things heavily laden with sarcasm that sometimes you wondered how he kept such a straight face while doing it.

One of the other star singers who rose to fame in the 1990s was Balaji Shankar. Balaji was a protégé of Sangita Kalanidhi D.K. Jayaraman, the brother of D.K. Pattammal. 'I started performing solos after the demise of my Guru, Jayaraman sir. That time, I was given a lot of encouragement by Karaikudi Mani sir, who was extremely fond of my Guruji. He had organized a lecture at the Russian Cultural Centre. It was about how mridangam embellishes music in different ways. I was singing and Mani sir was playing the mridangam. Balamurali sir was the chief guest for that programme. The writer Mahadevan had also attended it to cover the programme. He had spoken to Balamurali sir, on the phone, who had apparently commented about my voice and expressed an interest to meet me. So Mahadevan sir called me and asked me to go and meet him. I had not heard too much of his music. Coming from the D.K. Jayaraman/D.K. Pattammal tradition, my exposure to other kinds of music was limited. Nevertheless, I went and met him and he said he would teach me a few of his compositions. We started with Varnams. "*Gaana Sudha Rasa, Mahaniya Madhura Murthy,*" recollected Balaji Shankar.

Balamuralikrishna taught him his compositions and Balaji even performed them in his concerts. Balaji shared a lot of his experiences of being a student of Balamuralikrishna. 'He has never practised any music. In his house, Annapoornamma or anybody has never seen him once with the tambura or going through any practice. He was brilliant in yoga. Once he told me that a good voice requires a good body, and the next minute he did Shirasasana and stood on his head. I was shocked. Another time, when I accompanied him at The Music Academy, he was running a high fever and kept on coughing. Even after getting on to the stage, he kept struggling with an irritating cold and cough. Anybody else in that place would have been so tense. But he looked completely relaxed. He asked for some coffee and after that when he opened his mouth to sing 'Omkaarakarini', his voice effortlessly reached the upper octave and he gave a three-hour concert. It didn't feel like he was suffering from a high fever,' added Balaji as he showed me the precious copy of *Suryakanthi*, which Balamuralikrishna had specially autographed for him.

Balaji demonstrated several compositions of Saint Tyagaraja and Dikshitar in addition to what he had learnt from Balamuralikrishna. He gave details of how Balamuralikrishna gave him so many lessons in the nuances of Ragam, Taalam and Sahityam. At the peak of his career, Balaji suffered from severe sinusitis and tonsillitis. He underwent a surgery, which complicated the situation further. As a result of this, he began finding it difficult to sing for long hours. 'When I told my problem to Guruji, he gave me an advice that worked very well. He asked me to practice or sing entire songs in falsetto using the voice in my head. Initially, I didn't understand this, but later I realized how wonderfully it worked. It was one of the most scientific approaches to reactivating my voice,' said Balaji. Being the disciple of one of the greatest masters of voice culture, Balamuralikrishna's tips to aid Balaji's voice were something that he himself had gone through at one time.

In an older interview with me, Cleveland Sundaram mentioned his interactions with Balamuralikrishna about the same. 'When my voice broke, I was left stranded and extremely clueless. I struggled a lot and worked on my voice. I carefully studied what kind of effect the five elements have on the body and mastered how to deal with them. The voice that I have today didn't come to me just like that. I put in some amount of hard work. The music, however, was a different deal,' recollected Sundaram about his conversations with Balamuralikrishna. 'As clichéd as it all might sound, Balamurali sir would often say, "I don't know any music, but music knows me. Music sings through me." Now I am able to relate to his state of mind and understand what he meant,' said young maestro Abhishek Raghuram, who himself discovered an incredible change in his own voice and approach to music from a decade ago.

'Initially I thought he was just teaching randomly off his head or whatever came to his mind. But in retrospect, he had a pattern. He had a set of ten songs that he would open with. These included some of his own, and a couple of traditional Kritis. After these ten songs, there would be some kind of an assessment to tell you that you have crossed stage one. And only he knew at what point. I realized I had graduated to the third level when he asked me what I wanted to learn that day,' recollected Ragavan Manian, when I asked him about Balamuralikrishna's teaching methodology. 'He had developed his own teaching methodology, none of it was prescribed by the usual set of books or teachers in the standard ways. After all, wasn't he the first principal of the Vijayawada College who had helped design the entire syllabus? What was I thinking? There was obviously a well laid-out path and pattern. It was just that he never made it seem so. He never made us students feel that there was this organised way. Which is why we were under the impression that his style of teaching was chaotic!' added Ragavan.

This methodology not only helped Balamuralikrishna assess the disciples, but also gave him a good insight into their overall aptitude in grasping the finer nuances of Carnatic music. If he found someone who was incapable of learning, he told them in the most indirect of ways. 'Initially I had a problem with the language. I didn't know Telugu and I thought he didn't know Tamil. My father who had come had told him that if he gave the lyrics, my father would write them down in Tamil and that would help me learn the compositions later. He didn't say anything. He simply asked for the pen and paper and in front of our eyes, he began scribbling the entire composition in impeccable Tamil!' added Ragavan about how effortlessly his Guru reached out to teach him.

One of the students who came to Balamuralikrishna having been drawn to his music was Krishnakumar. 'I am basically from Trivandrum. My mother is from Tuticorin. When Guruji initially shifted from Vijayawada to Madras, he was staying in a rented accommodation in a building where my aunt was also his neighbour. That was my family's first introduction to him. I was not even born then. My father Prof. Kalyanasundaram was a very well-known professor in mathematics, who shifted to Trivandrum. He was also a great art lover and was involved with a number of music organizations. Those years, Trivandrum hardly had any hotels. It would be difficult for many visiting artistes to get decent food. So our home became a venue for many artistes, who would be welcomed every now and then. Many great vidwans visited our house. So Guruji also came to our house in the 1970s. My first recollection of attending his concert was driving with my father all the way to Nagercoil, where he was performing. I can say my actual musical journey began then. It was such a magical concert. T.V.G. sir was playing the mridangam and he was playing Swarams on the mridangam. I was a small kid and I knew nothing about music. But this left a big impression on my mind. Guruji sang all the srutis and went to the Anu Mandra Sthayi. M. Chandrasekharan who was accompanying him on the violin couldn't play those srutis. Guruji was showing all the srutis that even a violin could not reproduce. This stayed in my mind for a long time. After that I continued with my academics and was learning music on the side in Trivandrum from one Neyyattinkara Mohanachandran. In summer vacations I would visit my uncle in Madras and go to Guruji's house and learn. That is how it started,' said Krishnakumar. He gradually became a disciple and later caregiver of Balamuralikrishna in his last years.

While there were several musicians who came to him and learnt some of his compositions, there were many others who grew up listening to him and took inspiration. "'We were always listening to Guru Garu's music and knew him from a distance. But later, he became very close to us. If we had any doubts in Sahityam, we would go to him and he always took time to clarify it. We also learnt a couple of his compositions and sang them. He was extremely happy. Though we didn't learn much from him, we gave him a Gurusthanam and revered him. He was equally very loving. No trip to Madras was complete without visiting Guru Garu,' recollected D. Sheshachari of the famous singer duo, the Hyderabad Brothers.

Top-notch vocalists, they also hailed from the Tyagaraja Shishya Parampara from their mother's side. 'My first tryst with his music was that my mother loved his music. My childhood memories of his music were his rendering of "Devadideva" and "Nagumomu". My Guru M.L.V. Amma was a very close friend of Balamurali ji. M.L.V. Amma had great admiration for Balamurali sir. Whenever they met at functions or in public events, they openly expressed their warmth and admiration towards each other. Each one would praise the other. So by default, I too grew up admiring his music over a period of time. The first twelve years of my life, I grew up in Bangalore. I have attended a number of his concerts at the Fort High School grounds, Chowdiah hall and other popular venues, and enjoyed his musical creations,' recollected Carnatic vocalist Sudha

Raghunathan. Sudha had grown up in the 1970s and made big news in the Carnatic world when she won a number of competitions at a very early age. One of the famous quotes attributed to her came from Subbudu, who wrote, 'If I'm marooned on an island and if I am granted permission to bring along with me three things I like a lot, I would list the following: an audio-visual cassette of Sudha singing; second, betel leaves and tobacco; and third, poet Kannadasan's works.'

These reviews really boosted Sudha's image. Many years later, Sudha got the opportunity to work closely with Balamuralikrishna. 'Shashikiran, who organizes the Bharat Sangeet Utsav, was responsible for this collaboration. He always thinks of something new and so this time around he told me that I will be performing with Balamurali Ji. I was shocked. I said I can't. How will I even match his mastery! Shashi cajoled me to do it,' recollected Sudha about her famous collaboration. There was another occasion, which was the marriage of the son of dancer Shobhana, where they performed together with Haridwaragamangalam Palanivel on the thavil. 'I visited Balamurali Ji in his house and asked him what sruti he would sing in. He said, "I will sing whatever sruti you sing in." He was so casual, you could see a genius talking. I next asked him what are the songs, and he said "We will see then." I wasn't convinced about this, so I pleaded with him and said that I would bring a recorder to make notes. The first song was "Gana Sudha Rasa" and then he cracked a joke saying how he wrote a song about me. I remember he sang "Vatapi" in Hamsadhwani and "Sundari Nee" in Kalyani and Shobhaane. We finished with a Behag Thillana. This was the little interaction with him at home. After that we got busy with our schedules. This concert was received very well and several other organizers came forward to request presenting the same,' recollected Sudha.

The same collaboration was presented at the Cleveland Tyagaraja Aradhana. In Cleveland, they were joined by Chitraveena Ravikiran. 'I thought it was going to be very challenging and I would have to follow him timidly. But it wasn't anything like that. He made me feel like an equal and we sang along. This is the sign of a great musician. Because of that, it gave me courage to sing further, especially in the higher notes. He would just turn around and smile. It was interesting because Ravikiran was another prodigy by himself. So it was a double challenge for me, sharing a stage with both of them. Nothing was rehearsed, none of it was curated. Everything was spontaneous, the way it happened on stage. Each one picks up wherever they think they can enter, even the Swarams. The final Korvais and all of it was so casually done but with a lot of finesse. It was terrifying at the same time and a very interesting experience,' said Sudha about the collaboration. 'Sitting next to such a great maestro, you can feel those vibes. Today we use the terms "maestro", "prodigy", "genius" and so on, very flippantly. But he was all of those put together and more in a genuine way.' The Cleveland festival really cemented their friendship and Sudha would frequent Balamuralikrishna. 'I knew he loved fried foods. So I would go with Bajjis or Seppankezhangu roast, which we make very well in our house. I would spend time with him, upstairs in his room. It was like a friendship that M.L.V. Amma left behind as a legacy. He would often talk reminiscently about M.L.V. Amma and the great music she made.'

Sudha also learnt a couple of his compositions like 'Omkaarakarini' in Lavangi and gradually they became great friends. 'These interactions gave me the courage and impetus to request him to sing at my son Kaushik's wedding. He accepted and said he would sing. His manager in the meantime accepted another concert on the same day in Bhubaneswar. There was some communication gap between them. And the invitations were printed and when I went to give it, the manager said he was not available. I was shocked. I rushed to his house immediately and was literally in tears saying how he forgot his commitment to my son's wedding. He was calm and cool, pacifying me, telling me not to worry. On the day of the wedding, there was yet another tension. The function was starting by 6 p.m. He was stuck in traffic and didn't show up till 7.30 p.m. I had so many guests and I was really tense, whether the concert was going to happen or not and what would people think that I had just put his name on the cards. It would be so embarrassing! And then he came and sat on the stage and began the Varnam Amma Anandadayini. That was it! The hall was filled with his music, everybody sat and listened. I went to pay my respects to him and he called me and made me sit next to him. I remember, I was so emotional that I cried, and he pacified me like a father.

It was such a beautiful concert. I think that evening everyone carried the melody home,' said Sudha.

In fact, he had stopped accepting wedding kacheris long ago. So his singing at this wedding was an allowance for his friendship. Sudha Raghunathan was honoured with the Sangita Kalanidhi award by The Music Academy in 2013. To commemorate the occasion, a special coffee table book titled *Sampoorna* was being released. 'We couldn't think of anybody else releasing it, except Guruji. The book has a CD with messages from many musicians and public personalities. For the release of the book, he came in (at) the last minute and gave his blessings. That I think is something I will cherish all my life,' said Sudha about one of the last times she interacted with him closely.

The Carnatic field is pretty cutthroat. Power-hungry veterans, publicity-hungry mediocre artistes, performance-hungry half-baked youngsters, anxious parents of younger musicians and so on. Sibling rivalry, musician parents promoting their mediocre children over deserving disciples, nepotism, favouritism and many such issues have dogged the field for a long time. However, there have also been many individuals within the field generously encouraging of new talent. One of the prime examples was Chembai Vaidyanatha Bhagavatar, who encouraged a number of vocalists and instrumentalists. Balamuralikrishna belonged to the same league. Be it his students or other musicians who sought his guidance, he never hesitated from encouraging talented youngsters.

'This was after my marriage to Vasanthi. She herself is a flute artiste, whose family ancestry goes back to the musician Sangita Kalanidhi Pazhamaneri Swaminatha Iyer, who was a disciple of Maha Vaidyanatha Iyer. I had given a concert after which I met Guruji with her. There was somebody from that concert who remarked to Guruji, "I heard Sekar singing. He sings just like you." To which Guruji replied, "Yes he is a very good singer. In fact, he sings better than me." I was shocked. This is a day and age when a father doesn't promote his son. And here was my Guruji being so generous in his praise in front of a third person,' recollected Thiruvaiyaru P. Sekar choking with emotion. 'I immediately asked Guruji, "But Guruji you have not heard that concert. Why did you praise me this way?" To which he remarked: "You must have sung well

only. Otherwise, why will Vasanthi marry you?" Saying so, he giggled.'
Sekar and Vasanthi's daughter Mahati was named after the Ragam created
by Balamuralikrishna. She also trained under him from a young age.

While he could be generous with his students, he wasn't any different
with other musicians who sought his advice. Aruna Sairam was yet another
musician who gained from his sage advice. 'I have been a great fan of
Balamurali sir and heard him performing while growing up in Bombay.
He was a superstar. Those years sitar player Aravind Parekh would organize
a seminar at the NCPA (National Centre for the Performing Arts) in
Bombay. It was in one such seminar that he too spoke. In the lunch hour,
I mustered some courage to go up to him and tell him that I was his fan
and I wanted to meet him. I didn't know exactly why, but it was just an
act of hero worship. He promptly gave me his phone number and asked
me to call him when I visited Madras. Many years later, after I migrated to
Madras, one day I called on him. There was no particular agenda to meet
him. I just wanted to take his blessings. So he asked me to visit him. I took
an appointment and went. After I met Poornamma downstairs, I went up
to Guruji and I was so awestruck by his powerful presence, I didn't know
what to talk. He was very cordial and began talking. I didn't know what to
ask and I blurted out: "Guruji, how do you sing the way you do?" feeling
totally shy and awkward about what I just asked,' recollected Aruna.

'My interactions with him were not very many. But this is one meeting
that I will never forget. He asked me to sit down and lift my chin and
hum a Sruti or a tune. This way he asked me to do a circle of all the eight
directions. This exercise was like a precious gift he gave me. At that time in
my performing career, I was looking for answers to many things. And what
he prescribed had taken care of many of those things. I follow it till date
before all my concerts,' continued Aruna as she demonstrated the exercise
that she got from him. Balamuralikrishna could assess a musician's ability
and requirement and give them sage advice

It was not just mainstream performing musicians who gained from
him. Several friends and associates, too, recollected their memories of
him. One of them was Meenakshi Rajmohan, whose sister Vidushi Rama
Kausalya was an old friend and acquaintance of Balamuralikrishna from
Thiruvaiyaru. In the mid-1980s, Balamuralikrishna took some time

off from his hectic schedule to go and stay with them at their house in Thillaisthanam Agraharam. He stayed for three weeks, and during that time, he taught Meenakshi, who was then carrying her first child. 'He would narrate a number of stories about his childhood. He was very sentimental about his mother and how she had predicted that he would become a musician one day. How he never drank milk because he was not fortunate to have his mother's milk,' recollected Meenakshi. Her daughter Madhuvanthi Badri added: 'He taught her Mahati first. It was the day of Vijayadashami and my mother was about to deliver me soon. I had the Bhagyam of being a Prahalada and learning indirectly. Towards the end of the three weeks, my mother gave him conjunctivitis. He took her goggles and returned them later, with a cute little note of thanks.'

In his collection of essays titled *Amritavarshini*, the eminent musicologist and scholar Malladi Suribabu calls Balamuralikrishna a 'Sangeeta Meru Shikharam'. Recollecting his interaction with Balamuralikrishna, he wrote, 'My sons (Malladi Brothers) had recorded the Tyagaraja Pancharatna Kritis for *India Today*. Though these are known to everybody, the Pathantaram varies according to different musical styles. So we took the album and went to his house to take his suggestions. "The Sahityam is the life of Tyagaraja's Pancharatna Kritis. People here are swallowing the Sahityam and singing. Everybody should know the meaning and significance of the words. Wouldn't Tyagaraja's Atma feel hurt if everybody just sings with a herd mentality?" he asked. He then asked whether my sons would like to learn a Swati Tirunal Kriti that he set to tune in Ragam Desakshi. How affectionate! They not only learnt it in half-an-hour from him but he also recorded and sent it with them. How beautifully he tuned the Kriti "Saraseeruha Naabha Mudaaram Kalaye" in Ragam Desakshi! He also taught them a Thillana in Ragam Shivaranjani. Balamuralikrishna was the only Telugu vidwan who had the purity of Swaras, the clarity of pronunciation and knew the meaning of the words in the Sahityam and sang these Keertanams with emotion. There are many singers with singing defects like singing with the nose or with their eyes closed or beating their thighs too hard with Taalam or looking condescendingly at their audiences. But Balamuralikrishna was beyond all of these "Gaayaka Doshas". With an-ever smiling face, constantly encouraging his accompanying artiste and with a special musical rapport with his audience, right from the beginning of the concert till the Mangalam, he is a unique singer. He is a Gayaka Shiromani, who practised all his music in his last birth and sang to his heart's content in this birth.'

It was not just singers who sought his advice. There were other musicians who turned to him too. 'My introduction to Balamurali sir was through "Oru Naal Podhuma". As a young student of my Guru Vikku Vinayakaram, I had the opportunity to know him at close quarters,' recollected Dr S. Karthick, a ghatam artiste. A multi-faceted person, Karthick is a singer and composer, in addition to being one of the senior most-Ghatam Vidwans in the Carnatic field. 'Guru Garu, as I addressed him, was extremely fond of me too. In addition to performing for his concerts, and travelling with him, I had the good fortune of having an extremely personal bond with him. He treated me like his son. He performed for my marriage and at my Gruha Pravesham. My son would call him "Balu Thatha".' recollected Karthick. Karthick was one of the few musicians who shared an enviable proximity with him.

The other musician who went to him, inspired by his music, was P. Unnikrishnan. In numerous interviews he gave, he mentioned how music happened by accident and he became the disciple of Sangita Kalanidhi Ramanathan. 'I went to seek Balamurali sir's blessings. I was particularly fascinated by his Thillanas. So I went and learnt from him, not just a few Thillanas, but also a few of his compositions from his *Janaka Raga Kriti Manjari*. In addition to being such a genius of a musician, which he undoubtedly was, he was such a nice human being and extremely generous. You could stay in his company for hours together and he would regale you with endless stories. It was his humility that made him a sweetheart. I don't think there is anybody who met him and was not moved by him,' said Unnikrishnan.

While well-known musicians sought him out, he himself was always encouraging of youngsters even if he didn't know them. S.J. Jananiy was one of the few who was fortunate to become his student in later years. She was already a student of Neyveli Santhanagopalan and had recorded a number of albums. '"It was for my album on "Kanda Sashti Kavacham" and "Sri Venkateshwara Suprabhatham", which was released by Balamurali sir in 2008. In fact, both my Gurus were present on the occasion. Balamurali sir released it and Santhanagopalan sir received the first copy. After that he asked me if I would sing his compositions. I was more than overjoyed as I didn't expect this kind of a blessing. I was very willing and told him I would love to learn. He asked me to check with my Guru first. When I went to Neyveli sir and told him, he was extremely pleased and told me to learn as much as I can,' recollected Jananiy. She soon became his student. 'He first taught me his "Kunthalavarali" Thillana. He would tell me once and I would learn it and go home and take my notes. He began picking up different compositions from the seventy-two Melakartas that he did and taught me two or three a day. This way we completed the entire seventy-two. In addition to these were the compositions in the Ragam that he created. We would go through the Aarohanam and Avarohanam once, after that he would give a few swara exercises and then we continued into the Kritis. I had the good fortune of learning from him for a dozen years,' recollected Jananiy.

She also gave music for the movie *Prabha*, directed by Nandhan. 'The movie had a women-based theme and I was selected to be the music director. I wanted Guruji to sing in it. He gladly agreed. In fact, when I gave him the lyrics and the tune, he started singing them. In between he told me, "You are the music director. Don't say 'yes' for everything I sing. Feel free to correct me and make me sing as you want it for the movie." Even during the recording sessions, he would be humming the tune all through. He is such a legendary and iconic figure. He needn't be doing all that. I learnt how one can be a thorough professional from him,' said Jananiy. In the movie, Balamuralikrishna sang 'Poove Pesum Poove' in a duet with her. This was the last song he ever sang for any movie.

There has always been a criticism about many musicians that their children were not as successful as they were in the same field. Balamuralikrishna was not spared either. He had six children, and none of them was a full-time musician. When I spoke to them, it was clear that he didn't want them to be musicians. As a musician himself, he had faced a number of problems, both in his personal and professional life. No father would want their children to suffer, going through these problems again and again. Hence, he decided that his children would not be full-time musicians even though his oldest daughter Ammaji and the youngest daughter Mahati did learn music. One of his granddaughters, Mahati's daughter Mahima, was one of the few family members who learnt music from him since her childhood. Each day, on returning home from school, she would go and learn music from him.

One of the last students who joined Balamuralikrishna was young Shyam Ravishankar, for whose Arangetram, Balamuralikrishna was the chief guest. Shyam was learning the keyboard and later began learning the violin. After he joined Balamuralikrishna as a student, he learnt a number of compositions. When they were not in a class at home, Shyam would drive him to the beach. Even in his earlier interviews, Balamuralikrishna mentioned how he enjoyed the sea breeze. It was some kind of a strange myth that the salty sea breeze is not good for a singer's throat. There were other odd misconceptions like singers should always drink hot water, must not eat anything cold and must always have mild boiled food in order to maintain their vocal cords. Balamuralikrishna did the total opposite of all these things. He loved eating ice-creams, enjoyed fried foods and loved the sea breeze. In fact, in the documentary made on him earlier, he takes Penaz Masani to the beach and eats an ice-cream on camera, saying none of these affected him.

Several other musicians like Krishna Kumar and his wife Binny, and Sharath joined him in later years and became his students. He was always generous and willing to teach anyone who came to him. He believed that 'Vidhya' and 'Vaidhya' should always be available to everyone and not have a price tag. He never charged a single rupee from any of his students. Shyam recollected how he made him drive to the nuts-and-spices shop nearby and got him to purchase a little peppermint, saying that was the only Gurudakshina he would accept.

In January 2004, the Kanchi Mutt was commemorating the golden jubilee year of their pontiff Sri Jayendra Saraswathi who was heading the institution. On that occasion, Balamuralikrishna was honoured with a special certificate. That year Prasar Bharati, the public service broadcaster, was commemorating its seventy-fifth year. It was also the golden jubilee of the famous Aakashvani Sangeet Sammelan, where Balamuralikrishna had sung countless times. A grand ceremony was organized at the Lalitha

Kala Thoranam in Hyderabad. The then chairman of Prasar Bharati, M.V. Kamath, the CEO, K.S. Sarma, and others honoured a long list of eminent stalwarts who had contributed to the field of Indian music and radio. These included M.S. Viswanathan, Lata Mangeshkar, Manna Dey, and Dr Bhupen Hazarika in the field of film music. Pt Jasraj, Gangubai Hangal, Pt Bhimsen Joshi, Kishori Amonkar, Ustad Bismillah Khan, Sharan Rani, Pt Ravishankar and Pt Kishan Maharaj in Hindustani music. M.S. Subbulakshmi, D.K. Pattammal, N. Ramani, M.S. Gopalakrishnan, T.N. Krishnan, T. Mukta, T.K. Murthy, Palghat Raghu, Nedunuri Krishnamurthy and Dr Balamuralikrishna for Carnatic music. They were all honoured with the National Artiste Award on 29 March 2004. This was a homecoming of sorts for Balamuralikrishna, whose contribution to radio programming with the famous Bhakti Ranjani shone like a crest jewel in the history of Prasar Bharati and All India Radio.

The same year, Kanchi Mutt gave him the Lifetime Achievement Award. Shanmukhananda Fine Arts Sangita Sabha in Bombay, where Balamuralikrishna had given countless memorable concerts, made him an honorary patron. In the December season that year, the Nungambakkam Cultural Academy honoured him with the title of 'Sangita Kala Shiromani'. The award was given to him by Nalli Kuppuswamy Chetti, the textile merchant who was a great patron of the arts and a good friend of Balamuralikrishna for several decades.

Even as his music gradually attracted the curiosity of a younger generation of musicians willing to experiment, there was yet another element of his music which was going to be embraced and loved unequivocally in a completely different world that he wasn't associated with. This was the world of classical dance.

In Love with Dance

Other than the traditional music for dance that was already available, a lot of 'new' music had been adapted in the last several decades. While modern composers like Veena Sheshanna of Mysore, Mysore Maharaja Jayachamaraja Wodeyar, Patnam Subrahmanya Ayyar, Harikesanallur Muthaiah Bhagavatar, Poochi Srinivasa Iyengar, Tiger Varadachariar,

Mysore Vasudevachar and later composers like Rallapalli Ananthakrishna Sarma and Madurai N. Krishnan were fairly popular in the concert world, it took a while for the compositions of many of these to easily fit into the world of classical dance.

In numerous interviews, Balamuralikrishna said that he never composed for dance. But today it is impossible to believe so. His compositions have become so integral to the world of Bharatanatyam and Kuchipudi. Several other classical dance forms like Mohiniyattam from Kerala and Odissi from Odisha have also taken his compositions for their choreographies. If one takes a detailed look at his compositions, you realize how flexible and suitable they are for the purpose of classical dance. If Lalgudi G. Jayaraman is one of the composers who became famous in the classical dance world in the twenty-first century, the other is Balamuralikrishna. While there are his Varnams and Kritis, what became the most popular and caught the imagination of the dance world were his Thillanas. In fact, Balamuralikrishna published a book of his Thillanas as early as 1974. He would often sing many of these in his concerts right from the 1950s. Though we do not have the exact details of what was the first Thillana he ever composed, a preliminary study would reveal that these were all works of a mathematical brain. Amongst the earliest Thillanas that he composed were the ones in Hindolam, Brindavani, Dwijavanti, Kunthalavarali, Chakravakam, and Kadanakuthuhalam which are not extremely complicated to choreograph for a dancer with a good sense of rhythm.

This association with dance goes back to the 1960s. As a producer of the Bhakti Ranjani programme for All India Radio, Balamuralikrishna had already worked with the dance music of Balantrapu Rajanikantha Rao. Having sung for several Yakshaganams and dance productions, he was well equipped with the vocabulary of various dance forms.

The credit for making Balamuralikrishna's works popular in the world of Bharatanatyam in modern times goes to V.P. Dhanajayan and his wife Shanta Dhananjayan. Dhananjayan fondly remembered, 'We have been ardent admirers of Balamuralikrishna sir. Suddenly an opportunity knocked at our door to choreograph his Kunthalavarali Thillana, a controversial composition, brought to us by V.A.K. Ranga Rao, saying that no other artiste was willing to perform it. Mainly because of its contemporary structure with complicated patterns, which is not in the usual pattern of a Thillana. We grabbed the suggestion of V.A.K. Ranga Rao. If I remember correctly, it was in 1974. Before we started composing, we wanted our musicians to learn it directly from Balamurali sir. So we contacted him over the phone and fixed a few sessions for learning. That was the first connection with him, he was very cordial and surprised that we chose a controversial composition. We were also controversial artistes like him at that time, because we were performing newly choreographed items with innovative texture. The critics of that period used to compare us with sir, saying "in Carnatic music Balamuralikrishna and in Bharatanatyam the Dhananjayans are radicals". Anyway, we didn't mind that, but took it as a compliment. We invited him to come home to watch the composition, and he came with so much enthusiasm and watched me performing it. He was in tears and commented, "It looks like I composed the music for your dance—the dance and music gelled so much that they seem inseparable." That was a big compliment for us. After learning the music directly from sir, we initially composed it as a solo and I performed it since Shanta was carrying my second son. The Thillana was an instant hit with connoisseurs and became viral in the Bharatanatyam scene. Later, we composed it for both of us and did it several times in the country and abroad. People used to ask us for this Thillana. So this was the first-ever composition of Balamuralikrishna taken in the Bharatanatyam repertoire. This has given him the inspiration to do more such compositions which he acknowledged once in public on his seventy-fifth birthday concert in Delhi, for Kerala's Swaralaya cultural organization. On the day, we performed a couple of his compositions in his honour and this Thillana was the finale. We became very close to each other and he would come for our performances very often, irrespective of us not performing his songs.'

Later, in the year 1987, they were invited to the USSR Festival in India and wanted to do his Kadanakuthuhalam Thillana as a Nirtta-Tarangini group ensemble item. 'This was critiqued as "Choreographic Marvel" in the USSR press. When I sent my musicians to learn the music from him directly, he changed his original Sahityam and composed a new Sahityam for the last Charanam of the Thillana. He very cleverly incorporated our names into that (Dhananjayan and Shanta). I was a little embarrassed to

compose that. He came to see the final presentation of his Thillana at home.
I performed it with his original Sahityam. He stopped the performance
and insisted us to do the new Sahityam with our names and told me to
compose dance on the spot before him. So we did it. This Nritta-Tarangini
was again a huge hit and now it is a favourite item of connoisseurs all over
the globe. With our support and suggestions, our disciples conceived an
entire programme of Balamuralikrishna's compositions for an evening
titled "Murali Maadhuri,"' Dhananjayan said.

He recalls that the first ever public recognition and award Naatya
Sudhaarnava was presented to them by Balamuralikrishna's cultural
organization Murali Ravali in Hyderabad in 1982 through the then Chief
Minister Anjiah. After the award function, they were to perform, but the
electricity suddenly went off. To engage the audience, Balamuralikrishna
addressed them in the light of an oil lamp. 'He said, "My critics are under
the impression that I cannot sing without a mic. Now there is no mic or
any electric gadgets. I will sing until the light comes." He began singing
and the audience became silent. The audience was surprised that his voice
could reach the last row. This was a revelation to many Rasikas. I cherish
this incident very vividly,' said Dhananjayan.

Balamuralikrishna's critics did make unfavourable remarks, and in no
uncertain terms, the most famous of them being Subbudu. An acerbic
tongue, caustic wit and blunt opinion often masked his intelligence and
remarks, which many artistes looked forward to. He had some kind of
love-hate relationship with Balamuralikrishna. While he admired his voice
and musical genius in public, he often criticized his compositions. To this,
Balamuralikrishna didn't respond, except to say that 'Subbudu lacked
good knowledge of both Sanskrit and Telugu.' That was an undeniable
fact. In an interview, Balamuralikrishna said, 'Sometimes he likes the
artiste, sometimes the music, sometimes both, and sometimes none!'

The other dancer who shared a long-standing relation with
Balamuralikrishna is Padma Subrahmanyam. The daughter of the famous
film director K. Subrahmanyam, Padma is an academic who did pioneering
research on Bharata's *Natya Shastra*.

'Balamurali anna first visited our house in the early 1960s. He had
not yet migrated to Madras. The famous painter K.R. Venugopal Sarma

who painted the portrait of Tiruvalluvar was a friend of my father. He brought Balamurali anna to our house and arranged a private concert. We were all stunned by his voice and music! My father encouraged him to shift to Madras when he was in two minds about it. Our house was the hub of a lot of cultural activities and gathering spot for many artistes, as my father was the President of IPTA, the Indian People's Theatre Association. The other person who was associated with IPTA and was close to my father was the music director Salil Chowdhury (1923–95). My father introduced Balamurali anna to Salil-da. They had a lot of musical jamming sessions. It was after one of Balamurali anna's concerts in our house that Salil-da created one of his evergreen melodies. He heard Balamurali anna singing Vatapi Ganapatim and was so struck by it that he took the tune and created Jaatose Nahi Bolu Kanhaiya that became a huge hit. In the 1970s, when Balamurali anna was the head of the Tyagaraja Aradhana in Thiruvaiyaru, me and Kannan's mother learnt music from him. One year Kannan was playing veena at the Aradhana. He happened to be wearing a similar jibba. He was performing on the stage, somehow the audiences thought he was Balamuralikrishna's son and went to him and started saying that your son is playing good veena. It was quite hilarious, even funnier was that Balamurali anna did not deny that. That is the kind of bond they shared. Kannan was so inspired by the Ragam Mahati that Balamurali anna invented that he even named his daughter Mahati. In fact, the day Mahati was born, the same evening Kannan composed a Thillana in Ragam Mahati. That year we also sang at the Tyagaraja Aradhana. Shyamala Manni, that is, Kannan's mother, Kannan and me, all three of us learnt from Balamurali anna. In fact, we learnt Tyagaraja's 'Baagaayanayya' in Ragam Chandrajyoti and performed it at the Tyagaraja Aradhana. Poornamma was so fond of me. Whenever I danced, she would attend many of my shows. The love was mutual,' Padma Subrahmanyam said.

She continued about how she danced to his compositions. 'I think I was the first dancer to take his compositions and dance to them. I performed the Hindolam Thillana. His birthday celebrations were held at the Russian Cultural Centre with a whole evening of his compositions. It was presided over by Chembai Vaidyanatha Bhagavatar. Kannan's father

Balakrishnan and Balamurali Anna were extremely close friends. So one was Balu anna and another was Bala anna for me. Balu anna had a slip disc and was in bed. That time Balamurali anna came and said, "I will sing the Navagraha Kritis, and keep it by your bedside. Listen to them every day – that particular Kriti of the day, whichever was relevant." He recorded them in a small transistor and kept them by my brother's bedside. There were only two days for the programme, and he had asked me to choose whatever I wanted to amongst the Varnams he composed. I hadn't decided as yet. I asked him for 'Omkara Pranava'. From a long time, I was always attracted to anything abstract. I always like to take anything challenging. So I told him that he had written it as a Taana Varnam. "If you gave me the Sahityam for all the swaras tomorrow morning, I will perform it day after." It was like a very friendly challenge. "Seri, I will do it tonight," he said. So the Sahityam for the swaras was specially written for me. He actually did it and recorded a tape and sent it to me which I learnt and performed the next evening. Shyamala sang in the programme, Chembai was presiding. He kept exclaiming "Guruvayurappa! Guruvayurappa!" That moment is still in front of my eyes,' recollected Padma Subrahmanyam.

The more important event was the unplanned collaboration that happened the year Balamuralikrishna got the Sangita Kalanidhi. 'I was performing at The Music Academy that year. I had presented something called "Sukha Laasyam". Normally, the dancer performs to the rhythmic phrase embedded in the music of the dance. They don't dance to the music. So I said I'm going to dance to the music, without the rhythm. I am dancing to the Swarasthanams and to the Gamakams. This total synchronization to the music and movement, pitch and octave, the ornament in each swara, like how there is Gamakas for the Swarasthanams, I said there is what is called "Rechaka" which is Gamaka in the body. Because I am a musician, I can feel it. "Sukha Laasyam" cannot be taught to someone who cannot sing. Like music is produced by putting your fingers on different parts of the fretboard of the veena, likewise "Rechakas" come out from different parts of the body. I normally compose all the music for my dance. I rarely use outside music. Balamurali anna was one of the rare musicians whose music I took to. My mother had composed and given name to a Ragam called "Harini" (deer), which was full of leaps and "Vakra Prayogams". The Sahityam contained the word "Murali". I used to dance to this. So one day, Balamurali anna asked me "What is that you do in something new called "Harini"? People are asking me about it and thinking I have composed it. I am also agreeing when they think that way. You better show me what this sounds like. Moreover, 100 years from now, people will think that is my composition and more than all that, they might end up thinking all my compositions are yours!'

'This way we used to have many pleasant and intellectual discussions. So that morning at the Academy, anna was present. I said I will perform "Sukha Laasyam" for which I have composed music in Thodi Ragam. Once the music starts, Shyamala will sing the Ragam, I will perform for the Ragam and then the composition starts. Shyamala Manni had begun singing, when I stopped her and said "if she sings, you all will think this is pre-set. In this august assembly of so many musicians, I welcome any one of you to come and sing a Ragam of your choice and I will perform." At that time, famous writer and critic N.M. Narayanan got up and so I thought he is going to sing. But he left the hall. The audience suddenly started shouting Balamurali anna's name. Then he came up and said: "I thought somebody else may like to sing, that is why I waited. Otherwise I would have come earlier." He turned towards Shyamala and asked her to tune the shruti to Madhyamam, which was his range. He said he is going to sing "Yadukula Kambhoji". I nodded in affirmation and then he began singing. He sang for a few minutes to which I danced. After that he said something very important in Tamil: "There are artistes who think that creativity is like a bubble which will go away or disappear. I want to say if there is real creativity, it cannot be dammed. So what she did and what I did here is something which cannot be dammed and this will be recorded somewhere else."' Saying this, he pointed his finger up as he got off the stage.' This impromptu performance of both made news across the world of music and dance for a long time.

Recollecting some more of her association with Balamuralikrishna, Padma Subrahmanyam added, 'In fact, on an earlier occasion when my father passed away, an organization in Hyderabad was unveiling his portrait. For that occasion, they requested Balamurali anna to come and I was going to dance. So we were all travelling in the train together. We were in cabins next to each other. That is when he composed "Maruluminchera", a Javali in Ragam Chenchurutti. And he asked me to perform it at the function in Hyderabad.'

Balamuralikrishna and Padma Subrahmnayam shared a great friendship and loved each other as any siblings would. 'On every 1st of January, he had a sentiment. He would say: "Give me at least Rs 10 from your hands. You are like Mahalakshmi, so you have to give me something." I would normally write a cheque of Rs 100, which I would give him. Once when I went with that, Poornamma was so excited about our performance earlier, that she was completely carried away in the middle of cooking and cleaning her stove, and came and hugged me without realizing she had completely soiled my new saree with her curry. I can never forget all these memories and the amount of love he and his family had for me.'

The friendship between them automatically translated into them working together without any conscious effort. Padma Subrahmanyam recollected a time when he taught her a song over the telephone. 'Shankara Nethralaya was having a programme at The Music Academy, and I was dancing for them. My car was passing by The Music Academy, behind which Balamurali anna stayed. In the car, my brother Bala was joking and saying: "Are you going to dance about the eyes, since it is for Shankara Nethralaya?" I immediately thought that was a great idea. In an earlier kacheri, I had heard Balamurali anna singing one of his own compositions "Kamaladalayatha Lochana Mulave", set to Ragam Bahudaari, on the eyes of the lord. So I told my brother that I will learn that song from Balamurali anna and dance to it. Saying so, we reached home. I called Balamurali anna and told him my idea. He taught me the song on the phone. He would sing, I would follow and Shyamala Manni would take the notes down. I danced the entire piece with my eyes. I remember Seeta Ratnakar, who was then with the Doordarshan, wanted to record it. We recorded it in the next week itself. This was broadcast on the national programme of dance. The composition was so beautiful!'

Bharatanatyam dancer Sudharani Raghupathy, who hails from Bangalore (Bengaluru), has also choreographed a number of his compositions. Being an older friend of their family, Balamuralikrishna even performed at the wedding reception of Sudharani and Raghupathy in

Bangalore. Years later, when the famous 'Mile Sur Mera Tumhara' project happened, Sudharani was one of the few selected artistes present on the beach listening to Balamuralikrishna singing 'Isaindha Namm'.

The other dancer who had a wonderful long association with him was Alarmel Valli. 'Growing up in Madras, it was mandatory to go to all the season's kacheris. What was remarkable about Balamurali sir's music was how everyone could relate to it (in) some way. His music reached out and touched many age groups. His voice was like molten gold. You cannot but be drawn to the beauty and emotional depth of his style. This must have been in the 1980s. I was being taken in a car in Calgary in Canada. It was nighttime. Those days you had only cassettes. The host began playing a Thillana of Balamurali sir. I think it was the Kadanakuthuhalam Thillana. The car was suddenly filled with a lilting light. I couldn't sit still. I remember I found myself almost dancing sitting on the seat. On enquiring, I was told that this was a Thillana by Balamurali sir. I requested them to make a copy of it for me. I heard it a number of times and Amma said how danceable it was. So I began choreographing it. The thing with his music is that there is sheer joy and sensuousness. I always believed that music has elements of dance and poetry in it. In Balamurali sir's music, the dance of the notes is vividly visible in the mind's eye. His music has an intrinsic quality of dance in it. And that is why it suits dance. For us dancers, half of our work is done. The moment you listen to it, you see a visual in it. There are many shades and textures in his music, which is why it is such a joy to bring it out in movement. I decided to do his Kadanakuthuhalam Thillana. The composition gave a lot of scope to play around with the notes. My singer Prema Ramamurthy was a student of Balamurali sir. The tune seems very simple but within that simplicity, is a lot of complexity. I don't know if Balamurali sir thinks like a dancer, but somehow his stream of consciousness is aligned with yours. He seems to know every nuance in the movement like a dancer would negotiate while doing choreography. When I listen to his music, it comes across that there is a dancer in him. He very instinctively and intuitively gives an expression to the dance of the notes in his music,' recollected Alarmel Valli. She presented his Thillanas as a solo in her *Margam*.

Years later, she and the Odissi dancer Madhavi Mudgal collaborated on a project called "Samanvaya". Here, they performed the Kadanakuthuhalam Thillana to an entirely different choreography. This was probably the first time that Balamuralikrishna's compositions were being presented in Odissi. 'We didn't want to do this thing of dancers coming together on the final stage where the music is just present, while each dancer is doing their individual thing. From the beginning we decided to work the choreography out, where we are two halves of a whole. Both Bharatanatyam and Odissi, but without any discord or visual disparity for a viewer. I remember the first time we were doing it. We danced for many hours and saw that all of that had come to just about two minutes. It was a slow process. We wanted to play with contrasts and with similarities. Each Avartana, we had to find commonalities of movement, do justice to the joy of the music and the space, without compromising our styles. Sometimes we would deliberately use movements which were opposite but done together. For me it was a learning process to be dancing in tandem with someone, and for her it was a totally new experience working with Carnatic music,' recollected Valli about the making of "Samanvaya". This was presented to a packed Music Academy in Madras and later in Delhi and in several international venues like Theatre De La Ville and so on. Valli also performed in Bombay at the sixtieth birthday celebrations of Balamuralikrishna earlier.

One of the other dancers who actually recorded an entire *Margam* based on the compositions of Balamuralikrishna was Rama Vaidyanathan. 'In 2008, we did a proper video shoot of this for two days at the Bharatiya Vidya Bhavan in Chennai,' remembered Rama. The whole idea was to document an entire *Margam* with the compositions of Balamuralikrishna to show his versatility as a Vaggeyakara, who had composed everything from start to finish for a traditional Bharatanatyam recital. 'Balamurali sir was sitting in the front row. He was the only member of the audience in the entire empty hall. Before that I had gone to his place several times and he explained to me the intricacies of all the compositions that I was going to perform. I also needed my singer, Ramya Sundaresan Kapadia, to learn all of these from him. I remember I choreographed the Keertanam "Brihadeeshwara Mahadeva" in Ragam Kanada. Each and every piece that he gave I could easily understand. But this one Keertanam, I somehow couldn't get a grip on it. I knew the meaning and everything, but I couldn't interpret it properly in dance. Just to do a word-to-word Padaartha would be very pedantic. I needed to put in some kind of energy and I knew something was missing. But I couldn't put my finger on it. Though I had choreographed the whole piece, I was not happy with it,' recollected Rama.

The Keertanam was written by Balamuralikrishna when he was a teenager. It is a part of the *Janaka Raga Kriti Manjari*. Rama finally decided to consult him. He then patiently explained the history behind it, saying, 'I was only 16 or 17 when I went to Thanjavur. I visited the Brihadeeshwara temple and I stood in front of the huge Shivalingam and this Keertanam poured out of me and I began "Brihadeeswara Mahadeva Brovumu Maha Prabhuva". After that, my mind was blank. Then I did a Pradakshinam of the entire temple and came and stood again and the Anupallavi came to my mind, "Sahaja Kaarunya Vikshana Saadu Sujana Samrakshana". After that again my mind went blank and I did another Pradakshinam and returned to the Garbhagraham. Then the Charanam came to my mind, "Mamata Paashamula Taalanu Shamana Vairi Dayalekanu". Then I did another Pradakshinam and completed the rest of the Keertanam, "Kamaniya Murali Gana Sama Sangeetamu Ledannu". This way I finished the entire song.'

'When he narrated this incident to me, I somehow felt the image of lord Brihadeeswara was rising within his mind as he went around doing those Pradakshinams. He must have been ruminating, and the seed of the idea must have been slowly growing. So every time he returned back to the Garbhagraham, the output was this new creation. So I incorporated this into the choreography of the Keertanam. The moment I incorporated that, somehow the entire piece took a totally different energy. It got infused with some strange kind of divinity. I myself felt very happy with it and that is how I recorded it,' added Rama. The shooting was done with a two-camera setup and was set to be released as a CD, but that didn't happen. 'We also recorded a Varnam in Thodi, a Padam in Ragam Murali and a Thillana in Dwijavanti,' added Rama. "Murali" was yet another Ragam created by Balamuralikrishna. It was born out of the thirty-fourth Melakarta Ragam Vagadeeswari.

Almost all the Thillanas that Balamuralikrishna composed have been regularly performed by many dancers. Two fairly difficult Thillanas were the 'Gati Bedha Priya' Thillana set to a Ragamalika and the 'Thaaya Ragamalika' Thillana set to Adi Taalam. Both of these were performed by Parshwanath Upadhye, one of the finest male Bharatanatyam dancers. The 'Gati Bedha Priya' Thillana was composed in such a way that the rhythm cycle changes in every Charanam along with the Ragam. If this wasn't complicated enough, the name of the Ragam occurs within the Sahityam of the composition. 'The composition is actually very beautiful and all the five Taalam Gatis come. So all the Jaatis change while the speed remains the same. This is very challenging. It is difficult in terms of changeover while dancing. First we tried this for a group choreography. I had done a programme called 'Sadgati' with five dancers. So it was easy to work with five Jaatis, giving a dancer each of them. We had a live orchestra with two singers and I thought it would be a challenging musical conversation between the musicians and the dancers. It worked out very well. Then I converted that into a solo,' recollected Parshwanath. The composition is tightly packed with almost zero breathing space between the rhythm cycles. 'While choreographing it for dance, I had to take a few liberties. While shifting from Trisra to Chaturasra or Khanda to Chaturasra, dance-wise it wasn't showing out as much as it was in the music. The smooth transition sounds very well when sung in a kacheri. But when it comes to choreographing for dance, I thought inserting a pause between two cycles was required. So I did half Avartanam in the pause and changed the Gati. So in the pause, when I go back there is a *Takita Dhikita* and then the Gati changes to the next,' he added.

The Thillana begins with Ragam Gurupriya in the Pallavi and Anupallavi, and goes to Ragam Rasikapriya set to Trisra Gati in the first Charanam, to Ragam Gayakapriya set to Misra Gati in the second Charanam, to Ragam Sunaadapriya set to Sankeerna Gati in the third Charanam and finally, Ragam Karaharapriya—set to Khanda Gati in the fourth Charanam. After each Charanam you return to the Anupallavi first and end with the Pallavi before you get to the next Charanam. A truly mind-boggling mathematical feat for a composition and that too a Thillana. This was the same Thillana Balamuralikrishna ended his famous

Sangita Kalanidhi concert with at The Music Academy. As Parshwanath said laughing over the phone, 'Normally nobody sits for a Thillana in a dance performance. They see the Varnam and leave.' But this did not seem to matter to the composer Balamuralikrishna. Though it was a Thillana, it was highly embellished like a piece of silver filigree work.

'In the other Thillana, which was the Thaaya Ragamalika Thillana, the entire Thillana is in Chaturasram. While the scale changes, it starts in one scale and the next Ragam shifts to another scale. The challenge is to come back to the original Shadjamam. It was a bigger challenge for the singer than for me,' said Parshwanath. This Thillana begins with the Pallavi set to Ragam Kalyani and the Anupallavi to Ragam Sankarabharanam. The first Charanam is in Mohanam, the second in Hindolam and the third in Darbari Kanada. 'In this Thillana, Balamurali sir mentions the Panchabhootas. So I made use of Bhoomicharis and Aakashacharis in the transitions,' he added.

The Seventy-Fifth Year

On 10 April 2005, the Karnataka Lalit Kala Academy in Bangalore honoured him with the Lifetime Achievement award on the occasion of the common New Year festival of Ugadi that both states, Andhra Pradesh and Karnataka, celebrate. On 16 April, the Kerala-based organization Swaralaya headed by Justice Balakrishna Erady conferred upon Balamuralikrishna the prestigious Swaralaya Puraskaram along with a purse of Rs 1 lakh and a sculpture by Soman Dev. On 25 April, Balamuralikrishna was selected by the French government for the Chevalier des Arts et Letters award, the highest civilian recognition by the government of France. He was the first Carnatic musician and the second south Indian to receive this honour after the famous Tamil cinema actor Sivaji Ganesan. In a report in *The Hindu* dated 6 May, Garimella Subramaniam wrote, 'Balamurali's innate capacity to absorb the facets of foreign cultures and transmit the same through his music is indeed rare. The Kedaram song "Kanula Panduga Russia, Ita Kanaraadendu Eersha" comes to mind. Written in the solitude of a Russian hotel, way back in the 1980s, the Charanam describes the absence of poverty and the principle of "To each according to his needs" in

practice in the erstwhile USSR—"Yevari Joli Vaaridi Ita Joliki Paniledu."
The French honour accorded to Balamuralikrishna by the country's
Minister of Culture and Communication, Renaud Dohnedieu De Vabres,
underscores the global recognition of Carnatic music as a distinct genre.'

The Percussive Art Centre in Bangalore was founded by the
ghatam vidwan K. Venkataraman, who played a number of concerts for
Balamuralikrishna over the years. It grew to be a premier organization
in Bangalore. On 31 May, it honoured Balamuralikrishna with the title
of 'Sangita Kala Shiromani'. Another organization, The Manav Seva
Kendra in Bangalore, honoured him with the title of 'Sangita Saraswathi'
on 25 June.

On 6 July, Balamuralikrishna turned seventy-five. On 25 July, a
grand celebration was organized by his students and fans at The Music
Academy. This was presided over by the then chief minister of Tamil
Nadu J. Jayalalitha and Dr Pratap C. Reddy, the chairman of Apollo
Hospitals. The cultural programmes arranged that evening included
seventy-five singers singing the Varnam of Balamuralikrishna and seventy-
five dancers dancing his Thillana. In addition to that, a special Taala-
Vaadya programme presenting Balamuralikrishna's Panchamukhi Taalam
was presented by ghatam vidwan Vikku Vinayakaram and his disciples.
Balamuralikrishna gave a concert where he presented a new Ragam and
named it after the chief minister as he sang 'Jaya Jaya Lalithe'. One could
see how happy Jayalalitha was, sitting in the first row.

One of the greatest qualificationss of Balamuralikrishna was his
elephantine memory. If anything made an impression on his mind, it never
left him. As a child, he had travelled almost every week from Vijayawada to
Madras by train along with his Guru Pantulu and his father. In an earlier
interview he mentioned how he would barely sleep and sat up all night,
staring outside the window watching the countryside. He knew every
major and minor train junction along the way, and knew when the train
would stop at what junction and for how long. This childhood memory
he would recreate decades later by rattling off all the station names from
Vijayawada to Madras, much to the amusement of his audiences. That
concert on July 25 saw him performing this feat for the chief minister. As
he began from Vijayawada and reached Madras Central, the entire Music

Academy exploded with applause. In the speech that followed, Jayalalitha was an embodiment of humility. She was the artiste there and not a shrewd politician. She extolled Balamuralikrishna's musical achievement and praised him to the heavens. She said,

> I came here today to honour Dr Balamuralikrishna but he has honoured me in a way I never expected. He has created a new raga, he has composed a kirti in this new raga, he has named this raga after me and he has dedicated this raga and kirti to me. This is an honour I never dreamt of and something I will cherish with utmost humility till the end of my days. While speaking here, many referred to Dr Balamuralikrishna as Padma Vibhushan. It is my firm conviction that Dr. Balamuralikrishna deserves no less than the Bharat Ratna. A day will come when we will be able to influence even at the Centre and god-willing when such a day comes, I will see to it that Dr Balamuralikrishna is awarded the Bharat Ratna. By awarding the Bharat Ratna to him, India will only be honouring herself. After seeing his rendition, hearing his rendition of the new raga which he has composed and dedicated to me I would like to say that if I have one wish, it is this: If there is another janma, another birth, I would like to be born as a disciple of Dr Balamuralikrishna. I would like to learn Carnatic music under his tutelage and become such a great singer that my Guru should say Sabhaash after hearing me sing.

One could see the softer and artistic side of Jayalalitha that had gone into hibernation after her image as a politician took over her persona. She conferred on him the title of 'Gandharva Gana Samraat'. Unlike her other engagements, she stayed for the entire length of the evening's programme. This event made a major splash in the national media.

In the same year, the Tirumala Tirupati Devasthanam honoured Balamuralikrishna as a 'Lifetime Asthana Vidwan'. The appointment was conveyed on the phone by the then chief minister K. Rosaiah. The person responsible for this was R.V. Ramanamurthy, who was then the chairman of the State Cultural Council. For the occasion, he composed a Kriti

'Sthana Balamu Neeku, Asthana Balamu Naaku'. He also sang a number of popular Annamacharya Keertanams on that occasion.

Balamuralikrishna continued giving performances through these years. In a review about his performance at the Thyaga Brahma Gana Sabha, Sulochana Pattabhiraman called him 'Markandeya of Carnatic Music' in *The Hindu* dated 21 April 2006. She writes, 'The voice in mint condition, the spirit soaring with infectious zest and enthusiasm and sheer joy in singing were affirmations of the dictum, "What is age, but a number." . . . The breathtaking, sruti aligned karvais on the Tara Sthayi Shadjam would have posed a challenge to musicians half Balamuralikrishna's age . . . The full-throated prayogas steeped in the classical idiom, traversing the entire gamut of the fourth octave were indeed dream displace. Similarly, the powerful forays in the Mandra Sthayi, straight from the music manual, were remarkable outputs . . . As one left the auditorium, a member of the housefull audience was heard to sum up the performance adequately, "Not a dull moment."' Balamuralikrishna was accompanied by S. Varadarajan on the violin, G. Vijayaraghavan on the mridangam and S. Karthick on the ghatam.

It was always known that Chembai Vaidyanatha Bhagavatar had greatly admired Balamuralikrishna and his music for several decades. Balamuralikrishna too had great respect for the veteran. The Guruvayur Temple, of which Chembai was a staunch devotee all his life, dedicated an award in his memory, calling it the Sri Guruvayurappan Chembai Puraskaram. In September 2007, the Devaswom board minister announced the award for Balamuralikrishna. The award was given to him by the veteran music composer V. Dakshinamurthy in a ceremony held in Guruvayur. It was not just in India that Balamuralikrishna was receiving these honours. The same year, his concert in New York was a grand success. To celebrate this, the New Jersey State Assembly honoured him with a recognition. The resolution was read out by the Deputy Speaker Upendra Chivukula and passed by the Speaker Joseph Roberts Jr on that occasion. The function was held in New York at the Plane View Bethpage auditorium in Long Island. Several dignitaries, including Harry Anand, Mayor of Laurel Hollow; Dr Ajay Gondanay, Deputy Consul General of India in New York; Dr Prakash Swamy, the President of the Sri Vari Foundation; and others were present.

On 9 February 2008, the University of Mysore honoured Dr Balamuralikrishna with an honorary DLitt at the eighty-eighth annual convocation. This was his seventh doctorate he was receiving. For a primary school dropout, who would have imagined that he would be decorated with seven university doctorates? In many interviews later, Balamuralikrishna would laugh about it saying with childlike glee, 'I never studied or went to school, but I have seven doctorates.'

In the last quarter of 2009, Doordarshan Chennai organized a special function at the Narada Gana Sabha to commemorate its golden jubilee year. On that occasion, Balamuralikrishna was honoured for his contribution to All India Radio.

On 19 February, the Kerala-based Pazhassiraja Charitable Trust honoured Balamuralikrishna with the title of 'Sangeetha Retna'. The function was held at the Rashtrapati Bhavan. Carnatica was an organization founded by musician Shashikiran. He and his brother Ganesh both learnt music from Balamuralikrishna briefly. They performed together as the Carnatica Brothers. They have also been organizing numerous festivals. The Bharat Sangeet Utsav is one of the festivals they conceived which became extremely successful. They conferred the lifetime achievement award on Balamuralikrishna on 30 October. Balamuralikrishna sang for movies whenever he was offered. *Graamam*, produced and directed by Mohan Sharma, was one of the last ones. Balamuralikrishna won the best classical music singer award presented by the Kerala State Chalachithra Academy for this.

This way numerous awards kept coming his way, and Balamuralikrishna gracefully received them. He was healthy and travelling extensively in and outside India. All his concerts were always successful. There were rarely any occasions when he gave a lacklustre concert. The voice continued to soar above three octaves effortlessly. In the twilight years of his life, Balamuralikrishna was as sprightly as a teenager.

As we had seen, Balamuralikrishna was adept at building musical bridges with other genres. He had in the past performed a jugalbandi with the Hindustani flute maestro Pt Hariprasad Chaurasiya. But that didn't stop him from encouraging a younger artiste like Ronu Majumdar. Ronu was also a brilliant Hindustani flautist, a student of Pt Vijayaraghava Rao, whom Balamuralikrishna knew earlier. They went on a successful concert tour to the US in 2011 and later to Bangladesh. In September 2011, Balamuralikrishna was honoured for his contribution to Indian classical music by Global Indian Music Academy. He also received the prestigious Swati Puraskaram instituted by the government of Kerala.

In the summer of 2015, Balamuralikrishna's eighty-fifth birthday celebrations were ushered in. His student Krishnakumar organized a function at the Bharatiya Vidya Bhavan, where several musicians like K.J. Yesudasa and Aruna Sairam were present. Balamuralikrishna cut the cake and made a brief speech. One could see he was not doing very well.

Saraswathi

Anybody associated with Balamuralikrishna in the last three decades of his life would have interacted with and met Saraswathi. Saraswathi Sundaresan trained in Bharatanatyam under Pandanallur Shanmugasundaram Pillai. She also learnt a few items like the Navasandhi Kautuvams from Sudharani Raghupathy. She was one of the earliest to create a production of dance around the compositions of Balamuralikrishna, calling it 'Murali Gana Sudha'. She toured with the production, going to various cities across India. She slowly endeared herself into being his manager and handling his office affairs. I remember meeting her in the mid-1990s along with the critic Subbudu. She was an organizer who ran the 'Vipanchee Trust'. There were many good things about her communication skills and efficiency. She was also shrewd, and knew how to promote herself as a dancer even though she wasn't known as an exceptional dancer. One can go back to her career as a dancer and see there is nothing much to write home about. She was, however, a good teacher and trained a number of students. It has been a fact in the dance world that most performers don't make great teachers and vice versa. She belonged to the similar category.

Over the years, in his advancing years, Balamuralikrishna couldn't handle his hectic profession. Saraswathi became a filter for anyone who approached Balamuralikrishna. While some of this was probably necessary, there were occasions when it led to things turning sour. In fact, my own initial interactions with Saraswathi began on a confrontational note. It was only when she realized that I was a classical music and dance critic and a writer, and that my earlier interviews with Balamuralikrishna were liked by him, that she slowly began to ease up. But there were many others who faced her ire later. Though many people complained to Balamuralikrishna about Saraswathi, he paid no heed. As a result of his silence, Saraswathi began assuming more authority than usual. Almost everyone I interviewed mentioned how she ought to have known her limits. She would reportedly constantly try to keep him away from home and family. In his professional life, if anyone had to reach Balamuralikrishna, they had to go via her.

Several organizers complained that she demanded a lot of money. They would give it because of their love for Balamuralikrishna's music, but later they would learn that payment never reached Balamuralikrishna. Cleveland Sundaram mentioned how they signed a contract of several lakhs of rupees to record Balamuralikrishna's entire repertoire of Tyagaraja Kritis. A large part of the payment was already made. It was well-known that Balamuralikrishna thoroughly enjoyed visiting casinos on several of his foreign tours. 'It was very easy to get him to agree to perform concerts in destinations that had casinos,' recollected Pt Ajoy Chakrabarty, who sang over fifty jugalbandis with him. Balamuralikrishna would boast that he never lost money ever in a casino, but only won. He would inevitably win a large amount of money, which he would give to Saraswathi because she was his manager. What happened to all that remains a mystery!

Balamuralikrishna's students also complained of her unnecessary interference. Krishnakumar had begun an academy of music with Balamuralikrishna in Ernakulam, with the help of Apple Academy. 'When Saraswathi got to know Guruji was frequenting Kerala with me, she promptly made sure that the whole project came to an end,' recollected Krishnakumar. She also tried to usurp the famous Sooryakanta Bhavanumu which Pattabhiramayya so lovingly built, saying that she was going to convert it into some kind of a memorial. This news became public soon and was the talk of the town, both in Tamil Nadu as well as in Andhra. The family intervened and saved the Bhavanamu, which still stands secure in Satyanarayanapuram in Vijayawada. In 2013, Saraswathi went for a medical check-up and slipped in the bathroom and died on

13 July. With her demise, a lot of things were left incomplete, a lot of questions unanswered. Where is the famous 'Gandapendaram'?

And all the other honours, gold medals, bracelets that she was entrusted with? Dr Jayalakshmi, an old friend, recollected an incident, when Balamuralikrishna called her home and showed her a huge heap of jewels, including his famous 'Gandapendaram', countless gold bracelets studded with diamonds and rubies, and more. He joked to her saying he had more jewellery than she. He also mentioned that Saraswathi was going to create a memorial for him, where she would keep all this memorabilia on display. Balamuralikrishna's family were not even aware of how much was missing. 'Obviously we never really bothered to see. We knew he had everything. It was in the bank lockers, as far as we knew. It was only after his demise, we found everything missing,' recollected his grandson Vibhu. The family was helpless. Nobody knew whom to ask or hold accountable. In any other country, these precious items would have been proudly displayed in a museum to flaunt a musical legacy. Imagine losing the tanpura of a Tansen or the stylus of Thiruvalluvar? That loss belongs to everyone!

Balamuralikrishna was a human being with all the frailties and vulnerabilities of a human being, after all! And which human is exempt from making mistakes? If he was all that perfect, he would have been a god. There is a beautiful sloka in the Panchatantra that explains how even the mighty can fall to the call of fate.

पौलस्त्यः कथमन्यदारहरणे दोषं न विज्ञातवान्
रामेणापि कथं न हेम-हरिणस्यासम्भवोऽलक्षितः ।
अक्षैश्चापि युधिष्ठिरेण सहसा प्राप्तो ह्यनर्थः कथं
प्रत्यासन्न-विपत्ति-मूढमनसां प्रायो मतिः क्षीयते ॥ - पञ्चतन्त्रम् 2.4

How did Rāvaṇa fail to see that it is wrong to abduct another's wife!
How did Rāma fail to see that a golden deer could never exist!
How did Yudhiṣṭhira fail to see that gambling would lead to misery?
Generally, the understanding of one declines by impending calamity.

The Last Concert

This seemed to be the beginning of the end. Balamuralikrishna realized how he had been taken for a ride. All he could do was repent in his old age. He became an emotionally fragile person, and dealing with him became increasingly difficult by the day. However, he never once allowed that to affect his music. He continued to give concerts assisted by his student Krishnakumar. On 18 February 2016, Balamuralikrishna gave his last concert in the village of Anakapalli in Andhra Pradesh. He sang at the Ravugopala Rao Kalakshetram in a concert organized by Dhadi Ratnakar who heads the Diamond Hits Organization. M.S.N. Murthy on the violin, V.V. Ramanamurthy on the mridangam and Rayaprolu Baladinakar on the ghatam accompanied him. Though he was frail, when he opened his mouth to sing, the voice continued to effortlessly soar three octaves. Accompanying artistes half his age couldn't match up to his musical brilliance.

When not giving concerts, he continued to teach students like Shyam who visited him every day. But there was something that was not okay about him anymore. His youngest daughter Mahati who stayed nearby visited him every day. In his own diaries he wrote how fond he was of her. The older son Abhiram and daughter-in-law Krishnaveni visited him often. In Madras at home, his daughter-in-law Rekha and her son Vibhu took utmost care and concern. They say that when a person ages, he becomes extremely childlike. This has been true of hundreds of artistes in the past. They need the care and concern that a child requires. Vibhu would take care of him like that. It was a role reversal of sorts. Balamuralikrishna never had any known health problems like diabetes or hypertension, which one usually expects in veterans of his age. He was healthy and sang with his robust voice till the final concert.

'The Hyderabad-based dance Guru Hemamalini Arni once told me that male classical singers often hit their peak post-seventy lasting pretty much into the nineties. Their craft chiselled to perfection after a lifetime of sadhana coupled with the wisdom that comes after being cooked to tenderness in the pressure cooker of time. Balamuralikrishna, she said, was the perfect example. I couldn't disagree. His concerts in the years preceding his death were as good, if not better than when he was younger,' wrote journalist and author T.R. Vivek, who is a serious Carnatic music connoisseur.

Several of his friends like T.V.G. would come visiting him to keep him in good humour. His student Shyam would come for classes and that would continue with them going for a drive to the beach. On 21 November 2016, Shyam visited him and he took a promise to have one of their regular beach visits the next day. On 22 November, he had his lunch and took a nap in the afternoon and woke up in another world. For someone who sang all the songs of Saint Bhadrachalam Ramadasu and Saint Tyagaraja, who wrote in their love and admiration of lord Rama, Balamuralikrishna made his exit on a Navami. He probably had a kacheri to enthral the gods above.

The news of Balamuralikrishna's demise enveloped the world of music with gloom. Several of his colleagues and students rushed to his house to pay their respects. Tributes began pouring in from across the country. Classical musicians, film professionals, politicians, bureaucrats and almost everyone from every walk of his life has something to share. He should have ideally been given state honours, but the then head of state J. Jayalalitha was herself battling for life. She, too, made her exit on 5 December. She had expressed her wish to be reborn as his student. Maybe she went on to pursue that. That December season, many artistes and sabhas paid their respects to Balamuralikrishna. While many made loud proclamations, several other artistes handled it differently. For example, I remember attending Vidwan Abhishek Raghuram's Music Academy concert where he sang a medley of compositions of Bhadrachala Ramadasu as a musical tribute. There were no grand announcements. Just a subtle heartfelt tribute.

It was as if he needed to be taken care of, even in the heavens. Two months after he passed away, Annapoornamma also made her final exit. She was his lifelong partner, now in another world too. It was as if she was living only for him. Having taken care of his large family all her life, she was an embodiment of selfless love. Everyone who came in touch with her remembers her warmth. Grandson Vibhu remembered what an efficient homemaker and money-manager she was. She had mastered the art of keeping such a large family together. In addition to that, she was an embodiment of endless hospitality to the constant stream of guests, students and music colleagues at all times. The old saying which goes behind every successful man is a strong woman would stand cent per cent in this case.

Annapoorna was the reason, and a very strong one at that, for Balamuralikrishna's successful career as a musician. She managed that part of his life which would have easily consumed him. Setting him free to indulge in his musical creativity, she took on the humongous burden he would have otherwise come under. In that sense, she was a brilliant and ideal traditional Hindu housewife. Her only concern was Balamuralikrishna. Her world began and ended with him. Not even his music, for that matter. She would rarely attend his concerts, unlike wives of other musicians who were regular first-rowers. She belonged to a different generation of strong women whose sensibilities were deeply rooted in traditional family values.

As Jayalakshmi pointed out in an interview, 'If she wanted to, she could have easily left Balamuralikrishna in the middle of all his controversies. The world around was gossiping right through the 1960s when Abhayam came around till the years of Saraswati. But she would say one thing. "If I leave him and go, who will take care of him? He is a great musician and there is nothing he hasn't achieved in his professional career. The bad name would have been his. Not mine!" This was her nature. She was always very giving. A true Annapoona in her very character and nature!' She was already bed-ridden in his last months. It actually felt like a design ordained by divine intervention. The grand matron of the Mangalampalli home followed her husband like a Maha Pativrata. She had been that all her life. She continued it in her demise too. The children and family were devastated, to say the least. It was too much of a personal tragedy to take in such a short time. It took them a while to get back to normal.

With the exit of Balamuralikrishna, an era of Carnatic music came to an end. What he left behind was a large corpus of extraordinarily original work.

No other artiste in the history of Carnatic music enjoyed the kind of name, fame, popularity, and spotlight or faced dissension like Balamuralikrishna did in modern India. There were diehard fans of his, who loved everything he did, and there were his critics, who were confused about what they didn't agree with. But he was not a figure one could ignore. His music spanned several genres and touched many lives. In his essay titled 'Balamuralikrishna – the Musical Polymath', noted Sanskrit scholar Shatavadhani Dr Ganesh wrote,

> When we think about his talent and scholarship, cogitate about his achievements and personality, we feel that a legendary saga has passed by. Beyond the specialities and eccentricities of his personality, what attracted the world by the force of its brilliance was his art. To put it simply, Balamurali made people fall in love with music and cherish it. He is among the few who made Carnatic music accessible to all ears. The hallmark of a great artiste is that his art is appreciated by both scholars and laymen alike. If not, at least he produces art that evokes doubt, fear, admiration, and jealousy among the scholars who analyse it. And as for the lay listeners, he makes them consume his art with wonder cum love and concentration. In that sense, Balamurali was an unparalleled musical talent who attracted Pundits and laymen, young and old alike with his music.

In a moving tribute to his Guru, Ragavan Manian writes, 'I have had the privilege of discussing Guruji's legacy with him on numerous occasions. I tried to recall some conversations with a hope that I will find an answer in them. In those discussions, his attitude had ranged from passionate to fatalistic. The range of attitudes was understandable, for he was impossible to classify. Most eulogies to him read like roster lists of awards and achievements, the breadth and depth of (which) boggle the mind. There can be no boxing his genius. Indian music (Bharatiya Sangeetham) was his second nature, and with this broad vista, there was not a single idiom that he hadn't fully internalised and worked his magic upon. Voice, instruments, opera, cinema, language, movement – he was monarch of all that he surveyed. His purported muse was the ancient and revered goddess of music. Given this, how can anyone carry forward his legacy?'

Manian's sentiments echo with hundreds of fans and Rasikas across the world. They had said that the greatest musicians, especially Indian classical art performers like Pt Bhimsen Joshi, Pt Ravishankar and Kishori Amonkar, were 'one-piece-make'. One can take Balamuralikrishna's name in the same breath and say that he too was of that make.

It was indeed true that both Panditas and Paamaras were in awe of Balamuralikrishna. One is reminded of the poem written by the great poet Chellapilla Venkata Sastry, one-half of the iconic duo of 'Tirupati Venkata Kavulu', whose contribution to Telugu literature is unparalleled. He wrote:

గాత్రం ప్రమాతమే గాక ప్రాతమును స యితము కంటికి రెప్పగా ప్రేపుడుబోచి బాల మురళి శ్రీ కృష్ణుని బాల మురళి కృష్ణడేలుత మాయిష్య మెచ్చాసంగి

ఈ ముజ్జగంబులడుగుల ఏ మహితు డిమిడ్చి యిచ్చె ప్రిందునకున్ స్వ రామము, నిల నల సౌక్షా ద్యామనుడు భరించు దృష్టి వా చెడకుండన్

రెండు న ఎనిమిది కూడిన నిండుగ నొకటగు నటంచు నిన్ గానముతో పండించే కనకదుర్గ యే పండుగగా నేడు మమ్మ బాలమురళి

నా వలెనే వృద్ధుడవై నా వలెనే కీర్తిగాంచి నావలెనే శ్రీ దేవీ పదభక్తుడవై భూవలయము తిరుగు మోయి మురళీకృష్ణా!

After praising him and his music, Sastry blesses him saying 'May you become as aged and as popular as me, and may you go around the world!' Rich and generous blessings from a poet laureate.

The great Viswanatha Satyanarayana called him an 'Avataramurti' and poet Puttaparthi Narayanaacharyulu called him a 'Gandarva Vidya Paarangatudu'. If you thought these were common sentiments shared by old world scholars, Balamuralikrishna's contemporaries were no less. Playback singer P.B. Sreenivos wrote:

एक है गायक लाखों में !
मन है एक अनेकों में !
बात रसीली धुन है सुरीली !
लगता है हर अदा निराली !
मुख है प्रकाश का दर्पण !
रसमय है प्रतिभा का दर्शन !
लीन है स्वर में इनका तनमन !
की है इन्होने अदृत प्रगति !
जनम जनम की जो है सुकृति !
यश है इन का गगन-विशाल !
हो बेजोड़ हरेक कमाल !

These kinds of accolades would have made anyone headstrong and arrogant. That was also one of the accusations against Balamuralikrishna. Many times his silence was presumed to be arrogance. He would calmly respond with his old favourite 'Mouname Nee Bhasha O Mooga Manasa', the famous number that he sang earlier. But those who interacted with him at close quarters knew how childlike he was. Sometimes it was impossible to believe the same person had created so many musical marvels and the next moment he was sitting and discussing cricket. On one side he would discuss the intricacies of a Ragam with his student, and the next morning he was being entertained by the President of India. He was no exception to being eccentric, like many other geniuses. But his eccentricities never overshadowed his persona as a musician.

What counts is how he inspired a whole generation of artistes. His compositions continued to be performed by the best of the younger generation Carnatic vocalists like Saketharaman, Trichy Pradeep Kumar, Abhishek Raghuram, Kunnakudi Balamuralikrishna, Sandeep Narayanan and others. And instrumentalists like flute Vidwan JB Sruti Sagar and the prodigious veena vidwan Ramana Balachandran. It was his music that inspired several fans to name their children after him. The young Carnatic vocalist Kunnakudi Balamuralikrishna's name was inspired by him. Several others named their children after his creations. His student Sekar named his daughter 'Mahati' after the Ragam created by Balamuralikrishna. He is probably one of the few classical stalwarts whose statue adorns several places. The famous Tummalapalli Kalakshetram in the heart of the city of Vijayawada has life-size statues of a whole host of Telugu luminaries. Among writers, poets, actors and other public personalities, is a beautiful statue of Balamuralikrishna seated in a concert pose. Earlier in 2020, another life-size statue was unveiled at his birthplace in Sankaraguptam. In the remote village of Sevalaperi, on the bank of the Tamraparani river in the Tirunelveli district of Tamil Nadu, lived T.R. Sankara Iyer, a great devotee of goddess Durga. Balamuralikrishna visited him over half a century ago and promised him that he would help him build the temple to goddess Durga.

Keeping his word, he not only mobilized enough funds, but had the temple constructed and consecrated according to all the needed Shastras in the year 2000. As a tribute to this great service, the villagers and the temple authorities honoured Balamuralikrishna by having a statue of him as one of the many statues that decorate the Rajagopuram. This was yet another rare and unheard of honour for a musician in his own lifetime. To be immortalized on the Rajagopuram of a temple would mean to be remembered forever, as long as the temple continues to function.

The lane in Satyanarayanapuram where Sooryakanta Bhavanamu stands has been named 'Balamuralikrishna Street' in his honour. The government of Andhra Pradesh announced an annual award with a purse of Rs 10 lakh in honour of Balamuralikrishna. This was yet another rare state honour that no other classical musician has received in the twenty-first century. In one of his older speeches, he had mentioned how the Saint Tyagaraja was still alive because his music and compositions were sung day in and day out. Balamuralikrishna as a composer, wrote over 400 compositions, in his lifetime he gave over 25,000 concerts, he published a number of articles and books and he recorded several hundreds of hours of his music for posterity. Thanks to technology, a good part of it is available and accessible to everyone. He was probably one of the few classical musicians whose professional career as a performing artiste was under the media glare from day one. Balamuralikrishna immortalized himself through his music. In an older interview, Balamuralikrishna had mentioned that he was living many lives at one time. It is not possible to document every little thing he did. It might require much more than this. What I have done is to tell you in concise, a short story from each of those lives. This is but a biography of the many things he did.

The famous Sanskrit poet Bhartrihari of the fourth century in his Niti Shatakam wrote:

जयन्ति ते सुकृतिनो रससिद्धाः कवीश्वराः ।
नास्ति तेषां यशःकाये जरामरणजं भयम् ।।२०।।

Victorious and auspicious
the lordly poets perfect in poetic taste.
Their body–fame—has no
Fear born of old age and death.

Balamuralikrishna was indeed a 'Rasasiddha' in the true term of the word. He experienced rasa and shared it with his audiences, making them true 'Rasikas'.

Acknowledgements

Another tome can be written about the amount of goodwill Dr Mangalampalli Balamuralikrishna left behind. Everyone who met him had a story to tell. It only took me a little effort to reach out and see the overwhelming response hundreds of Rasikas gave from across the world. It was a tremendous and moving experience. I owe a great deal of gratitude to so many people. The list is long, and I have tried to include everyone who helped me in this massive project.

HH Sri Sri Sri Bharathi Theertha Mahasannidhanam and HH Sri Sri Vidhu Shekhara Bharathi Sri Sannidhanam of Dakshinamnaya Sharada Peetham, Sringeri, for their abundant blessings. As they blessed their 'Asthana Vidwan' Dr Mangalampalli Balamurali Krishna, it was their overflowing grace and compassion that helped me complete this project. It is at their holy feet that I place this humble work of mine.

A very special note of immense gratitude to Sri Deviprasad Rambhatla Garu, for enabling a research grant in the memory of his parents, Rambhatla Balatripurasundari Garu and Rambhatla Krishna Rao Garu. They were fans and friends of Balamuralikrishna and hosted him often. I dedicate this work to them, in memoriam. A very special mention of gratitude and thanks to my dear friend Sri Ramachander Poodipeddi Garu, for not only pushing me into this further but also getting me in touch with several important people who helped me in my research. Also, for sourcing out several old records and texts of Dr Balamuralikrishna.

In Tamil Nadu (Chennai/Thanjavur/Srirangam /Madurai/Coimbatore): First and foremost, the family members, sons, daughters-in-law and grandchildren of Dr Mangalampalli Balamuralikrishna, for the warmth with which they welcomed me and shared their stories. His sons, Sri Abhiram ji, Sri Sudhakar ji, Sri Vamsee Mohan ji, his daughters, Smt Ammaji, Smt Lakshmi ji in Bangalore, Smt Mahati ji, daughters-in-law Krishnaveni ji and Rekha ji, and granddaughter, Mahima ji, for valuable inputs; and Balamurali Vibhu, the wonderful grandson who is working hard to keep his grandfather's memory alive. This would have been impossible without the support of the whole family.

Shri Murali, president of the Music Academy, Madras, archivist, scholar and critic V.A.K. Ranga Rao Garu and B.M. Sundaram, for sourcing old images; Shri Pappu Venugopala Rao Garu, for his time and valuable inputs; historian and raconteur Sriram Venkatakrishnan and Sharada Sriram, for being a great source of support; Dr Prema Nandakumar and Sri Nandakumar in Srirangam, for sharing their invaluable wealth of knowledge and precious memories; Dr Rama Kausalya of Marabu Foundation in Thiruvaiyaru, Meenakshi Rajmohan and Madhuvanti Badri. Vakeel Ganesan and Sri Panchanadam in Thanjavur. Sri Balachandran and Sharanya Balachandran from Tiruvannamalai, journalist and editor Sri T.R. Vivek.

Mridangam maestros: nonagenarian T.K. Murthy, T.V. Gopalakrishnan, Karaikudi Mani, Guruvayur Dorai, Kamalakar Rao, Srimushnam Raja Rao, Thiruvarur Bhaktavatsalam, Pathri Satish Kumar and K.S.R. Aniruddha.

Violinists: nonagenarian Dwaram Mangathayaru, M.K. Chandrashekhar and the late T. Rukmini, who gave me invaluable inputs into the mathematical mind of Balamuralikrishna; Ms Kanyakumari, Lalgudi Vijayalakshmi, Lalgudi G.J.R. Krishnan, M.A. Sundaresan, M.A. Krishnaswamy, Mysore Nagaraj, Mysore Manjunath and B.V. Raghavendra Rao.

Vocalists: Vidushi R. Vedavalli, Sri Madurai T.N. Sheshagopalan, Sri Unnikrishnan, Sri Sanjay Subrahmanyan, Vidushi Sudha Raghunathan, Vidushi Bombay Jayashree, Vidushi Aruna Sayeeram, Sri Rajkumar Bharathi, Sri Balaji Shankar, Carnatica brothers Shashikiran and Ganesh. Instrumentalists: (chitraveena) Ravikiran, (veena) E. Gayathri, (kannan) Balakrishnan, (mandolin) U. Rajesh, (flute) Shashank, (ghatam) Karthik.

Bharatanatyam artistes: Dr Padma Subrahmanyam, Dr Sudharani Raghupathy, Sri V.P. Dhananjayan and Shanta Dhananjayan, Alarmel Valli, Priya Murle, Rama Vaidyanathan, Parshwanath Upadhye and Adithya P.V.

Kuchipudi artistes: Seeta Rathnakar, Rathna Kumar, Manju Bharghavi, Jaikishore Mosalikanti.

Younger generation Carnatic musicians: Vidwan Abhishek Raghuram, Trichy Pradeep Kumar, Sandeep Narayan, (veena) Ramana Balachandran, (flute) Vidwan J.B. Sruti Sagar, J.B. Keerthana.

Students of Dr BMK: Dr B.M. Sundaram, Dr Prema Ramamurthy, Thiruvaiyaru P. Sekar, Sri Vijayaraghavan, Sri Mohana Krishna, Smt. Mahati, Raghavan Manian, Krishnakumar and Binny Krishnakumar, Cuddalore S.J. Jananiy, Shyam Ravishankar.
    Y. Prabhu and Shashwati Prabhu of Sri Krishna Gana Sabha, the Mylapore Fine Arts Club, Indian Fine Arts,

From the Tamil cinema fraternity: actor Kamal Hassan, music director Shri Ilayaraja ji, Shri A.R. Rahman, Shri K.V. Sekhar, playback singer Smt P. Susheela Amma, the late S.P. Balasubramaniam ji, film critic Baradwaj Rangan.

Friends of Dr BMK: Dr Ayyagari Lakshmi Garu, Dharanikota Jayalakshmi, Dr Sarma Garu, Sri Hari Garu, for opening the world of Sri Hari Achyutarama Sastry Garu, journalist and writer Sri Garimella Subramaniam Garu.

In Hyderabad/Telangana: Sri Ramanachari, veteran journalist Sri Putturi Venkateshwara Rao, scholar and writer Nanduri Parthasarathy and the wonderful archives of his journal *Rasamayi*, director of culture Mamidi Harikrishna, Carnatic vocalists Hyderabad brothers Sri Raghavachari and Sri Seshachari, morsing Vidwan Ghantasala Sathya Sai, violinist (late) Peri Srirama Murthy, violinist Purnachander Rao, who took time out to give me numerous interviews. Veena artiste Ayyagari Syamasunder, K. Krishna Mohan, who helped me access several newspaper archives and images.

In Andhra Pradesh (Vijaywada/Guntur/Kakinada/Vishakapatnam/ Srikakulam/Nellore/Tirupathi): Nonagenarian violinist Sri Annavarapu Ramaswamy Garu, Malladi Suribabu Garu, Malladi brothers Sreeramprasad Garu and Ravikumar Garu, mridangam artiste Parupalli Phalgun, vocalist Modumodi Sudhakar, mridangam vidwan Vankayala Ramanamurthy, archives of the All India Radio in Vijaywada, Ranga Rao in Nellore. Harikatha exponent M.V. Simhachala Shastry Garu, archivist and collector Girija Shankar ji in Guntur, for opening out his vast cassette collection, Polisetty Hari Prasad Garu and Polisetty Shyam Sundar Garu of the Sringeri Peetham temple in Guntur.

A special mention of the precious Annamaya Granthamala in Guntur, Ravi Krishna and Sri Lanka Suryanaraya Rao Garu of the Annamaya Granthamala, for generously sharing their archives.

In New Delhi: Shekhar Sen, former chairman of the Central Sangeet Natak Akademi, Mrs Rita Swami Chaudhary, former secretary of the Central Sangeet Natak Akademi, the librarian and office staff, Pritpal Singh, head of the photo archives, 'Chinamma' Sukanya Pt Ravishankar, sarod maestro Ustad Amjad Ali Khan saab and Mrs Subbalakshami Khan, for sharing their experiences, Amaan and Ayaan Ali Bangash.

Maharashtra (Mumbai/Pune): the family of (late) Vidushi Kishori Amonkar, especially her son, Vibhas Amonkar, the family of Bharat Ratna Pandit Bhimsen Joshi ji in Pune, Shubhada Mulgund, the daughter of Bhimsen ji, the president and staff of Shanmukhananda Sabha, bansuri artiste Pandit Ronu Majumdar, Pandit Nayan Ghosh, Santoor maestro (late) Pt Shiv Kumar Sharma ji, (late) Pandit Jasraj ji for giving their time and interviews.

Karnataka (Bangalore/Mysore/Dharwad/Kaiwaram/Mantralayam): H.S. Tyagaraja of the Harikere family, (late) Vidushi Shyamala Bhave, violin maestro Dr L. Subramaniam and Kavita Krishnamurti, the family of Vidushi Gangubai Hangal, musicologist (late) Ra Satyanarayana of Mysore, violinist duo vidwans Mysore Nagaraj and Mysore Manjunath, Prof. Yogananda of the Advaita Sharada and the Samskrutika Sampatti Project. Ghatam vidwan Giridhar Udupa, Mr Prasad and the Bangalore Gayana Samaja, Sri Rama Seva Mandali, Sanskrit scholar and writer Dr Shatavadhani R. Ganesh, Kuchipudi artiste Manju Bharghavi, Mr Mahesh of Sangeeta Records, who shared his archives, Mr Krishna of Sangeeta Records, who helped with information. Bharatanatyam dancer Praveen Kumar.

In Sringeri: V.R. Gowrishankar, CEO, Sringeri Sharada Peetham, Sri Anand of the Adwaita Shodha Kendra.

In Kerala (Thiruvananthapuram/Cochin/Palakkad): vocalist K.J. Yesudas ji, Prince Rama Varma, (late) film director Lenin Rajendran, Mohiniyattam dancer Neena Prasad.

In West Bengal (Kolkata/Shanti Niketan): Pandit Ajoy Chakraborty, Kaushiki Chakraborty, the archives of the Visva-Bharati University, Ustad Rashid Khan.

In the United States of America: Ravi Joshi ji, who generously shared his experiences and images from his private collection. 'Cleveland' Sundaram ji, for sharing his experiences. K.V. Ramaprasad.

YouTube has been another great source of information. The music channel dedicated to Balamuralikrishna's music, run by Srinivasa Murthy Garu of Bangalore, is a precious archive. I could find several missing links from this. Shri Raju Asokan and Shri Jayram V. Sataluri have also uploaded several old recordings that helped me during my research. Though I have never met all these three fans of Balamuralikrishna's music, I am deeply indebted to them for their generosity in sharing such precious music and making it available to the world at large. It is a research scholar's paradise!

A whole bunch of friends generously provided their skills and time. My dear friend Vikram Venkateshwaran in Chennai, who waded through the draft and gave me invaluable feedback. Lalita Thiruvengadam, editor of the Narthaki website in Chennai, who patiently edited an earlier draft, going through it multiple times.

My dear friend Bharatram Uppili Aravamudan, who meticulously polished a number of archival images, improving their quality. My student Saranga Sharma in Thanjavur, for editing an early rough draft.

Special note of thanks to my very patient literary agent, Kanishka Gupta, who survived my tantrums and other writerly quirks, and my wonderful editor, Swati Chopra ji at Penguin Random House, for having the faith in my work and me. After Swati changed jobs, Elizabeth Kuruvilla took over and continued the work ahead with much patience and persistence.

My mother, father and sister: this is for you!

Finally, to the memory of all the great stalwarts of Dakshina Bharata Shastriya Sangeetam from the Telugu-speaking lands who continue to inspire!

'Endaro Mahanubhaavulu, Andariki Vandanamulu!'

All royalties from the sale of this book will go to the Dr M. Balamuralikrishna Memorial Trust, Chennai.

References and Bibliography

1. *Sangita Sampradaya Pradarsini*, Subbarama Dikshitulu, Vidya Vilasin Press, Ettayapuram, 1904.
2. *Gandharva Kalpavalli: Being a Self-Instructor in Music*, P.S. Ramulu Chetti, first edition, India Printing Works, Madras, 1911.
3. *Abhinaya Svayambodhini*, Devulapalli Veeraraghavamurti Sastri, Saraswati Mudraksarasala, Kakinada, 1915.
4. *A Family History of Venkatagiri Rajas*, Alladi Jagannatha Sastri, Addison Press, Madras, 1922.
5. *Golkonda Kavula Sanchika*, ed. and pub. Suravaram Pratapa Reddy, 1934.
6. *History of Classical Sanskrit Literature*, M. Krishnamachariar, Madras, 1937.
7. *Andhra Vijnana Sarvaswam* (Telugu Encyclopaedia), Telugu Bhasha Samiti.
8. *Classical Bhagawata Mela Dance Drama*, E. Krishna Iyer, Marg 19, 1966.
9. *Andhra Samsthanamulu Sahitya Poshanamu*, Prof. T. Donappa, 1969.
10. *Andhra Nataka Ranga Charita*, Mikkilineni Radhakrishna Murthy, Renuka Granthamala, 1969.
11. *Andhra Vaggeyakara Charitamu*, Balantrapu Rajanikanta Rao, Vishalandhra Publications, Vijayawada, 1958.

12. *Nataratnalu*, Mikkilineni Radhakrishna Murthy, Seetaratnam Granthamala, Vijayawada, 1980.

13. *Folklore of Andhra Pradesh*, Acharya Biruduraju Rama Raju, National Book Trust, New Delhi, 1978.

14. *Contribution of Andhras to Sanskrit Literature*, Acharya Biruduraju Rama Raju, Hyderabad, 2002 and 2007.

15. *Karnataka Sangeeta Pragati: Andhrula Seva* (Telugu), Dr S. Umadevi, Navodaya Bookhouse, Hyderabad, 2011.

16. *Glimpses of Indian Music*, Gowry Kuppuswamy and M. Hariharan, Sundeep Prakashan, Delhi, 1982.

17. *Carnatic Music Composers: A Collection of Biographical Essays*, Dr B. Dayananda Rao (ed.), the Triveni Foundation, Hyderabad, 1995.

18. *Tolinaati Gramophone Gayakulu* (two volumes), Modali Nagabhushana Sharma, Creative Links Publications, Hyderabad, 2012.

19. *Sangita Maharushulu: Vaggeyakarulu*, Narumanchi Subba Rao, Shivasri Publishers, Tenali, 1962.

20. *The Dance Compositions of the Tanjore Quartet*, K.P. Sivanandam (ed.), Tharmapushanam S. Rathinaswamy Chettiar Endowment, 1992.

21. Back issues of *Ganakala* magazine, 1963–74.

22. Back issues of *Natyakala* journal, 1967–72.

23. Centenary souvenir of 'Saraswati Gana Sabha', Kakinada, 2002.

24. Golden jubilee souvenir of 'Tyagaraja Baktha Sabha', Bhimavaram, 1970.

25. Silver jubilee souvenir of 'Tyagaraja Gana Sabha', Hyderabad, 1992.

26. Golden jubilee souvenir of 'Tyagaraja Narayanadasa Seva Samiti', Rajahmundry, 2002.

27. Dr Dwaram Venkataswamy Naidu birth centenary souvenir, Vizainagaram, 1993.

28. Maharaja Pusapati Alaknarayan Gajapati birth centenary festival souvenir, Vizainagaram, 2002.

29. *Abhinaya Darpanam of Nandikeswara*, Prof. P.S.R. Apparao (tr.), Natyamala Publications, Hyderabad, 1997.

30. *The Vizainagaram Music Manuscripts*, Vissa Appa Rao, Journal of the Madras Music Academy, 1952.

31. 'Bhagawata Mela: The Telugu Heritage of Tamil Nadu', Arudra, *Sruti*, 22, 1986.

32. 'Telugu Dance Traditions of Tanjore Court', Arudra, *Shankmukha*, 14, 1988.

33. *Javalilu: Svarasahitamu*, N.C. Parthasarathi and Dvaraka Parthasarathi, Andhra Pradhesh Sangeeta Nataka Academy, Hyderabad, 1980.

34. *Daksinaatyula Naatyakala Charitam*, Nataraja Ramakrishna, Vishalandhra Publishers, Hyderabad, 1968.

35. *Tanjore as a Seat of Music during the 17th, 18th and 19th Centuries*, S. Seetha, University of Madras, 1981.

36. *When God Is a Customer: Telugu Courtesan Songs by Kshetrayya and Others*, A.K. Ramanujan, Velcheru Narayana Rao and David Shulman, University of California Press, Berkley, 1994.

37. *The Sangita Sara of Sri Vidyaranya*, S. Ramanathan, The Journal of the Music Academy, 1980.

38. *Karnataka Sangita Vahini*, Ra. Sathyanarayana, Kannada Pusthaka Pradhikara, 1980.

39. 'Later Sangita Literature', Dr V. Raghavan, *Bulletin of the Sangeet Nataka Akademi*, 17, 1960.

40. *Telugu Saints and Sages*, vol. 1, Acharya Biruduraju Ramaraju, Prof. M. Sivarama Krishna (tr.), Sri Sai Publications, Hyderabad, 2005.

41. *Report of the first All India Music Conference*, Baroda Printing Works, Baroda, 1916.

42. *Gayaka Sarvabhowma Parupalli Ramakrishnayya Pantulu Jeevita Charitra* (Telugu), Kona Venkataraya Sharma, 1940.

43. *Sri Tyagaraja Swamy Shata Varshikotsava Sanchika*, Vissa Appa Rao (ed.), Andhra Ganakala Parishat, Rajamundry, 1947.

44. *Another Garland: Biographical Dictionary of Carnatic Composers and Musicians*, book 3, N. Rajagopalan, Carnatic Classicals, Madras, 1994.

45. Gayaka Sarvabhouma Golden Jubilee Aradhana Festival souvenir, Vijayawada, 2001.

46. *Ponduri Parthasarathi, Rasamayi,* monthly magazine, July 2001 issue.
47. *Two Men and Music,* Janaki Bakhle, OUP, 2005.
48. *Gayaka Sarvabauma Parupalli Ramakrishnayya Pantulu,* P.N. Muralidharan, Chennai Fine Arts, December 2012.
49. Prof. Ritha Rajan, Sahapedia Online, https://www.sahapedia.org/veena-dhanammal-1868%E2%80%931938
50. *Journal of the Music Academy,* volumes 4–8, 1933–37.
51. *The Spiritual Heritage of Tyagaraja,* text in Devanagari with an English translation by C. Ramanujachari. Introduction by Dr V. Raghavan. Foreword by S. Radhakrishnan. Sri Ramakrishna Math, Madras, 1958.
52. Old issues of *Andhra Patrika.*
53. Old issues of *Gruhalakshmi.*
54. Personal interview with Annavarapu Ramaswamy.
55. *Manuscripts of Andhra,* Prof. Ramaswamy, Bangalore.
56. *Andhra Gazette,* 1930.
57. Interview with Nookala Chinna Satyanarayana, *Surabhi* magazine, December 2010.
58. *Janaka Raga Kriti Manjari,* Mangalampalli Balamuralikrishna, Welcome Press, Guntur, 1952.
59. Thyagaraja bicentenary souvenir, the Mulakanadu Sabha, Madras, 1947.
60. *Ananda Vikatan,* old issues, 1940–45.
61. *Grihalakshmi,* March 1949 issue.
62. *Saptaswaralu* (Telugu book), Mangalampalli Suryanarayana, privately published, 1975.
63. *The Devadasi and the Saint: The Life and Times of Bangalore Nagarathnamma,* Sriram V., East West Books, Chennai, 2007.
64. *Splendour of Swaras,* B.M. Sundaram, Siddhi Books, 1996.
65. *Murali Madhuri* (Telugu book), V. Banda, Bharathiradha Publications, Eluru, 2003.
66. 'Rasamayi', *Samskrutika Maasa Patrika,* edited and published by Nanduri Parthasarathi, January 2003 issue, Hyderabad.
67. 'Sajeeva Swaralu: Interview with Prayaga Vedavati', AIR, Vijayawada.

68. 'Bahumukha Pratibhashali: Balamurali', radio programme by M. Chittaranjan, AIR, Vijayawada.

69. *Kasbekar, Asha, Pop Culture India!: Media, Arts, and Lifestyle*, ABC-CLIO, p. 132, ISBN 978-1-85109-636-7.

70. 'The Voice Next Door', *Caravan*, 1 December 2012, retrieved 30 October 2014.

71. 'An Anthem, Almost', Daily News, 20 August 2009, retrieved 30 October 2014.

72. *Strictly Personal: Manmohan and Gursharan*, Daman Singh, HarperCollins Publishers India, p. 62.

73. *Four Score and More: The History of the Music Academy*, Sriram V. and Malathi Rangaswami, East West Books, Chennai, 2009.

74. *Harikesanallur Dr L Mutthaih Bhagavatar: A Biography*, Dr Meera Rajaram Pranesh, Vanamala Center for Art and Culture, Bangalore, November 2014.

75. *Tyagaraja Keertanalu: Vishesha Vivaranamu*, vol. 1, Kalluri Veerabhadra Sastri, Swadharma Swarajya Sangha, Chennai, 1975.

76. *Sri Hari Achyutarama Sastry Gari Rachanalu*, K.S.R. Balakrishna Sastry, Hyderabad, July 2015.

77. *Thirty Second Thrillers: Tales That Tell the Stories Behind the Ads We Love*, K.V. Sridhar, Bloomsbury India, 2017.

78. *Sringara Padamulu: Pracheena Agnata Kavikrutamu*, P. Sitapati and K. Venkateswara Rao (eds), Andhra Pradesh Government Oriental Manuscripts Library and Research Institute, Hyderabad, 1972.

79. *Vaggeyakara Ratna Brahmasri Hari Nagabhushanam Gari Divyanama Keertanalu*, K.S.R. Balakrishna Sastry, Hyderabad, 2015.

80. *Fidelu Naidu Garu*, M. Ravikrishna (ed.), VVIT Book Series, no. 4, Guntur, 2019.

81. *Naanna: Nenu*, Bujjai, Creative Links, Hyderabad, 2013.

82. 'Swan Song?', *Illustrated Weekly of India*, Bombay, November 1985.

83. 'Jealousy Had Killed Many a Genius', *Times of India*, July 1986.

84. 'An Enigma (Four Parts)', Naarada, *Economic Times*, Bombay, 1986.

85. https://www.livemint.com/Leisure/oa8LYCxvv6140d53015NpN/The-making-of-a-musical-prodigy.html

86. https://baradwajrangan.wordpress.com/2014/10/17/master-of-arts/

87. https://mohannadkarni.org/bhimsen-joshi-is-75/

88. *Andhra Samsthanamulu Sahitya Poshanamu, Thomati Donappa*, Pravarthana Publications, 1969.

89. *Harikatha Bhikshuvu, Srimath Panditaradhyula Sambamurthy Ayyavari Jeevana Darshanam*, M.S. Suryanarayana, 2018.

90. *Marapuraani Maneeshulu*, Tirumala Ramachandra, AJO-VIBHO-KANDALAM Foundation, Hyderabad, 2001.

91. *Telugu Harikatha Sarvasvam*, Thomati Donappa, Telugu Academy, Hyderabad, 1978.

92. *Viprula Gotra Rushula Charitra: Pravara Manjari*, compiled by N. Durgamallikarjuna Sharma, Vasishta Cultural Association, Secunderabad, 2018.

93. *Rajarajecharam*, Kudavayil Balamsubramanian, Kannamma Balasubramanian, Thanjavur, 2015.

94. *Madhu Murali*, commemorative volume, Abhinandana Sanchika, HSVK Ranga Rao, Nellore, 2010.

95. *Saptaswaralu, Mangalampalli Suryanarayana*, Sahiti Samsta, Bhimavaram, 1971.

96. *Voice of the Veena: S. Balachander*, Vikram Sampath, Rupa Publications, 2012.

97. *Srinivasa Iyer: Life and Music*, Subrahmaniam V. and Sriram V. Semmangudi, Westland Books, Chennai, 2006.

98. *Collected Writings on Indian Music*, vols 1–3, Dr V. Raghavan Centre for Performing Arts, in association with Sangeet Nataka Akademi, New Delhi, 2007.

99. *Musical Composers during Wodeyar Dynasty, 1638–1947*, Dr Meera Rajaram Pranesh, Vee Emm Publications, Bangalore, 2003.

100. *Starlight, Starbright: The Early Tamil Cinema*, Randor Guy, Amra Publishers, Chennai, 1997.

101. *South Indian Music Book*, vols 1–6, Prof. P Sambamoorthy, the Indian Music Publishing House, Madras, 1972.

102. *An Incurable Romantic: The Musical Journey of Lalgudi Jayaraman*, Lakshmi Devnath, HarperCollins, 2013.

103. *Endaro Mahanubhavulu: Dr Avasarala (Vinjamuri)*, Anasuya Devi, Chennai, 2011.

104. *Asamana Anasuya (Naa Gurinchi Nene): Avasarala (Vinjamuri)*, Anasuya Devi, Vanguri Foundation of America, INC, Houston, Texas, 2015.

105. Interviews with:

T.V. Gopalakrishnan, Dr Prema Nandakumar, Sri Balasubramanian, Dr Padma Subrahmanyam, Sudharani Raghupathy, Alarmel Valli, Rama Vaidyanathan, Parshwanath Upadhye, V.P. Dhananjayan, Shyamala Bhave, Vidwan Abhishek Raghuram, Kunnakudi Balamuralikrishna, Vidwans Raghavachari and Sheshachari, Sandeep Narayanan, Chitraveena Ravikiran, Carnatica brothers: Shashikiran and Ganesh, Giridhar Udupa, Sri K.V. Ramanachari in Hyderabad, Sri Malladi Suribabu Garu in Vijayawada, Sri Annavarapu Ramaswamy, Mr Mohanakrishna, Krishnakumar, Venkataraghavan, Balaji Shankar, Balachandran, Rajkumar Bharati, P. Unnikrishnan, Sudha Raghunathan, Bombay Jayashri, Seeta Ratnakar, Aruna Sairam, S.J. Jananiy, Shyam Ravishankar, Ghantasala Satya Sai, 'HMV' Raghu Mama, Shyam Ravishankar, M.A. Sunderasan, M.A. Krishnaswamy, P. Purnachander, Vijayawada Jayalakshmi and Mr Sarma, Garimella Subramaniam, Aralikatte Babu, Dr Lakshmi Ayyagari, Thiruvaiyaru P. Sekar and Mrs Vasanthi, Mahati, Ragavan Manian, Hari Sree Ramachandra Sharma, Ghatam S. Karthick, Harikere Srikanta Iyer Thyagaraja, Ronu Majumdar, Vibhas Amonkar, T.N. Krishnan, Dr L. Subramaniam, M. Chandrasekharan, Lalgudi Vijayalakshmi, R. Vedavalli, Sri Anand of Advaita Shodha Kendra, Dr B.M. Sundaram, Dr V.A.K. Ranga Rao Garu, Cleveland Sundaram, Trichy Pradeep Kumar, Saketharaman, Vakeel Ganesan and Mr Panchanadam in Thanjavur, Vidushi Rama Kausalya in Thillaisthanam, Mrs Meenakshi Rajmohan, Mrs Madhuvanthi Badri, Dr Mysore Nagaraj and Dr Mysore Manjunath, veteran journalists Sri Puttur Venkateshwara Rao and Nanduri Parthasarathi in Hyderabad, Dr Pappu Venugopala Rao, Sri R.T. Chari and Mrs Ranganayaki, Sri Y. Prabhu of Krishna Gana Sabha, Sri Harishankar of Narada Gana Sabha, Mrs Shubhalakshmi Khan, Ayaan Ali Bangash and Amaan Ali Bangash, Ms Sunita Buddhiraja, Mrs Hema Ramani Iyer, Dinakaran, Ravi Palagummi, Parupalli

Phalgun, Modumudi Sudhakar, Prof. Yogananda, Mr Dinakar, Ms Padma and Shylaja, Mangalampalli Vijayamohana Muralikrishna, Srinivas Joshi, Ravi Joshi in America, Mr Ramaprasad of Sri Rama Seva Mandali Bangalore, Prema Ramamurthy.

The Family Members of Dr Mangalampalli Balamuralikrishna

Mr Abhiram and Mrs Krishnaveni, Mrs Durga Suryakantam (Ammaji) and Colonel Subramanaiam, Mrs Lakshmi and Mr Ramachandra Rao, Mrs Mahati Srinivas, Mrs Mahima and, last but not the least, Mr Balamurali Vibhu, who patiently took time out for everything through this entire project.